Web Dynpro for ABAP®

 PRESS

SAP PRESS is a joint initiative of SAP and Galileo Press. The know-how offered by SAP specialists combined with the expertise of the publishing house Galileo Press offers the reader expert books in the field. SAP PRESS features first-hand information and expert advice, and provides useful skills for professional decision-making.

SAP PRESS offers a variety of books on technical and business related topics for the SAP user. For further information, please visit our website: *www.sap-press.com*.

Brian McKellar, Thomas Jung
Advanced BSP Programming
2005, 492 pp., ISBN 1-59229-049-3

Jörg Beringer, Karen Holtzblatt
Designing Composite Applications
2006, 192 pp., ISBN 1-59229-065-5

Horst Keller
The ABAP Quick Reference
2005, 212 pp., ISBN 1-59229-057-4

W. Heuvelmans, A. Krouwels, B. Meijs, R. Sommen
Enhancing the Quality of ABAP Development
2004, 504 pp., ISBN 1-59229-030-2

Ulli Hoffmann

Web Dynpro for ABAP®

Galileo Press

Bonn • Boston

ISBN 978-1-59229-078-9

1st edition 2006, 1st reprint 2008

Translation Lemoine International, Inc., Salt Lake City, UT
Editor Stefan Proksch
Copy Editor Nancy Etscovitz and John Parker, UCG, Inc., Boston, MA
Cover Design Nadine Kohl
Layout Design Vera Brauner
Production Iris Warkus
Typesetting Typographie & Computer, Krefeld
Printed and bound in Germany

© 2006 by Galileo Press
SAP PRESS is an imprint of Galileo Press,
Boston (MA), USA
Bonn, Germany

German Edition first published 2006 by Galileo Press.

All rights reserved. Neither this publication nor any part of it may be copied or reproduced in any form or by any means or translated into another language, without the prior consent of Galileo Press, Rheinwerkallee 4, 53227 Bonn, Germany.

Galileo Press makes no warranties or representations with respect to the content hereof and specifically disclaims any implied warranties of merchantability or fitness for any particular purpose. Galileo Press assumes no responsibility for any errors that may appear in this publication.

All of the screenshots and graphics reproduced in this book are subject to copyright © SAP AG, Dietmar-Hopp-Allee 16, 69190 Walldorf, Germany.

SAP, the SAP logo, mySAP, mySAP.com, mySAP Business Suite, SAP NetWeaver, SAP R/3, SAP R/2, SAP B2B, SAPtronic, SAPscript, SAP BW, SAP CRM, SAP Early Watch, SAP ArchiveLink, SAP GUI, SAP Business Workflow, SAP Business Engineer, SAP Business Navigator, SAP Business Framework, SAP Business Information Warehouse, SAP interenterprise solutions, SAP APO, AcceleratedSAP, InterSAP, SAPoffice, SAPfind, SAPfile, SAPtime, SAPmail, SAP-access, SAP-EDI, R/3 Retail, Accelerated HR, Accelerated HiTech, Accelerated Consumer Products, ABAP, ABAP/4, ALE/WEB, BAPI, Business Framework, BW Explorer, Enjoy-SAP, mySAP.com e-business platform, mySAP Enterprise Portals, RIVA, SAPPHIRE, TeamSAP, Webflow and SAP PRESS are registered or unregistered trademarks of SAP AG, Walldorf, Germany.

All other products mentioned in this book are registered or unregistered trademarks of their respective companies.

Contents at a Glance

	Introduction	13
1	On the Development of Web-Based Applications	23
2	WD4A Framework	37
3	Developing WD4A Applications	95
4	Multi-Component Applications	185
5	Dynamic Component Applications	225
6	Reusing WD4A Components	261
7	Integrating WD4A Applications	293
A	Classes and Interfaces	317
B	Bibliography	353
C	The Author	354
	Index	355

Contents

Introduction 13

1 On the Development of Web-Based Applications 23

1.1   Mainframe and Client Server Systems 24
1.2   Business Server Pages 27
1.3   Web Dynpro Framework 29
1.4   Web Dynpro for ABAP for Future Use 35

2 WD4A Framework 37

2.1   Web Dynpro Explorer 37
    2.1.1   View Elements 39
    2.1.2   View Designer 41
    2.1.3   "Hello World" 43
2.2   Relationships Between Application and Component 51
2.3   Visual Parts 53
    2.3.1   Interface Views and Plugs 53
    2.3.2   View Layout 56
    2.3.3   Windows 60
2.4   View Controller and View Context 61
    2.4.1   Context Property Cardinality 63
    2.4.2   Singleton and Lead Selection Context Properties 66
    2.4.3   Supply Function Method 70
    2.4.4   Sample Applications 71
2.5   Controllers and Controller Methods 78
    2.5.1   Hook Methods 80
    2.5.2   Instance Methods 82
    2.5.3   Event Handler Methods 82
    2.5.4   Fire Methods 83
    2.5.5   Additional Information About Context 84
2.6   Navigation, Inbound Plugs, and Outbound Plugs 87
2.7   Phase Model 91

3 Developing WD4A Applications 95

3.1   Transferring Parameters from a URI 95
    3.1.1   Reading and Displaying Parameters 96
    3.1.2   Controlling the Navigation Via Parameters 98

3.2		Influencing the Request/Response Cycle	103
	3.2.1	Automatic Triggering of Requests	104
	3.2.2	Automatic Triggering of Requests with User Interaction	106
	3.2.3	Automatic Forwarding	109
3.3		Implementation of Selection Options	111
	3.3.1	Using Dropdown Lists	112
	3.3.2	Using Radio Buttons	121
3.4		Presentation of Tree Structures	125
	3.4.1	Sequential Building of Tree Structures	126
	3.4.2	Recursive Tree Structures	131
3.5		User Guidance per RoadMap and Messages	137
	3.5.1	Structure of the RoadMap Application	138
	3.5.2	Message Handling	148
3.6		Presenting Tables	152
	3.6.1	Table Output and Row Selection	152
	3.6.2	Selection of Single or Multiple Rows	157
	3.6.3	Changing Single Cells Using Variants	159
3.7		Calling Popup Windows	163
	3.7.1	Message Popups	164
	3.7.2	Query Popups	166
	3.7.3	Popups with Navigation	168
3.8		Using Input Helps	171
3.9		Internationalization	172
	3.9.1	Online Text Repository	173
	3.9.2	Assistance Class	175
3.10		Customization, Configuration, Personalization	176
	3.10.1	Implicit and Explicit Configurations	177
	3.10.2	Configuring Components and Applications	177

4　Multi-Component Applications　185

4.1		A Model of Layer Separation	185
	4.1.1	Strict Separation	187
	4.1.2	Light Separation	188
	4.1.3	Strict versus Light Separation	189
	4.1.4	MVC Concepts in the WD4A Framework	190
4.2		Defining WD4A Component Usages	192
	4.2.1	Embedding Windows of Used Components	194
	4.2.2	Calling Methods of Used Components	195
	4.2.3	Triggering Cross-Component Events	196
	4.2.4	External Context Access Using Direct Mapping	197
	4.2.5	External Context Access Using Reverse Mapping	198

	4.3	Componentizing an Application	200
		4.3.1 Structure of the Sample Application	201
		4.3.2 Implementing the Components	202
		4.3.3 Result of Componentization	218
		4.3.4 Redesigning the Sample Application	218
		4.3.5 Overview of Used Components and Sample Applications	224

5 Dynamic Component Applications — 225

	5.1	Types of Dynamic Changes	225
		5.1.1 Dynamic Modification of the Properties	226
		5.1.2 Dynamic Modification of the UI Hierarchy	229
		5.1.3 Dynamic Binding of Properties	234
		5.1.4 Dynamic Modification of the Context	235
		5.1.5 Dynamic Modification of Action Assignments	236
	5.2	Dynamic Programming—A Sample Application	237
		5.2.1 Dynamic Display of Address Data	237
		5.2.2 Creating Business Partners	241
		5.2.3 Metadata for the Address Formats	242
		5.2.4 Implementation and Layout of the Component	246

6 Reusing WD4A Components — 261

	6.1	Comparing Classes and Components	261
	6.2	ALV Component SALV_WD_TABLE	263
		6.2.1 Using the ALV Component	264
		6.2.2 Accessing the ALV Configuration Model	267
	6.3	OVS Component WDR_OVS	270
	6.4	SO Component WDR_SELECT_OPTIONS	275
	6.5	Developing Input-Help Components	282
		6.5.1 Implementation of the Input-Help Component	283
		6.5.2 Using the Input-Help Component	286
	6.6	Enhancements of Components	288

7 Integrating WD4A Applications — 293

	7.1	Integration into the SAP NetWeaver Portal	293
		7.1.1 Triggering Portal Events	294
		7.1.2 Registration to Portal Events	295
	7.2	Graphical Display of Data	297
		7.2.1 Using the BusinessGraphics View Element	299
		7.2.2 Connecting the Data Source	303

	7.3	Interactive Forms Via Adobe Integration	308
		7.3.1 System Requirements for Interactive Forms	309
		7.3.2 Scenario for Using Interactive Forms	309
		7.3.3 Using the InteractiveForm View Element	311

A Classes and Interfaces ... 317

	A.1	Component	317
		A.1.1 IF_WD_COMPONENT	317
		A.1.2 IF_WD_COMPONENT_USAGE	320
		A.1.3 IF_WD_COMPONENT_USAGE_GROUP	324
		A.1.4 IF_WD_PERSONALIZATION	325
	A.2	Context	326
		A.2.1 IF_WD_CONTEXT	326
		A.2.2 IF_WD_CONTEXT_NODE	328
		A.2.3 IF_WD_CONTEXT_NODE_INFO	329
		A.2.4 IF_WD_CONTEXT_ELEMENT	332
		A.2.5 CL_WD_CONTEXT_SERVICES	332
	A.3	View	335
		A.3.1 IF_WD_ACTION	335
		A.3.2 IF_WD_VIEW	336
		A.3.3 IF_WD_VIEW_CONTROLLER	337
		A.3.4 IF_WD_VIEW_ELEMENT	338
		A.3.5 IF_WD_VALIDATION	338
	A.4	Window	339
		A.4.1 IF_WD_WINDOW	339
		A.4.2 IF_WD_WINDOW_CONTROLLER	341
	A.5	Integration	341
		A.5.1 CL_WDR_PORTAL_OBNWEB_SERVICE	341
		A.5.2 IF_WD_PORTAL_INTEGRATION	342
		A.5.3 CL_WD_ADOBE_SERVICES	342
	A.6	Application	342
		A.6.1 IF_WD_APPLICATION	342
	A.7	Other	343
		A.7.1 IF_WD_CONTROLLER	343
		A.7.2 IF_WD_MESSAGE_MANAGER	344
		A.7.3 IF_WD_NAVIGATION_SERVICES	346
		A.7.4 CL_WD_CUSTOM_EVENT	348
		A.7.5 CL_WD_RUNTIME_SERVICES	348
		A.7.6 CL_WD_UTILITIES	349

B	Bibliography	353
C	The Author	354

Index 355

Introduction

After you have read this book and implemented the examples and scenarios, you will have ample knowledge to implement the new SAP user interface strategy based on the WD4A (Web Dynpro for ABAP) framework. The goal of this book is to create a foundation that can be used with the SAP Help Portal (*http://help.sap.com*) and the SAP Developer Network (*http://sdn.sap.com*) to meet the requirements and challenges of new projects regarding Web Dynpro for ABAP and to find a solution whenever questions arrise.

The WD4A framework enables you to use different methods for solving a problem. For example, program fragments can be created either manually or by using a code wizard. The layout can be designed by adding view elements to the UI tree, or by using *Drag&Drop* in the layout preview. For this reason, the procedures presented in this book use rather basic and easy-to-comprehend methods; however, there may be a specific design procedure for which a different control sequence is used and is not mentioned here. It's up to you to use your intuition and curiosity to find other solutions, and in so doing, enhance the knowledge that you will gain in this book.

Audience

This book is intended for ABAP application developers who are familiar with the ABAP Development Workbench and the user interface development methods available, and who now want to implement business processes and their user interaction based on the WD4A framework.

This book will help you to better support users, and it will help you with problems that can arise during the migration to the WD4A framework, for example, the separation of business and presentation logic while observing the Model View Controller (MVC) concept, or addressing component-based reuse-focused software development. This book will discuss general concepts for designing and developing web-based systems and specifically detail their specifications when they are implemented within the WD4A framework.

Before and while this book was being written, there existed great communication between the first application developers using the WD4A framework and the groups responsible for the design and implementation of the framework. Therefore, new ideas and suggestions for enhancing and extending the

Introduction

WD4A framework reached the responsible departments very quickly. It is assumed that the WD4A framework will be continuously developed and extended by new functionalities. Therefore, this book should encourage you to discover these new features, to test them, and, ultimately, to integrate the growing library of view elements in your applications.

If you already gained some experience in developing web applications based on Java Server Pages (JSP), Business Server Pages (BSP), or other technologies, you might be surprised at the restrictive handling of the WD4A framework when it comes to the manual integration of JavaScript. This restriction was introduced in order to enable the WD4A applications to support emerging client technologies that don't use JavaScript for client-side flow control.

Prerequisites

Because the WD4A framework was developed completely in ABAP Objects, you will encounter object-oriented concepts throughout the implementation. Therefore, a sound knowledge of object-oriented ABAP programming is integral for understanding the topics discussed in this book; we cannot go into detail regarding the concepts of object-oriented programming and its implementation in ABAP Objects.[1]

You should be familiar with handling classes and interfaces in ABAP Objects and with the most common ABAP language items. WD4A applications integrate a number of technologies like HTTP, HTML, CSS, XML, and client-side scripting. These are not specific to the WD4A framework, but are the foundation for every other web application. The objective of the WD4A framework development is to encapsulate the complex and specific details and connections of these technologies so that they will eventually become transparent to you and you can then completely focus on implementing the program logic.

To reproduce the examples given in this book, you can download a test version of SAP NetWeaver Application Server ABAP from the SAP Developer Network (*http://sdn.sap.com*) that can be installed locally on your PC. In the **Downloads · SAP Evaluation Software · Web AS** area, navigate to the **Sneak Preview SAP NetWeaver 04s—Full ABAP Edition with Web Dynpro for**

---

[1] Whenever it makes sense, publications and sources that provide additional useful information for specific areas will be referenced. SAP PRESS, in particular, offers a wide range of literature in this respect *(http://www.sap-press.com)*. Additional references are listed in the bibliography (see Appendix B).

ABAP package. For detailed information about the installation process and system requirements, go to the **Installation Guide** file.

To better understand the WD4A framework, you should be at least somewhat familiar with the following topics:

- Communication processes in HTTP or HTTP request/response cycles
- Particularities of programming within distributed development environments
- Differences between client-side and server-side scripting
- Purpose and use of design patterns in programming

The parameters to be used for designing layouts are based on *Cascading Style Sheets* (CSS) standards. It is therefore helpful to have a certain overview of CSS language items and units.

Structure

For most developers, the actual implementation is the quickest way to become familiar with a new technology. The structure of this book is therefore based on using simple examples and scenarios in the introductory sections to illustrate the concepts. By our first presenting the architecture of the WD4A framework, you'll be introduced to the most important steps of component and application development. ABAP Objects constructs belong to the essential part of a WD4A application so that another focus should also be on the presentation and discussion of program fragments that can be used to solve problems.

- **Chapter 1** deals with some particularities regarding the design and the development of web-based applications. Based on the functionalities of the BSP technology and its predecessors, you will get to know the characteristics and advantages of the WD4A framework. The present status and the concepts behind it will be closely examined. When developing WD4A applications, the component is the most important part; WD4A applications can be composed of one or more components. The component-based software development therefore facilitates reuse and reduces development costs.
- **Chapter 2** introduces you to the WD4A development environment, the Web Dynpro Explorer that is integrated in the Object Navigator. First, you learn about the immediately visible parts, such as the component controller, view, window and application. Then, when you have the knowledge

necessary to create your first simple components, you learn how to design a simple, structured view, and embed it in a window.

Using three differently structured "Hello World" applications, you get your first insight into using the context, the data binding, the view element properties, and the implementation of supply function methods, followed by the other parts of the framework. These include the functions of the inbound and outbound plugs, the functions of the actions and their event handler methods, the parts of the context and of the framework controller methods. The framework controller methods are called at different times in the phase model of the WD4A framework and form a kind of user exit of the framework that enables you to influence the programmatic process.

▶ **Chapter 3** builds on your newly acquired abilities and knowledge in order to help you develop more complex components based on the available view elements. By implementing scenarios that might be familiar to you from web applications based on other technologies (e.g., periodic polling of the web browser, automatic forwarding, etc.), additional relationships are shown that exist within the WD4A framework among component, window, and view elements.

Whereas the components created and described so far used only simple view elements like the `TextView` view element, this chapter introduces important view elements contained in the view element library of the WD4A framework and describes their function. Dropdown lists and radio buttons are different with regard to their usage, but they are based on the same concepts with regard to their implementation and handling in the WD4A framework. They are discussed using example applications. Additionally, you learn how to output messages about the user via the message manager. The most complex and most commonly used view element when visualizing business data is the `Table` element. For this element, we'll show you display formats and properties and discuss the handling of cell variants. This chapter also provides procedures for implementing popups and using the `RoadMap` and `Tree` elements. It concludes with a list of the input help concepts implemented in the WD4A framework.

▶ **Chapter 4** deals with the concepts required for developing multi-component applications. Examples whose structure is based on the Model View Controller concept are developed. The layout is defined separately from the business logic, and the data provision for the view can be implemented in methods of the view controller. The view controller therefore also controls the view. Based on this concept, even more complex applications can be separated into different components: UI components that organize the arrangement of view elements. The main component or controller component is responsible for instantiating the use and its lifetime; the model component is responsible for data storage and program logic. The various components communicate by using context and events that are accessible via their interfaces.

When implementing the componentization, the context, as a data container, and its mapping types are the central parts. Context data can be defined in the component, in the view, and in the window controller. By defining the context nodes as interfaces, mapping components can access and change the data of other components. The concept of direct and reverse context mappings is described in this context.

▶ During the design phase of complex WD4A applications, requirements that change program processes and layout structures at runtime can emerge. To be able to consider these requirements when developing components, the WD4A framework enables the dynamic programming of components. The concepts that pertain to the ability to program dynamically will be described in **Chapter 5**. You'll learn how you can add view elements to the UI hierarchy of the layout definition at runtime and thereby dynamically influence their properties. We will also show you how context node attributes can be added and the properties of dynamically created view elements can be bound against them. For action-triggering view elements like the `Button` element, actions can also be defined at runtime in dynamic programming, which then trigger event handler methods generated by the WD4A framework.

These concepts of dynamic programming will be illustrated in an example application: business partner addresses will be presented in the client under consideration of the format used in the respective country. Because parts of the address and their arrangement can be different from country to country, the arrangement of the view elements will be created dynamically at runtime. Additionally, parameters are determined from the address data at runtime. These parameters can be dynamically generated to enable the localization of the respective business partner via Google Map, by using a *Uniform Resource Identifier* (URI).

▶ In **Chapter 6**, the concepts already presented are extended for reuse in the WD4A framework. By reusing existing components, current resources can be used more efficiently. The idea of reusability of software modules has been examined, propagated, and applied for many years. Accelerated

17

development cycles and cost reduction are two main reasons for further promoting these concepts.

The WD4A framework now enables you to build component-based business applications from the user interface and to structure them in a reusable way. Based on the componentization described in Chapter 4, this chapter will show you how to implement the use of the ABAP List Viewer (ALV) component, the object value selector component, the select options component, and the user-specific development of input-help components. For the tabular presentation of data, the ALV component provides extensive personalization and configuration options that are described in detail. Input helps support the user when editing forms. Simple input helps based on the ABAP Dictionary can be implemented very quickly by selecting the context attribute type. For more complex selection scenarios, they can be implemented in a component to be available to other WD4A applications.

▶ **Chapter 7** finally deals with the integration possibilities of WD4A applications. These include the integration in the SAP NetWeaver Portal and the resulting possibilities for implementing client-side eventing. Using the SAP NetWeaver Portal, scenarios are enabled by integrating applications that are based on other web technologies. This enlarges the integration potential in heterogeneous system landscapes.

The integration of business graphics in WD4A components enables the presentation of charts and geographic map material. In this context, you can anticipate default implementation steps. From different chart types and chart rendering methods—comparable to those given in Microsoft Excel—you can select the display format that best meets your needs. We will present the numerous possibilities with an example that uses the Google Web APIs service as a data source. You will also get to know a scenario that shows the integration of the Adobe Document Service in the WD4A framework, which enables the creation of interactive PDF forms that can be edited both online and offline.

Conventions

The WD4A framework uses the term *context* for describing structured data storage within the controller. The main parts of the context are *context nodes* and *context attributes*. From the names of context nodes and context attributes, along with some extensions, the WD4A framework generates the names of the type definitions and interfaces. The length of these names, however, is limited to 30 characters. You should keep this in mind when selecting the names of context nodes and context attributes. For example, creating a context node named EXAMPLE_NODE in the V_DEFAULT view results in the type definition if_v_default=>element_example_node being stored in an interface. The total length to be observed results from the element_ and example_node parts. Therefore, the part of the type definition following the => character combination cannot exceed a maximum of 30 characters.

To unify the IDs and to better distinguish the individual view elements, as far as they are mentioned in this book, we will identify them using the prefixes shown in Table 1.

View Element	ID Prefix	Example ID
BusinessGraphics	BGR_*	BGR_SALES
Button	BTN_*	BTN_SAVE
ButtonRow	BTR_*	BTR_DETAILS
Caption	CPT_*	CPT_COLUMN
DropDownByIndex	DDI_*	DDI_COUNTRY
DropDownByKey	DDK_*	DDK_REGION
FileUpload	FUD_*	FUD_CONTRACT
Group	GRP_*	GRP_FORM
HorizontalGutter	HOG_*	HOG_ROADMAP
InputField	INP_*	INP_NAME
InteractiveForm	IFO_*	IFO_CUSTOMS
Label	LBL_*	LBL_INPUT
LinkToAction	LTA_*	LTA_SEARCH
LinkToURL	LTU_*	LTU_VENDOR
RadioButton	RBT_*	RBT_MALE
RadioButtonGroupByIndex	RBI_*	RBI_GENDER
RadioButtonGroupByKey	RBK_*	RBK_TYP
RoadMap	RMP_*	RMP_DIMENSIONS
RoadMapStep	STP_*	STP_DIMENSION
Table	TBL_*	TBL_ADDRESS
TextEdit	TXE_*	TXE_INFO

Table 1 Prefixes of Used View Element IDs

Introduction

View Element	ID Prefix	Example ID
TextView	TXV_*	TXV_INTRO
TimedTrigger	TTR_*	TTR_NOTIFY
TransparentContainer	TCO_*	TCO_TABLE
Tray	TRY_*	TRY_FORM
Tree	TRE_*	TRE_SIMPLE
TreeNodeType	TNT_*	TNT_FOLDER
TreeItemType	TIT_*	TIT_FILE
ViewContainerUIElement	VCU_*	VCU_ROADMAP

Table 1 Prefixes of Used View Element IDs (cont.)

For component elements, the prefixes listed in Table 2 are selected.

Element	Prefix	Example
Window	W_*	W_DEFAULT
View	V_*	V_DEFAULT
Inbound-Plug	IP_*	IP_START
Outbound-Plug	OP_*	OP_EXIT

Table 2 Prefixes of Component Elements

For distinguishing different parts within the components, the font style conventions shown in Table 3 are used:

Component Part	Example
View element	TextView
View element ID	TXV_INTRO
Property	text
Property value	header1
Context node	CONTENT
Context attribute	MANDT

Table 3 Identification of Component Parts

Component Part	Example
Controller attribute	mv_*, ms_*, mt_*, mr_*
Controller actions	DO_SET_COUNTER

Table 3 Identification of Component Parts (cont.)

Additionally, the WD4A framework contains the reserved keywords from Table 4.

Reserved Keywords		
CONTROLLER	CONTROLLER_NAME	COMMAND
COMPONENT	EVENT	EVENT_NAME
F_APPL_CLASS	F_ROOT_INFO	F_ROOT_NODE
FIRST_INIT	PLUG	PARAMETERS
RESULT	VIEW	VIEW_NAME

Table 4 Reserved Keywords in the WD4A Framework

The names of components and applications used in this book have the prefix ZEXP_*. All components and applications described in the following chapters and sections and using this prefix are available for download in two formats on the web pages of the book under *http://www.sap-press.com* or *www.sap-press.de/1214* respectively. You can either load the examples as a transport into your installation of the SAP NetWeaver Application Server ABAP, or implement them manually using screenshots and ABAP statements in TXT format.

In some of the screenshots, German user interface elements appear. Where these words are referred to in the text, we have provided the English translation in parentheses.

Acknowledgement

When compiling the contents of this book—already during the development phase of the WD4A framework—I had the great advantage to gain insights into the design, to cooperate on additional functionalities, and to build up the necessary expertise in this environment thanks to independent web projects (based on previous SAP technologies).

Introduction

Whenever I had to become familiar with areas that were still unknown to me, I could rely on the knowledge of the respective SAP experts. Without their valuable support, this book would not have been possible.

I would like to thank Rüdiger Kretschmer, Brian McKellar, and Dirk Feeken for their suggestions and tips regarding Web Dynpro. When I was working on the technical details and specific scenarios, I could always rely on the direct feedback of Regina Breuer, Thomas Szuecs, Ariane Buster, Uwe Klinger, Aiga Uhrig, Klaus Ziegler, Stefanie Mayer, and Heidi von Geisau—thank you all, and may you continue having great ideas and fun developing! For their time spent reviewing the material, their tips regarding the contents and the structure, I would particularly like to thank Regina Breuer, Uwe Klinger, Thomas Szuecs, Thomas Weiss, and especially my editor Stefan Proksch. When I was reviewing and designing specific scenarios and examples, I got great support from Nestor Sosa, Thorsten Kampp, and Dirk Jennerjahn. My biggest thank you, however, goes to Claudia for her love, support, and understanding for the enormous amount of time that is taken up by such a project.

Additionally, I could always rely on the WD4A forum in the SAP Developer Network (SDN) when I was compiling the topics and contents. The forum, which was only accessible to SAP-internal users until the official market launch of the WD4A framework, gave me a detailed insight into the developers' questions and problems that arose during their adjustment to the new UI technology. Predicated on this basis, I could design parts of this book, compose individual subject areas, and develop examples from the scenarios described therein.

In this way, even before the first version of the WD4A framework to be released to the market was finalized (Release SAP NetWeaver 2004s), I could draw on the extensive experience and procedures of application developers during the making of this book, and hopefully pass on their wisdom in a sensible way.

Web-based applications for mapping business processes have gained importance in the past few years, especially due to the increasing acceptance of the Internet. This chapter will deal with technologies that already exist in the ABAP environment for developing web-based applications and with the basic concepts of the WD4A framework.

1 On the Development of Web-Based Applications

In the past, great effort went into the architecture and design of the development of web-based applications. Before even the first line of business process logic could be implemented, various characteristics of Internet communication had to be considered:

- The *Hypertext Transfer Protocol* (HTTP) is the communication protocol for the Internet. It is based on a *request/response* model. This means that the web browser sends a request to the server, which then processes the request and sends a response back to the web browser. The server, however, does not retain any information about the application status between two request cycles.

- When it comes to user-friendliness, the basic functionalities of a browser-based user interface are limited. Initially, the Internet was used as a means of communication for presenting static texts, rather than a way to process dynamic business data. The *Hypertext Markup Language* (HTML) determines the logical structure of a document and therefore provides only limited options for presenting user interface elements or receiving user input.

- Web-based applications are usually open to a large number of users. Enterprises take advantage of the popularity of web browsers in order to expand their clientele and their number of suppliers in a cost-efficient way. The developers of web-based applications therefore need to consider such factors as internationalization, navigation options, and the interactions that entail often hundreds of pages. Numerous systems in a heterogeneous system landscape must be smoothly integrated. In many cases, this involves the backend systems of an enterprise so that security aspects are adhered to in order to protect the enterprise data.

The characteristics mentioned here have led and still contribute to the development of tools and frameworks that simplify the development of web-based applications, or at least try to remove the disadvantages posed by the web browser. An important reason for using the web browser in the past, and what accounts for its current predominance as an application client— despite the high effort involved regarding architecture and design—is the low cost factor.

If there is a need to increase the number of users of an application, a web browser makes this consideration almost moot. Because the web browser is part of the standard software that exists on almost every system, the communication and presentation framework is standardized. This is different with proprietary client technology that needs to be installed and maintained for every additional user. Web-based applications enable you to integrate suppliers and customers worldwide into the communication process without making a noticeable effort. Even within enterprises, the web browser asserts itself as the preferred client technology, its low installation and maintenance cost both convincing arguments for its popularity.

1.1 Mainframe and Client Server Systems

This has not always been the case, however. Figure 1.1 gives you an overview of the UI technologies developed in the SAP environment up until today.

At the beginning of the development of complex systems for implementing business software, there were the mainframe systems. Several terminals were connected to a mainframe system that performed the entire processing of the data and sent it to the terminal for presentation and user interaction. SAP R/2 is an example of business software that was developed for mainframe systems.

A terminal presentation of the R/2 screen is shown in Figure 1.2. The terminal was used to display data and existed without additional hardware for processing tasks. The user could use the keyboard to navigate to the various fields presented on the terminal, make entries and changes, and send the data back to the mainframe for processing.

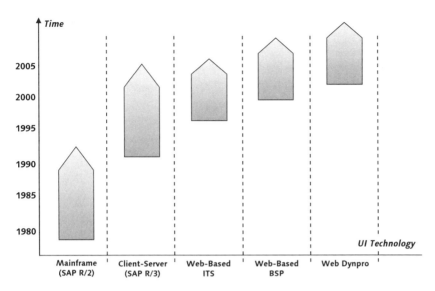

Figure 1.1 SAP Developments in the Area of UI Technologies

With the market launch of SAP R/3, mainframe systems were replaced with systems based on the client/server architecture. SAP R/3 used the resources existing on the client system (PC or workstation) to provide a *graphical user interface* (GUI) to make user interaction more comfortable and to shift various tasks from the central system to the client. The resources provided by the client systems in the form of computing capacity could now be used to enable the user to work more efficiently and productively. This client/server concept is based on the networking of systems and the distribution of tasks within the network.

The client technology of SAP R/3 was made up of the SAP GUI that was developed in different versions for the multitude of operating systems and platforms that existed on the market, like OS/2, Microsoft Windows, Mac OS, UNIX, Java, and others.

With the Internet gaining more and more importance, however, the web browser again reduced the function of the client system to data display, input, and transfer, similar to the situation that existed at the time of the mainframe systems. The critical difference, though, is the number of users that accessed the applications. While during the mainframe period, these were small groups of ten or more people within an enterprise, today, there are now hundreds, thousands, and even more users within and outside an enterprise. They access the application from client systems running numerous different operating systems and platforms.

1 | On the Development of Web-Based Applications

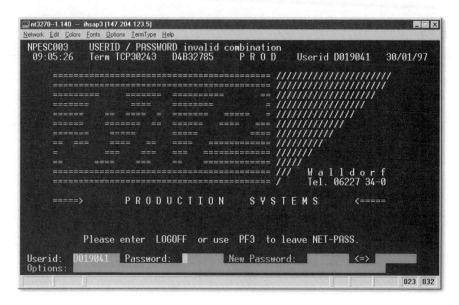

Figure 1.2 Terminal Screen on SAP R/2

Accessing the extended number of users can be most cost-efficiently achieved by using standardized client technologies. Naturally, the application running on the server must also support the client to be connected. Because the R/3 basis system did not support the relevant communication protocols like TCP/IP and HTTP until the end of the 1990s, SAP introduced the *Internet Transaction Server* (ITS). ITS enabled users to retrieve the relevant transactions via a web browser. And it handled the conversion of the SAP GUI to HTML pages that could be presented in the web browser.

Although this simplified the web integration of R/3 applications, it did have its disadvantages when it came to usability, because the emulation of R/3 screens in the browser was not part of the original GUI concept and therefore neither the type of data flows nor the presentation elements could be optimized for web applications. The runtime drawbacks, in particular, which occurred due to the emulation because the conversion process was very time-consuming, required new solutions. Additionally, users were not presented with the user interfaces familiar to them from other web-based applications, or the control elements were not optimized for the interfaces in web browsers, respectively. Therefore, the simplification of the development process for web-based applications, which was achieved via ITS, did not necessarily result in a simplified use of the application for the user. More alternatives were required.

In many cases, however, the use of the web browser, which was and is limited to simple processes within applications or for more complex processes, either leads to higher implementation costs or to control sequences that are unsatisfying to the user. It would be desirable to have a client technology that combines the benefits of user-friendliness that can be achieved, for example, via the SAP GUI with the cost-efficient increase of the number of users that is enabled by the web browser.

With the development of the *Internet Connection Framework* (ICF) and the *Internet Communication Manager* (ICM), the way was paved for the direct connection of the R/3 application server to the Internet. This resulted in the opportunity to develop programming models where server-side statements are built into the definition of the logical document structure.

1.2 Business Server Pages

This new approach of developing web-based applications on an ABAP system led to the so-called *Business Server Pages* (BSP). With their introduction, the development of browser-based applications was directly supported, as they were known from other technologies and platforms, for example, *Active Server Pages* (ASP) or *Java Server Pages* (JSP).

In the development of BSP applications, ABAP-based script code and HTML are combined. When the BSP page is processed on the server, the page is read, the ABAP code is executed, and the response is constructed accordingly. The integration of HTML and ABAP statements via ICF and ICM enables a direct access to application server contents like function modules, data type definitions, and database tables.

BSP applications are developed in the ABAP Workbench and are integrated in the ABAP runtime environment. They usually consist of several BSP pages that define the user interface functionality and contain the ABAP code, and an *application class* in which the application logic is implemented. As an example, Listing 1.1 shows a simple BSP page with statements for outputting five lines of text in different font sizes.

```
<%@page language="abap" %>
<html>
    <body>
        <h2><p><center>A simple BSP example!</center></p></h2>
           <% do 5 times.%>
              <font size = <%= sy-index %> >
```

```
            <p><center>Hello BSP world!</p></center>
         </font>
      <% enddo.%>
   </body>
</html>
```

Listing 1.1 BSP Example with ABAP Code

You should think of the programming model of plain BSP applications as a thin abstraction layer propped up on the HTTP request/response model. This abstraction layer provides support for the following tasks:

- Reading field contents from the request
- Integrating ABAP code for accessing data and functionalities of the respective server
- Composing the response

If elements arranged on the BSP page, like buttons or links, are used at runtime, one of two possible actions can be executed:

1. If the BSP page contains client-side code that was loaded into the web browser along with the page, processes within the client can be triggered. These processes don't necessarily lead to a communication with the server.
2. On the other hand, depending on the HTML statements for the respective UI element (a button, for example), a request can be sent to the server immediately. One example would be the **Submit** button in a form.

Using the BSP technology, it was now possible to clearly minimize response times and to enable application developers to design and implement browser-based applications according to the users' needs; the requirement for cost-efficiently increasing the number of users was therefore met by introducing the BSP technology. But, if you compare functionalities of applications developed in SAP GUI to those based on BSP running in the web browser, you will notice that SAP GUI applications still show a higher degree of user comfort. Complex applications that are called in the web browser are often more difficult to handle, or the development effort to adapt them to meet the SAP GUI level of user comfort is very high.

In SAP GUI, the display of input help for a field of the ABAP Dictionary structure and taking over the selected value, for example, requires only the assignment of the input help name within the structure definition. The implementation of the same functionality using BSP is more complicated (i.e., several additional steps are required) and starts with calling the respective API that determines the data for the input help. The determined data is then prepared according to the output on the client. For its presentation, a separate popup window must be programmed. Using the appropriate JavaScript statements, the selected value is displayed in the input field that called the input help, and the popup window is closed.

This shows that the implementation of the BSP programming model, despite its many advantages, is very complex, because you need to distinguish between client-side and server-side code and you have to deal a lot with the HTTP request/response cycle. A complex structuring of the areas for the presentation logic and the application logic can quickly lead to incomprehensible processes.

On the other hand, there is a great amount of flexibility regarding creative presentation options that are exact down to the pixel, and regarding the influence on programmatic processes, because the BSP programming model has over time been extended by two key functionalities:

- With *BSP extensions*, it became possible to create reusable UI element libraries that facilitated a more comfortable interaction and the display of more complex data structures. The library elements can be reused and encapsulate their complexity.
- The separation of presentation, control, and program logic according to the *Model View Controller concept* improves the comprehensibility and maintainability of BSP applications.

These extensions and the *HTMLB tag library* that was developed by SAP, based on the BSP extensions, provide developers with an open and extensible development and implementation environment. This environment facilitates the design and implementation of high-quality, scalable, and reusable web applications within an ABAP system.

1.3 Web Dynpro Framework

The weakest point in the development process of the web-based applications presented so far is that almost half of the development time is spent on the solution of less important tasks like the adaptation to communication protocols, platform-specific functionalities, and virtually standardized user interactions. These implementations for providing an infrastructure distract the development team from the crucial contents of the development process — the implementation and automation of business processes.

The SAP Web Dynpro concept is now based on establishing a model-driven framework that facilitates the development of quickly reusable and combinable applications. The underlying technologies, like communication protocols and presentation techniques, are to be encapsulated for the developer so that he or she can focus on the actual task of implementing business cases.

Developers using the *WD4A framework* (Web Dynpro for ABAP), for example, don't have to deal with the design issue that is typical of the BSP programming model: whether an input validation should be implemented using client-side or server-side code. By shifting recurring processes in an application to the abstraction layer of the framework, the WD4A framework increases the productivity of the development process.

The WD4A framework is based on a metadata model that describes the elements of the user interface. During the development process, executable statements (ABAP Objects classes) are generated from the metadata that assume the task of composing the user interface at runtime. The process-related logic, the implementation of event handlers, and the dynamic influence on the user interaction are implemented using ABAP statements. The WD4A framework enables you to influence the process at different times using application-specific implementations and to react to user actions by implementing event handlers.

User interfaces can be developed in the WD4A framework by using two techniques: *declarative* and *dynamic*.

- If the layout and the navigation processes are clear at the time of development, the user interface and the navigation can be implemented using declarative programming. This is supported by the various Web Dynpro tools of the ABAP Workbench, like the view designer for arranging and positioning UI elements in the form of WYSIWYG editor (what you see is what you get). This kind of implementation will probably be used in most cases, because the type of interface items and their category are usually known at the time of development.
- The technique of dynamic programming is used when the structure of the user interface can partially or entirely be determined at runtime only, or when the WD4A component to be developed is to have certain generic properties to allow for reusability.

Another benefit of the WD4A framework is that different frontend technologies or clients can be supported, regardless of the requirements requested by the functional specifications of the application to be implemented. Developers of WD4A components cannot influence the rendering mechanism; it is entirely reserved to the WD4A framework and is there to ensure the independence of the application regarding different client technologies. The use of different rendering mechanisms should not result in interventions and changes to the implementation of the WD4A application. Figure 1.3 compares the different ABAP-based web technologies with regard to their degree of abstraction.

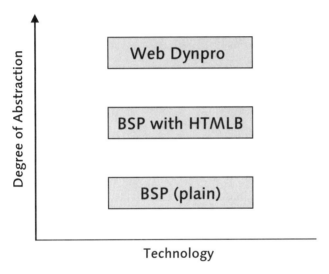

Figure 1.3 ABAP-Based UI Technologies

The characteristics of the plain BSP development and those of the extension of the BSP programming model by the HTMLB tag library were already discussed in Section 1.1.2. In Web Dynpro, these approaches are consequently implemented and form the basis of the model-driven architecture underlying Web Dynpro. The WD4A framework additionally provides several generic services like the access to simple and complex input helps and message management; in BSP, these functions must be developed manually. Declarative programming is implemented when designing the layout, defining the navigation, and declaring data structures.

Another benefit of Web Dynpro is the component-based development, which is predicated on reusability, and therefore helps with cost reduction during the development process. The idea of component-based software development has already existed in the software community for quite a long time. In the past, it was commercially used, particularly in the area of middleware technologies like COM, CORBA, JavaBeans, and so forth. The component-based approach of the WD4A framework, however, focuses primarily on the frontend or presentation layer, respectively. Basically, the development of WD4A applications is no longer based on object-oriented classes, but on a sophisticated component concept. In general, component-based software development is regarded as an extension of object-oriented programming. A WD4A application can be composed of one or more WD4A components. On the one hand, the goal here is for a better structuring of an application; on the other hand, the goal is to facilitate the reuse of WD4A components. The premise for the WD4A framework is to simplify recurring basic development processes, starting from the user interface.

More than in any other area of software development, new technologies and concepts arise very quickly in the web environment. For web-based applications, there is therefore a great demand for increased productivity and support for investments. In this respect, model-driven architectures and component-based software development form the basic concepts on which the WD4A framework is based. The introduction of component-based software development should be another step towards the industrialization of the software developing process; the intention here is to make application development more cost-efficient, to make software maintenance easier, and to ensure reusability.

The present discussions compare advantages and disadvantages of existing client technologies. On the one hand, these are *thin clients* like the web browser; on the other hand, they are *rich clients* where the client is strongly bound to the server, one such example being SAP GUI. The new generation combining the advantages of thin and rich clients is called *smart clients*. An exact classification of the individual technologies is difficult. In fact, there are slight overlaps in the list of characteristics of thin and rich clients and smart clients. The definition of smart client characteristics tries to bundle the benefits of previous client technologies and to reduce their drawbacks. Figure 1.4 shows some characteristics and examples that can be assigned to the different groups. Please note that not every example shown necessarily possesses all characteristics listed.

Client Technology Properties	Rich Client	Smart Client	Thin Client
High requirement of resources in client system (heavy footprint)			
Close link beween presentation and process logic			
User-friendliness			
Web-service support			
Easy installation and maintenance			
Low requirement of resources in client system (small footprint)			
Constant connection to server			
High development costs for applications			
Examples	MFC-based clients SAP GUI Eclipse	Java Web Start Windows Smart Client SAP Smart Board	Internet Explorer Firefox Opera

Figure 1.4 Overview of Present Client Technologies

One of the main goals when developing the WD4A framework was to make the user interface development independent of changing client technologies. The technology changes from the mainframe system to the client/server architecture and from the client/server architecture to browser-based systems required a great conversion effort for connecting the application logic to the new client technology. This should no longer become necessary for applications based on the WD4A framework in the case of an emerging change, for example, from browser-based applications to various developments in the area of smart client technology.

In the WD4A framework, the user interface development is implemented in an abstraction layer that keeps the client technology away from the UI developer, or it encapsulates it. The developer's responsibility is to take care of only those parts and processes that are relevant to the user interface, irrespective of the client-specific techniques and protocols. This includes the UI controls and data flows to be implemented. The developments done by the developer are stored as metadata. The WD4A framework then uses various client implementations at runtime that prepare this metadata for communication with and presentation on the client. For this reason, the UI developer is not confronted with HTML tags or JavaScript functions in the WD4A framework, for example, because they are specific to the presentation of contents and the implementation of processes in web browsers. In fact, the client implementation defined for the web browser, the *Server-Side Rendering* (SSR), takes over the implementation of metadata and generates HTML pages with integrated JavaScript functions.

Figure 1.5 shows the embedding of client implementations into the Web Dynpro runtime. The diagram shows two implementations: server-side rendering and XML implementation. The XML implementation is presently used for eCATT scenarios as well as for the Windows smart client integration that is also referred to as *SAP Smart Board*.[1]

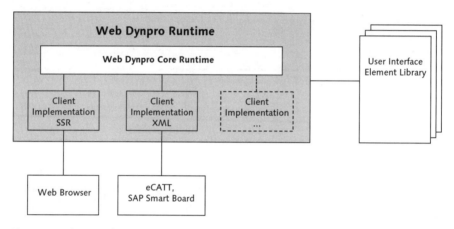

Figure 1.5 Client Implementations in the WD4A Runtime

The idea of decoupling user interface development from the client technology to be used, which is the basis of the WD4A framework client implementations, can be compared to the database interface existing since the market launch of SAP R/3. Database system vendors use inconsistent SQL statements (*Structured Query Language*) in their programming interfaces. Therefore, the appropriate SQL statements need to be observed in every application specific to the database that is to be used for data retention in the production operation. To relieve the developers of business process applications from this additional implementation effort and to simplify maintenance, the database interface was introduced in SAP products. The developers use a query language that is based on ABAP statements (*Open SQL*). The statements of this language are converted to the vendor-specific standard SQL statements at

---

1 At the time this book was written, the Windows smart client integration was still in beta phase. Therefore, later changes or different names are possible.

runtime. During the development process, it is therefore not necessary to consider the database systems on which the application is eventually operated (see Figure 1.6).

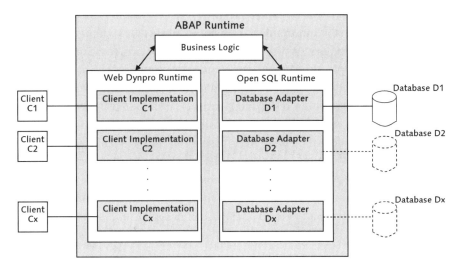

Figure 1.6 Structure of the ABAP Runtime

This shows that both the declarative approach of the WD4A framework for processing and presenting data in the presentation layer and the older database interface for persisting data in the database layer increasingly support the developers in dedicating themselves to their main task—the automation of business processes. This minimizes the effort for implementing recurring and non-core tasks.

1.4 Web Dynpro for ABAP for Future Use

Every new technology requires investments in the educational area. The development of web-based applications using Business Server Pages cannot be accomplished without comprehensive knowledge in HTML, CSS, JavaScript, or without architecture-specific expertise. At regular intervals, new technologies and platforms evolve that require training phases and new experience. Because the WD4A framework abstracts the implementations in the user interaction area, it is easier when developing business process applications to appropriately react to new technologies, to adapt existing products, or to offer new, innovative products. The WD4A framework provides a great deal of functionality that makes the development of web-based applications more efficient and therefore removes some disadvantages that were caused by the BSP/ITS technology.

We can assume that enterprises will take their first step towards browser-based development using the WD4A framework. The number of smart client products is still small, and the development of proprietary clients is still too expensive for customers. With its strict separation of presentation and business application logic, the WD4A framework also simplifies the maintenance of web-based applications. For implementations based on BSP, however, there is a very high degree of freedom for the developer team that can also result in applications that are very difficult to maintain. The WD4A framework also has the advantage that enterprises don't have to fear a loss of their investments when client technologies change. Instead, client implementations can easily be adapted to new protocols and display formats while complex applications are not affected. The web browser will therefore maintain a significant position in the world of client technologies in the years to come.

This chapter introduces the WD4A framework in detail. It will explain the terms and relations that are necessary for developing components and applications. Simple examples will enable you to become familiar with the operation of Web Dynpro tools.

2 WD4A Framework

2.1 Web Dynpro Explorer

Web Dynpro Explorer is completely integrated in the ABAP Workbench and serves as a development environment for the WD4A (Web Dynpro for ABAP) framework. Web Dynpro Explorer (see Figure 2.1) is called via Transaction SE80, where you select the **Web Dynpro Comp./Intf.** entry in the object list selection.

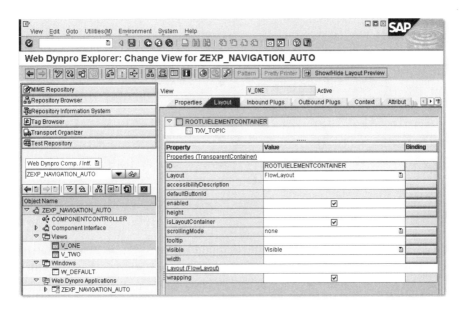

Figure 2.1 Web Dynpro Explorer

After starting Web Dynpro Explorer, you can either call an existing WD4A component or create a new component. The *object tree* of the component is

37

displayed in the lower left area. It allows you to display and edit the various parts of the component.

We'll now describe the primary structure and the underlying relationships within the WD4A framework. For the purpose of simplification and to make concepts easier to understand, we'll take a closer look at the basic parts of this framework and explain how they are interrelated in the following sections.

Figure 2.2 shows the view of the object tree of a component. The **component**, in this case ZEXP_INTRODUCTION, is a unit of cohesive processes and presentations, which has several interfaces. WD4A components can be used in other WD4A components, but they cannot be executed separately.

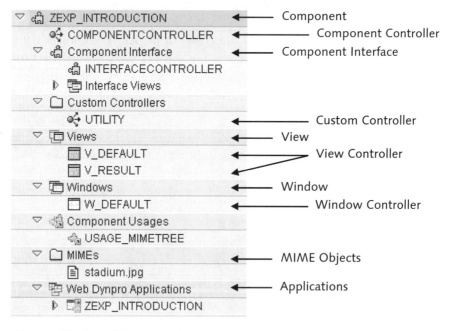

Figure 2.2 Structure of a Component

To execute a component, it must be defined in an application that is listed in the **Web Dynpro Applications** area. The WD4A application defines the entry point of a component and can be called via a Uniform Resource Identifier (URI).

The **component interface** determines the interface that would be available to other components within the WD4A framework when defining a usage. The component interface consists of a visual part, the interface view, and a logical part, the interface controller, which can be assigned context, methods, and events. The **view** is used for defining individual visual interfaces to the user. The **window** is for defining the arrangement and navigation of views and is the interface to the application. In the **MIMEs** area, you can store files consisting of different file formats locally to the component.

Let us now look at the controllers of a WD4A component. The **component controller** is automatically generated when a new component is created and exists as a superior controller within a component. The **custom controller** is used to group subareas of other controllers of the same component that have similar functionalities. The **view controller** deals with user interaction. The **window controller** is a global controller. Contrary to the view controller, the window controller is visible to all other controllers within the component.

2.1.1 View Elements

View elements are the smallest parts of a view. They can describe graphical, visible areas in the client and invisible areas of the layout. View elements are grouped in a *view element library* that you can access within a view via the **Layout** tab. The area under the Layout tab is also referred to as a *view editor*. To open the view editor, you must select a view from the object tree. Figure 2.3 shows the access to the view element library during the layout composition for an example view named V_CONFIRM.

The view is determined by a hierarchical tree structure of the view elements. The top node of this tree structure is the ROOTUIELEMENTCONTAINER, which is generated by default when a view is created.

Figure 2.4 shows the arrangement of view elements in the example view V_CONFIRM. The example contains two TransparentContainer view elements with the IDs TCO_LEFT and TCO_RIGHT. These two view elements form the invisible frame for additional view elements. Under each TransparentContainer view element, there is a Group view element. The IDs of these Group view elements are GRP_PERSON and GRP_PRODUCT. Each group contains Label view elements, InputField view elements, and one Button view element.

At runtime, this arrangement results in the client output shown in Figure 2.5. Another significant aspect for the presentation is the layout category to be selected. In this case, the MatrixLayout was used. Section 2.3.2 will address the differences and characteristics of the various layout categories in detail.

2 | WD4A Framework

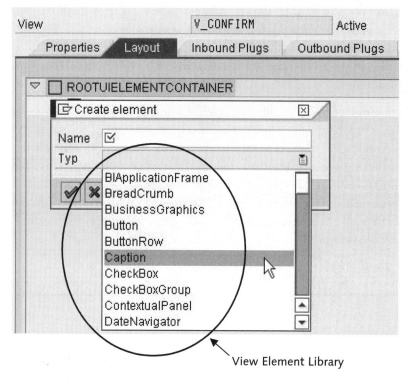

Figure 2.3 Access to the View Element Library in the View Editor

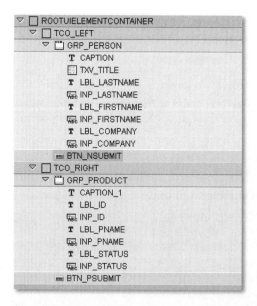

Figure 2.4 Example of the Arrangement of View Elements

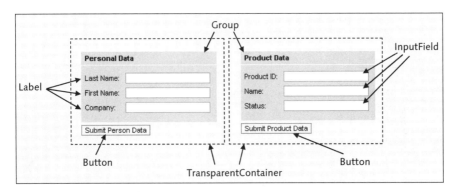

Figure 2.5 Presentation of View Elements in the Client

2.1.2 View Designer

The **Layout** tab allows you to switch to the view designer. Using the view designer, you can position view elements in a WYSIWYG editor using Drag&Drop. By clicking **Show/Hide Layout Preview**, you can display or hide the view designer (see Figure 2.6).

Figure 2.6 Displaying the Layout Preview

The view designer groups the view elements into various areas that correspond to their use or complexity. Currently, there are nine of these categories: **Standard Simple**, **Standard Complex**, **Standard Container**, **ActiveComponent**, **Adobe**, **BusinessGraphics**, **BusinessIntelligence**, **OfficeIntegration**, and **Pattern** (see Figure 2.7).

Just as the number of view elements will change with further releases and support packages, the assignments and categorization might change over time as well. The sole purpose of these groupings is to clarify and simplify the selection at development time. You should note that these groupings do not affect the runtime behavior of the view elements.

2 WD4A Framework

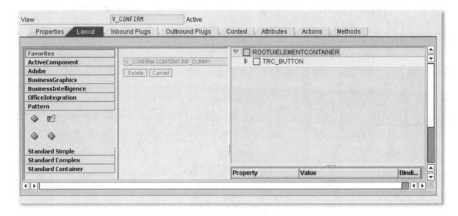

Figure 2.7 Grouping of View Elements in the View Designer

Aside from the aforementioned categories, there is a distinction of *simple* and *composite* view elements. Composite view elements contain additional lower-level view elements in the view element hierarchy. In the V_CONFIRM view example, the TransparentContainer view elements and the Group view elements are composite view elements. The InputField view elements, the Button view elements, and the Label view elements are simple view elements.

Every view element has a number of **properties** that control its appearance in the client, value assignments, and executable actions. The values of the properties can be assigned statically at the time of development and influenced dynamically at runtime. The properties of a view element are shown in the lower half of the view editor when the view element is selected (see Figure 2.8).

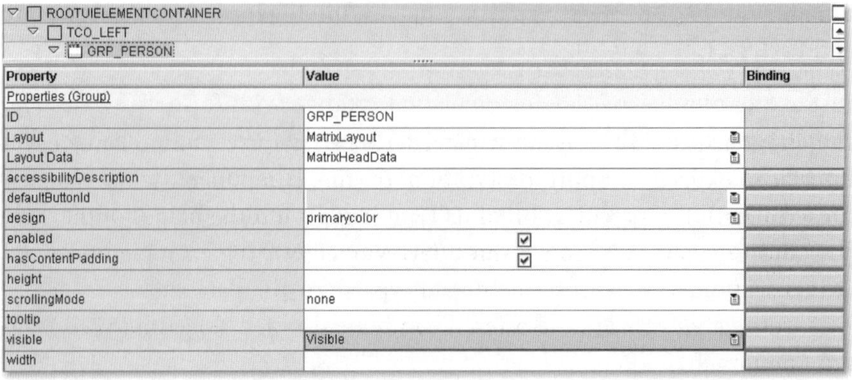

Figure 2.8 Properties of the Group View Element

2.1.3 "Hello World"

Now that you know the basics for handling the WD4A framework, you will create your first component by setting a view element property that will output the text "Hello World" on the client. For this purpose, the text is assigned as a fixed value to the **text** property of the TextView view element.

To create the component, in the object list selection of the Repository Browser (Transaction SE80), select the **Web Dynpro Comp./Intf** entry. Then, in the input field, enter the name of the component to be created; in our example, this is "ZEXP_HELLOWORLD_VIEW" (see Figure 2.9).

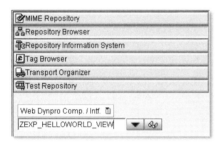

Figure 2.9 Creating a Component

After you press Enter, the general query for creating the object is displayed (see Figure 2.10). Confirm this query with **Yes**.

Figure 2.10 Query for Creating the Component

The input mask that is now displayed (**Web Dynpro: Component/Create Interface**) expects a short description of the component to be created (**Description**), the specification of its type (**Type**), and the names of the window and the view (**Window Name/View Name**). For the example presented in this section, you can use the default values or the data shown in Figure 2.11, respectively. From the offered component types, select the **Web Dynpro Component** value.

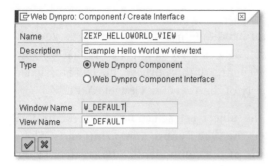

Figure 2.11 Input Mask for Component Definition

The query following the input of the description, type, view, and window of the component refers to the selected namespace and depends on the configuration of the system on which you implement the examples (see Figure 2.12). WD4A components (like classes, function modules, programs, BSP applications, etc.) starting with the letter "Z" or "Y" are created in the customer namespaces.

These namespaces are reserved for customer-specific developments and the creation of test programs. You can confirm the corresponding message and continue with the creation.

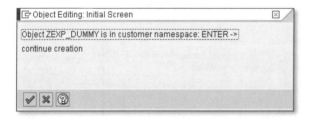

Figure 2.12 Namespace Information

If you don't want to transport the examples discussed in this book, in the next query (**Create Object Directory Entry**), you should ensure that you save the component as a local object (see Figure 2.13). In this case, you don't need to specify a package name; all data belonging to the component is stored locally in the $TMP package.

As a result of these steps, there is now an inactive version of the ZEXP_HELLOWORLD_VIEW component. Depending on the SAP Web Application Server version used or the support packages that are installed, there is either a view named V_DEFAULT or a window named W_DEFAULT. If the view or the window does not exist, they are now added to the component.

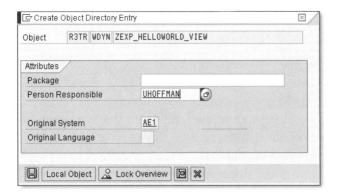

Figure 2.13 Saving the Component as a Local Object

For this purpose, right-click on the component name in the object list on the left side of the Web Dynpro Explorer and select **Create · View** in the context menu. The context menu also enables you to create additional windows, custom controllers, or the actual Web Dynpro application, for example (see Figure 2.14).

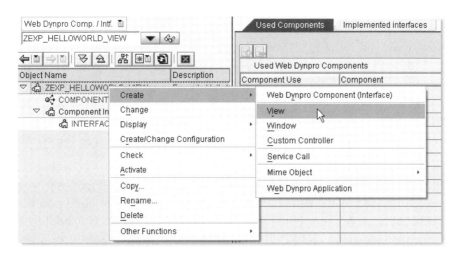

Figure 2.14 Adding a View to the Component

As with every object created in the ABAP Workbench, you are prompted to enter the name and the description of the view. Name the view "V_DEFAULT" (see Figure 2.15).

2 | WD4A Framework

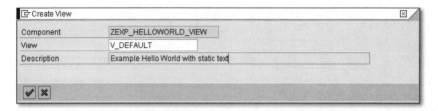

Figure 2.15 Input Mask for Creating the View

After saving the view, the object tree of the component shows a new node (**Views**) listing the view with the name V_DEFAULT. If you use the same procedure to create a window called W_DEFAULT (**Create · Window** in the component's context menu), it is also displayed in the component's object tree on the left side of the screen under the **Windows** node (see Figure 2.16).

Figure 2.16 Component with a View and a Window

Now double-click the V_DEFAULT view to select it. The right window of the Web Dynpro Explorer now displays the view editor—the **Layout** tab is the default setting—with the areas for presenting and defining the layout properties, the inbound and outbound plugs, the context, the attributes, the actions, and the methods of the view. The view layout is built hierarchically based on the ROOTUIELEMENTCONTAINER, or is composed in the layout preview (see Figure 2.4 and Figure 2.17).

The layout preview is designed as a WYSIWYG editor. Via Drag&Drop, you can position individual view elements from the view element library on the layout preview. Another possibility for designing the layout is to add view elements underneath the ROOTUIELEMENTCONTAINER node. Using the superior node in the hierarchy, you can add new nodes and change their position in relation to other view elements. The method you use for designing the layout does not affect the final result and is therefore dependent on your personal preferences or the preferences of the individual developer. In the following descriptions, we will modify only the hierarchy under ROOT-UIELEMENTCONTAINER.

2.1 Web Dynpro Explorer

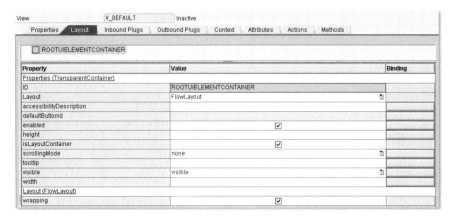

Figure 2.17 View Editor of the Component After Creating the View

Now let's continue developing the component by designing the view layout. To output the text line, we'll use the `TextView` view element. Right-click on the ROOTUIELEMENTCONTAINER node. In the context menu, select the **Insert Element** entry. In the displayed dialog box, select the type and enter the name of the view element. Select the **TextView** entry and enter the name "TXV_HELLO" (see Figure 2.18).

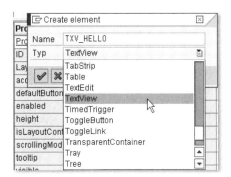

Figure 2.18 Selection and Definition of a View Element

The view element is now displayed beneath the ROOTUIELEMENTCONTAINER node, and its properties are shown in the lower right window. The majority of properties were assigned the default values of the WD4A framework. Now assign the string to be output—"Hello World from View!"—to the **text** property. To get a clearer presentation of the client output, we change the **design** property by selecting the **header1** value (see Figure 2.19). The configuration of the `TextView` view element `TXV_HELLO` is now complete.

design	header!	
enabled		✓
hAlign	auto	
layout	native	
semanticColor	standard	
text	Hello World from View!	

Figure 2.19 Setting Properties in the TextView View Element

We will now embed the view in the window. To execute this step, in the object list of the component on the left side of the Web Dynpro Explorer, open the **Window** node and double-click on the W_DEFAULT window to select it. The window editor is now displayed on the right side of the Web Dynpro Explorer, containing the areas for presenting and defining the characteristics, the window structure, the inbound and outbound plugs, the context, the attributes, and the methods for the window. By default, the WD4A framework displays the **Window** tab (see Figure 2.20).

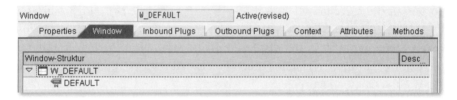

Figure 2.20 Window Editor of the Component

To embed the V_DEFAULT view in the W_DEFAULT window, right-click on the window name and select the **Embed View** entry from the context menu. From the input help of the dialog box now displayed, select the V_DEFAULT view and confirm your input (see Figure 2.21).

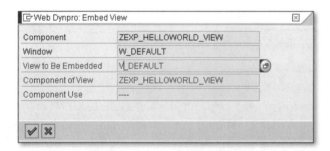

Figure 2.21 Selection of the View to Be Embedded in the Window

The view is added to the window structure. Because it is the first view in the window structure, it is automatically marked with the DEFAULT property.

This means that when the window is called, the V_DEFAULT view is displayed as the first view. The entire component, consisting of the W_DEFAULT window and the V_DEFAULT view, can now be saved and activated.

For this purpose, we will create the Web Dynpro application and assign the ZEXP_HELLOWORLD_VIEW component in the last step. Like the view and the window, the application is created via the component name in the object list. Position the mouse on the component name in the object list on the left side of the Web Dynpro Explorer, right-click on it, and select **Create · Web Dynpro Application** from the context menu. By default, the displayed dialog box specifies the component name as the name of the application. Use this proposal, complete the description of the Web Dynpro application, and confirm your input (see Figure 2.22).

Figure 2.22 Creating an Application

On the right side of the screen, you now see a page for defining the **properties** of the application (see Figure 2.23). The WD4A framework presets the name of the component to be used with the name of the component from which the application was created. In this case, this is the ZEXP_HELLOWORLD_VIEW component. The settings of the **Interface View** and **Plug Name** can also be used as suggested by the WD4A framework. The value of the **Interface View** field specifies the window that is called at application startup, and the value of the **Plug Name** field specifies the startup inbound plug that is to be triggered when the window is called (see Section 2.3.1).

Once you have saved the Web Dynpro application, it can be started. For this purpose, you can either copy the URL from the **Property** page of the application editor to the address line of your web browser, or select the **Test** entry from the application context menu in the object tree (see Figure 2.24).

Using the default values, when embedding the view in the window and configuring the application, results in the process that is illustrated in Figure 2.25 (i.e., when the ZEXP_HELLOWORLD_VIEW Web Dynpro application is started).

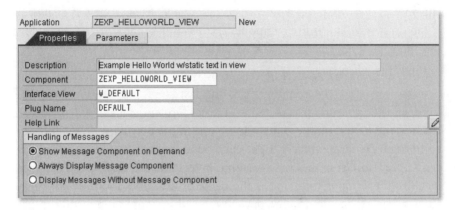

Figure 2.23 Specifying the Properties of an Application

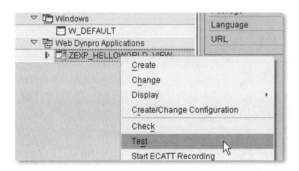

Figure 2.24 Starting the Application

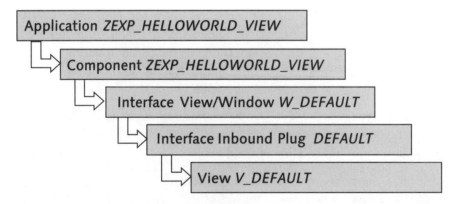

Figure 2.25 Process When Starting the Application

The client calls the ZEXP_HELLOWORLD_VIEW WD4A application. This application is assigned to the component of the same name, ZEXP_HELLOWORLD_VIEW.

The W_DEFAULT window is marked as the interface view and is therefore called with the inbound plug identified as **startup**. In the window, the V_DEFAULT view is set as the default view and is therefore displayed first. The result of the client output is shown in Figure 2.26.

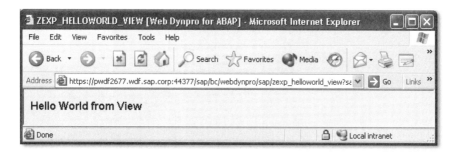

Figure 2.26 Text Output When Using a Default Value in the View Element

2.2 Relationships Between Application and Component

The basic concepts of the WD4A framework are predicated on reuse and componentization. The thought here is that it should be possible to structure web applications in different components, which can be implemented in various applications. WD4A components can be called by applications, but also used by other components. Therefore, it is not the application that is the central part of the WD4A framework, but the component.

At runtime, WD4A applications do not contain any data or information about the program processes, the layout structure, or the events to be triggered. They exist completely independent of the components. The application defines the address, the component to be called, and the entry point within this component, and therefore simply serves as a link between the user and the components.

WD4A applications are the higher-level module that facilitates the access to the functions of a component set as the entry point via the URI. If functions are required that are provided by other components, the embedding of these functions and the access to them are not controlled via the application, but by defining uses for these functions within the entry component. This ability to define component uses means that projects can be ideally grouped into individual fields of functions, which, in turn, can be realized by implementing components.

The following example illustrates the relationship between application and component. Let us assume that the components A, B and C shown in Figure 2.27 implement the functions listed in Table 2.1. Using the three components, we now want to create an application that enables a user to select a vehicle type from a list. In another step, the data of the respective manufacturer and the data of the vehicle parts are to be output for the selected vehicle type.

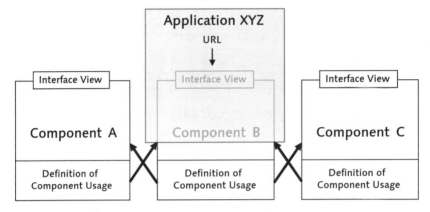

Figure 2.27 WD4A Application with Component B as the Entry Point

Component	Component Function
A	Presentation and editing of vehicle part data
B	Presentation and editing of vehicle type data
C	Presentation and editing of vehicle manufacturer data

Table 2.1 Example Functionality of Three WD4A Components

It is assumed that appropriate uses have been defined for the components and that they communicate via the generated interfaces. Because component B outputs the startup overview for the vehicle type data, it is defined as the entry component (see Figure 2.27). After the user has selected a vehicle type at runtime, component B accesses the interfaces of components A and C to request and output the corresponding information about the vehicle parts and the vehicle manufacturers of the selected vehicle type. As you can see, the application does not influence the process; rather, all functions are controlled within component B.

Now we will modify the discussed scenario slightly and look at the required changes that affect the application. The modification is made so that the user will select a manufacturer from a list of vehicle manufacturers at the beginning. For the selected manufacturer, the corresponding vehicle types should be listed. After selecting a type, the corresponding vehicle parts will be output. All this information is still provided unchanged by the components A, B, and C; however, the definition of the application will change. Because the list of vehicle manufacturers is to be displayed first in this scenario, an application must be defined with component C as the entry point (see Figure 2.28). After selecting the manufacturer, component C uses the interface to component B to use its function for retrieving the vehicle type data of the selected manufacturer. In the same way, component C accesses component A via component B to present the vehicle parts data. You can see that no programmatic changes of the application are required, but that the processes are designed entirely by the components.

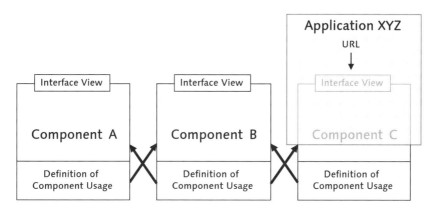

Figure 2.28 WD4A Application with Component C as the Entry Point

2.3 Visual Parts

Figure 2.27 and Figure 2.28 show examples of the relationships between applications and components within the WD4A framework. In the areas presenting the components, there is a box labeled Interface View. We will now look into the characteristics of the interface views.

2.3.1 Interface Views and Plugs

Every created window also corresponds to an interface view. The interface view allows for the connection of application and component. When component uses are defined, the interface view facilitates the embedding into the window of the component that defines the use.

For creating and defining an application, the following items are required:

- The entry component
- The interface view of the entry component, which shows the startup screen
- The inbound plug of the interface view that is to be triggered during the application startup and whose event handler method edits potential passed parameters and start conditions

In order for the inbound plugs of a window to be available for selection—as inbound plugs of the interface view when the application is defined—they must be defined accordingly in the window controller. The plugs should be identified as **Interface** and you will need to select the **startup** type. In Figure 2.29, the inbound plugs IP_A, IP_B and IP_C were identified as interface plugs and are therefore displayed in the interface view (see Figure 2.30).

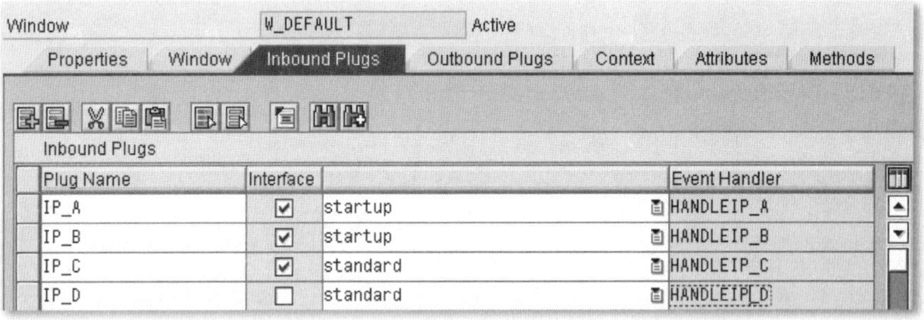

Plug Name	Interface		Event Handler
IP_A	✓	startup	HANDLEIP_A
IP_B	✓	startup	HANDLEIP_B
IP_C	✓	standard	HANDLEIP_C
IP_D	☐	standard	HANDLEIP_D

Figure 2.29 Identification of Inbound Plugs in the Window Controller

Plug Name		Description
IP_A	startup	
IP_B	startup	
IP_C	standard	

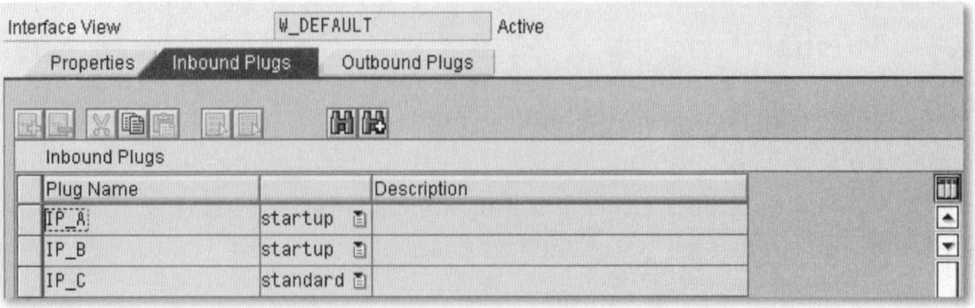

Figure 2.30 Interface View with Inbound Plugs

Inbound plug IP_D is not visible in the interface view and can only be used within the component for interacting with other windows. Of the three inbound plugs that are visible in the interface view, IP_A and IP_B are of the **startup** type and are available to the application for being defined as entry points. Inbound plug IP_C is of the **standard** type and is not accessible to the application. This plug type is used for communicating within component usages. In Figure 2.31, the IP_A and IP_B inbound plugs can be selected by the application; however, the application can use only one plug as a startup plug.

Figure 2.32 once again illustrates the inbound plug's configuration of a window in the window controller, as it was set for this example.

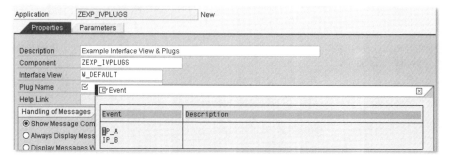

Figure 2.31 Selection of the Startup Plug

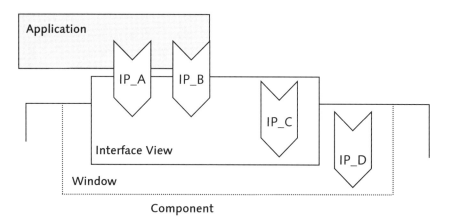

Figure 2.32 Graphical Presentation of the Inbound Plug Definitions

When creating the application, you need to decide which one of the two startup plugs, IP_A or IP_B, is to be used. For a component use, the IP_C inbound plug would be visible in the components that define the use. The

IP_D inbound plug is addressable only within its own component. The windows of a component can define any number of inbound plugs. When a user creates a new component, the WD4A framework automatically adds a window containing an inbound plug of the **startup** type called DEFAULT. This default plug can be renamed, and more plugs can be created. The components can also have several windows. For every window, however, the WD4A framework generates exactly one interface view with a default startup inbound plug.

2.3.2 View Layout

The layout of a view describes the characteristics of a visual part of the screen. A view can contain several view elements that represent data, receive user actions, or control other processes in the client (see Table 2.2).

View Element	Function
TextView	Present text sequences in the client
Button	Enable the user to trigger events
TimedTrigger	Implement client-side scripting to automatically trigger request/response cycles

Table 2.2 Examples of Using View Elements

View elements are processed in the view editor using the **Layout** tab. Initially, the view elements are added to the ROOTUIELEMENTCONTAINER node. Every view element has several properties that control its characteristics like display format and functioning.

The superior node in the view element hierarchy determines the layout of the view elements arranged under this node. There are four layout categories (see Table 2.3).

Layout Category	Characteristic
FlowLayout	Row-based arrangement of view elements with automatic adaptation to the client's window size
RowLayout	Row-based arrangement of view elements where the user controls the line breaks

Table 2.3 View Layout Categories

Layout Category	Characteristic
GridLayout	Column-based arrangement of view elements with a preset number of columns
MatrixLayout	Column-based arrangement of view elements where the number of columns is not preset

Table 2.3 View Layout Categories (cont.)

When a new view is created or composable view elements are added, the default layout category is the FlowLayout. Note that depending on the layout category, there are different properties that need to be set for the view element. For the MatrixLayout layout category, for example, you need to specify for every view element to be added whether it is to be arranged within a column of the same row (**MatrixData** value) or in the first column of a row (**MatrixHeadData** value). For the RowLayout layout category of a UI container, you need to differentiate between the values **RowData** and **RowHeadData** when determining the arrangement of view elements.

We'll show the characteristics of the four layout categories using several examples. If you have five view elements to display, they are presented in the client using the four layout categories as follows:

▶ **FlowLayout**
If you use the FlowLayout layout category, all elements are displayed sequentially. You cannot force line breaks. The presentation is automatically adapted to fit the size of the client window (see Figure 2.33).

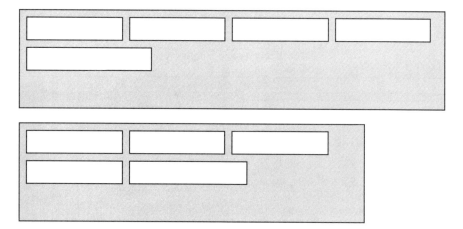

Figure 2.33 FlowLayout Presentation in Different Window Sizes

2 | WD4A Framework

▶ **RowLayout**
If you use the `RowLayout` layout category, every element is displayed in its own column. The column widths therefore differ from row to row. Line breaks are forced via the **RowHeadData** property (see Figure 2.34).

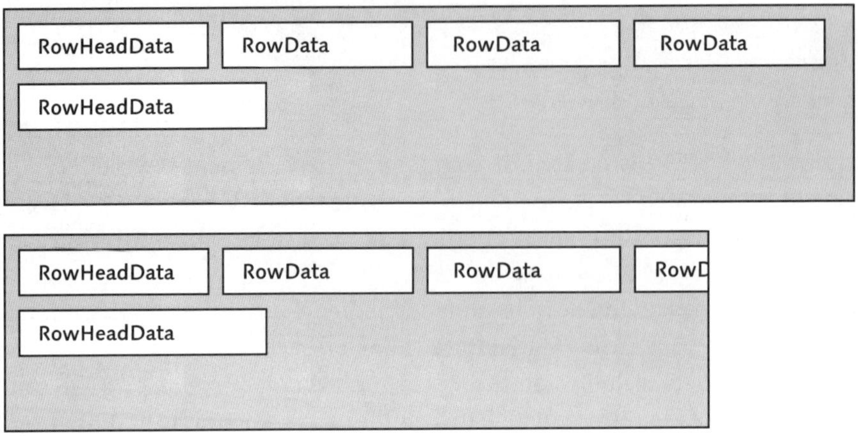

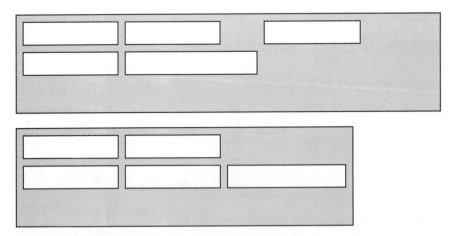

Figure 2.34 RowLayout Presentation in Different Window Sizes

▶ **GridLayout**
The `GridLayout` layout category arranges all elements depending on a number of columns to be defined. Line breaks are also inserted if the client window is not large enough to display the view element. In the example shown in Figure 2.35, the `GridLayout` was defined for three columns.

Figure 2.35 GridLayout Presentation in Different Window Sizes

▶ **MatrixLayout**

The `MatrixLayout` layout category arranges the view elements in columns, where a new column is determined by the **MatrixHeadData** property of a view element. Therefore, it is neither necessary nor possible to define the number of columns at the time of development. The display is adapted to fit the size of the client window using the **stretchedHorizontally** and **stretchedVertically** properties (see Figure 2.36).

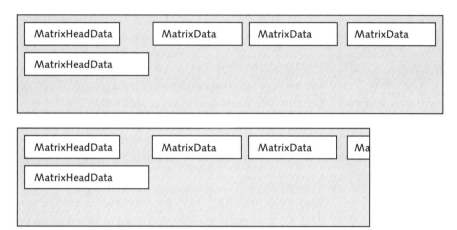

Figure 2.36 MatrixLayout Presentation in Different Window Sizes

If you want to influence the size of the view elements' presentation, you can use the units of measurement in Cascading Style Sheets (CSS). The units of measurement and their relations are listed in Table 2.4.

Unit of Measurement	Type	Relation
em	Relative	Highest/widest letter of the parent element
ex	Relative	Smallest/narrowest letter of the parent element
px	Absolute	Pixel
%	Relative	Percentage related to the size of the parent element

Table 2.4 CSS Units of Measurement for Controlling the View Layout

Within a component, you can define several views. You can navigate among the views via inbound and outbound plugs to be determined. When editing the views, you can also define the plugs. The navigation is determined by linking the plugs in the component windows that embed the respective views. In the simplest case, there is only one view that, by default, is assigned the **default** characteristic when it is embedded in a window. At runtime, this view is therefore displayed as the first view. A window always contains exactly one view with the **default** characteristic.

2.3.3 Windows

In the previous sections, the term *Window* was mentioned several times in the descriptions of application, component, interface view, and view. In this section, we will elaborate on the characteristics of a window.

The window is the collective of the visual part of the component and facilitates the definition of the navigation. Every component can consist of several windows, and every window can consist of several views. Within the window, you can determine the navigation among the individual views. At runtime, a window can display only one view at a time. If several views are to be displayed, they must be grouped within a main view using `ViewContainerUIElement` view elements.

The views are embedded in windows, and the same view can be used in several windows. In Figure 2.37, for example, **View A** is used in **Window 1** and **Window 2**, and **View B** is used in **Window 1** and **Window 3**. You cannot use or embed the same view twice in a window.

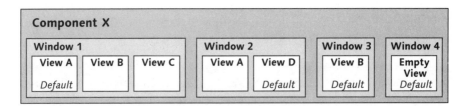

Figure 2.37 Example of Embedding Views in Windows

In every window, there is at least one view, which is marked as the default view and is first displayed when the window is called. In Figure 2.37, this is **View A** in **Window 1** and **View D** in **Window 2**. The WD4A framework marks the view that was embedded first as the default view; however, this characteristic can be transferred to another view at any time as soon as it has been embedded in the window. Since **Window 3** and **Window 4** each contain only one view in Figure 2.37, this view is automatically marked as the default view when it is embedded.

The *empty view* is a special case. The WD4A framework always generates it in a window if no other view has been embedded. In Figure 2.37, this applies to **Window 4** because it does not contain a view at the time of generation and is therefore assigned an empty view by the WD4A framework, which is marked as the default view at the same time.

The window is the superior unit of the views and is responsible for defining the navigation and for providing the interface to the application and to other components defining the component as a usage. The navigation possibilities are described in Section 2.6. Windows are called from the application or other components via inbound plugs that are coupled with event handler methods. For every window, you can define several inbound plugs. For every plug, the WD4A framework creates event handler methods in which you can implement the corresponding logic that specifies the processes to be executed when the plug is called. Within the event handler methods of the inbound plugs, transferred parameters can be evaluated or context attributes can be initialized, for example.

2.4 View Controller and View Context

Every view contains a controller that maintains the view data in the *view context*. On the one hand, the controller provides functionalities for populating the context with data that is then output via the view. On the other hand, it provides functionalities for processing user input and actions.

The context is comparable to a hierarchical tree structure and consists of context nodes and context attributes. The properties of view elements can be bound against context nodes and context attributes. This binding enables the controller at runtime to extract data from the http request, to assign the values to the binding context and, conversely, to compose the HTTP response using the values from the context (see Figure 2.38).

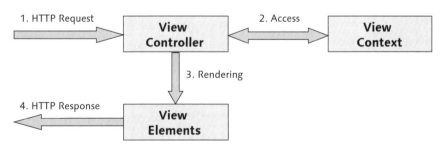

Figure 2.38 Context Controller View Structure According to MVC

The context binding via the view controller decouples the view elements from the application logic or the model, respectively. Thus, the layout information exists separately from the program content and logic. The concept behind this structure is based on the *Model View Controller Design Pattern* (MVC). In Chapter 4, we'll explore the details and the development of MVC-based WD4A applications.

Context nodes can have any combination of other context nodes and context attributes as lower-level elements in the tree structure. This does not apply to context attributes; they are always the leaf elements in a tree hierarchy. A context node is typically used for grouping context attributes and other lower-level context nodes.

For example, if you want to build an input mask for a customer's contact data, you would create a CUSTOMER context node and under this node, you would create one appropriate context attribute for every field of the input mask; in this example, the attributes COMPANY, CITY, ZIP_CODE, and STREET are displayed (see Figure 2.39). To store the data of a potential contact person of the customer, you could now create another group context node named CONTACT under the CUSTOMER context node. This context node would store the context attributes that pertain to the data of this contact person: FIRST_NAME, LAST_NAME, EMAIL, and PHONE.

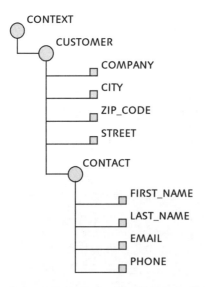

Figure 2.39 Example of the Structure of a View Context

Up to now, we dealt with the grouping possibility within a context, that is, with grouping related attributes under a context node; however, you should note that the context also provides several configuration options that influence its behavior at the time of initialization and during the remaining runtime of the WD4A application. We will describe these options in the following sections.

2.4.1 Context Property Cardinality

The number of context node elements to be created is determined by the **Cardinality** property. When creating the context as it is structured in Figure 2.39, if you accept the default settings at runtime, an instance with one element is created first (see Figure 2.40).

This is absolutely sufficient for the example shown of presenting a simple input mask. But, if several customer entries were to be created and presented in a table, then several elements of the context node would be required. Every created context node element would then contain the data for one customer entry.

Property	Value
Nodes	
Node Name	CONTENT
Dictionary structure	
Cardinality	1..1
Selection	0..1
Initialization Lead Selection	✓
Singleton	✓
Supply Function	SUPPLY_CONTENT

Figure 2.40 Default Context Node Settings

If the value assigned to the **Cardinality** property amounts to **1..1** for presenting a simple input mask, the **Cardinality** property must change to either **0..n** or **1..n** to present the data of several customers, depending on whether or not there is an entry when the table is initially displayed. The **Cardinality** property can be assigned a maximum of four different values that define not only the number of elements, but also the behavior at the time of context initialization. The options that can be selected are listed in Table 2.5.

2 | WD4A Framework

Value	Characteristic
1..1	At the time of context initialization, exactly one element is created that is maintained at runtime.
0..1	At runtime, a maximum of one context element can be used.
1..n	At the time of context initialization, one or more elements can be created, but at least one element must exist at runtime.
0..n	At runtime, any number of context elements can be used.

Table 2.5 Values for the Cardinality of Context Nodes

It is important that you understand the selection options listed in Table 2.5, because runtime errors can easily occur if the configuration is not correct. Therefore, we'll go through some hypothetical scenarios and discuss the right selection for the **Cardinality** property. The example of inputting and presenting customer data will remain the basis for all further discussions.

As we mentioned earlier in this chapter, the **Cardinality** property of the CUSTOMER context node would be set to a value of **1..1** to present the input mask. This means that at the time of initialization exactly one element of the CUSTOMER context node is created with the respective attributes. Additionally, we shall assume that we can define exactly one contact person per customer. Therefore, the **Cardinality** property of the CONTACT context node would be set to **1..1** as well. With this setting, within the only element of the CUSTOMER context node, there is exactly one element for the CONTACT context node (see Figure 2.41).

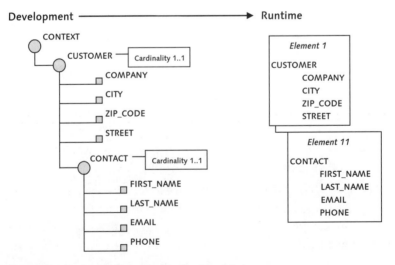

Figure 2.41 Context Node with a Cardinality of 1..1

Therefore, you would use the value **1..1** of the **Cardinality** property for context nodes to whose attributes the view elements are bound that are displayed in input masks, for example. If the **Cardinality** property were set to a value of **0..1** or **0..n** in this case, this would lead to a runtime error because the element that is required at the time of initialization and that contains the attributes to be bound does not exist. The application expects at least one element, but finds only an empty node. An example of such a runtime error is presented as an extract from Transaction ST22 in Figure 2.42.

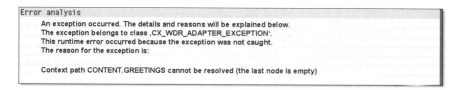

Figure 2.42 Runtime Error Caused by a Wrong Cardinality

The value **1..n** could be assigned, but would unnecessarily occupy system resources at runtime because the WD4A framework assumes that several elements of the context node are used at runtime.

We will now assume that already existing customer entries are to be read from the database and presented to the user in a table in the client at the time of initialization. For this purpose, the structure of the view context remains unchanged as shown in Figure 2.41, that is, there is data for every customer according to the context attributes of the CUSTOMER context node.

If the value **1..1** of the **Cardinality** property were kept as shown in the previous example, only one element would be created at runtime and it would only be possible to display the data of a single customer using this element. The WD4A framework, however, prevents the use of a cardinality of **1..1** or **0..1** for the display of tables and would terminate with a runtime error.

To present all existing customer entries, a value of **1..n** or **0..n** must be used for the **Cardinality** property of the CUSTOMER context node; however, the value **0..n** would make sense only if you assumed that there might be changes related to the number of customer entries (e.g., due to deletions) at runtime. The value **0..n** is particularly important to prepare for the inevitable time when, due to the deletions, there are no more customer entries left (i.e., there are no more elements of the CUSTOMER context node either). If in such a scenario the **Cardinality** property were set to a value of **1..n**, and if the last customer entry and therefore the last element of the CUSTOMER context node were deleted, the WD4A framework would respond with a runtime error.

Figure 2.43 shows an overview of the configuration of the CUSTOMER context node and its behavior at runtime with an assigned cardinality of **1..n**. Because the cardinality of the CONTACT context node remains set to **1..1** (assuming that every customer has only one contact person), for every element of the CUSTOMER context node, there is exactly one element of the CONTACT context node.

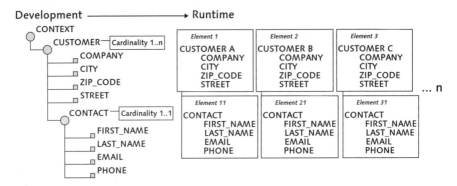

Figure 2.43 Context Node with a Cardinality of 1..n

The presented scenarios show that a good understanding of the context properties is crucial to avoid errors and indefinable states at program runtime.

2.4.2 Singleton and Lead Selection Context Properties

To explain the **Singleton** property, we will further extend the previous scenario discussed in Section 2.4.1. We assumed that at the time of initialization the data of several customers is read from the database to populate the context. The **Cardinality** property of the CUSTOMER context node is set to the value **1..n**. Therefore, there are several elements: one for every customer entry. Up to this point, we assumed that there is exactly one contact person for every customer entry, which means that the **Cardinality** property of the CONTACT context node is set to **1..1**.

This specification is now changed to allow several contact persons to exist for every customer. In this case, the **Cardinality** property must be changed to **0..n** or **1..n**. Figure 2.44 shows the structure of context node elements at runtime after the initialization has been completed and the context has been populated. For our example, we will assume that the database contains two customer entries with three contact persons each. Therefore, two elements will be created for the CUSTOMER context node at runtime, Element 1 and Element 2.

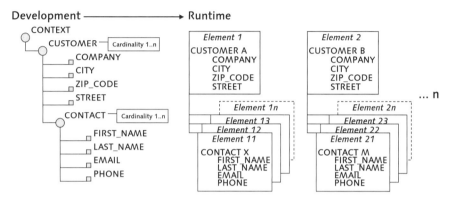

Figure 2.44 Grouping Elements with the Cardinality 1..n

For the CONTACT context node, there are now two groups with three elements each: Element 11, Element 12, and Element 13 are assigned to the parent context node element, Element 1; and Element 21, Element 22, and Element 23 are assigned to the parent context node element, Element 2. For every one of these *groups of elements*, the WD4A framework creates a new instance of the context node.

In our example, the WD4A framework creates an instance of the CUSTOMER context node with two elements and two instances of the CONTACT context node with three elements each. This shows that for a considerable depth of the tree structure, due to several existing levels of lower-level nodes and an accordingly large data volume, the time required for building the tree structure at runtime—the instantiation of the context node and the creation of elements, as well as the system resources required for these tasks—can very easily have a negative effect on the program runtime.

An alternative to this is the **Singleton** property of a context node. By default, this property is set for every context node to be created and indicates that there can only be one instance of the respective context node at runtime. This instance always refers to one element of the higher-level node, which is, in this case, called a *lead selection*. In other words, if the **Singleton** property of a lower-level context node is set, all elements of the lower-level context node can be built for exactly one element of the higher-level context node. This

2 | WD4A Framework

element of the higher-level node—for which all lower-level elements are created—is the lead selection. Because this property is difficult to understand, we'll refer again to our customer data example. The left side of Figure 2.45 shows the settings as they are made at design time.

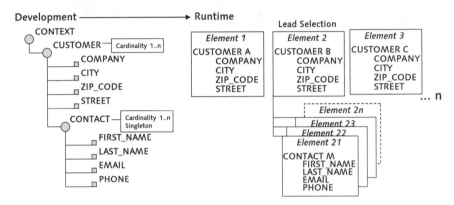

Figure 2.45 Using the Lead Selection

For the CUSTOMER context node, the **Cardinality** property is set to **0..n** and the **Singleton** flag is set. The same settings apply to the CONTACT context node. At runtime, an instance is created with the elements of the CUSTOMER context node. For context nodes that are arranged immediately under the root node, there is always only one instance, that is, these nodes are always **Singleton** nodes because the root node is always represented by only one element.

In Figure 2.45, there are three elements for the CUSTOMER context node, but only for Element 2 of the CUSTOMER context node were the elements of the CONTACT context node created. In this case, Element 2 is the lead selection. The element maintained as the lead selection can either be determined at the time of populating a context node, or the initialization can be left up to the WD4A framework. This is achieved via the **Initialization Lead Selection** property of the respective context node (see Figure 2.46). If the property is set, the WD4A framework determines the first element from the list as the lead selection.

Property	Value
Nodes	
Node Name	CONTENT
Dictionary structure	
Cardinality	1..1
Selection	0..1
Initialization Lead Selection	✓
Singleton	✓
Supply Function	SUPPLY_CONTENT

Figure 2.46 Initialization Lead Selection

If you flag a context node as **Singleton**, whenever the lead selection of the higher-level context node is changed the elements of the lower-level context node will be rebuilt. Furthermore, the data of the previous list of elements is no longer available. If necessary, it must be read and saved beforehand. The lead selection can be changed by a user action; one such example is the selection of a table row in a table whose **selectionMode** property is set to the value **single**. At runtime, the application has different methods for influencing the lead selection at the respective context node object. These methods are listed in Table 2.6.

Method	Lead Selection
set_lead_selection	Sets the lead selection to the element in the element list that is specified by a reference
set_lead_selection_index	Sets the lead selection to the element in the element list that is specified by an index
move_first	Sets the lead selection to the first element in the element list and provides a reference to the new lead selection
move_last	Sets the lead selection to the last element in the element list and provides a reference to the new lead selection
move_next	Sets the lead selection to the following element in the element list and provides a reference to the new lead selection
move_previous	Sets the lead selection to the previous element in the element list and provides a reference to the new lead selection
move_to	Sets the lead selection to the element in the element list that is specified by an index and provides a reference to the new lead selection

Table 2.6 Methods of Setting/Changing the Lead Selection

Setting the lead selection via the index to the second element of a context node named TEST would be implemented in the controller methods as follows:

```
DATA lr_node    TYPE REF TO  if_wd_context_node.
...
lr_node = wd_context->get_child_node( 'TEST' ).
lr_node->set_lead_selection_index( index = 2 ).
```

Listing 2.1 Setting the Lead Selection Using the Index

Using **Singleton** context nodes, system resources can be handled more efficiently. Only one instance with all elements of the context node is created and maintained at a time, contrary to completely building a tree structure as illustrated in Figure 2.44. But, **Singleton** context nodes require a very good understanding of the processes at runtime, and a slightly higher development effort is necessary to avoid data inconsistencies when changing the lead selection. The decision regarding whether to use **Singleton** context nodes does not only depend on performance and complexity factors, but also on the view elements chosen that bind to the respective context nodes and context attributes.

For example, when using the Tree view element and presenting recursive tree structures, the context nodes to be bound against must not be configured as **Singleton** context nodes. The same holds true when the DropDownByIndex view element is used for selecting values in table rows. The context node providing the list of elements, which are the selection values of the dropdown list, must also not be a **Singleton** context node, because every table row requires an instance with the elements of the context node.

2.4.3 Supply Function Method

The view controller has numerous methods that are applied during the program run, either when an HTTP request is received, or when an HTTP response is composed, and that afford the developer with the option to influence these processes at different times. Additionally, there is the possibility of adding methods to the controller that can take over various functions depending on their type. This includes the *supply function methods*.

Supply function methods are used for populating the context attributes of the context node elements. If it exists, the supply function method is always called before a read access when the context node element that is accessed by reading is in an invalid state. This is the case after the initialization of a component, or a context node can explicitly be invalidated during the program run. After the initialization of a component, there are elements for all context nodes that are not populated or bound, respectively. If a context node is assigned a related method for the **Supply function** property, this method is executed.

Within the supply function method, the data is procured and the elements of the context nodes are populated. For populating, the WD4A framework provides a number of options that should be used according to the **Cardinality** property of the context node and depending on the user input (see Table 2.7).

Value of the Cardinality Property	Possible Populating Methods
0..1 or 1..1	bind_element(), bind_structure(), set_attribute(), set_static_attributes()
0..n or 1..n	bind_elements(), bind_table()

Table 2.7 Context Population Methods Depending on the Cardinality Property

When using the bind_*() methods, you need to consider that the entire node is filled and the elements are already created. Using the set_*() methods, you can explicitly access individual attributes of elements; however, the elements must already exist. The bind_element() and bind_elements() methods have a generic interface and thereby facilitate the transfer of instances of if_wd_context_element() and DATA, or even the transfer of references to objects. The bind_structure() and bind_table() methods optimize the performance in cases where context nodes are based on data types that were defined in the ABAP Dictionary.

2.4.4 Sample Applications

At this point, you've learned about the basic parts and various functions of the WD4A framework that should enable you to create simple WD4A components and applications. We will now put your newfound knowledge to practical use. To illustrate the development process, we'll use the concepts that were introduced in the previous sections to describe the development procedure. The following sample applications have a common goal: the output of a line of text in the client. The example in Section 2.1.3 achieved this goal by setting a property of the view element. In the following examples, the text is assigned by the **default** parameter of a context attribute, or by binding itself to the context node within a supply function method.

When dealing with the examples introduced in this section, the individual consecutive steps for the implementation are shown and described. Every example is based on only one component containing a window that provides a startup inbound plug for the interface view. The window, in turn, contains only one view; the layout of the view is restricted to only one view element.

"Hello World" from the Context

In contrast to the ZEXP_HELLOWORLD_VIEW component in Section 2.1.3, the **text** property of the view element will now be bound to a context attribute of the view context. Therefore, the fixed value that was assigned to the view property is overwritten by the value of the context attribute. The context attribute has a **Default Value** property that should now contain the line of text to be output.

The advantage of using context attributes or the context in general is that you get a stricter separation of layout data from program content and logic (see Section 2.4). Again, we will discuss the individual steps of implementing the context using an example component called ZEXP_HELLOWORLD_CTX. The easiest way of creating the ZEXP_HELLOWORLD_CTX component is to copy the ZEXP_HELLOWORLD_VIEW component developed in Section 2.1.3 and to make the appropriate changes that are described in detail below.

After you created or copied the new ZEXP_HELLOWORLD_CTX component, go to the V_DEFAULT view and select the **Context** tab on the right-hand side. You will see two windows, each containing the root node CONTEXT. The window to the left represents the context of the V_DEFAULT view; the right window shows the context of the component controller (see Figure 2.47).

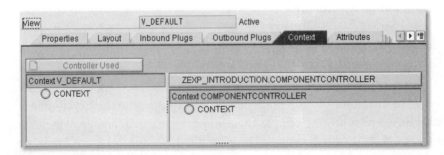

Figure 2.47 Display of the Context of a View

By default, every view can access the context of the component controller. If usages are defined on other components, the right window cannot only represent the context of its own component controller, but also the context of the component controllers for which a usage was defined.

Usages are defined on the **Properties** tab of the view (see Figure 2.48). Here, the WD4A framework automatically enters the component controller of its own view when the view is created. For uses from other components, the developer must specify this accordingly. The concepts for defining component uses are addressed in Chapter 4 and Chapter 6. To implement the example component ZEXP_HELLOWORLD_CTX in this section, only the view context is important and that is supplemented here.

Used Controllers/Components			
Component Use	Component	Controller	Description
	ZEXP_HELLOWORLD_CTX	COMPONENTCONTROLLER	

Figure 2.48 Definition of Component Uses in the View

Select the root node CONTEXT. In the lower right half of the screen, a table is displayed showing the **Properties** of the context node. The properties of the root node CONTEXT are fixed and cannot be changed. We will now create a new context node under the root node and add an attribute. Right-click on the root node CONTEXT and select **Create · Node** from the context menu (see Figure 2.49).

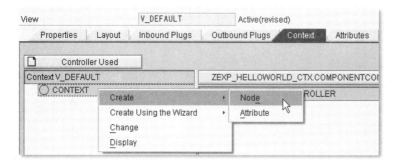

Figure 2.49 Creating a Context Node

In the input mask, assign the name "CONTENT" to the new context node. All other suggested values can remain unchanged. Check to ensure that the **Car-**

2 | WD4A Framework

dinality property is set to **1..1** by default (see Section 2.4.1) and then confirm your input.

In the next step, an attribute is added to the newly created context node. In the context menu of the CONTENT context node, select the **Create · Attribute** entry. In the displayed input mask, enter "GREETING" as the **Attribute Name**, and under **Type**, select **STRING**. The remaining default data remains unchanged (see Figure 2.50).

After you confirm your input, the properties of the newly created GREETING attribute are displayed in the lower pane. Now we will assign the text line to be output to the context attribute. In the **Value** field of the **Default Value** property, enter the text "Hello from WD4A Context!"(see Figure 2.51). All other properties of the attribute remain unchanged.

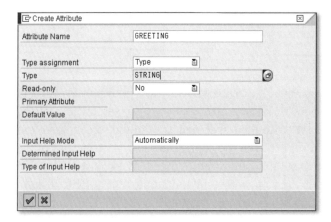

Figure 2.50 Creating a Context Attribute

Context V_DEFAULT	ZEXP_HELLOWORLD_CTX.COMPONENTCONTROLLER
▽ ○ CONTEXT	Context COMPONENTCONTROLLER
▽ 🗐 CONTENT	○ CONTEXT
╰ GREETING	

Property	Value	
Attribute		
Attribute Name	GREETING	
Type assignment	Type	🗐
Type	STRING	
Read-only		☐
Primary Attribute		☐
Default Value	Hello from WD4A Context!	
Input Help Mode	Automatically	🗐
Determined Input Help		
Type of Input Help		

Figure 2.51 Context Attribute with the Default Value Set

To ensure the output in the client, we must bind the attribute to the **text** property of the `TextView` view element `TXV_HELLO`. For this step, select the **Layout** tab. If you created the component `ZEXP_HELLOWORLD_CTX` by copying the component `ZEXP_HELLOWORLD_VIEW`, which was recommended at the beginning of the section, the `TextView` view element with the ID `TXV_HELLO` should already exist in the layout. If it does not yet exist, add the view element as described in Section 2.1.3. Then, in the rightmost column of the **Property** table of the view element, at the **text** property click on the **Binding** button. A display frame appears that represents the structure of the view context of the `V_DEFAULT` view (see Figure 2.52).

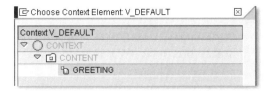

Figure 2.52 Selection of the Context Attribute to Be Bound

Mark the context attribute `GREETING` and confirm your input. In the **Property** table of the view element, the **text** property is now marked as bound. The path to the bound context attribute is specified as follows:

`[NameOfView].[NameOfContextNode].[NameOfContextAttribute]`

Figure 2.53 shows the result, in our example `V_DEFAULT.CONTENT.GREETING`.

layout	native
semanticColor	standard
text	V_DEFAULT.CONTENT.GREETING
textDirection	inherit

Figure 2.53 Binding a Property to a Context Attribute

Once you have saved the component, it can be activated. Create the application for the component and start it in the client. The text should be output as shown in Figure 2.54.

2 | WD4A Framework

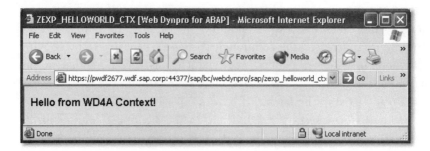

Figure 2.54 Text Output Via the Default Value in the Context Attribute

"Hello World" from the Supply Function Method

The previous sections showed how to output text by assigning fixed values to the **text** property of a view element and to the **Default Value** property of a context attribute. Now, we want to perform the assignment or the population of a context attribute via the supply function method.

For this purpose, in the view editor select the **Methods** tab. Create a new method named SUPPLY_CONTENT and mark it as a method of the **Supply Function** type (see Figure 2.55). You can also enter the name and confirm it when editing the properties of the context node in the input field of the **Supply Function** property. In this case, the method is automatically created under the **Supply Function** method type.

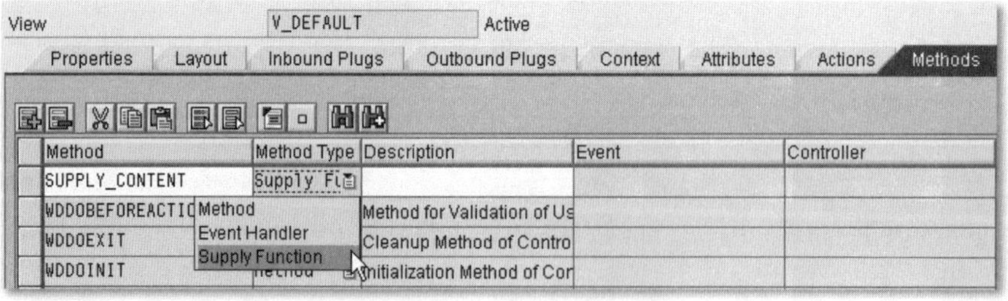

Figure 2.55 Creating Supply Function Methods

A double-click brings you to the editor of the method. In the signature of all supply function methods, the WD4A framework provides two parameters by default that facilitate an easy access to the context node and the corresponding parent element (if present) to be edited (see Figure 2.56). Listing 2.2 shows how to populate the only element of the CONTENT context node at runtime via the appropriate statements in a newly created supply function method.

76

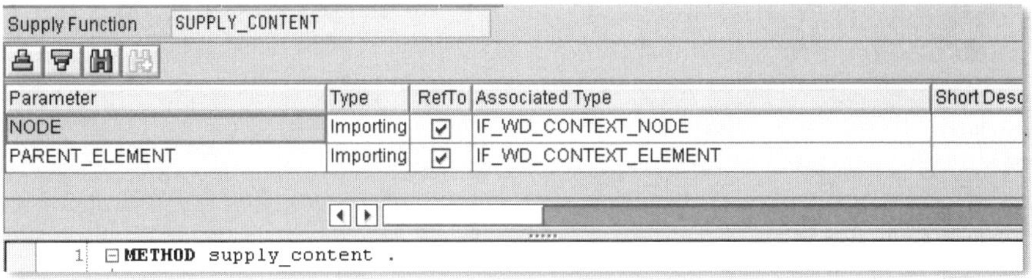

2.4 View Controller and View Context

Supply Function	SUPPLY_CONTENT				
Parameter		Type	RefTo	Associated Type	Short Desc
NODE		Importing	✓	IF_WD_CONTEXT_NODE	
PARENT_ELEMENT		Importing	✓	IF_WD_CONTEXT_ELEMENT	

```
1  METHOD supply_content .
```

Figure 2.56 Structure of Supply Function Methods

```
METHOD supply_content.
   DATA  ls_content     TYPE  if_v_default=>element_content.
   ls_content-greeting = 'Hello World - from Supply Function Method!'.
   node->bind_structure( new_item = ls_content ).
ENDMETHOD.
```

Listing 2.2 Implementing the Supply Function Method

For the specifications made in the view context, the WD4A framework creates local type definitions as parts of an interface generated for the view. These types are private to the view controller and can be used in its methods. The naming convention for the generated type of an individual context node element looks as follows:

`if_[NameOfView]=>element_[NameOfContextNode]`

Replace the brackets with the respective names to receive the appropriate data type of the context node element. For our example, this looks as follows:

`if_v_default=>element_content.`

The text is assigned by accessing the attribute of a structure type, as it is common in ABAP. Because the value of the **Cardinality** property of the context node is **1..1**, we can use the methods `bind_element()` or `bind_struture()` that are listed in Table 2.7. We know that we are editing a structure, `ls_content`, and will therefore populate the context node using the `bind_struture()` method that is specifically adapted to structures.

The supply function method must now be assigned to the appropriate context node. In the view editor, go to the **Context** tab and select the CONTENT context node. Position the cursor in the **Supply Function** property field. A selection icon appears to the right of the input field. If you click on this icon, a popup opens displaying the newly created supply function method for

77

selection. After you confirm your selection, the name of the method is transferred into the **Property** field (see Figure 2.57).

Property	Value
Nodes	
Node Name	CONTENT
Dictionary structure	
Cardinality	1..1
Selection	0..1
Initialization Lead Selection	☑
Singleton	☑
Supply Function	SUPPLY_CONTENT

Figure 2.57 Assignment of the Supply Function Method for the Context Node

After saving and activating the component, the application can be created and started. The result of the client output is shown in Figure 2.58.

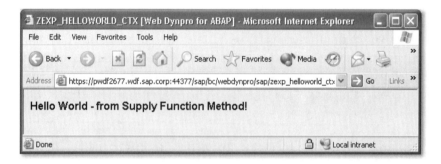

Figure 2.58 Text Output Using the Supply Function Method

The aforementioned examples show a determining characteristic of the WD4A framework: support for the development of complex applications based on declarative statements, while minimizing program lines to be created manually. For your information, our examples were developed with a very low effort with regard to ABAP programming, even though the developed components were very straightforward in their structure and flow.

2.5 Controllers and Controller Methods

Up to now, we have dealt primarily with the view controller. Other controllers of the WD4A framework include the component controller, the custom controller, the window controller, and the interface controller.

As you can see from working with the view controller, the controllers provide the functionality for flow control and for linking the areas of data storage and data display. The component controller plays an integral role in this respect. Its context data, events, attributes, and methods are visible within the entire component—provided the **public** setting has been selected for the attributes—and can be accessed by all lower-level controllers within a component. Furthermore, the component controller allows you to provide the component's interface to other components via methods, events, and context nodes to be specifically identified. The methods, events, and context nodes of this interface then make up the interface controller. The interface controller itself cannot be changed separately; modifications to the interface must always be performed via the component controller. The attributes, methods, context nodes, and actions defined in the view controller, however, are visible only within the same view and their existence is inextricably tied to that of the view. The characteristics of all controller types are listed in Table 2.8.

Controller	Function	Visibility	Lifetime
Component controller	Provides global services and data within the component	Component-wide	Depends on component
Interface controller	Provides services and data to the component being used	Cross-component	Depends on component
Custom controller	Provides services and data to view groupings	Component-wide	Depends on component
Window controller	Provides services and data to the window	Component-wide	Depends on window
View controller	Provides services and data to the view	Local to the view	Depends on view or component

Table 2.8 Controllers of a Component

The parts of the individual controllers vary. Except for the interface controller, all other controllers have a common context, methods, and attributes (see Table 2.9). The interface controller contains the context nodes, methods, and events identified as the interface in the component controller. If the controllers control visual parts of the component, like the view or the window, the controllers contain elements for specifying the navigation, such as the inbound and outbound plugs. Within the view, actions can be defined to which events of specific view elements (like the onAction event of the Button view element) can be bound.

Controller	Layout	Inbound Plug	Outbound Plug	Context	Attribute	Actions	Events	Methods
Component controller				x	x		x	x
Interface controller				x			x	x
Custom controller				x	x		x	x
Window controller	x	x	x	x	x			x
View controller	x	x	x	x	x	x		x

Table 2.9 Parts of Controllers

Every action has an event handler method that is called when the bound event is triggered by the view element. The event handler method of every action is automatically created when the action is defined. On the **Methods** tab, the event handler method can be identified via the **Event Handler** method type and the ONACTION prefix; event handler methods of inbound plugs can be distinguished by the HANDLER prefix. In the component controller, events can be defined to which other controllers can be registered. If such an event is triggered, the controllers that are registered to the event can execute corresponding event handler methods and therefore individually react to the respective event.

In every controller, you can implement a number of different types of methods. Their name, calling time, and function can be predefined as fixed and unchangeable by the WD4A framework or determined by the developer. In Section 2.4.3, we already had a closer look at the supply function methods. All other types of methods are introduced in the following sections.

2.5.1 Hook Methods

Every controller has a number of default methods that enable the developer to interfere in the program flow at certain times. In their initial state, these methods do not contain statements. The methods are called in a sequence specified by the phase model (see Section 2.7), and the logic added by the developer is executed. The methods provided by the respective controller depend on the controller type. The availability per controller is shown in Table 2.10.

Hook Method	Component Controller	View Controller	Window Controller	Custom Controller
wddoinit()	x	x	x	x
wddoexit()	x	x	x	x
wddobeforenavigation()	x			
wddopostprocessing()	x			
wddomodifyview()		x		
wddobeforeaction()		x		
wddoonclose()			x	

Table 2.10 Hook Methods

- wddoinit()
  This method is called immediately and only after the instantiation of the controller. Here, you should implement statements that are for initializing the controller.

- wddoexit()
  This method is called at the end of a controller's lifetime and should be used for executing closing statements.

- wddobeforenavigation()
  This method is run by the component controller before the navigation stack is processed. Here, you can validate input and influence the navigation accordingly.

- wddopostprocessing()
  Because you cannot determine the calling time of supply function methods exactly, this method is for performing exception handlings of the supply function methods. With this method, no more changes should be made to the context.

- wddomodifyview()
  This method is called before the view is rendered. Here you have the option to directly access the view element objects. This is mainly applied in dynamic programming.

▶ wddobeforeaction()
This method is run before the action triggered by the user is executed. User input should be verified when this method is used. You have the option to access the context and to output messages via the message manager.

▶ wddoonclose()
This method is called when a modal popup is closed. Here you can execute terminating statements for the data shown in the popup or for your input.

2.5.2 Instance Methods

In all controllers, you can implement user-defined methods. Similar to ABAP Objects classes, you can define methods and parameters for these methods. Furthermore, you can identify instance methods of component controllers as interface methods. They are then displayed in the interface controller of the component and can be called by other components for defining a use.

Instance methods should be called in their own controller via a self-reference wd_this; this works similarly to the self-reference me in ABAP Objects. wd_this is the reference to the interface of its own controller and therefore facilitates the access to all functionalities of the class that are generated from the controller. The generated functionalities can change with future versions of the WD4A framework; using wd_this, the compatibility of your developments remains ensured.

Therefore, the call of a create_quote() method without parameter passing implemented in a controller would read as follows:

```
wd_this->create_quote( ).
```

All methods are public and can be called within a component by other controllers. This requires that an appropriate usage has been defined for the controller in which the method was implemented.

2.5.3 Event Handler Methods

Event handler methods are implemented to respond to events of controllers, to events of inbound plugs, and to actions that come from the client. If you want to create an event handler method, which registers to an event that can be triggered within another controller, you can freely assign its name on the **Methods** tab. Then, you can select the **Event Handler** method type and select the event to which to react. The implementation, as usual, is done in the method editor.

Figure 2.59 shows the creation of the event handler method `set_status()` that registers to the CHANGE_STATUS event created in the component controller.

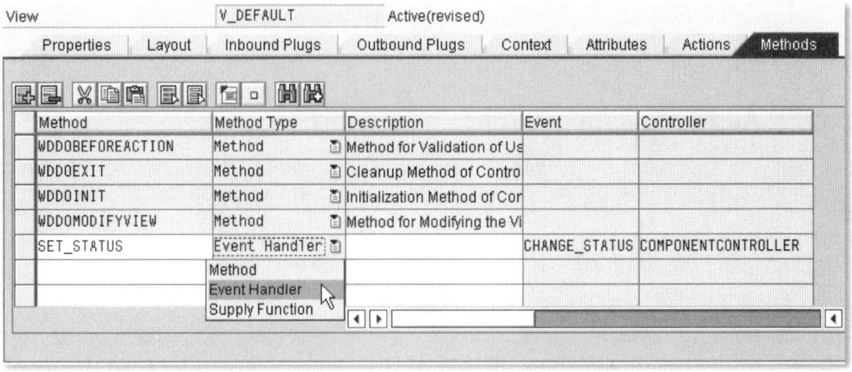

Figure 2.59 Registration to an Event of the Component Controller

Event handler methods that react to actions can only be created in view controllers. Actions are extensions of events that are triggered in the client either by the user or by client-specific statements. The action is defined on the **Actions** tab in the view controller and assigned to the property of a view element (e.g., the **onAction** property of the Button view element). The corresponding event handler method is created automatically by the WD4A framework and receives the prefix ONACTION.

For example, if you define the SAVE action on the **Actions** tab, the corresponding event handler method `onactionsave()` is displayed on the **Methods** tab and can be implemented using the appropriate statements. When inbound plugs are created in view and window controllers, automatic event handler methods are created by the WD4A framework as well. If the inbound plug of a view or a window is called at runtime, this corresponds to calling its event handler method. Here you can implement the appropriate statements, as you would when passing.

2.5.4 Fire Methods

A fire method is created by the WD4A framework when you define an outbound plug in the view or window controller. Contrary to the previous methods, however, you cannot implement fire methods. The statements to be executed when they are called are entirely controlled by the WD4A framework. Nevertheless, you can still define transfer parameters during the development stage that are then populated with values when this method is called at runtime.

A fire method of an outbound plug is called via the following statement:

```
wd_this->fire_[NameOfOutboundPlug]_plg( ).
```

2.5.5 Additional Information About Context

Section 2.4 describes the characteristics of the context in the view controller. As you can see in Table 2.9, all other controllers have a context for data maintenance as well. The concepts described in Sections 2.4.1 and 2.4.2 regarding cardinality, Singleton context nodes, and the lead selection also apply to these controller contexts.

The differences between the contexts of the various controllers are the availability of the data stored in the context and the possibility of binding view elements to context nodes and context attributes. Data stored in the context of the view controller is only available during the lifetime of the view. The lifetime of a view can be limited to its visibility or, if configured accordingly, controlled by the WD4A framework (see Figure 2.60).

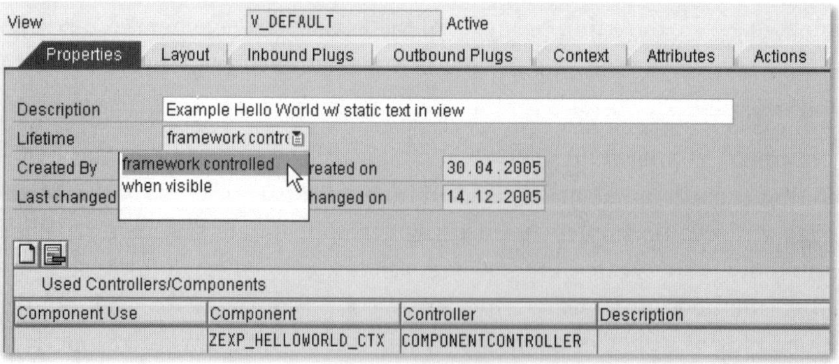

Figure 2.60 Configuration of the Lifetime of a View

This is the default setting when a view is created. The **framework controlled** setting usually corresponds to the lifetime of the component in which the view is displayed. But even with a component-based lifetime, you cannot access the data of a view context from other views. The data in the context of the view controller is always only available within the same view.

In this respect, the context of the component controller allows you to provide and maintain the data across several views. If you wanted, you could access the context of the component controller via a view controller method and edit or copy the data accordingly. The WD4A framework provides a simpler option, however, of establishing a connection between the context data of the component controller and that of the view controller, which is made possible by *mapping*.

To access the data of a context node of the component controller from a view context, you need to define a mapping to a context node of the component controller for the appropriate view controller context node. There are two ways to define the mapping. The first option is that you can choose **Define Mapping** from the context menu of the appropriate context node in the view controller, and then select the appropriate node from the list of component controller context nodes (see Figure 2.61).

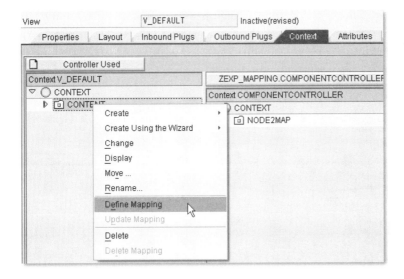

Figure 2.61 Context Mapping Via the Menu

The second option is to define the mapping from the context node of the component controller via Drag&Drop. You click on the appropriate context node in the component controller (right side of the window) and drag and drop the node to the view controller context node to be mapped (left side of the window, see Figure 2.62). As when using the mapping menu option, please note that the structure of the context nodes to be mapped must be identical, that is, the structure of the context nodes and the context attributes must be the same. The entire context node is always mapped and this includes all attributes and other context nodes that are arranged below the context node.

Figure 2.62 Context Mapping Using Drag&Drop

If this is not the case, the WD4A framework suggests to the mapped context node to delete and recreate the context node to be mapped. A simpler option, particularly for more complex context nodes, is to copy the context node of the component controller to the view controller and then perform the mapping. This can be done easily in a single step by mapping via Drag&Drop to the root node CONTEXT of the view controller (see Figure 2.63). Figure 2.64 shows the view to a view controller with a CONTENT context node displayed in the left part of the window.

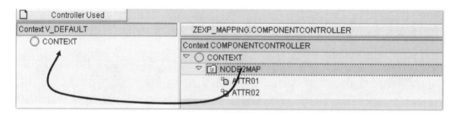

Figure 2.63 Copying and Mapping Context Nodes

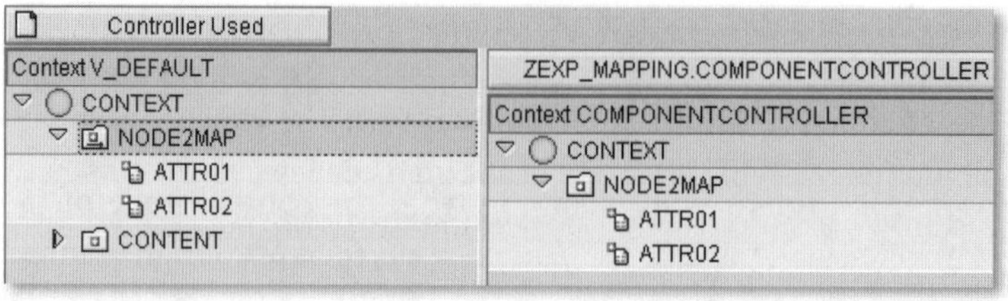

Figure 2.64 View Controller After Copying and Mapping

The component controller is shown on the right side and has a context node to be mapped named NODE2MAP. To copy and map the NODE2MAP context node, it is moved to the CONTEXT root node in the view controller. The mapped NODE2MAP context node is now displayed in the view controller (in the left part of the window) with all its attributes and potential lower-level context nodes; a mapped context node is marked with a small arrow in the folder icon.

Note that the NODE2MAP context node in the view controller and the NODE2MAP context node in the component controller exist separately at the time of development. Although you can make changes to the attributes of the NODE2MAP context node in the component controller only, these changes are not automatically reflected in the view controller. Only after you perform a separate step to update the mapping (**Update Mapping**) in the view controller are these changes transferred to the mapped context node (see Figure 2.65).

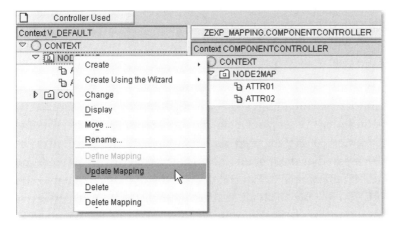

Figure 2.65 Update the Data of the Mapped Context Node

2.6 Navigation, Inbound Plugs, and Outbound Plugs

The visual parts of components are view and window. The view is composed of the view elements; the window is for grouping the views and for specifying the navigation. You can navigate through the views of the same window of a component, the views of different windows of a component, and windows (interface views) of different components.

The navigation is initiated at runtime by triggering outbound plugs that are defined in the view or the window controller. On the **Window** tab of the window controller, the outbound plugs of the source view are linked to the inbound plugs of the target view during the development phase. For example, if you want to navigate within a component from a view V_ONE to a view V_TWO, you must perform the following steps:

1. Definition of an outbound plug in the view V_ONE
2. Definition of an inbound plug in the view V_TWO
3. Linking the outbound plug of V_ONE to the inbound plug of V_TWO in the window controller of the component
4. Inserting the fire method for the outbound plug of V_ONE in the place of the program logic from which the navigation is to be triggered

By default, the WD4A framework creates an inbound plug named DEFAULT for every new window. This inbound plug is marked as an interface plug and is of the type **startup**. This facilitates the simple configuration when creating a WD4A application, because then you always need to determine a window (interface view) with an inbound plug as the entry point (see Section 2.3.1). For view and window alike, you can define several inbound and outbound plugs.

The definition of navigation links specifies which inbound plug is called by which outbound plug. When an inbound plug is created, a corresponding event handler method is generated automatically (see Figure 2.66). The event handler method of the inbound plug is displayed on the **Methods** tab and can be used, for example, to control the transfer of passed parameters. It is processed before the view is built.

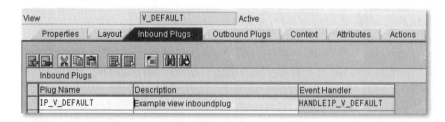

Figure 2.66 Inbound Plug with Event Handler Method

When an outbound plug is created, the WD4A framework generates no programmable event handler method, but a fire method that cannot be implemented. The fire method of the outbound plug shown in Figure 2.67 is called as follows:

`wd_this->fire_op_v_default_plg( ).`

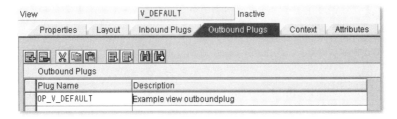

Figure 2.67 Outbound Plug in a View

The easiest way to integrate the fire method generated by the WD4A framework, however, is to use the **Web Dynpro Code Wizard** that you can start via the main menu using the **Edit · Web Dynpro Code Wizard** option, via the shortcut **Ctrl+F7**, or via the appropriate toolbar icon (see Figure 2.68).

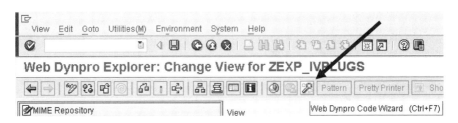

Figure 2.68 Calling the Web Dynpro Code Wizard

The Web Dynpro Code Wizard enables you to insert the following ABAP code fragments:

- Method calls in the same controller
- Method calls from used controllers
- Instantiation of used components
- Trigger the navigation
- Read context node/attribute data
- Create messages in the message manager
- Method calls within the portal integration
- Method calls within the personalization

When calling the fire methods of outbound plugs, parameters that are evaluated in the event handler methods of the inbound plugs can be transferred. Here, it is essential that the names of the parameters in the outbound plug and in the inbound plug to be linked are the same. Moreover, the parameters must always be transferred as well. The following is the call of a fire method transferring two parameters:

```
wd_this->Fire_op_v_default_plg( first_name = lv_firstname
                                last_name  = lv_lastname ).
```

In the event handler method of the inbound plug to be linked, which belongs to the view to which you want to navigate, these parameters must be defined as importing parameters. Figure 2.69 shows the event handler method handleip_v_index() of the inbound plug IP_V_INDEX of the view V_INDEX with the manually added parameters FIRST_NAME and LAST_NAME. These parameters match the parameters of the outbound plug OP_V_DEFAULT of the view V_DEFAULT (see Figure 2.70). The plugs are linked in the window controller on the **Window** tab.

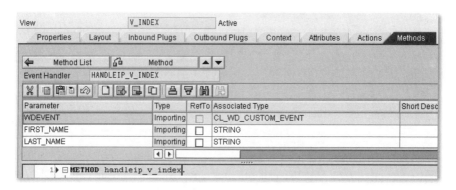

Figure 2.69 Inbound Plug Event Handler with Importing Parameter

In Figure 2.71, the views V_DEFAULT and V_INDEX were embedded in the W_DEFAULT window. Both views each contain an inbound and an outbound plug. The outbound plug OP_V_DEFAULT of the view V_DEFAULT was linked to the inbound plug IP_V_INDEX of the view V_INDEX. This linking is achieved by selecting the **Create Navigation Link** option in the context menu of the appropriate outbound plug and by entering the inbound plug of the view to which you want to navigate in the following popup. Regarding the example in Figure 2.71, the navigation from the view V_DEFAULT to the view V_INDEX would be triggered at runtime by calling the fire method of the outbound plug OP_V_DEFAULT.

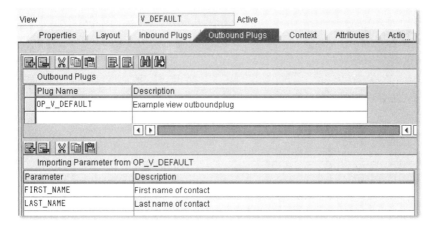

Figure 2.70 Outbound Plug with Parameter

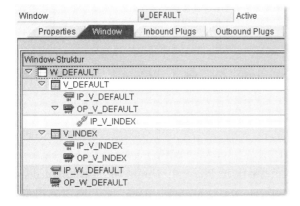

Figure 2.71 Specifying the Navigation Via Plug Linking

2.7 Phase Model

The phase model shows the individual steps that are processed and executed sequentially and without repetition within a request/response cycle; however, depending on the error states that are detected by the WD4A framework, single phases may be skipped. The schematic procedure is outlined in Figure 2.72, and the individual phases are described in detail below.

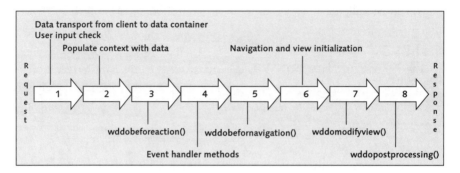

Figure 2.72 Phases of a Request/Response Cycle

▶ **Phase 1**
The data in the incoming request is converted from the client-specific format to a client- and protocol-independent format and is then available to the WD4A framework for further processing. The user input is checked against the type definitions and user-specific settings (e.g. date formats) specified in the context.

▶ **Phase 2**
The context is populated with the data. Error messages that were generated during the input evaluations in Phase 1 are processed in the message manager.

▶ **Phase 3**
Here you can perform your own input checks that surpass the checks performed by the WD4A framework in Phase 1. The input checks must be implemented in the method wddobeforeaction() that is called for every visible view of the component.

▶ **Phase 4**
At the beginning of Phase 4, the input made by the user has been checked and resides in the context. Now the event handler methods are processed. If an error state has been detected, you go directly to Phase 8 (wddopostprocessing()), and all other events such as triggering a navigation are ignored. In an error-free process, the onaction() methods are called.

▶ **Phase 5**
Within the method wddobeforenavigation(), which is processed in the component controller of the current component, you can conduct more complex checks of the contents of different contexts. This may be necessary for complex applications that also use embedded components. If errors are detected in this phase and the navigation must be interrupted,

you must call the `cancel_navigation()` method of the interface IF_WD_COMPONENT.

- **Phase 6**
  The navigation is performed in this phase. The event handler method of the inbound plug, of the view to which to navigate, is called. If the view is displayed for the first time, the method `wddoinit()` of the view controller is processed.

- **Phase 7**
  Phase 7 gives you the option to change the statically fixed layout of a view at runtime by processing the method `wddomodifyview()`. Within this method, the entire UI hierarchy of the respective view can be accessed, and view elements can be deleted or added, and their properties changed. But, you should not make changes to the context or add error messages to the message manager, because this could result in indefinable states within the application.

- **Phase 8**
  The method `wddopostprocessing()` enables you to process exception conditions that have arisen when supply function methods were called. At this stage, however, no more changes should be made to the context.

In this chapter, we'll take a closer look at the development of WD4A (Web Dynpro for ABAP) applications. Our goal here is to clarify the coherences that exist within a component among component controller, view controller, and window controller. To do this, we'll introduce several typical web scenarios, as well as a number of more complex view elements, for presenting tree structures and tables, for example.

3 Developing WD4A Applications

3.1 Transferring Parameters from a URI

Parameters and their values that are part of the Uniform Resource Identifier's (URI) *query component* can be attached to the URI of an application or website to be called. The query component can be used in many ways. Two potential scenarios are the transfer of data between two applications that call each other or the control of actions on the server.

The WD4A framework implements the transfer of parameter value pairs in the URI's query component as follows:

[parameter_name]=[parameter_value]

The first parameter pair is attached to the URI using the ? character; all other parameter pairs are separated by the & character. Otherwise, the restrictions for query components listed in RFC 2396[1] apply; reserved characters are ;, /, ?, :, @, &, =, +, ,, and $. A URI with two parameter value pairs could therefore have the following format:

http://www.google.com/search?hl=com&q=webdynpro

---

1 RFCs (requests for comments) deal with standards as well as advanced ideas, concepts, and descriptions about the Internet.

3 | Developing WD4A Applications

3.1.1 Reading and Displaying Parameters

Using the example ZEXP_PARAMETER_APP, we will now show how URI parameters can be passed to an application and evaluated in the WD4A framework. In the WD4A framework, you must define the parameters that are expected in the event handler method of the component window inbound plug that is marked as the startup plug. In every component, the name of this inbound plug is preset in the window as a DEFAULT; however, every other inbound plug created by the user can be marked as the startup plug. The parameters first_name and last_name are defined as **Importing** parameters in the event handler method handledefault(), and therefore, their names must match the name in the URI exactly.

In the method, the values are read and assigned to the context attributes (see Figure 3.1). In this case, the context in the windows controller consists of a context node named CONTENT and two **STRING** attributes named FIRST_NAME and LAST_NAME.

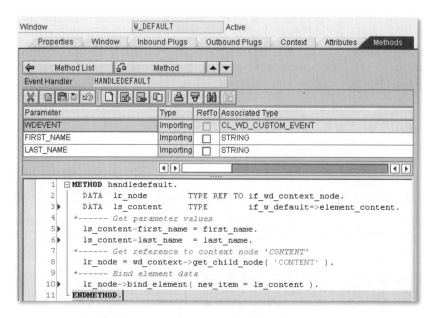

Figure 3.1 Event Handler Method of the Startup Inbound Plug

In the WD4A application, the parameters defined in the inbound plug can be assigned default values (see Figure 3.2). This is not mandatory, but results in a clean solution because the lack of parameters in the URI would lead to a runtime error. Therefore, for both parameters, FIRST_NAME and LAST_NAME, a **Value** of **any_name** is specified.

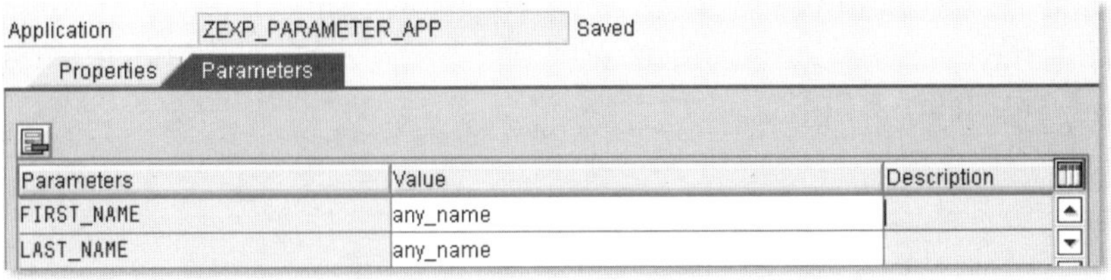

Figure 3.2 Preassignment of the Application Parameters

The window controller must be defined in the V_DEFAULT view as **Used Controller** (see Figure 3.3). In the **Properties** tab, click on the creation icon on the left-hand side and select the controller name W_DEFAULT. How the window controller will be used must be defined in order to map the context node of the window controller in the view controller (see Figure 3.4). In the view layout, you can then bind the attributes FIRST_NAME and LAST_NAME to the **text** property of the TextView view elements that are responsible for the output of the parameter values.

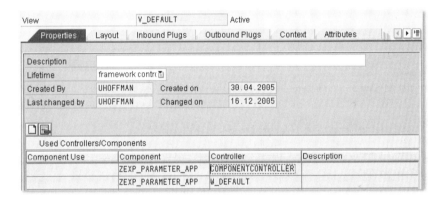

Figure 3.3 Defining the Use of the Window Controller

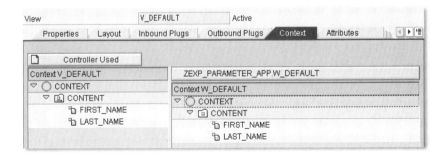

Figure 3.4 Mapping the Window Controller Context

After the initial call of the application without the parameters transferred in the URI, the default values defined in the application characteristics are displayed (see Figure 3.5).

Figure 3.5 Client Output without Parameters in the URI

If you complete the URI in the **Address** line accordingly, by adding parameter names and values, the result should correspond to the display shown in Figure 3.6. Here, the parameters `first_name` and `last_name` were assigned the values **John** and **Doe**.

Figure 3.6 Display of the Parameters Passed in the URI

3.1.2 Controlling the Navigation Via Parameters

In addition to simply displaying the parameters passed via the URI, they can also be analyzed on the server and used to control processes or calls. We will illustrate this by using the implementation of another component named ZEXP_PARAMETER_NAV. The navigation to various views will be implemented based on URI parameter values at program runtime. If the `target_view` parameter is set to a value of **one**, the view V_ONE will be displayed; if the `target_view` parameter is set to a value of **two**, the view V_TWO will be displayed.

To implement this example, in the view editor, create two views named V_ONE and V_TWO for the component ZEXP_PARAMETER_NAV. You can minimize the effort necessary for the layout, since we only need some indication in the display that the navigation was performed to the right view. It is therefore sufficient if you integrate a `TextView` view element that outputs a distinguishable text as shown in Figure 3.7 or Figure 3.8.

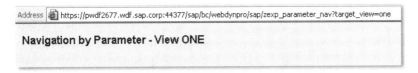

Figure 3.7 Result with Parameter One

Figure 3.8 Result with Parameter Two

The views additionally each require an inbound plug, which is triggered based on the transferred URI parameter value. Depending on the triggered inbound plug, the appropriate view is displayed. Name the inbound plug for the V_ONE view IP_V_ONE and the inbound plug for the V_TWO view IP_V_TWO. Figure 3.9 shows an example of the inbound plug definition for V_ONE.

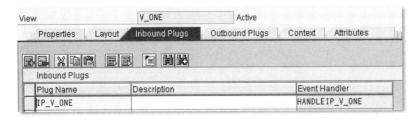

Figure 3.9 Definition of the Inbound Plug in the View V_ONE

Now that we have completed the tasks to be performed in the view editor, we are ready to move to the window editor. As described in Section 2.3.1, you need to indicate an inbound plug of the window marked as a startup plug when you create the application. This plug is the link between the application URI and the component window. Usually, the view that is displayed first within the window is the view that has the **Default** property set. There is always only one view that is marked as the default view. Consequently, the identification of the default view must be confirmed or changed during the development phase. The WD4A framework always sets the first view embedded in the window as the default view.

However, you can transfer this identification to another view as well. If the view V_ONE was set as the default value view, and without previously evaluating the URI parameters, V_ONE would be displayed first at application startup. We will now override the default behavior implemented in the WD4A framework by evaluating the URI parameter target_view in the event handler of the window's startup plug and by making the corresponding decisions about the further navigation that is necessary. The navigation is influenced by triggering outbound plugs of the window that are each bound to an inbound plug of the respective view. Additionally, it is necessary to define the outbound plugs of the window and link them to the inbound plugs of the view.

The outbound plugs are defined in the window editor. Name the outbound plug that performs the navigation to the V_ONE view OP_TO_V_ONE and the second outbound plug OP_TO_V_TWO. The plugs are defined in the **Outbound Plugs** tab, as shown in Figure 3.10.

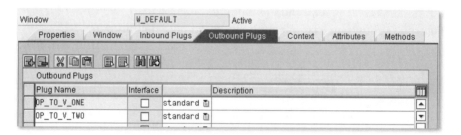

Figure 3.10 Definition of Outbound Plugs in the Window

The linking of the window's outbound plugs to the view's inbound plugs takes place in the window structure editor. For this purpose, open the context menu by right-clicking on the outbound plug OP_TO_V_ONE and select the **Create Navigation Link** option (see Figure 3.11). In the following popup window, you can select the target view and its inbound plug; in our ZEXP_PARAMETER_NAV example, this is the inbound plug IP_TO_V_ONE. Repeat this step for the outbound plug OP_TO_V_TWO by linking it to the inbound plug IP_V_TWO. Alternatively, you can also link the plugs using Drag&Drop.

In the last step, the evaluation of the URI parameter target_view, which is performed at runtime, must be implemented in the event handler method of the window's startup plug. For this purpose, you need to define the parameter as it is shown in the URI as an import parameter of the event handler method (see Figure 3.12).

3.1 Transferring Parameters from a URI

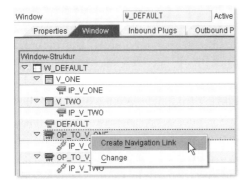

Figure 3.11 Define Navigation Link

When a window is defined, the WD4A framework automatically creates an inbound plug named DEFAULT and marks it as the startup plug. At this time, the WD4A framework also creates the corresponding event handler method named handledefault().

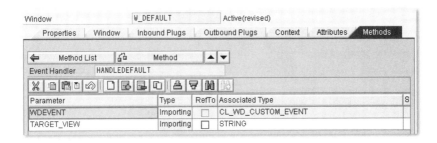

Figure 3.12 Definition of the URI Parameter as the Import Parameter

The statements for evaluating the parameter and triggering the navigation, which are to be implemented in the event handler method, are presented in Listing 3.1. Depending on the value for the import parameter target_view, the two outbound plugs of the window are triggered.

```
METHOD handledefault.
  CASE target_view.
    WHEN 'one'.
      wd_this->fire_op_to_v_one_plg( ).
    WHEN 'one'.
      wd_this->fire_op_to_v_two_plg( ).
  ENDCASE.
ENDMETHOD.
```

Listing 3.1 Implementing the Event Handler Method

Figure 3.13 again illustrates the coherences between the outbound plug of the window and the inbound plugs of the views. The outbound plugs OP_TO_V_ONE and OP_TO_V_TWO are parts of the W_DEFAULT window; the inbound plugs IP_V_ONE and IP_V_TWO are parts of the respective view. A view cannot be directly called in the event handler method, but is always called by triggering outbound plugs, which, in turn, must be linked to the respective inbound plug of the view.

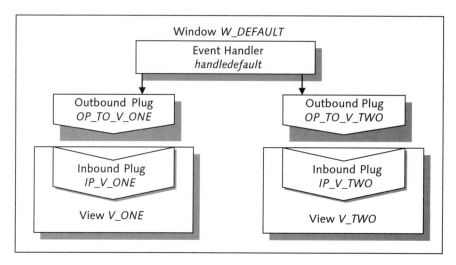

Figure 3.13 Controlling Views to Be Displayed Using the Event Handler

As explained in Section 3.1, the lack of the parameter target_view in the URI would lead to a runtime error. To prevent this from occurring, you can pre-assign the parameter with a value in the parameter definition of the application; in our case, this is a value of **one** (see Figure 3.14). This means that if the parameter target_view is missing, the view V_ONE is always displayed.

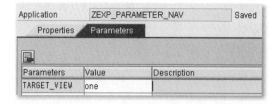

Figure 3.14 Definition of a Default Value for the URI Parameter

Another exception that might occur at the runtime of the application would be an undefined value that could be passed to the parameter target_view in the URI. Fortunately, this value can be intercepted within the program logic. To do this, you would extend the CASE control structure in Listing 3.1 by a statement block in which you deal with the exception:

```
WHEN OTHERS.
  [...]
```

Another option would be to determine the view to be displayed if none of the window's outbound plugs are triggered, by defining the default view in the window W_DEFAULT.

Since we left the default values of the WD4A framework unchanged, if the URI parameter target_view was not defined, the view V_ONE (i.e., the default view) would always be displayed in our example. If the view V_TWO will be displayed if the target_view value cannot be evaluated, this view would have to be marked in the window as the default view.

3.2 Influencing the Request/Response Cycle

An important characteristic of HTTP is the request/response cycle coming from the client. On the server, the response to the request received from the client is created and then returned to the client. The server cannot be the initiator of the roundtrip, nor can it send data to the client when there is no active HTTP request/response cycle (see Figure 3.15).

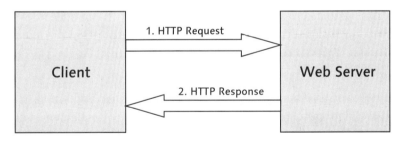

Figure 3.15 Client/Server Communication

In most cases, the trigger of a client request is a user action like a click on a button or a link on the page displayed by the client. On the server, the incoming request is analyzed, and the response is composed based on the action performed by the user and then sent to the client.

3.2.1 Automatic Triggering of Requests

In special application scenarios, it is sometimes desirable to update the data displayed by the client without the user having to become active. An example would be the flow of an asynchronous process on the server and the corresponding notification of the user after the process has completed or errors have occurred. If the TimedTrigger view element is used, the WD4A framework enables periodic requests to be sent from the client to the server and therefore to either update information that is displayed in the client or to visualize status changes in the client that occurred on the server.

The implementation of the view element TimedTrigger consists of JavaScript functions that are not visible to the user, that is, the embedding of the view element in the view and the values of the properties do not affect the layout and the arrangement of the remaining view elements. The function and the use of the TimedTrigger view element will be explained in detail in the following section. In a first component to be implemented, the client is to output a value that is incremented on the server with every roundtrip.

For this purpose, create a component named ZEXP_TTRIGGER_APP. The component consists of a view V_DEFAULT with two TextView view elements and a TimedTrigger view element TTR_COUNTER. The view element TXV_TOPIC is used to display the static text "Number of server round trips:". The **text** property of the TXV_COUNTER view element is bound to a context attribute and represents the server round trips.

To achieve this, you need to create a new node named CONTENT in the context of the view controller and underneath a **STRING** context attribute named COUNTER. This context attribute should contain the current value of the counter.

In the next step, you assign the name of the action to be called with every client request to the property **onAction** of the TimedTrigger view element. But first you need to define an action in the view editor of the V_DEFAULT view. Select the **Actions** tab and name the action SET_COUNTER. With the definition of the action, the WD4A framework creates the event handler method at the same time; it is called onactionset_counter() (see Figure 3.16).

The method onactionset_counter() has the task of incrementing the value of the context attribute COUNTER with every server roundtrip. Listing 3.2 shows the processes to implement.

3.2 Influencing the Request/Response Cycle

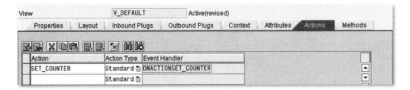

Figure 3.16 Definition of an Action

You can add the listing to the currently empty event handler method by double-clicking on the name of the event handler method within the definition of the action, or by using the **Methods** tab to change to the editor.

```
METHOD onactionset_counter.
  DATA  lr_context_node    TYPE REF TO     if_wd_context_node.
  DATA  lv_counter         TYPE            i.
*------ Get reference of context node 'CONTENT'
    lr_context_node = wd_context->get_child_node( 'CONTENT' ).
*------ Get value of node attribute 'COUNTER'
    lr_context_node->get_attribute( EXPORTING name = 'COUNTER'
                                    IMPORTING value = lv_counter ).
*------ Increment attribute
    lv_counter = lv_counter + 1.
*------ Set new value of node attribute 'COUNTER'
    lr_context_node->set_attribute( EXPORTING name  = 'COUNTER'
                                              value = lv_counter ).
ENDMETHOD.
```

Listing 3.2 Implementation of the onactionset_counter() Method

Additionally, the **delay** property of the TimedTrigger view element is for determining the time interval between the requests that are triggered by the client. Set its value to "3" (see Figure 3.17).

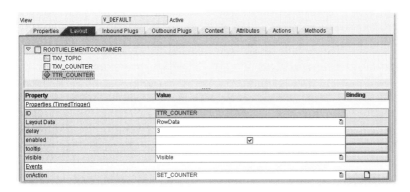

Figure 3.17 View Layout of the Component ZEXP_TTRIGGER_APP

To initialize the counter after the application startup, you finally need to implement the initialization in the `wddoinit()` method of the view controller. Use the specifications shown in Listing 3.3.

```
METHOD wddoinit.
  DATA  lr_context_node       TYPE REF TO     if_wd_context_node.
  lr_context_node  = wd_context->get_child_node( 'CONTENT' ).
  lr_context_node->set_attribute( EXPORTING name  = 'COUNTER'
                                            value = 0 ).
ENDMETHOD.
```

Listing 3.3 Initialization of the Counter

Now that the processes in the event handler methods and in the `wddoinit()` method have been determined, all necessary steps for implementing the component are completed. Now just create the WD4A application in order to test the component. The result displayed in the client should match the output shown in Figure 3.18.

Number of server round trips: 15

Figure 3.18 Client Output for Counting Server Round Trips

Due to the way in which we implemented the `TimedTrigger` view element in the `ZEXP_TTRIGGER_APP` component, the sending of requests from the client to the server begins immediately after the application has been started and is repeated in intervals of three seconds each.

3.2.2 Automatic Triggering of Requests with User Interaction

Let us now assume that we could trigger the shown procedure only after a user action was defined. A potential scenario would be that a user makes entries in a web form. When the data is saved, an asynchronous process is started on the server, the progress of which is to be displayed in the client via a periodic query of the process status.

The goal of the following application is to initially leave the `TimedTrigger` view element inactive after startup and not to start the periodic sending of requests in the client until a button is clicked. The number of triggered server round trips is again made visible by using a counter in the client.

For the implementation, copy the `ZEXP_TTRIGGER_APP` component to a new component named `ZEXP_TTRIGGER_USR`. In the layout of the `V_DEFAULT` view in the view element `TTR_COUNTER`, delete the definition of the action in the **onAction** property. This results in the `TimedTrigger` view element being inactive after application startup. It is activated dynamically at runtime, but we'll deal with that later. First, in the `V_DEFAULT` view, under the existing view elements, add a `Button` view element named `BTN_TRIGGER_ACTIVATE`. The action that is triggered when the button is clicked should be called `SET_TT_ACTIVE`. As a label, we will use "Activate TimedTrigger"; assign this text to the **text** property.

The WD4A framework assigns the name `onactionset_tt_active()` to the event handler method that is generated for the action; its implementation is shown in Listing 3.4. It consists of a single line in which the controller attribute `mv_tt_active` is set.

```
METHOD onactionset_tt_active.
  wd_this->mv_tt_active = abap_true.
ENDMETHOD.
```

Listing 3.4 Event Handler Method for the Button Action

This controller attribute is of the **WDY_BOOLEAN** type; possible values are `abap_true` and `abap_false` and it contains the information for activating the `TimedTrigger` view element at runtime (see Figure 3.19). Controller attributes are defined in the **Attributes** tab of the controllers; the attribute is predefined with the value `abap_false` in the `wddoinit()` method.

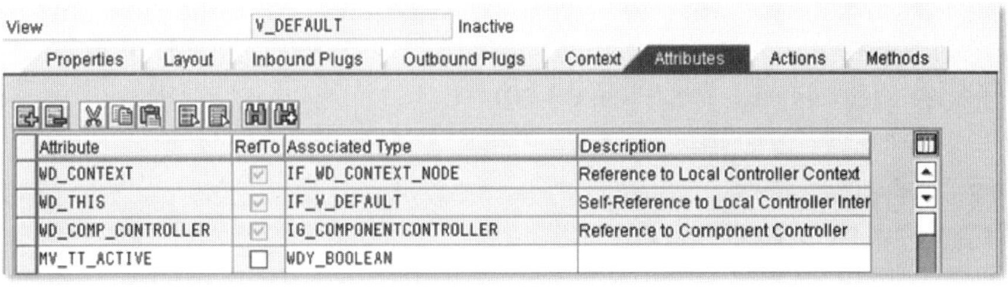

Figure 3.19 Creating View Controller Attributes

After the button has been clicked, this attribute is set to the value `abap_true` in the event handler method `onactionset_tt_active()` at runtime. Depending on the view controller attribute `mv_tt_active`, the `TimedTrigger` view element is then activated in the `wddomodifyview()` method; the appropriate ABAP code can be taken from Listing 3.5. After the application has been started, the implemented methods wddoinit() and wddomodifyview() are first processed. The TimedTrigger view element remains inactive, because its **onAction** property is not set. If the user now clicks on **Activate TimedTrigger**, the view controller attribute mv_tt_active is set in the event handler method of the button, and the action SET_COUNTER is assigned to the view element TTR_COUNTER when the wddomodifyview() method is processed.

```
METHOD wddomodifyview.
    DATA    lr_timedtrigger    TYPE REF TO        cl_wd_timed_trigger.
*------ Get reference to timedtrigger control
    lr_timedtrigger ?= view->get_element( 'TTR_COUNTER' ).
*------ Activate/Deactivate timedtrigger control
    IF lr_timedtrigger IS BOUND.
        IF wd_this->mv_trigger_active EQ abap_true.
          lr_timedtrigger->set_on_action( 'SET_COUNTER' ).
        ELSE.
          lr_timedtrigger->set_on_action( '' ).
        ENDIF.
    ENDIF.
ENDMETHOD.
```

Listing 3.5 Dynamic Action Assignment of the TimedTrigger View Element

The implementation of the event handler method set_counter() remains unchanged as compared to the example component ZEXP_TTRIGGER_APP (see Section 3.2).

When you have created and started the application, the counter initially keeps its initial value of **0**. Only after the button **Activate TimedTrigger** has been clicked, does the periodic sending of requests from the client to the server begin, along with the incrementing of the counter variable in intervals of three seconds each (see Figure 3.20).

Figure 3.20 Server Round Trips Triggered by the User

Another way of implementing the user-controlled activation would be by using a context attribute to which the **enabled** property of the TimedTrigger view element is bound, which replaces the controller attribute mv_tt_active. When the button is clicked, the context attribute is set in the event handler method and the view element is activated. The action can therefore be determined at the time of development, and the dynamic assignment in the wddomodify() method is omitted.

3.2.3 Automatic Forwarding

In Section 3.1, we showed how to decide which view should be displayed if there are several views by evaluating URI parameters. The evaluation of the URI parameter took place in the window and specifically in the event handler method of the startup plug. Now, we will now find out how deciding which view to display can be shifted from the window controller to the view controller of the default view. This would be necessary, for example, if context data of the view controller is to be considered.

This example is based on the common Internet scenario of automatic forwarding to a resource other than the one specified in the URI. To transfer this scenario to a WD4A component, we implement two views. When the application is started, a view other than the default view is called.

As the component name for this example, we choose ZEXP_NAVIGATION_AUTO. In the window editor of the component, create a window W_DEFAULT, and in the view editor, create two views named V_ONE and V_TWO. The two views each contain only a TextView view element that is assigned a text to identify the respective view. Figure 3.21 shows the layout structure of the view V_ONE. The view contains the TextView view element TXV_TOPIC, and the **text** property has been assigned the text "Example Navigation—View ONE". The text is to enable us to differ the displayed views at runtime.

In the next step, V_ONE and V_TWO are to be embedded in the window; make sure that the identification of view V_ONE as the default view remains unchanged. To define navigation from the view V_ONE to the view V_TWO, the appropriate plugs need to be created. For the view V_ONE, this would be an outbound plug named OP_TO_V_TWO; for V_TWO, an inbound plug named IP_V_TWO. The steps that are processed after the application has been started are shown in Figure 3.22.

3 | Developing WD4A Applications

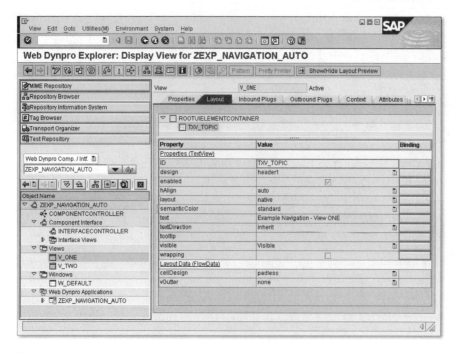

Figure 3.21 Creating the Views

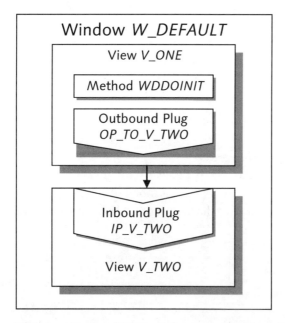

Figure 3.22 Process of Automatic Forwarding to a Second View

In the `W_DEFAULT` window, you can thus define a link between `OP_TO_V_TWO` and `IP_V_TWO` (see Figure 3.23). If the application were started now, `V_ONE` would be displayed because it is specified as the default view. To navigate to the second view `V_TWO` per forwarding without user interaction, the output plug `OP_TO_V_TWO` is triggered in view `V_ONE` in the `wddoinit()` method by calling the fire method:

`wd_this->fire_op_to_v_two_plg( ).`

Insert this statement in the `wddoinit()` method.

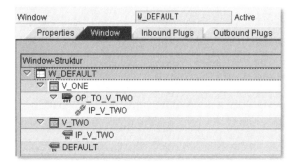

Figure 3.23 Linking the View Plugs

The triggering of the outbound plug at runtime could now be made dependent on various conditions. You can try this out yourself and make the triggering of the outbound plug dependent on the user name or the system time. Remember that whenever the condition is not met, the default view is displayed.

3.3 Implementation of Selection Options

Up to now, we tried to imitate some familiar scenarios from web-based applications in Web Dynpro for ABAP using simple WD4A components and applications. We did not deal much with the design elements of the application interface—the examples displayed only simple text output—but focused on the technical aspects and described processes that occur in common HTTP request/response cycles.

In the following sections, we'll develop components by integrating the extensive view element library of the WD4A framework, emphasize its particularities, and describe the implementation of the different characteristics of the view elements. A web application is only met with user acceptance if it has a user-friendly interface that can be used intuitively.

The WD4A framework provides an extensive selection of view elements. Their diverse functionalities simplify the development of standardized and recurring processes, thereby enabling you to focus on the design of efficient and intuitive user interactions, instead of your having to deal with implementations that recur in every application, like the transferring of input values or the handling of user actions.

3.3.1 Using Dropdown Lists

We will begin with dropdown lists. The WD4A framework provides two different view elements, DropDownByIndex and DropDownByKey, which differ in the implementation of the provision of selection data.

In a sample application, the design of a text is to be controlled by selecting a value from a dropdown list. This means that the **design** property of the TextView view element is set depending on the value selected from the list. Regarding the text design types used in the sample application, we will content ourselves with **emphasized**, **header1**, **header2**, and **header3** to keep matters simple; however, the **design** property provides many more types (see Figure 3.24).

Property	Value	Binding
Properties (TextView)		
ID	TXV_TOPIC	
Layout Data	RowHeadData	
design		
enabled	emphasized	
hAlign	header1	
layout	header2	
	header3	
semanticColor	header4	
text	label	
textDirection	inherit	

Figure 3.24 Property Design of the TextView View Element

The goal of the implementation is to change the design of a given text ("Example Dropdownlist—ByIndex") that is displayed in the client with every new selection from the values provided in the dropdown list (see Figure 3.25). Technically, this means that an event should be triggered with every change of the value in the dropdown list that is underneath the text. This event will lead to a change of the **design** property of the TextView view element that represents the text.

Figure 3.25 Selection of the Design Type

In the following two sections, we'll show how this functionality can be developed using the `DropDownByIndex` or the `DropDownByKey` view element, respectively.

DropDownByIndex

The component that will be developed first will be named `ZEXP_DDLB_INDEX`. The layout of the component's `V_DEFAULT` view consists of the `TextView` view element `TXV_TOPIC`, the `Label` view element `LBL_DESIGN`, and the `DropDownByIndex` view element `DDI_DESIGN` (see Figure 3.26).

With every selection of a value from the dropdown list, an action is to be triggered to change the lead selection of the elements in the corresponding context nodes. The action is named `DO_TEXT_DESIGN`, defined in the **Actions** tab and assigned to the **onSelect** property of `DLB_DESIGN`. The `DropDownByIndex` view element requires a context node that provides the values to the selection list. This context node should have the cardinality **1..n**, which means that the selection list can either contain one or more entries. In the example, the context node `TEXT_DESIGNS` is created in the view controller of `V_DEFAULT` for this purpose (see Figure 3.27). If an initial row is to be displayed for a selection list, the **Cardinality** property of the context node is set to **0..n**. In this case, the WD4A framework automatically inserts an empty row.

We will add two context attributes to the context node: the attribute `KEY` for the key of the respective selection list entry and the attribute `VALUE` for the description of the entry. The attribute `VALUE` is bound to the **texts** property of the view element `DLB_DESIGN` in the view's layout so that the descriptive texts are displayed in the selection list. The attribute `KEY` is bound to the **design** property of the `Label` view element and determines the design for representing the text.

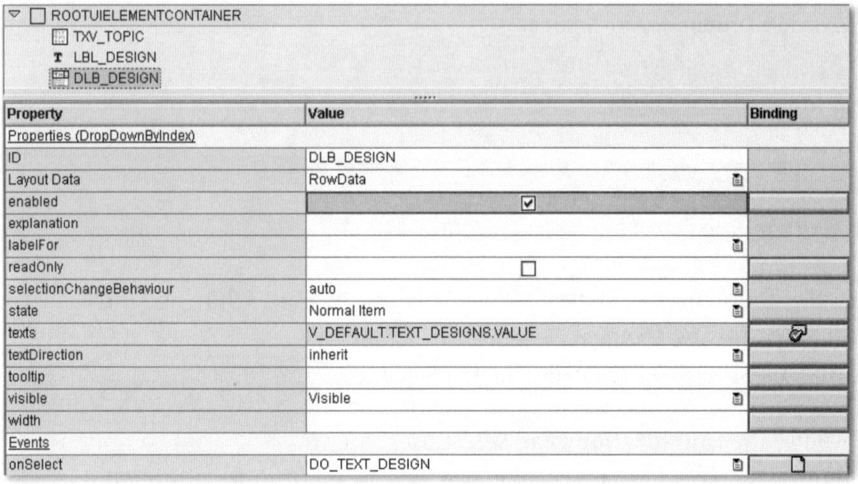

3 | Developing WD4A Applications

Property	Value		Binding
▽ ☐ ROOTUIELEMENTCONTAINER			
▭ TXV_TOPIC			
T LBL_DESIGN			
🗔 DLB_DESIGN			
Properties (DropDownByIndex)			
ID	DLB_DESIGN		
Layout Data	RowData		
enabled	☑		
explanation			
labelFor			
readOnly	☐		
selectionChangeBehaviour	auto		
state	Normal Item		
texts	V_DEFAULT.TEXT_DESIGNS.VALUE		🔗
textDirection	inherit		
tooltip			
visible	Visible		
width			
Events			
onSelect	DO_TEXT_DESIGN		

Figure 3.26 View Elements of the View

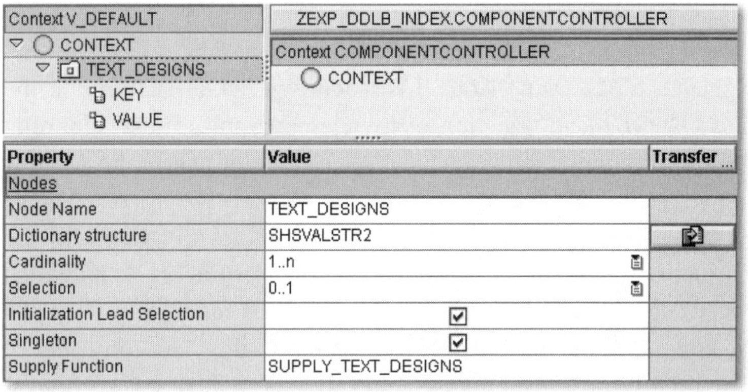

Context V_DEFAULT	ZEXP_DDLB_INDEX.COMPONENTCONTROLLER
▽ ◯ CONTEXT	Context COMPONENTCONTROLLER
▽ 🗔 TEXT_DESIGNS	◯ CONTEXT
🔑 KEY	
🔑 VALUE	

Property	Value	Transfer
Nodes		
Node Name	TEXT_DESIGNS	
Dictionary structure	SHSVALSTR2	📋
Cardinality	1..n	
Selection	0..1	
Initialization Lead Selection	☑	
Singleton	☑	
Supply Function	SUPPLY_TEXT_DESIGNS	

Figure 3.27 Definition of the Context in the View Controller

To populate the context node, implement the supply function method `supply_text_designs()`: In this method, the key value pairs are composed as an internal table and bound to the context node (see Listing 3.6).

```
METHOD supply_text_designs.
  DATA  ls_text_design  TYPE  if_v_default=>element_text_designs.
  DATA  lt_text_designs TYPE  if_v_default=>elements_text_designs.
*----- Create value key list of different text designs
  ls_text_design-key = cl_wd_text_view=>e_design-emphasized.
  ls_text_design-value = 'emphasized'.
  APPEND ls_text_design TO lt_text_designs.
  ls_text_design-key   = cl_wd_text_view=>e_design-header1.
```

```
    ls_text_design-value = 'header1'.
    APPEND ls_text_design TO lt_text_designs.
    ls_text_design-key   = cl_wd_text_view=>e_design-header2.
    ls_text_design-value = 'header2'.
    APPEND ls_text_design TO lt_text_designs.
    ls_text_design-key   = cl_wd_text_view=>e_design-header3.
    ls_text_design-value = 'header3'.
    APPEND ls_text_design TO lt_text_designs.
*----- Fill context node TEXT_DESIGNS
    node->bind_table( new_items = lt_text_designs ).
  ENDMETHOD.
```

Listing 3.6 Supply Function Method of the Context Node TEXT_DESIGNS

Because the **Initialization Lead Selection** property of the context node TEXT_DESIGNS remains unchanged, the lead selection referring to the selected element of the selection list is initialized with the index "1" after the application has been started. This means that the lead selection is set to the first element of the context node. Therefore, the first entry of the selection list—in our example, the design type **emphasized**—appears to be selected in the display, and the text is displayed according to the design (see Figure 3.28).

Figure 3.28 Initial Client Output

With every new selection from the dropdown list, an action—and therefore a server round trip—is triggered that leads to a change of the lead selection of the elements of the context node TEXT_DESIGNS. The event handler for the action does not need to be implemented; the change of the lead selection is handled by the WD4A framework. Because the KEY context attribute of the context node TEXT_DESIGNS is bound to the **design** property of the TextView view element, it always contains the key value of the lead selection. Therefore, the design of the text always corresponds to the value selected in the dropdown list.

Now the application is to be changed so that the preselected value of the selection list represents a value other than **emphasized**. This can be achieved by manipulating the lead selection. Due to the settings of the context node TEXT_DESIGNS chosen in the previous example, the lead selection is set automatically when the context node is populated (**Initialization Lead Selection** property). If this preference is changed, the setting of the lead selection is the default. Then, after the context node has been populated, the lead selection must be specified accordingly; otherwise, an error is triggered at runtime.

To set the lead selection of the context node, you have two options. You can use the set_lead_selection_index() method via the index, where the index must be passed as an integer value; or, you can use the set_lead_selection()method, whereby a reference to the element is passed that is designated as the lead selection. Because we used an internal table to populate the TEXT_DESIGNS context node in our example, we set the lead selection via the index. Add the following program line to the end of the supply_text_designs() method:

node->set_lead_selection_index(index = 2).

The second entry in the internal table of the possible TextView designs contains the **header1** type. When the application is run again, this value is preselected in the dropdown list, and the text above it is displayed in the corresponding design (see Figure 3.29).

Figure 3.29 Output with a Changed Lead Selection

DropDownByKey

Another means of presenting selection lists is provided by the view element DropDownByKey. Via the node info of the context node, we need to store a *value set* at the attribute info of the attribute to which the selectedKey property is bound. This value set, in turn, corresponds to an internal table. The node info and the attribute info contain the description data for the respective context node and its attributes. As a value set, the WD4A framework expects the composition of a list of key value pairs of the **WDY_KEY_VALUE_TABLE** type.

The attribute info of a context attribute is determined via the context node info. If the **selectedKey** property of the DropDownByKey view element is bound to this attribute, the values stored in the attribute info of KEY are displayed in the selection list. The key of the value selected by the user can be determined from the bound attribute by evaluating the lead selection.

3.3 | Implementation of Selection Options

We will illustrate this procedure using an example. For this purpose, copy the component ZEXP_DDLB_INDEX to the component ZEXP_DDLB_KEY. In the view layout, replace the DropDownByIndex view element with DropDownByKey. In the context of the view controller of V_DEFAULT, the cardinality of the context node TEXT_DESIGNS is changed to a value of **1..1**. The VALUE attribute is no longer required and can be deleted. The supply function method can be removed as well (see Figure 3.30).

In the wddoinit() method of the view controller, the selection value pairs of the dropdown list are now composed. The same entries are used here as in the component ZEXP_DDLB_INDEX that has just been described. The value set to be passed to the attribute info must be of the **WDY_KEY_VALUE_TABLE** type and is added to the context attribute KEY of the context node TEXT_DESIGNS. Listing 3.7 contains both the statements for composing the value set and the calls for writing the attribute info.

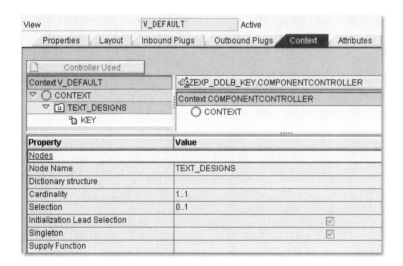

Figure 3.30 Context of the View Controller

```
METHOD wddoinit.
  DATA  lr_node_info TYPE REF TO        if_wd_context_node_info.
  DATA  ls_value     TYPE               wdy_key_value.
  DATA  lt_value_set TYPE               wdy_key_value_table.
*----- Create value key list of different text designs
  ls_value-key   = if_wdl_standard=>textviewdesign_emphasized.
  ls_value-value = 'emphasized'.
  APPEND ls_value TO lt_value_set.
  ls_value-key   = if_wdl_standard=>textviewdesign_header1.
```

```abap
        ls_value-value = 'header1'.
        APPEND ls_value TO lt_value_set.
        ls_value-key   = if_wdl_standard=>textviewdesign_header2.
        ls_value-value = 'header2'.
        APPEND ls_value TO lt_value_set.
        ls_value-key   = if_wdl_standard=>textviewdesign_header3.
        ls_value-value = 'header3'.
        APPEND ls_value TO lt_value_set.
*----- Retrieve node
        lr_node_info = wd_context->get_node_info( ).
        lr_node_info = lr_node_info->get_child_node( 'TEXT_DESIGNS' ).
*----- Set attribute info
        lr_node_info->set_attribute_value_set( name = 'KEY'
                                               value_set = lt_value_set ).
ENDMETHOD.
```

Listing 3.7 Setting the Attribute Info for DropDownByKey

In the view layout, the context attribute KEY is then bound to the **selectedKey** property of the DropDownByKey view element. To apply the design type to the text to be displayed after the selection has been changed, you need to bind the **design** property of the view element TextView to the KEY attribute of the context node as well. The definitions that are transferred to the W_DEFAULT window remain unchanged.

When you start the application after it has been created, the resulting output in the client corresponds to that of the ZEXP_DDLB_INDEX application. Every new selection of the design type triggers a server round trip, and the change of the design type becomes visible in the displayed text (see Figure 3.31).

Figure 3.31 Client Output of ZEXP_DDLB_KEY

The DropDownByKey view element should be used, particularly if existing fixed values from the Data Dictionary are to be provided as default values. It is then not necessary to compose the value list in the wddoinit() method; you only need to assign the appropriate data type from the Data Dictionary to the context attribute. All other functions—like determining the default values, preparing them in an internal table, and presenting the values—are then performed by the WD4A framework.

We'll clarify these procedures again by using an example. The component that we'll be implementing is named ZEXP_DDLB_KEY_DDIC; you can just copy the component we developed last, ZEXP_DDLB_KEY, and adapt it as needed. The initialization in the wddoinit() method is no longer required and can be deleted. For our example, the definition of the selection values is stored in the Data Dictionary in the data type **WDUI_TEXT_VIEW_DESIGN** that is based on the domain WDUI_TEXT_VIEW_DESIGN (see Figure 3.32).

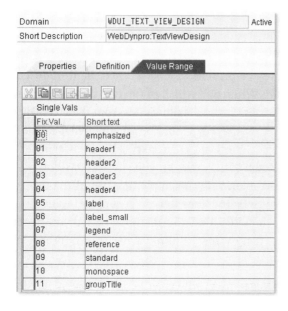

Figure 3.32 Fixed Values of the Domain for the TextView Design

The only step you need to perform in order to present the fixed Data Dictionary values in the view is to assign the data type to the context attribute in the view controller of the V_DEFAULT view. In our example, the KEY context attribute is now of the type **WDUI_TEXT_VIEW_DESIGN**. The layout of the view and the binding of the KEY context attribute remain unchanged.

After creating and starting the application, you can see that the list of selectable design types now corresponds to the entries in the WDUI_TEXT_VIEW_ DESIGN domain in the Data Dictionary (see Figure 3.33) and is no longer restricted to our four entries.

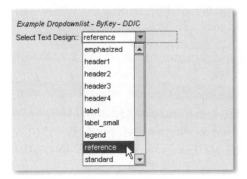

Figure 3.33 Client Output of ZEXP_DDLB_KEY_DDIC

Comparison of the Two Variants

The two available view elements for presenting selected text via dropdown lists raise the following question: When will which of the two view elements be active, that is, in which situations? If the default values from the Data Dictionary were to be provided, DropDownByKey would be an effective means of establishing a connection between the Data Dictionary and the user interface. For freely definable dropdown lists, however, you should consider various factors that can affect performance. For example, the use of the DropDownByIndex view element requires the creation of a context node, the instantiation of context node elements, and the manipulation of the lead selection. These steps can adversely affect runtime when the number of selection list entries is high.

However, DropDownByIndex is easier to handle than DropDownByKey. If you use DropDownByKey, the change of the attribute info affects all elements of a context node with cardinalities of **0..n** or **1..n**. You should therefore have a sound knowledge of the dependencies involved. Changes to the context node info are also very complicated and should only be made if you fully understand the potential of their affects. Furthermore, because the changes always affect all attributes of all elements of a context node, you should only use the view element DropDownByKey if the number of values in the selection list is very high, changes frequently, and will be influenced dynamically. Note that you can begin with a DropDownByIndex view element and switch to DropDownByKey, but only if the system performance noticeably deteriorates.

When using dropdown lists in table columns, using the DropDownByIndex view element is inevitable if selection lists with different values are to be displayed for different rows. The DropDownByKey view element cannot be used here, because the value set is always valid for all elements of a context node. For a table, this characteristic applies to every row and would therefore result in the same contents being displayed in every row.

3.3.2 Using Radio Buttons

The use of radio buttons is based on the same concepts that were described with regard to dropdown lists. Again, two types of view elements are distinguished: the `RadioButtonGroupByIndex` type and the `RadioButtonGroupByKey` type.

RadioButtonGroupByIndex

We'll use the same scenario for our example (i.e., the change of the design type for a text); however, now, we'll use radio buttons in the client instead of dropdown lists. Selecting a radio button triggers an action that leads to a change of the design type used for the presentation of text.

To implement the scenario, create a new component that we'll call ZEXP_RADIOBTN_INDEX. The layout of the V_DEFAULT view of the component consists of the view element TXV_TOPIC and the view element RDB_DESIGN of the type `RadioButtonGroupByIndex`. With every change of the selected radio button, an action will be triggered to change the lead selection of the elements in the corresponding context nodes. The action is named DO_TEXT_DESIGN and is defined in the **Actions** tab, and the **onSelect** property of view element RDB_DESIGN is bound to this action (see Figure 3.34).

The `RadioButtonGroupByIndex` view element requires a context node that provides the values for the individual radio buttons. This context node has a cardinality of **1..n**, which means that there is at least one radio button. As in the previous examples, we'll create this context node in the view controller of V_DEFAULT using the name TEXT_DESIGNS. Here again, the context node contains two attributes: the KEY attribute for the key and the VALUE attribute for the label of the respective radio button. This time, however, the VALUE attribute is bound to the **texts** property of the view element RDB_DESIGN in the layout of the view. Using this assignment, the descriptive texts for every radio button are displayed. The attribute KEY is bound to the **design** property of the TextView view element TXV_TOPIC and determines the design for representing the text. To populate the context node, you implement the supply function method `supply_text_designs()` in which the key value pairs are composed as internal tables and bound to the context node (see Listing 3.6).

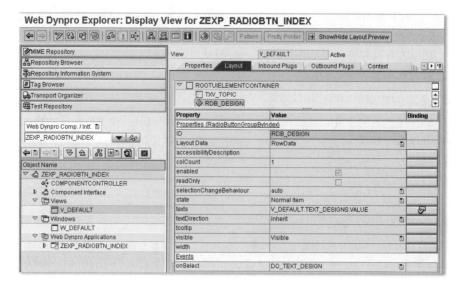

Figure 3.34 RadioButtonGroupByIndex Layout in the View Controller

Because the **Initialization Lead Selection** property of the context node TEXT_DESIGNS remains set, the lead selection for the radio button to be selected is initialized with the index "1", which means that it is set to the first element of the context node after the application has been run. Therefore, the first radio button in the list, which, in our example, represents the **emphasized** design type, is selected. The text is presented in accordance with the selected design (see Figure 3.35).

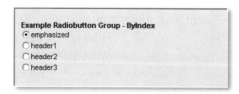

Figure 3.35 Client Output With RadioButtonGroupByIndex

With every new selection of a radio button, an action and therefore a server round trip is triggered, which leads to a change of the lead selection of the elements of the context node TEXT_DESIGNS. The event handler method for the action does not need to be implemented.

Again, the WD4A framework controls the change of the lead selection. Because the **design** property of the TextView view element is bound to the KEY context attribute of the TEXT_DESIGNS context node, it always contains the key value of the lead selection, which, in turn, causes the design of the text to correspond to the lead selection at all times, and therefore to correspond to the selected radio button as well. The only purpose of the event handler method `do_text_design()` is to enable the client to trigger the **onSelect** event when a radio button is selected. No additional programming effort is required within the event handler method. The WD4A framework accepts the change of the lead selection and the assignment to the corresponding property of the `TextView` view element.

RadioButtonGroupByKey

Another means of making a selection via radio buttons is provided by the `RadioButtonGroupByKey` view element (see Figure 3.36). As in the procedure using `DropDownByKey`, we have to store a value set at the info of a context attribute. This value set, in turn, corresponds to an internal table and must be of the **WDY_KEY_VALUE_TABLE** type. The attribute info of a context attribute is determined via the context node info.

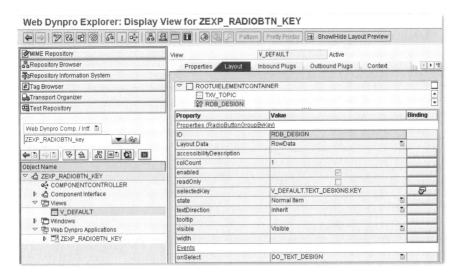

Figure 3.36 RadioButtonGroupByKey Layout in the View Controller

If the **selectedKey** property of the `RadioButtonGroupByKey` view element is now bound to the `KEY` attribute, the values stored in the attribute info of `KEY` are displayed and the selected radio button can be determined from the bound attribute.

We will again illustrate this using an example. For this purpose, copy the ZEXP_RADIOBTN_INDEX component from the previous section to the ZEXP_RADIOBTN_KEY component. In the layout of the view, replace RadioButtonGroupByIndex with RadioButtonGroupByKey. In the context of the view controller of V_DEFAULT, the cardinality of the context node TEXT_DESIGNS is changed to a value of **1..1**. The VALUE attribute is no longer required and can be deleted. The same applies to the supply function method supply_text_designs(). In the wddoinit() method of the view controller, the values of the radio buttons list are composed. The same entries as in the ZEXP_RADIOBTN_INDEX component will be used. The value set to be passed to the attribute info must be of the **WDY_KEY_VALUE_TABLE** type and is added to the context attribute KEY of the context node TEXT_DESIGNS (see Listing 3.8)

```
METHOD wddoinit.
  DATA lr_node_info TYPE REF TO    if_wd_context_node_info.
  DATA ls_value     TYPE           wdy_key_value.
  DATA lt_value_set TYPE           wdy_key_value_table.
*----- Create value-key list of different text designs
  ls_value-key   = cl_wd_text_view=>e_design-emphasized.
  ls_value-value = 'emphasized'.
  APPEND ls_value TO lt_value_set.
  ls_value-key   = cl_wd_text_view=>e_design-header1.
  ls_value-value = 'header1'.
  APPEND ls_value TO lt_value_set.
  ls_value-key   = cl_wd_text_view=>e_design-header2.
  ls_value-value = 'header2'.
  APPEND ls_value TO lt_value_set.
  ls_value-key   = cl_wd_text_view=>e_design-header3.
  ls_value-value = 'header3'.
  APPEND ls_value TO lt_value_set.
*----- Retrieve node
  lr_node_info = wd_context->get_node_info( ).
  lr_node_info = lr_node_info->get_child_node( 'TEXT_DESIGNS' ).
*----- Set attribute info
  lr_node_info->set_attribute_value_set( name = 'KEY'
                                         value_set = lt_value_set ).
ENDMETHOD.
```

Listing 3.8 Setting the Attribute Info for RadioButtonGroupByKey

In the layout of the view, the KEY attribute is now bound to the **selectedKey** property of the RadioButtonGroupByKey view element. To apply the design type to the text to be displayed, after the selection has been changed, you need to bind the **design** property of the view element TextView to the KEY attribute of the context node as well. The definitions in the window W_DEFAULT that were transferred from the previous example remain unchanged.

Again, you can start the application after its creation. The result shown in the client corresponds to that of the ZEXP_DDLB_INDEX application. Every other selection of the design type triggers a server round trip and the change of the design type becomes visible in the displayed text (see Figure 3.37).

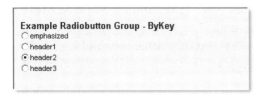

Figure 3.37 Client Output with RadioButtonGroupByKey

3.4 Presentation of Tree Structures

For the visual presentation of hierarchically structured data sets, the WD4A framework provides the Tree view element with two possible implementation techniques: sequential and recursive. A *sequential* implementation is used if the depth of the tree is known at the time of development. The *recursive* implementation is used if the tree depths of the individual nodes vary, or aren't known at the time of development.

Generally, when presenting tree structures, it is impossible to know how many lower-level nodes are under the root node, or how deeply a tree is nested. Therefore, the recursive technique is the implementation that is most frequently used. Aside from the two implementation techniques for presenting trees, there are also differences in controlling the chronological order of building the tree hierarchy. On the one hand, all elements can be loaded and the tree hierarchy can be completely created; on the other hand, only the parts that are visible to the user can be loaded. Performance and resources each play an important role, and they each must be considered on a case-by-case basis.

Figure 3.38 shows some examples of tree structures. The sample structures Structure 1 and Structure 2 show a regular nesting; the sample structures Structure 3 and Structure 4 have irregularly distributed lower-level nodes and leaf elements. Therefore, the sequential method would be appropriate for implementing Structure 1 and Structure 2, while the recursive method could be used for Structure 3 and Structure 4. In the following two sections, we'll address the details and differences inherent in these two techniques and further illustrate them with examples.

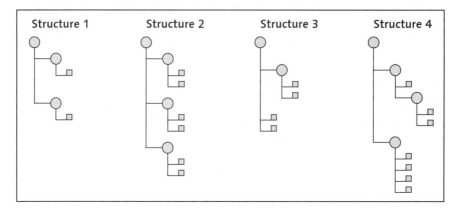

Figure 3.38 Examples of Tree Structures

3.4.1 Sequential Building of Tree Structures

As a result of the implementation of the example in this section, a two-level tree will be presented in the client with its nodes and elements. The tree has the three nodes, **Node A**, **Node B**, and **Node C**, each of which has several leaf elements (see Figure 3.39).

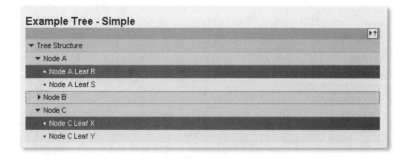

Figure 3.39 Presentation of a Simple Tree Structure

The component to be implemented is named ZEXP_TREE_SIM. In the context of the view controller, a context node CONTENT is created with a cardinality of **1..1**. Under this context node, the context nodes required for the Tree view element are composed. First, we need a context node for the tree node, which is named TREENODE, receives a cardinality of **1..n**, and is of the type

WDR_NAME_VALUE. From the DDIC structure (*Data Dictionary*) **WDR_NAME_VALUE**, we will use the attributes NAME and VALUE. Furthermore, we'll add an appropriate lower-level node that represents the leaf elements to the context node TREENODE. The name of this context node is TREELEAF. It is of the **WDR_NAME_VALUE** type as well, and uses the two attributes VALUE and KEY.

First, we will discuss the simpler variant where the complete tree structure is composed at the time of initialization. For this purpose, it is necessary that the **Singleton** property not be set for the context node TREELEAF (see Figure 3.40). This enables an instance of the TREELEAF context node with elements and appropriate values to be created for every element of the TREENODE context node. At runtime, the entire tree structure is therefore available, and when the views are changed by the user, that is, when the nodes are opened and closed, the previously determined lower-level node values and their leaf elements are accessed and displayed in the client.

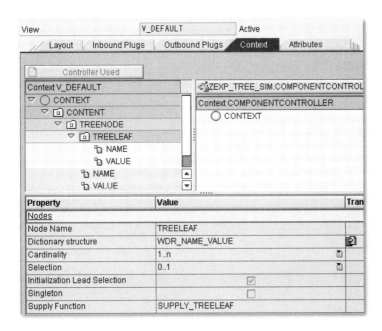

Figure 3.40 Characteristics of the Context

The context node is populated via supply function methods. The elements of the context node consist of value pairs, composed of a key and its description. From these, an internal table is built, and the context node is populated using the `bind_table()` method (see Listing 3.9).

```
METHOD supply_treenode.
  DATA  lt_node_items    TYPE    wdr_name_value_list.
  DATA  ls_node_item     TYPE    wdr_name_value.
  ls_node_item-name  = 'Node A'.
  ls_node_item-value = '10'.
  APPEND ls_node_item TO lt_node_items.
  ls_node_item-name  = 'Node B'.
  ls_node_item-value = '20'.
  APPEND ls_node_item TO lt_node_items.
  ls_node_item-name  = 'Node C'.
  ls_node_item-value = '30'.
  APPEND ls_node_item TO lt_node_items.
  node->bind_table( lt_node_items ).
ENDMETHOD.
```

Listing 3.9 Population of the TREENODE Context Node

The values for the lower-level nodes are set in a similar way. The supply function method of the TREELEAF context node is referred to as supply_treeleaf() (see Listing 3.10). At runtime, it is called for every element of the parent TREENODE context node. In order to distinguish which element is the respective caller, we evaluate the passed parameter PARENT_ELEMENT and then decide which values are assigned to the lower-level attributes.

```
METHOD supply_treeleaf.
  DATA  ls_leaf_item     TYPE    wdr_name_value.
  DATA  lt_leaf_items    TYPE    wdr_name_value_list.
  DATA  lv_value         TYPE    wdr_value.
  parent_element->get_attribute( EXPORTING name  = 'VALUE'
                                 IMPORTING value = lv_value ).
  CASE lv_value.
    WHEN '10'.
      ls_leaf_item-name  = 'Node A Leaf R'.
      ls_leaf_item-value = '11'.
      APPEND ls_leaf_item TO lt_leaf_items.
      ls_leaf_item-name  = 'Node A Leaf S'.
      ls_leaf_item-value = '12'.
      APPEND ls_leaf_item TO lt_leaf_items.
    WHEN '20'.
      ls_leaf_item-name  = 'Node B Leaf T'.
      ls_leaf_item-value = '21'.
      APPEND ls_leaf_item TO lt_leaf_items.
      ls_leaf_item-name  = 'Node B Leaf U'.
      ls_leaf_item-value = '22'.
      APPEND ls_leaf_item TO lt_leaf_items.
```

```
        ls_leaf_item-name  = 'Node B Leaf V'.
        ls_leaf_item-value = '23'.
        APPEND ls_leaf_item TO lt_leaf_items.
      WHEN '30'.
        ls_leaf_item-name  = 'Node C Leaf X'.
        ls_leaf_item-value = '31'.
        APPEND ls_leaf_item TO lt_leaf_items.
        ls_leaf_item-name  = 'Node C Leaf Y'.
        ls_leaf_item-value = '32'.
        APPEND ls_leaf_item TO lt_leaf_items.
    ENDCASE.
    node->bind_table( lt_leaf_items ).
ENDMETHOD.
```

Listing 3.10 Population of the TREELEAF Context Node

The layout of the view consists of the view element TXV_TOPIC representing the heading and the Tree view element TRE_SIMPLE representing the tree structure (see Figure 3.41).

The **dataSource** property of the view element TRE_SIMPLE binds to the context node CONTENT. The view element for the presentation of the node—TreeNodeType—and the leaf elements—TreeItemType—of the tree are inserted underneath TRE_SIMPLE. The **dataSource** property of the TreeNodeType view element TNT_NODE binds to the context node TREENODE, the name of the node is determined by the context attribute VALUE. The bindings for the TreeItemType view element TIT_ITEM are similar to those of TreeNodeType: the **dataSource** property binds to the TREELEAF context node, and the VALUE attribute binds to the **text** property.

We can present another variant of the tree structure by setting the **Singleton** property of the context node TREELEAF, which represents the lower-level node. In this case, at the time of initialization, only an instance of TREELEAF is created, which is assigned to the lead selection of the parent context node (see Section 2.4.2). On the one hand, this reduces the storage space that is taken up by the application, because only a part of the tree structure has been composed and needs to be maintained; on the other hand, this reduces the time required at the time of initialization for the only partial building of the tree structure. However, whenever a parent node is opened, the underlying structure must be determined.

3 | Developing WD4A Applications

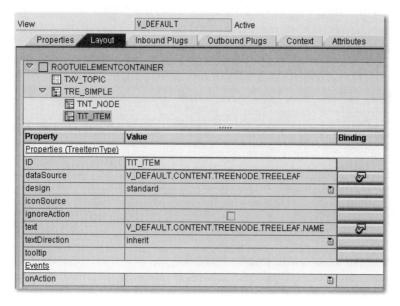

Figure 3.41 Binding of the Context to the Tree Elements

In our example, this is achieved by setting the lead selection in the event handler method—for the DO_LOAD event of the view element TNT_NODE—to the node manipulated by the user (see Listing 3.11).

```
METHOD onactiondo_load.
  DATA   lr_element     TYPE REF TO  if_wd_context_element.
  DATA   lr_node        TYPE REF TO  if_wd_context_node.
  DATA   lr_tree_node   TYPE REF TO  if_wd_context_node.
*--- Change lead selection
  lr_element = wdevent->get_context_element( 'CONTEXT_ELEMENT' ).
  lr_node      = wd_context->get_child_node( 'CONTENT' ).
  lr_tree_node = lr_node->get_child_node( 'TREENODE' ).
  lr_tree_node->set_lead_selection( element = lr_element ).
ENDMETHOD.
```

Listing 3.11 Changing the Lead Selection

First, the corresponding element of the node selected by the user is determined, which is passed by the WD4A framework via the parameter WDEVENT to the event handler method. Then, in order to set the lead selection to this element, we still need a reference to the context node TREENODE.

The WD4A framework provides two options for setting the lead selection: via the index, or by specifying the element directly. Because we have a reference to the appropriate element due to the passed parameter, we choose the second variant.

The context node TREELEAF is now in its initial state. This causes the appropriate supply function method to be called, which populates the context node with data (see Listing 3.10). In the supply_treeleaf() method, the parent node is determined and this represents the changed lead selection. Therefore, the corresponding values of the attributes arranged underneath the context node can also be determined. Note that the values of the attributes of the previous lead selection are discarded, so only the tree structure corresponding to the current lead selection is available in the storage left in the application.

Using this technique, we create a division of the total duration that would be required for composing the tree structure. The respective substructure is only built when a node is opened.

3.4.2 Recursive Tree Structures

As a result of the implementation of the example used in this section, the tree structure of the MIME Repository of the server you are currently using is to be presented. The contents of the MIME Repository can usually be accessed via Transaction SE80 (see Figure 3.42). The MIME Repository consists of folders and files; every folder can contain several folders and files.

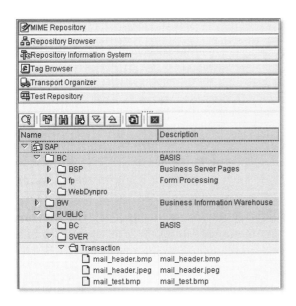

Figure 3.42 MIME Repository in the ABAP Workbench

We will now implement this presentation via a WD4A application using the Tree view element. You should note that the nesting of the tree structure of the MIME Repository could be changed by the user; for example, when a new WD4A component is created, you can store MIME objects in the central MIME Repository.

Because we cannot predict which additional nodes and corresponding MIME objects are added to the tree structure, we cannot assume that the structure has not been changed, or that the layout has evenly nested trees. The solution that we now must implement is to enable the presentation of unevenly nested trees and structures that are not fixed at the time of development (see Figure 3.43).

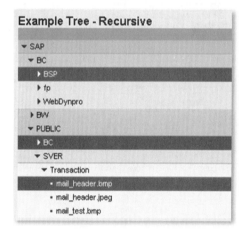

Figure 3.43 WD4A Application for MIME Repository Presentation

The component that we will implement is named ZEXP_TREE_REC. For the context of the view controller, first create a context node named CONTENT where the **Cardinality** property is set to **1..1**. Underneath the context node, the recursive context node is created by calling the context menu of the parent context node via the right mouse button, in our case CONTENT, and selecting the **Create · Recursion Node** entry (see Figure 3.44). In the following input mask, enter the name of the recursive context node ("MIMECONTENT"). At the same time, you must enter the recurring node, which, in our case, is the context node CONTENT (see Figure 3.45).

Thus, for the recursive context node, there is always an instance for every element of the parent context node at runtime. This means that the recursive context node may not be of the **Singleton** type; the value of this property refers to CONTENT, which is the context node that is to recur.

The context node MIMECONTENT can represent a folder or a file. Whether the context node represents a folder or a file is determined in the layout by using different view elements: TreeNodeType and TreeItemType. In contrast to TreeNodeType, the TreeItemType cannot contain any lower-level nodes.

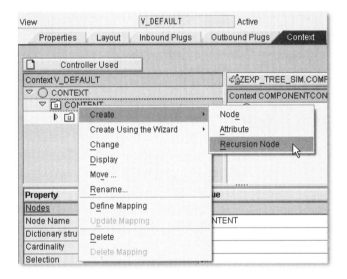

Figure 3.44 Creating a Recursive Context Node

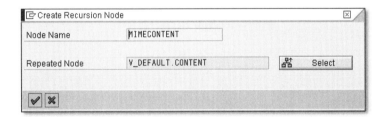

Figure 3.45 Determining the Context Node to Recur

For now, let's continue working with the context of the view controller and add the still required context nodes and attributes. For the CONTENT context node, we need three attributes (see Figure 3.46):

- The NAME attribute will represent the names of the nodes or folders, respectively.
- The CHILDREN_LOADED attribute is an indicator that will be used to avoid redundant loading processes. It may happen that the user selects a parent node, the substructures of which have already been determined. In this case, the loading process must not be repeated.
- The third required attribute, PATH, contains the information about the path of the selected node and is required to load additional child structures.

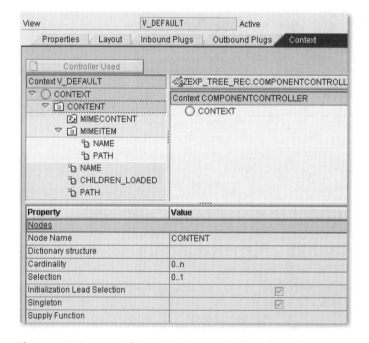

Figure 3.46 Context with Recursive Context Node and Attributes

Also for the leaf elements of the tree structure, which, in our example, are the actual MIME objects, an appropriate context node is required. It is named MIMEITEM, and its attributes are again NAME and PATH. An attribute for the indication of existing sublevel nodes or folders is not necessary because this context node represents the leaf elements in the tree structure.

Now let's start building the view layout (see Figure 3.47). We will need the Tree view element and its lower-level view elements for distinguishing the node type. The **dataSource** property of the view element TRE_RECURSIVE binds to the context node CONTENT. Below TRE_RECURSIVE, the two view elements for presenting the node and the leaf elements of the tree are inserted—`TreeNodeType` and `TreeItemType`. The property of the `TreeNodeType` view element `TNT_MIMEFOLDER` binds to the context node `CONTENT` as well. The name of the node is determined by the `CONTENT` context attribute `NAME`.

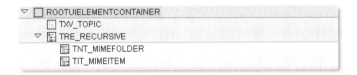

Figure 3.47 Layout for Presenting Recursive Trees

If the user selects a node, it is to present the next lower level. For this purpose, an appropriate action needs to be defined that we will call `DO_LOAD` and bind it to the **onLoadChildren** property of the view element `TNT_MIMEFOLDER`. The steps to be executed in the event handler `onactiondo_load()`, which is generated by the WD4A framework for that purpose, will be discussed later. The bindings for the view element `TIT_MIMEITEM` look as follows: the **data-Source** property binds to the `MIMEITEM` context node, and the `NAME` attribute binds to the **text** property.

At runtime, it is necessary to first initialize the tree. The top node of the MIME Repository is named **SAP**. In our example, this name is to be displayed in the client. For this purpose, the appropriate attributes of the `CONTENT` context node are set in the `wddoinit()` method of the view controller. The starting path that is stored in the `PATH` attribute is "/sap". (see Listing 3.12).

```
METHOD wddoinit.
  DATA  lr_current_node    TYPE REF TO   if_wd_context_node.
  DATA  lr_current_element TYPE REF TO   if_wd_context_element.
  lr_current_node    = wd_context->get_child_node( 'CONTENT' ).
  lr_current_element = lr_current_node->create_element( ).
  lr_current_element->set_attribute( name  = 'NAME'
                                     value = 'SAP' ).
  lr_current_element->set_attribute( name  = 'PATH'
                                     value = '/sap' ).
  lr_current_node->bind_element( lr_current_element ).
  lr_current_node->set_lead_selection( lr_current_element ).
ENDMETHOD.
```

Listing 3.12 Initialization of the Recurring Node

The initial screen with **SAP** as its top node is shown in Figure 3.48. If the user selects this top node, an event is triggered that calls the event handler method `onactiondo_load()`. The event handler method uses the node to determine the corresponding lower-level nodes or leaf elements using the stored path. This extensive determination process by calling the corresponding APIs can be found in Listing 3.13; the statements are implemented in the `onactiondo_load()` event handler method. The `properties()` method of the API MIME object determines whether the lower-level object is a node or a leaf element. Depending on the result, the determined entry is bound to the CONTENT context node or to the MIMEITEM context node.

Figure 3.48 Display After Starting the Application

```
METHOD onactiondo_load.
    DATA lr_node              TYPE REF TO       if_wd_context_node.
    DATA lr_mime_api          TYPE REF TO       if_mr_api.
    DATA lt_path_entries      TYPE              string_table.
    DATA lv_index             TYPE              sytabix.
    DATA lv_is_folder         TYPE              abap_bool.
    DATA ls_io                TYPE              skwf_io.
    DATA lt_ios               TYPE              skwf_ios.
    DATA lv_url               TYPE              skwf_url.
    DATA lv_path              TYPE              string.
    DATA lv_children_loaded   TYPE              string.
    DATA ls_mime_entry        TYPE if_v_default=>element_selected.
*----- Avoid redundant loading of data
    context_element->get_attribute(
                        EXPORTING name  = 'CHILDREN_LOADED'
                        IMPORTING value = lv_children_loaded ).
    CHECK lv_children_loaded = abap_false.
    context_element->set_attribute( EXPORTING name  = 'CHILDREN_LOADED'
                                              value = abap_true ).
*----- Create children elements
    context_element->get_attribute( EXPORTING name  = 'PATH'
                                    IMPORTING value = lv_path ).
    lr_mime_api = cl_mime_repository_api=>if_mr_api~get_api( ).
    lr_mime_api->get_io_for_url( EXPORTING i_url = lv_path
                                 IMPORTING e_loio = ls_io ).
```

```
*------ Get all children under a specific node
    CALL METHOD cl_skwf_folder_util=>ios_attach_get
        EXPORTING folder                     = ls_io
                  iotypeacc                  = ' '
                  x_prefetch_properties      = abap_true
        IMPORTING ios                        = lt_ios.
  LOOP AT lt_ios INTO ls_io.
    CALL FUNCTION 'SKWF_NMSPC_IO_ADDRESS_GET'
        EXPORTING io  = ls_io
        IMPORTING url = lv_url.
    ls_mime_entry-path = lv_url.
    SPLIT ls_mime_entry-path AT '/' INTO TABLE lt_path_entries.
    lv_index = LINES( lt_path_entries ).
    READ TABLE lt_path_entries INDEX lv_index INTO ls_mime_entry-name.
*---- Determine type of element
    CALL METHOD lr_mime_api->properties
        EXPORTING i_url       = ls_mime_entry-path
        IMPORTING e_is_folder = lv_is_folder.
    IF lv_is_folder = abap_true.
*---- Create a folder element
       lr_node = context_element->get_child_node( 'MIMECONTENT' ).
    ELSE.
*----- Create a file element
       lr_node = context_element->get_child_node( 'MIMEITEM' ).
    ENDIF.
    lr_node->bind_structure( new_item           = ls_mime_entry
                             set_initial_elements = abap_false ).
  ENDLOOP.
ENDMETHOD.
```

Listing 3.13 Determining the Lower-Level Structures of the MIME Repository

3.5 User Guidance per RoadMap and Messages

The RoadMap view element facilitates a secure user guidance via a multistep process. For applications that guide the users across several inputs and for steps that build on one another, we recommend that you use an additional help aid to assist users in their interaction with the application. The RoadMap view element always indicates the exact current position in the editing chain. In this section, we will first discuss some general aspects that should be considered when using the RoadMap view elements provided by the WD4A framework.

For the design of the user guidance, it is important to first determine the individual steps of the process. Every step and the resulting user interaction are implemented in the WD4A framework within a view that we'll refer to as a *single step view* in this section. The component also contains a view, the central parts of which are the `RoadMap` view element and the buttons for advancing in the editing chain. For clarification purposes, this view is referred to as a *main view* in this section.

To be called by the main view, every single step view requires at least one inbound plug. The navigation between the main view and the individual single step views takes place by triggering the outbound plugs that are connected to the respective inbound plug of the next single step view. This means that the main view needs one outbound plug for each single step view to be called.

For representing the **Next** button in the main view, there is a special design that marks the button with appropriate arrows. This can be specified in the layout of the main view using the **design** property of the respective button.

The context stores the information about the selected step and the application-specific data. Because the context cannot be accessed across several views, all data should be stored in the context of the component controller and provided to the view controller contexts via an appropriate mapping.

Controlling the process steps using the `RoadMap` view element requires a context node `ROADMAP` with two attributes, `STEP` and `NEXT_ENABLED`. The `STEP` attribute always holds the current process step in the overall process. Depending on the planned navigation options, more attributes for controlling the properties of view elements come into question. For example, if you want to enable the user to optionally navigate backwards, you would implement the control of the corresponding Back button via another attribute.

3.5.1 Structure of the RoadMap Application

In our case, we want to describe the use of the `RoadMap` view element using a forward navigation. The component is named `ZEXP_ROADMAP`. The `NEXT_ENABLED` attribute controls the activation of the **Next** button; in the last step of the process, the button is to be turned inactive.

The main view contains the `RoadMap` view element and corresponding `RoadMapStep` view elements that map the individual process steps. Additionally, a `ViewContainerUIElement` view element is needed as a placeholder for the individual single step views. The main view is then embedded in the window, and the single step views are embedded in the `ViewContainerUIElement` view element.

The navigation is defined by linking the outbound plugs of the main view to the inbound plugs of the single step views. The example component to be created for the `RoadMap` view element is to guide us through the conversion of units. The process consists of three steps:

1. Select the dimension.
2. Enter the original value and select the conversion units.
3. Calculate the target value according to the target unit and display the result.

The processes in the client are illustrated in Figures 3.49 through 3.51 using the example of a length conversion.

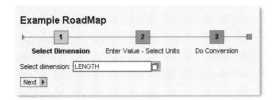

Figure 3.49 Select the Dimension

Figure 3.50 Enter the Source Value and Select the Units

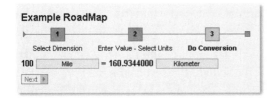

Figure 3.51 Calculate and Display the Result

3 | Developing WD4A Applications

The context of the component controller consists of four context nodes (see Figure 3.53):

- The ROADMAP context node has two attributes, STEP and NEXT_ENABLED.
- The DIMENSION context node contains a DVALUE attribute of the **DIMID** type. The input field, the **value** property of which is bound to the context attribute, is to provide an input help for selecting the dimension. Therefore, the **Input Help Mode** property of the DVALUE attribute is assigned the value **Dictionary Search Help**, and the search help to be used, **H_T006D**, is specified in the property beneath (see Figure 3.52).

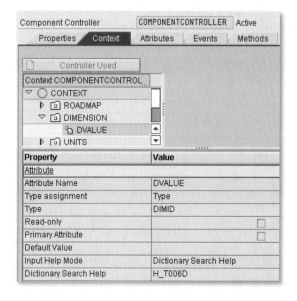

Figure 3.52 Assigning a DDIC Search Help to a Context Attribute

- The UNIT context node consists of two more context nodes, FROMUNIT and TOUNIT, to which the dropdown lists for selecting the units are bound. The **Cardinality** property is set to **0..n**. Both context nodes are populated by a supply function method that provides all appropriate units depending on the selected dimension; the name of this method is supply_unit(). The IVALUE attribute of the UNIT context node is for entering the value to be converted.
- The CONVERSION context node includes an attribute named CVALUE, which contains the converted value. To calculate the result, the supply_conversion() method is used (see Listing 3.19), which, as a supply function method, is assigned to the CONVERSION context node.

Now we will have a look at the methods in the component controller. To initialize the RoadMap view element, the appropriate attributes of the ROADMAP context node are set in the wddoinit() method. To distinguish the individual steps in the conversion process, we will introduce three identifications: STP_DIMENSION, STP_INPUT, and STP_RESULT. With every navigation event, the component controller also passes an identification (target parameter). The view has registered to the navigation event and responds, depending on the respective identification, by triggering the associated outbound plug. In the wddoinit() method of the component controller, the first step is initialized and receives the identification STP_DIMENSION (see Listing 3.14).

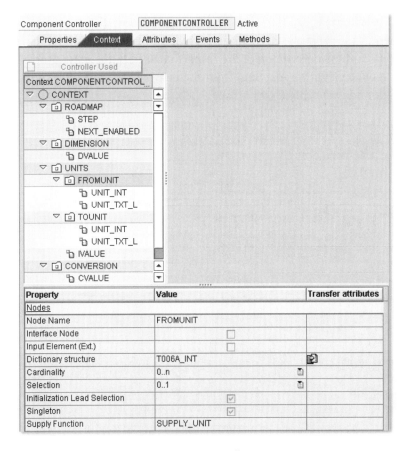

Figure 3.53 Context of the Component Controller

In the view controller of the V_DEFAULT view, there is a mapping from the component controller to the ROADMAP context node.

```abap
METHOD wddoinit.
  DATA lr_node TYPE REF TO if_wd_context_node.
  DATA ls_road TYPE    if_componentcontroller=>element_roadmap.
*--- Initialize roadmap
  lr_node = wd_context->get_child_node( 'ROADMAP' ).
  ls_road-step          = 'STP_DIMENSION'.
  ls_road-next_enabled = abap_true.
  lr_node->set_static_attributes( ls_road ).
ENDMETHOD.
```

Listing 3.14 Initialization of the RoadMap

To populate the dropdown lists that display the units and provide them for selection, we will use the UNITS_GET_FOR_DIMENSION API. In this process, the dimension and the language need to be passed. The result includes a table with the keys and the description of the respective unit. In the view controller of the V_UNIT view, the mapping from the component controller to the UNIT context node takes place (see Listing 3.15).

```abap
METHOD supply_unit.
    DATA    lr_node       TYPE REF TO if_wd_context_node.
    DATA    lv_dimension TYPE       dimid.
    DATA    lt_unit       TYPE
                                if_componentcontroller=>elements_fromunit.
    lr_node = wd_context->get_child_node( 'DIMENSION' ).
    lr_node->get_attribute( EXPORTING name  = 'DVALUE'
                            IMPORTING value = lv_dimension ).
    CALL FUNCTION 'UNITS_GET_FOR_DIMENSION'
      EXPORTING
        dimension           = lv_dimension
        language            = sy-langu
      TABLES
        units_of_measurement = lt_unit
      EXCEPTIONS
        dimension_not_found  = 1
        OTHERS               = 2.
    IF sy-subrc EQ 0.
      node->bind_table( new_items          = lt_unit
                        set_initial_elements = abap_true ).
    ENDIF.
ENDMETHOD.
```

Listing 3.15 Determining the Units of a Dimension

The `continue()` method (see Listing 3.16) of the component controller is called from the event handler method `onactiondo_next()` of the V_DEFAULT view and sets the next step in the process.

```
METHOD continue.
  DATA lr_node    TYPE REF TO if_wd_context_node.
  DATA ls_roadmap TYPE if_componentcontroller=>element_roadmap.
  DATA lv_step    TYPE        string.
*---- Determine current step
  lr_node = wd_context->get_child_node( 'ROADMAP' ).
  lr_node->get_attribute( EXPORTING name  = 'STEP'
                          IMPORTING value = lv_step ).
*---- Set next step depending on current step
  CASE lv_step.
    WHEN 'STP_DIMENSION'.
      ls_roadmap-step         = 'STP_INPUT'.
      ls_roadmap-next_enabled = abap_true.
    WHEN 'STP_INPUT'.
      ls_roadmap-step         = 'STP_RESULT'.
      ls_roadmap-next_enabled = abap_false.
    WHEN OTHERS.
      ls_roadmap-next_enabled = abap_false.
  ENDCASE.
  lr_node->set_static_attributes( ls_roadmap ).
  wd_this->fire_navigate_evt( ls_roadmap-step ).
ENDMETHOD.
```

Listing 3.16 Setting the Next Process Step

At the end of the process, the NAVIGATE event, to which the V_DEFAULT view has registered, is triggered. The event is created in the component controller in the **Events** tab and includes a TARGET parameter that is required for passing the identification of the new process step (see Figure 3.54).

As with the outbound plugs, the WD4A framework uses the defined event to generate a fire method that calls the event defined in Figure 3.54 using the following command:

```
wd_this->fire_navigate_evt( [ParameterValue] ).
```

The composition of the method name is determined by the following convention:

```
wd_this->fire_[NameOfEvent]_evt( ).
```

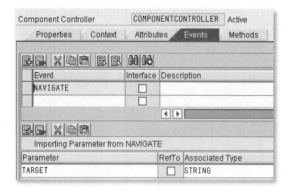

Figure 3.54 Definition of an Event and the Associated Parameters

The registration to the NAVIGATE event in the V_DEFAULT view takes place by defining an appropriate event handler method in the **Methods** tab. The name of the event handler method is on_navigate(). The event to be registered is entered via a display frame in the **Event** column (see Figure 3.55).

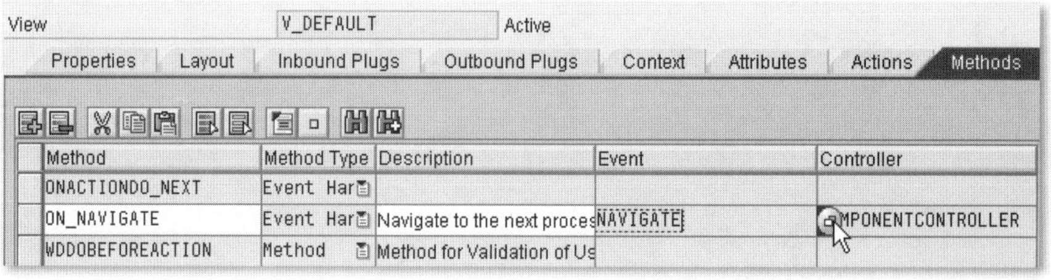

Figure 3.55 Registration to an Event

If this event is triggered by the component controller, the on_navigate() event handler is called in the view and triggers the corresponding outbound plugs, depending on the value of the passed parameter TARGET (see Listing 3.17).

```
METHOD on_navigate.
  CASE target.
    WHEN 'STP_DIMENSION'.
      wd_this->fire_op_to_v_dimension_plg( ).
    WHEN 'STP_INPUT'.
      wd_this->fire_op_to_v_units_plg( ).
    WHEN 'STP_RESULT'.
      wd_this->fire_op_to_v_result_plg( ).
  ENDCASE.
ENDMETHOD.
```

Listing 3.17 Navigation to the Next Process Step

The inbound plugs to which the outbound plugs of the V_DEFAULT view are linked are defined in the respective single step views. There are three single step views, V_DIMENSION, V_UNIT, and V_RESULT, with the inbound plugs IP_V_DIMENSION, IP_V_UNIT, and IP_V_RESULT. In the W_DEFAULT window, the outbound plugs of the V_DEFAULT view are linked to the corresponding inbound plugs of the respective single step view. In the window, V_DEFAULT and the single step views are first embedded in the VCU_ROADMAP view element (see Figure 3.56); then, the appropriate navigation links can be created.

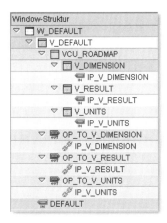

Figure 3.56 Linking Window Outbound Plugs and View Inbound Plugs

The V_DEFAULT view consists of the view element RMP_CONVERSION and three RoadMapStep view elements that represent the individual process steps (see Figure 3.57). The **selectedStep** property binds to the context attribute STEP of the ROADMAP context node and identifies the currently active process step in the client at runtime. Additionally, the layout of the view contains the view element VCU_ROADMAP as a placeholder for the single step views. The layout is finally completed by a ButtonRow view element, which, in our example, only contains a button for forward navigation in the process. The action DO_NEXT is assigned to the **onAction** property of the Button view element BTN_NEXT; the continue() method of the component controller is called in the event handler of the action (see Listing 3.18).

```
METHOD onactiondo_next.
  DATA lr_comp_controller   TYPE REF TO  ig_componentcontroller.
  lr_comp_controller =  wd_this->get_componentcontroller_ctr( ).
  lr_comp_controller->continue( ).
ENDMETHOD.
```

Listing 3.18 Calling the continue() Method in the Component Controller

The context of the V_DEFAULT view consists of the ROADMAP context node to which a mapping exists in the component controller from the context node of the same name. The views representing the individual process steps are V_DIMENSION, V_INPUT, and V_RESULT. The V_DIMENSION view consists of an input field for the dimension. The context of the V_DIMENSION view consists of the DIMENSION context node to which a mapping exists in the component controller from the context node of the same name. The input field is bound to the DVALUE context attribute of the DIMENSION context node for which an ABAP Dictionary search help has been specified. The search help allows the user to select from among all the dimensions existing in the system.

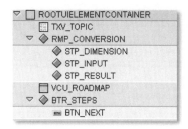

Figure 3.57 Layout of the V_DEFAULT View

Apart from the INP_VALUE view element for the value to be converted, the V_UNITS view (see Figure 3.58) consists of the dropdown lists for setting the source and target units of the conversion. The context of the V_UNITS view consists of the UNITS context node to which a mapping exists in the component controller from the context node of the same name. The properties of the view elements bind to the corresponding attributes of the UNITS context node.

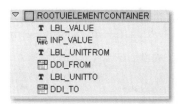

Figure 3.58 Layout of the V_UNITS View

The V_RESULT view (see Figure 3.59) finally displays the conversion result in the client. The context of the V_RESULT view consists of the CONVERSION and UNITS context nodes to which a mapping exists in the component controller from the context nodes of the same names.

Figure 3.59 Layout of the V_RESULT View

Important view elements in the view layout are the view element TXV_IVALUE for the source value, the view element INP_FROMUNIT for the source unit, the view element TXV_CVALUE for the result, and the view element INP_TOUNIT for the target unit. The properties of the view elements bind to the corresponding attributes of the CONVERSION and UNITS context nodes.

The converted value is calculated when the user navigates to V_RESULT. Because the CONVERSION context node is accessed, its supply function method supply_conversion() is called where the conversion takes place. The used APIs are the function modules CONVERSION_FACTOR_GET and CONVERT_TO_FRACT10. Listing 3.19 contains the calls for calculating the target value.

```
METHOD supply_conversion.
  DATA  lr_input_node   TYPE REF TO        if_wd_context_node.
  DATA  lr_sub_node     TYPE REF TO        if_wd_context_node.
  DATA  lv_fromunit     TYPE               t006-msehi.
  DATA  lv_tounit       TYPE               t006-msehi.
  DATA  lv_value        TYPE               string.
  DATA  lv_denominator  TYPE               f.
  DATA  lv_numerator    TYPE               f.
  DATA  lv_nomout       TYPE               dzaehl.
  DATA  lv_denomout     TYPE               nennr.
  DATA  ls_conversion   TYPE
                  if_componentcontroller=>element_conversion.
  lr_input_node = wd_context->get_child_node( 'INPUT' ).
  lr_input_node->get_attribute( EXPORTING name = 'IVALUE'
                                IMPORTING value = lv_value ).
  lr_sub_node     = lr_input_node->get_child_node( 'FROMUNIT' ).
  lr_sub_node->get_attribute( EXPORTING name = 'UNIT_INT'
                              IMPORTING value = lv_fromunit ).
  lr_sub_node     = lr_input_node->get_child_node( 'TOUNIT' ).
  lr_sub_node->get_attribute( EXPORTING name = 'UNIT_INT'
                              IMPORTING value = lv_tounit ).
  CALL FUNCTION 'CONVERSION_FACTOR_GET'
    EXPORTING
      no_type_check         = 'X'
```

```abap
              unit_in                = lv_fromunit
              unit_out               = lv_tounit
            IMPORTING
              denominator            = lv_denominator
              numerator              = lv_numerator
            EXCEPTIONS
              conversion_not_found = 1
              overflow               = 2
              type_invalid           = 3
              units_missing          = 4
              unit_in_not_found      = 5
              unit_out_not_found     = 6
              OTHERS                 = 7.
          IF sy-subrc <> 0.
            RETURN.
          ELSE.
            CALL FUNCTION 'CONVERT_TO_FRACT10'
              EXPORTING
                nomin                  = lv_numerator
                denomin                = lv_denominator
              IMPORTING
                nomout                 = lv_nomout
                denomout               = lv_denomout
              EXCEPTIONS
                conversion_overflow = 1
                OTHERS                 = 2.
            IF sy-subrc <> 0.
              RETURN.
            ELSE.
              ls_conversion-cvalue
                             = lv_value * ( lv_nomout / lv_denomout ).
            ENDIF.
            node->bind_structure( new_item           = ls_conversion
                                  set_initial_elements = abap_true ).
          ENDIF.
        ENDMETHOD.
```

Listing 3.19 Conversion Process

3.5.2 Message Handling

The presentation of messages in the client is controlled by the WD4A framework via the *message area*. By default, this area is arranged in the upper part of the screen (see Figure 3.60).

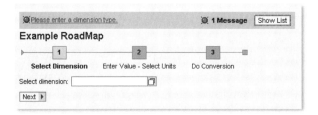

Figure 3.60 Default Output of Error Messages

You should note, however, that you can display the message area in other places of the screen. If you want to do so, you need to arrange the `MessageArea` view element accordingly in the view element hierarchy of the view. Figure 3.61 shows the positioning of the message output in the view editor below all other view elements. Figure 3.62 shows the corresponding output in the client.

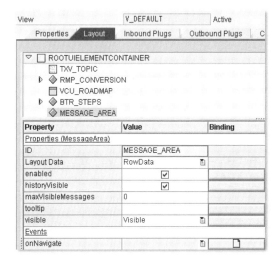

Figure 3.61 User-Defined Arrangement of the Message Area

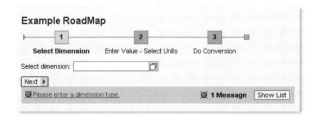

Figure 3.62 Client Output with Changed Position of the Messages

3 | Developing WD4A Applications

In the **Properties** tab of the application, you can configure whether the message area is to be constantly displayed even if there are no messages (**Always Display Message Component**), whether it is to be displayed only when there are messages (**Show Message Component on Demand**), or whether the messages are to be output without using the message area (**Display Messages Without Message Component**), that is, as a pure text display (see Figure 3.63).

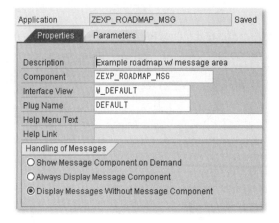

Figure 3.63 Options for Displaying Messages

The messages are created via the IF_WD_MESSAGE_MANAGER interface, using those simple texts that can be output as messages. Another option for displaying messages is the output of T100 messages via ID and number. This message type is known from the ABAP environment. Additionally, ABAP Objects exceptions can be used.

Table 3.1 lists the methods of the IF_WD_MESSAGE_MANAGER interface and their use in the different message types.

Method	Message Type
REPORT_ATTRIBUTE_ERROR_MESSAGE	Text
REPORT_SUCCESS	Text
REPORT_WARNING	Text
REPORT_ERROR_MESSAGE	Text
REPORT_FATAL_ERROR_MESSAGE	Text

Table 3.1 Methods of IF_WD_MESSAGE_MANAGER and Message Types

3.5 User Guidance per RoadMap and Messages

Method	Message Type
REPORT_T100_MESSAGE	T100
REPORT_ATTRIBUTE_T100_MESSAGE	T100
REPORT_ATTRIBUTE_EXCEPTION	Exception
REPORT_EXCEPTION	Exception
REPORT_FATAL_EXCEPTION	Exception

Table 3.1 Methods of IF_WD_MESSAGE_MANAGER and Message Types (cont.)

To react to user input, the hook method wddobeforeaction( ) is used in the appropriate view controller for implementation. Otherwise, you can create the messages in all other methods of the respective controller. The easiest way of implementing the access to the component message manager is to use the code wizard.

The logic for the message shown in Figure 3.60 or Figure 3.62 was implemented in the ZEXP_ROADMAP_MSG component in the wddobeforeaction( ) method of the view controller of the V_DIMENSION view. The goal of the validation in this example is to check the dimension input and to output a simple text message; the report_attribute_error_message( ) method is used for this purpose (see Figure 3.64).

Figure 3.64 Use of the Code Wizard for Implementing Messages

Listing 3.20 shows the input validation of the user for the displayed screenshots. The statements for the message creation were inserted by using the code wizard and were adapted accordingly.

```
METHOD wddobeforeaction.
  DATA  lr_current_controller  TYPE REF TO  if_wd_controller.
  DATA  lr_message_manager     TYPE REF TO  if_wd_message_manager.
  DATA  lr_node                TYPE REF TO  if_wd_context_node.
  DATA  lv_dvalue              TYPE         string.
  DATA  lr_sub_node            TYPE REF TO  if_wd_context_node.
  DATA  lr_element             TYPE REF TO  if_wd_context_element.
*--- Get message manager
  lr_current_controller ?= wd_this->wd_get_api( ).
```

```abap
    CALL METHOD lr_current_controller->get_message_manager
      RECEIVING
        message_manager = lr_message_manager.
*--- Read input data
    lr_node    = wd_context->get_child_node( 'DIMENSION' ).
    lr_element = lr_node->get_element( ).
    lr_node->get_attribute( EXPORTING name  = 'DVALUE'
                            IMPORTING value = lv_dvalue ).
    IF lv_dvalue IS INITIAL.
*--- Report message
      CALL METHOD lr_message_manager->report_attribute_error_message
        EXPORTING
          message_text   = 'Please enter a dimension type.'
          element        = lr_element
          attribute_name = 'DVALUE'.
    ENDIF.
ENDMETHOD.
```

Listing 3.20 Example of the Creation of Messages

3.6 Presenting Tables

To present data in a table, the WD4A framework implements the Table view element. At the time of development, this view element is assigned more lower-level view elements and is therefore also referred to as a *composite view element*. Lower-level view elements can be, for example, the Caption view element or the TableColumn view element.

The cells of the Table view element are arranged in rows and columns. In addition to the rows and columns, the Table view element consists of a *header* and a *footer area*. The characteristics and the population with data are managed via properties, as with all other view elements.

3.6.1 Table Output and Row Selection

The presentation of data using the Table view element requires several context bindings. Therefore, we will now address the creation of the context node and the attributes and describe this procedure by using the output of the country text table T005T, which is included by default in every delivered SAP system.

The component to be developed is named ZEXP_TABLE. In the view controller of the V_DEFAULT view, a context node COUNTRIES is created. The **Dictionary**

structure property is assigned the value **T005T**, and the **Cardinality** is assigned a value of **0..n**. Later, the **dataSource** property of the Table view element will be bound to this context node. For the **dataSource** property of the Table view element to bind to a context node, it must have a **Cardinality** property of **0..n** or **1..n**.

Via the context menu option **Create Using the Wizard · Attributes from Components of Structure** of the COUNTRIES context node, add the necessary attributes from the T005T table (see Figure 3.65).

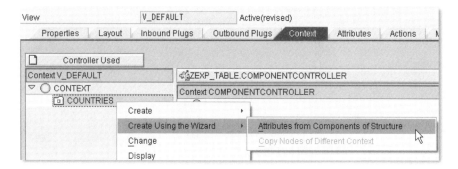

Figure 3.65 Definition of Context Attributes Via the Wizard

Then, all attributes of the T005T table are available for selection. Figure 3.66 shows the attributes to be used; the fields MANDT and SPRAS are not relevant for the output and are not selected.

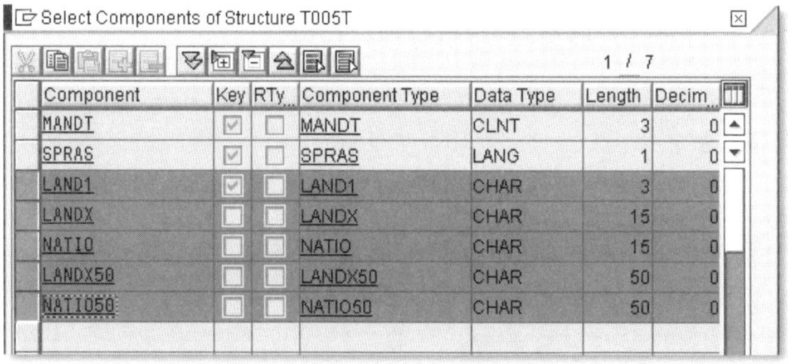

Figure 3.66 Selecting Attributes

Confirm your selection. With this step, the attributes are displayed as context attributes for the COUNTRIES context node with the type that was specified in the ABAP Dictionary (see Figure 3.67).

3 | Developing WD4A Applications

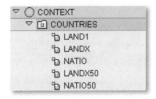

Figure 3.67 Context of the View Controller of V_DEFAULT

The context is populated via a supply function method. Name the **Supply Function** property of the COUNTRIES context node SUPPLY_COUNTRIES and navigate to the editor of the method. Listing 3.21 shows the required statements for populating the context.

```
METHOD supply_countries.
  DATA lt_countries    TYPE STANDARD TABLE OF t005t.
  SELECT * FROM t005t INTO TABLE lt_countries WHERE spras EQ sy-langu.
  IF sy-subrc EQ 0.
    node->bind_table( new_items = lt_countries ).
  ENDIF.
ENDMETHOD.
```

Listing 3.21 Implementation of supply_countries()

The context-related work is done. Now, we'll turn our attention to the layout and the view elements. As we mentioned above, the Table view element is a composite view element that can contain further lower-level view elements. In the view layout, first add the Table view element, which, in our example component ZEXP_TABLE, is named TBL_COUNTRY. With the TBL_COUNTRY view element, a Caption view element is automatically arranged under the TBL_COUNTRY node. Here, you can specify a table heading ("Countries and Nationality", see Figure 3.68).

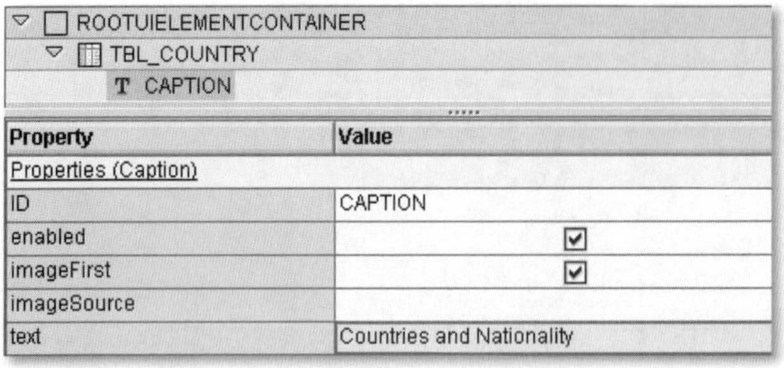

Figure 3.68 Table View Element with Lower-Level Caption View Element

Then bind the **dataSource** property of the TBL_COUNTRY view element to the COUNTRIES context node. The definitions of the table columns can be implemented in two ways: You can either configure the columns individually via the context menu of the Table view element (**Insert Table Column**), or you do this using a wizard with the specification of the context binding. Here, we will show you how to implement the definitions of the table columns using the simpler second way. From the context menu of the TBL_COUNTRY view element, select the **Create Binding** option. In the following window, the **Context-Knoten** ("context node") field is preset (see Figure 3.69) because we have already bound the **dataSource** property of the TBL_COUNTRY view element. But, you can still make changes here, or select the context node to be used in this step. In the table underneath, all context attributes are listed.

Create Context Binding for Table "TBL_COUNTRY"				
Context-Knoten	V_DEFAULT.COUNTRIES		Context	
Standard Cell-Editor	TextView			

Context Attribute	Cell Editor of Table Column	Bind	Name of Property to Be Bound
LAND1	TextView	✓	text
LANDX	TextView	✓	text
NATIO	TextView	✓	text
LANDX50	TextView	✓	text
NATIO50	TextView	✓	text

Figure 3.69 Context Binding Wizard for Table View Elements

The second column **Cell Editor of Table Column** enables the selection of the *cell editor* per column of the table to be presented. The cell editor describes the view element to be used to display or edit the cell contents of the column. In our example, the TextView view element was selected and defined as the cell editor for all columns of the table. The possible view elements that can be used as cell editors are displayed in Table 3.2.

View Element	
Button	Caption
Checkbox	DropDownByIndex
DropDownByKey	FileDownload
FileUpload	ValueComparison
Image	InputField
LinkToAction	LinkToURL

Table 3.2 Possible View Elements for Cell Editors

View Element	
ProgressIndicator	RadioButton
TextView	ToggleButton
ToolBarLinkToAction	ToolBarLinkToURL
TriStateCheckBox	

Table 3.2 Possible View Elements for Cell Editors (cont.)

The check box in the **Bind** column and the specifications in the **Name of Property to Be Bound** column determine whether and which property of the view element specified as the cell editor is to be bound to the respective context attribute. In our example, the **text** property of the TextView view element is bound to the context attributes of the COUNTRIES context node. The result of the assignments and inputs is shown in Figure 3.70.

As you can see, the TBL_COUNTRY view element has five TableColumn view elements, exactly one per every context attribute of the COUNTRIES context node. Every TableColumn view element has another Caption view element and a TextView view element. By default, the Caption view element belongs to every TableColumn view element and determines the column heading; if you do not enter anything here, the description of the data element is automatically retrieved from the ABAP Dictionary. The TextView view element has been selected as the cell editor for all columns of the table.

Figure 3.70 Columns and Cell Editors of the TBL_COUNTRY View Element

The most basic steps for outputting a table using the Table view element are now complete, and we can create and start the application. The result of the output is shown in Figure 3.71. Using the navigation elements in the lower area of the table, you can navigate per row, per page, or to the end or the beginning of the table, respectively.

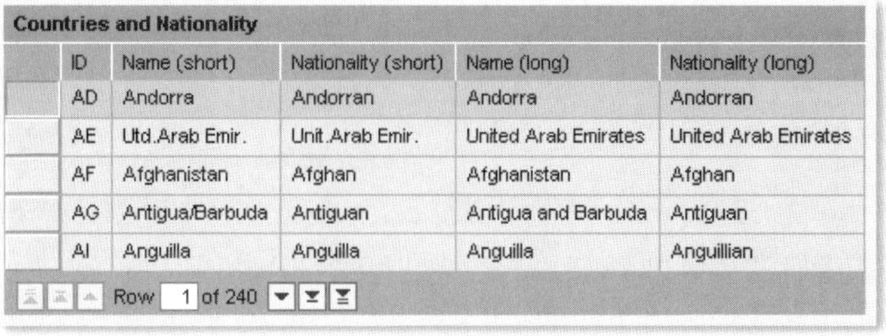
Countries and Nationality

ID	Name (short)	Nationality (short)	Name (long)	Nationality (long)
AD	Andorra	Andorran	Andorra	Andorran
AE	Utd.Arab Emir.	Unit.Arab Emir.	United Arab Emirates	United Arab Emirates
AF	Afghanistan	Afghan	Afghanistan	Afghan
AG	Antigua/Barbuda	Antiguan	Antigua and Barbuda	Antiguan
AI	Anguilla	Anguilla	Anguilla	Anguillian

Row 1 of 240

Figure 3.71 Client Output of T005T Using a Table View Element

3.6.2 Selection of Single or Multiple Rows

Now let's discuss some relationships between the presented table and the context. The individual rows of the table each correspond to the elements of the context nodes. If a new row in the table is selected, this results in a server round trip and a change of the lead selection of the context node to which the **dataSource** property of the `Table` view element has been bound. In its initial state, the first element of the context node is marked as the lead selection. Therefore, after the application has been started, the first table row is selected. If the user makes a new selection in the table, this selection can be determined at runtime via the following statement:

```
lr_element = lr_node->get_lead_selection( ).
```

As a prerequisite, the **onLeadSelect** property of the `Table` view element must have been assigned an action; only then can the element for the lead selection be determined in the associated event handler method. In our example, an action `ROW_SELECTED` may be defined and assigned to the **onLeadSelect** property for this purpose (see Figure 3.72). The implementation of the access to the lead selection in the event handler method `onactionrow_selected()` is shown in Listing 3.22.

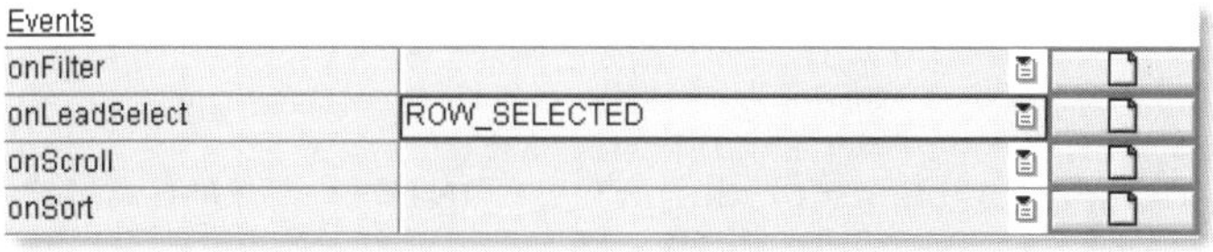

Figure 3.72 Action for Changing the Lead Selection

```
METHOD onactionrow_selected.
  DATA  lr_node      TYPE REF TO  if_wd_context_node.
  DATA  lr_element   TYPE REF TO  if_wd_context_element.
  DATA  ls_countries TYPE         if_v_default=>element_countries.
*--- Get lead selection
  lr_node    = wd_context->get_child_node( 'COUNTRIES' ).
  lr_element = lr_node->get_lead_selection( ).
  lr_element->get_static_attributes( IMPORTING
                                     static_attributes = ls_countries ).
ENDMETHOD.
```

Listing 3.22 Retrieving the Lead Selection

The `Table` view element also enables you to select several rows and to determine this selection in the event handler method. The multiple selections in the client are achieved by simultaneously pressing the **Shift** button and the table row selection. To determine this multiple selection at runtime, in the event handler method, you need to make changes to the properties of the context node and the `Table` view element. The **Selection** property of the COUNTRIES context node must be set to the **0..n** or **1..n** (see Figure 3.73). By default, this value is set to **0..1**, which means that either no or one row is selected at runtime.

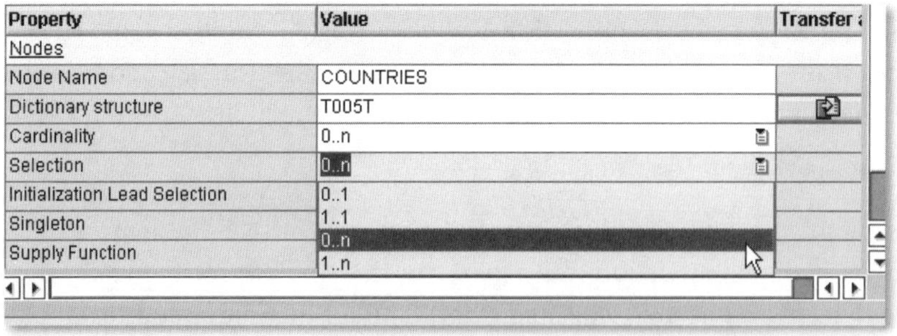

Property	Value	Transfer
Nodes		
Node Name	COUNTRIES	
Dictionary structure	T005T	
Cardinality	0..n	
Selection	0..n	
Initialization Lead Selection	0..1	
Singleton	1..1	
Supply Function	0..n	
	1..n	

Figure 3.73 Change to the Context for Multiple Selections

You also need to set the **selectionMode** property of the `Table` view element to the **multiple** value; the default value of this property is **single**. The selected rows of the table are then read using the following statement:

```
lt_elements = lr_node->get_selected_elements( ).
```

The internal `lt_elements` table is of the **WDR_CONTEXT_ELEMENT_SET** type. Here, you can determine whether or not you want the lead selection to be set as well. If you want the lead selection to be included in the output set of selected rows, you need to use the following statement:

```
lt_elements = lr_node->get_selected_elements(
                     including_lead_selection = abap_true ).
```

3.6.3 Changing Single Cells Using Variants

The properties of table cells are specified via the definitions for the table column. For example, the selection of the TextView view element as the cell editor for the **LAND1** column applies to all cells of this column. If you now want to change properties of individual cells of the same column, you can do this by defining *cell variants*.

We will describe the handling of cell variants with an example that illustrates the benefits of using a LinkToUrl view element, instead of the TextView view element in the **Name (short)** column in the country table output in Section 3.6.1 when the country identification "DE" occurs. When the links are clicked, the default web browser should display, and the Google search result for the country should be returned (see Figure 3.74).

Figure 3.74 Table Output with Different Cell Display and Linking

We will develop the example based on the ZEXP_TABLE component. The new component ZEXP_TABLE_VARIANT is created by copying the existing component.

The changes of a special cell of a column are identified via a key. In the layout, the key must be communicated to the **selectedCellVariant** property of the respective column. This is achieved by adding another attribute, in our case VARIANT, to the COUNTRIES context node to be bound (see Figure 3.75). The attribute is of the **STRING** type. The **selectedCellVariant** property of the TBL_COUNTRY_LANDX view element is then bound to this context attribute (see Figure 3.76).

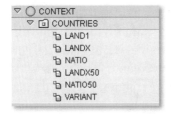

Figure 3.75 Adding an Attribute for the Variant Key to the Context Node

hAlign	auto		
isFiltered		☐	
resizable		☑	
selectedCellVariant	V_DEFAULT.COUNTRIES.VARIANT		
sortState	none		

Figure 3.76 Binding the selectedCellVariant Property in the View Layout

The **LANDX** column is the column where we want to exchange the cell editor. By binding the **selectedCellVariant** property of the view element TBL_COUNTRY_LANDX, every cell of the respective column can be assigned a unique key. Because we control the characteristics of the individual cells of the **LANDX** column, like cell editor and value assignment, completely via the variants, the binding existing from the ZEXP_TABLE component to the LANDX context attribute of the COUNTRIES context node still needs to be removed.

The key assignment is implemented in the supply function method supply_countries() of the COUNTRIES context node (see Listing 3.23). The method is extended so that after reading the database table T005T, the key is composed for every country entry using the country identification and the loop index. For example, for the first entry of the country table, the variant key would be "AD1", for the second entry "AE2", and so forth.

```
METHOD supply_countries.
  DATA lt_t005t       TYPE STANDARD TABLE OF t005t.
  DATA ls_t005t       TYPE                   t005t.
  DATA ls_countries   TYPE if_v_default=>element_countries.
  DATA lt_countries   TYPE if_v_default=>elements_countries.
```

```
    DATA lv_sytabix      TYPE string.
*--- Get country data
    SELECT * FROM t005t INTO TABLE lt_t005t WHERE spras EQ sy-langu.
    IF sy-subrc EQ 0.
*--- Create variant key
      LOOP AT lt_t005t INTO ls_t005t.
        lv_sytabix = sy-tabix.
        MOVE-CORRESPONDING ls_t005t TO ls_countries.
        CONCATENATE ls_countries-land1 lv_sytabix INTO
                                                 ls_countries-variant.
        CONDENSE ls_countries-variant NO-GAPS.
        APPEND ls_countries TO lt_countries.
      ENDLOOP.
*--- Bind data to node
      node->bind_table( new_items = lt_countries ).
    ENDIF.
  ENDMETHOD.
```

Listing 3.23 Composing the Variant Key

Let us now deal with the specification of the cell editor. Our objective here is to replace the cell editor of the TextView view element in the **Name (short)** column with a cell editor of the LinkToUrl view element whenever the country identification "DE" occurs, but cannot be achieved in a declarative way and instead must be implemented using the statements for dynamic programming in the wddomodifyview() method. Dynamic programming is discussed in more detail in Chapter 5.

The wddomodifyview() method includes a parameter VIEW as a reference to an object of the **IF_WD_VIEW** type that facilitates the access to an instance of the view at runtime. When the wddomodifyview() method is called, this view object contains all declaratively specified view elements and the corresponding layout, and therefore also the TableColumn view element TBL_COUNTRY_LANDX to be modified. Using the get_element() method, you can determine a reference to a view element.

In the country table, you must now determine the row that contains the entry for the "DE" country identification. When you locate this row, you can create the cell editor of the LinkToUrl view element by using the variant key and assigning it to the column reference. For all other country identifications, use the cell editor of the TextView view element. The corresponding process is as follows:

1. Create a new object of the desired view element and set the appropriate properties.
2. Create a new table cell object and assign the variant key.
3. Set the cell editor of the new table cell object to the view element object that is created in the first step.
4. Add the table cell object to the column reference.

The implementation of the statements for our example can be found in Listing 3.24.

```abap
METHOD wddomodifyview.
  DATA lr_standard_cell  TYPE REF TO cl_wd_table_standard_cell.
  DATA lr_table_column   TYPE REF TO cl_wd_table_column.
  DATA ls_countries      TYPE        if_v_default=>element_countries.
  DATA lt_countries      TYPE        if_v_default=>elements_countries.
  DATA lr_node           TYPE REF TO if_wd_context_node.
  DATA lr_textview       TYPE REF TO cl_wd_text_view.
  DATA lr_ltu            TYPE REF TO cl_wd_link_to_url.
  DATA lv_text           TYPE        string.
  IF first_time EQ abap_true.
*--- Get table column to be modified
    lr_table_column ?= view->get_element( 'TBL_COUNTRY_LANDX' ).
*--- Get table data which will be displayed
    lr_node = wd_context->get_child_node( 'COUNTRIES' ).
    lr_node->get_static_attributes_table(
                          IMPORTING table = lt_countries ).
    LOOP AT lt_countries INTO ls_countries.
*--- Determine cell which will be assigned the LinkToUrl UI element
*--- as cell editor
      IF ls_countries-land1 EQ 'DE'.
        lv_text = ls_countries-landx.
        lr_ltu = cl_wd_link_to_url=>new_link_to_url(
            view      = view
            reference = 'http://www.google.com/search?hl=en&q=germany'
            text      = lv_text ).
        lr_standard_cell =
                cl_wd_table_standard_cell=>new_table_standard_cell(
                            view        = view
                            variant_key = ls_countries-variant ).
        lr_standard_cell->set_editor( lr_ltu ).
        lr_table_column->add_cell_variant( lr_standard_cell ).
      ELSE.
*--- All other cells have a TextView UI element as cell editor
        lv_text = ls_countries-landx.
```

```
            lr_textview = cl_wd_text_view=>new_text_view(
                                                view = view
                                                text = lv_text ).
            lr_standard_cell =
                cl_wd_table_standard_cell=>new_table_standard_cell(
                            view        = view
                            variant_key = ls_countries-variant ).
            lr_standard_cell->set_editor( lr_textview ).
            lr_table_column->add_cell_variant( lr_standard_cell ).
          ENDIF.
        ENDLOOP.
      ENDIF.
ENDMETHOD.
```

Listing 3.24 Implementation for Changing the Cell Editor

3.7 Calling Popup Windows

For various reasons, it may be necessary to open popup windows in an application. These reasons include processes that require either the sending of short messages on the current processing status to the user, or a user interaction in order to continue the further processing of the program. More complex scenarios often require popup windows for controlling user entries and selection options.

The WD4A framework provides two basic options for calling popup windows. On the one hand, you can output data through a single view in a popup window and provide various buttons that enable the user to continue the processes by clicking on those buttons. This is enabled by using the methods `popup()` and `popop_to_confirm()` of the `CL_WD_POPUP_FACTORY` class. The second option, which contains a greater range of functionalities, involves the Window Manager (interface `IF_WD_WINDOW_MANAGER`) in order to implement an overlapping of several popup windows and facilitates the navigation among different popups.

Currently, popups can be displayed only as modal dialogs,[2] which means that the background window is locked for entries as long as the popup window is displayed. Amodal operation—the ability to make entries in the background window—is planned to be made available in a later version of Web Dynpro. The following three sections describe the use of the `popup()` and

---

[2] SAP NetWeaver Application Server ABAP (Release SAP NetWeaver 2004s SP4)

popop_to_confirm( ) methods of class CL_WD_POPUP_FACTORY, as well as the Window Manager in greater detail.

3.7.1 Message Popups

If you want to inform the user on the status of the program flow and output other messages as well that don't require any interaction with the user, the easiest way to do this is to use the popup( ) method of class CL_WD_POPUP_FACTORY. Let's look at component ZEXP_POPUP2NOTIFY to explain this a little further.

As you can see in Figure 3.77, the popup window to be displayed is supposed to present a simple message text next to an icon when a user clicks on the **Open Popup** button.

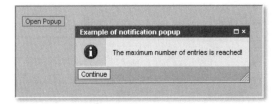

Figure 3.77 Output of a Message Text with Icon

The initial screen of our sample component merely contains this button, while the call of the popup is implemented in the event handler method of the associated Button view element. The information to be displayed in the popup window must be defined in a separate view. In our example, that's V_POPUP (see Figure 3.78).

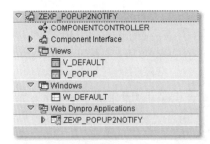

Figure 3.78 Structure of Component ZEXP_POPUP2NOTIFY

First, a reference to the component is determined in the event handler method onactionopen_popup( ). This reference is needed by the CL_WD_

POPUP_FACTORY class. You can use the `button_kind` parameter of the `popup()` method, which has the **WDR_POPUP_BUTTON_KIND** type, to define which buttons you want to display in the popup window. In our example, there is only one button that is used to confirm the message. This button is defined by the `CO_BUTTONS_OK` constant. Table 3.3 lists the possible key combinations that are defined in interface `IF_WD_WINDOW`. You can derive the button types from the names of the constants.

Names of Constants	
CO_BUTTONS_NONE	CO_BUTTONS_ABORTRETRYIGNORE
CO_BUTTONS_OK	CO_BUTTONS_CLOSE
CO_BUTTONS_OKCANCEL	CO_BUTTONS_YESNO
CO_BUTTONS_YESNOCANCEL	CO_BUTTON_ABORT
CO_BUTTON_RETRY	CO_BUTTON_IGNORE
CO_BUTTON_OK	CO_BUTTON_CLOSE
CO_BUTTON_CANCEL	CO_BUTTON_YES
CO_BUTTON_NO	

Table 3.3 Constants for Controlling the Selection Options

Another option for configuring the popup window is provided by parameter `message_type` that has the type **WDR_POPUP_MSG_TYPE**. You can use this parameter to define the type of icon that is to be displayed next to the message text. The icon types are also stored in interface `IF_WD_WINDOW` (see Table 3.4).

Names of Constants	
CO_MSG_TYPE_NONE	CO_MSG_TYPE_WARNING
CO_MSG_TYPE_INFORMATION	CO_MSG_TYPE_QUESTION
CO_MSG_TYPE_ERROR	CO_MSG_TYPE_STOPP

Table 3.4 Constants for Controlling the Display of the Message Type

Listing 3.25 shows the implementation of the event handler method.

```
METHOD onactionopen_popup.
  DATA lt_texts          TYPE       string_table.
  DATA lr_component_api TYPE REF TO if_wd_component.
  DATA lr_popup          TYPE REF TO if_wd_popup_to_confirm.
*--- Get reference to component controller
```

```
  lr_component_api = wd_comp_controller->wd_get_api( ).
*--- Open popup window
  CALL METHOD cl_wd_popup_factory=>popup
    EXPORTING
      component     = lr_component_api
      view_name     = 'V_POPUP'
      button_kind   = if_wd_window=>co_buttons_ok
      message_type  = if_wd_window=>co_msg_type_information.
ENDMETHOD.
```

Listing 3.25 Example of Using Method popup()

3.7.2 Query Popups

Popups that query the user should be implemented into the program flow when a file is to be deleted, for example. For this purpose, you can use the popup_to_confirm() method of class CL_WD_POPUP_FACTORY.

Unlike the popup() method described in the previous section, the number and type of buttons are defined here. The user can only confirm (**Yes**), reject (**No**), or cancel (**Cancel**) a query. We want to implement an example of this in component ZEXP_POPUP2CONFIRM (see Figure 3.79).

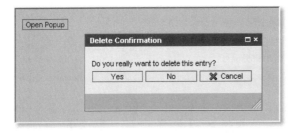

Figure 3.79 Delete Confirmation

The component consists only of a V_DEFAULT view and a W_DEFAULT window into which the V_DEFAULT view is embedded. No second view exists for designing the popup layout, which means that you can only output text in the popup. The V_DEFAULT view contains a Button view element that is used to trigger the popup display.

When the user clicks on the **Open Popup** button, the associated event handler method onactionopen_popup() is called. The query texts to be output are stored in a table of the **STRING_TABLE** type. Each row can contain a maximum of 255 characters. To be able to determine the corresponding user action, an event handler method must be registered that is called when a button is clicked. In our example, we'll call this method `ON_POPUP_TO_CONFIRM` (see Figure 3.80). The registration is carried out using the `subscribe_to_events()` method (see Listing 3.26).

Method	Method Type	Description
ONACTIONOPEN_POPUP	Event Handler	
ON_POPUP_TO_CONFIRM	Event Handler	Handle popup button events
WDDOBEFOREACTION	Method	Method for Validation of User Input

Figure 3.80 Creating the Event Handler Method on_popup_to_confirm()

```
METHOD onactionopen_popup.
  DATA lt_texts          TYPE string_table.
  DATA lr_component_api  TYPE REF TO if_wd_component.
  DATA lr_popup          TYPE REF TO if_wd_popup_to_confirm.
  DATA lr_view_controller TYPE REF TO if_wd_view_controller.
*--- Get reference to component controller
  lr_component_api = wd_comp_controller->wd_get_api( ).
*--- Create message text
  APPEND 'Do you really want to delete this entry?' TO lt_texts.
*--- Open popup window
  CALL METHOD cl_wd_popup_factory=>popup_to_confirm
    EXPORTING
      component      = lr_component_api
      text           = lt_texts
      window_title   = 'Delete Confirmation'
    RECEIVING
      popup_to_confirm = wd_this->mr_popup.
*--- Subscribe to popup events
  lr_view_controller = wd_this->wd_get_api( ).
  wd_this->mr_popup->subscribe_to_events(
         controller   = lr_view_controller
         handler_name = 'ON_POPUP_TO_CONFIRM' ).
ENDMETHOD.
```

Listing 3.26 Example of Using Method popup_to_confirm()

The `on_popup_to_confirm()` event handler method then tells you which button was clicked by the user. This enables you to react in the same way to the action.

Listing 3.27 shows the implementation of the event handler method without any additional actions.

```
METHOD on_popup_to_confirm.
  CASE wd_this->mr_popup->answer.
```

```
       WHEN if_wd_popup_to_confirm=>co_button_1_pressed.
*--- Act on "Yes" button pressed
       WHEN if_wd_popup_to_confirm=>co_button_2_pressed.
*--- Act on "No" button pressed
       WHEN if_wd_popup_to_confirm=>co_cancel.
*--- Act on "Cancel" button pressed
   ENDCASE.
ENDMETHOD.
```

Listing 3.27 Implementation of on_popup_to_confirm()

3.7.3 Popups with Navigation

In more complex scenarios that require navigation within a popup or within several popups, you must use the Window Manager. To describe this in more detail, we now want to implement a scenario in which the user can navigate between two different views within the same popup window. The content to be displayed in the views is not very important in this example. We will merely output different texts in order to distinguish the views from each other.

Figure 3.81 shows the popup window with the view V_ONE. A click on the **Navigate to view TWO!** button enables the navigation to the V_TWO view (see Figure 3.82), which is displayed in the same popup window. The user can then return to V_ONE or click on the **Close** button to close the popup.

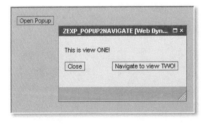

Figure 3.81 Display of View V_ONE in the Popup Window

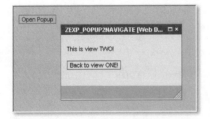

Figure 3.82 Display of View V_TWO in the Popup Window

We implement the example in component ZEXP_POPUP2NAVIGATE. For the implementation of the scenario, we need three views and two windows: V_DEFAULT is the initial view. This view contains only one Button view element with the label **Open Popup**. This view element is used to call the popup. The view is embedded into the W_DEFAULT window. W_DEFAULT is also used as an interface view for the application. The action that is assigned to the **onAction** property of the Button view element will be called OPEN_POPUP. Moreover, we'll create two views that will be used in the popup.

The views will be called V_ONE and V_TWO. Both views are then assigned an inbound and an outbound plug, which will each be called IP_V_ONE and OP_V_ONE as well as IP_V_TWO and OP_V_TWO.

The layout of V_ONE consists of a TextView view element and two Button view elements. The Button view elements are used to close the popup (BTN_CLOSE with the text, **Close**) and to navigate to view V_TWO (BTN_NAVIGATE with the text, **Navigate to view TWO!**). The layout of view V_TWO also consists of a TextView view element, and only one Button view element (BTN_NAVIGATE with the text, **Back to view ONE!**) that is needed to return to V_ONE. The window that will be displayed in the popup is assigned the name W_POPUP. Figure 3.83 displays the structure of component ZEXP_POPUP2NAVIGATE as well as the link between the views in the W_POPUP window.

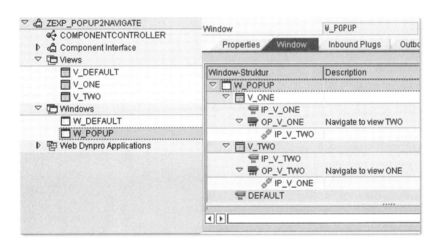

Figure 3.83 Component ZEXP_POPUP2NAVIGATE with Window Structure

The reference to the window object to be created is stored in the component controller in attribute MR_WINDOW that has the type **IF_WD_WINDOW**. This is necessary because apart from V_DEFAULT, the V_ONE view must also access the window object every time the **Close** button is clicked. Remember to mark the attribute as **Public**; otherwise, no other controllers will be able to see it (see Figure 3.84).

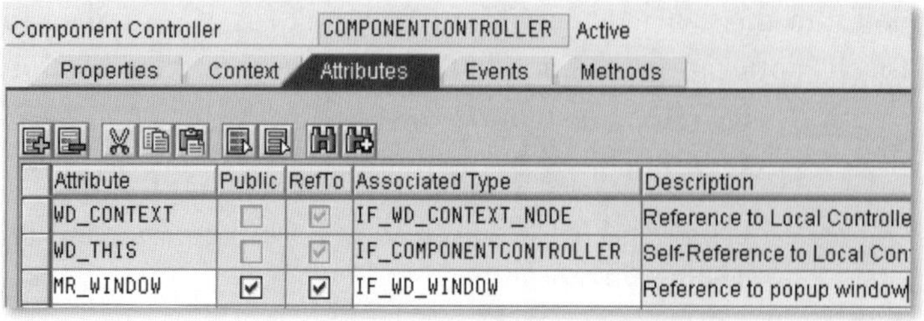

Attribute	Public	RefTo	Associated Type	Description
WD_CONTEXT		✓	IF_WD_CONTEXT_NODE	Reference to Local Controlle
WD_THIS		✓	IF_COMPONENTCONTROLLER	Self-Reference to Local Con
MR_WINDOW	✓	✓	IF_WD_WINDOW	Reference to popup window

Figure 3.84 Reference to the Window Object in the Component Controller

If the **Open Popup** button is clicked at runtime, the event handler method `onactionopen_popup()` creates a new window object for the W_POPUP window through the Window Manager of the component. The reference to the window object is stored in the `mr_window` attribute in the component controller. The display of the method, and hence the call of the popup, is initiated by the `open()` method. Listing 3.28 shows the implementation of the event handler method.

```
METHOD onactionopen_popup.
  DATA lr_window_manager  TYPE REF TO if_wd_window_manager.
  DATA lt_texts           TYPE         string_table.
  DATA lr_component_api   TYPE REF TO if_wd_component.
  DATA lr_popup           TYPE REF TO if_wd_popup_to_confirm.
  DATA lr_view_controller TYPE REF TO if_wd_view_controller.
  DATA lr_compcontroller  TYPE REF TO ig_componentcontroller.
*--- Get reference to component controller
  lr_compcontroller = wd_this->get_componentcontroller_ctr( ).
*--- Get component API
  lr_component_api = wd_comp_controller->wd_get_api( ).
*--- Get reference to window manager
  lr_window_manager  = lr_component_api->get_window_manager( ).
*--- Create window instance
  lr_compcontroller->mr_window = lr_window_manager->create_window(
                                  window_name  = 'W_POPUP' ).
*--- Display window
  lr_compcontroller->mr_window->open( ).
ENDMETHOD.
```

Listing 3.28 Implementation for the Creation of a New Window Object

The popup window that displays now allows the navigation between both views. The window object—whose reference has been stored in attribute mr_window in the component controller—is not accessed again until the **Close** button in view V_ONE is clicked. In the event handler method, the popup is closed by calling the close() method of the window object. Listing 3.29 shows the implementation of this event handler method.

```
METHOD onactionclose_popup.
  DATA lr_compcontroller  TYPE REF TO ig_componentcontroller.
*--- Get reference to component controller
  lr_compcontroller = wd_this->get_componentcontroller_ctr( ).
*--- Close window
  lr_compcontroller->mr_window->close( ).
ENDMETHOD.
```

Listing 3.29 Implementing Statements for Closing the Popup Window

3.8 Using Input Helps

Input helps or *F4 helps* support the user in entering data and they facilitate the interaction with an application. Whenever possible, you should use input helps when designing input scenarios. The WD4A allows you to define different types of input helps:

- Automatic assignment by the WD4A framework (**Automatically**)
- Assignment of a search help created in the ABAP Dictionary (**Dictionary Search Help**)
- Assignment of an OVS search help (**Object Value Selector**)
- Assignment of a user-defined search help (**User-Defined Programming**)

Input helps are defined via the **Input Help Mode** property of the context attribute to which the input field is bound (see Figure 3.85).

If you select the automatic assignment of a search help (**Automatically**) when assigning the **Input Help Mode** property of the context attribute, the WD4A framework first determines whether an ABAP Dictionary search help is available for the field. If not, the framework determines whether a check table—a table that contains permitted values for a field—is assigned to the field, which will then be displayed. Finally, the values from the domain of the field can be provided as an input help, if they are available.

3 | Developing WD4A Applications

Property	Value	
Attribute		
Attribute Name	DVALUE	
Type assignment	Type	🗂
Type	DIMID	
Read-only	☐	
Primary Attribute	☐	
Default Value		
Input Help Mode	Dictionary Search Help	🗂
Dictionary Search Help	Deactivated Automatically Dictionary Search Help Object Value Selector User-Defined Programming	

Figure 3.85 Defining the Type of Input Help to Be Used

If you select the **Dictionary Search Help** value when assigning the **Input Help Mode** property, the name of the ABAP Dictionary search help to be used must be assigned to the **Dictionary Search Help** property. You can create an ABAP Dictionary search help in the ABAP Dictionary (Transaction SE11).

The use of OVS and user-defined search helps requires the knowledge of how to define component usages. Chapter 6 will address these subjects in greater detail.

At runtime, the availability of an input help is indicated by an icon next to the input field (see Figure 3.86). The values that can be selected in the search help are displayed in separate tables in the popup window, and the value that is selected from the table is then transferred into the input field.

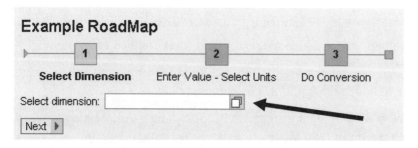

Figure 3.86 Input Field and Search Help

3.9 Internationalization

The concept of internationalization describes the possibility to control the output language of texts. This enables you to use an application in different countries with different languages without having to make changes to the implementation of the application. The WD4A framework provides support for multiple languages in several different ways.

Usually the client output of texts occurs in the language in which the user has logged on to the system. If the language hasn't been specified at logon, the system checks if the language has been defined via the URI parameter `sap-language`. If that is not the case, the system uses the language that's set in the client. Texts that are involved in the translation process include static texts and texts that have been assigned within definitions in the ABAP Dictionary:

- **Static texts**
  Static texts that are assigned to view element properties are available for translation, depending on the type of view element. The property values that are transferred to the translation process include, for example, texts from the `Label` view element, the `Caption` view element, the `Button` view element, and the `TextView` view element, as well as the content of the **tooltip** property of all view elements for which this property exists.

- **Texts from the ABAP Dictionary**
  If the properties of a view element are bound to context attributes that are based on an ABAP Dictionary type, the texts of the corresponding data elements are automatically used. This applies predominantly to the display of tables in which the description value for the data element is taken from the ABAP Dictionary to create the column header. The ABAP Dictionary value is not used if a specification exists for the **text** property of the `Caption` view element of each column.

Static texts cannot be used multiple times, as they are only valid for the property to which they have been assigned. You can reduce the translation effort by defining texts in the Online Text Repository (OTR) instead of static texts. You can then use an alias to reference the texts as often as you like, or you can use the functions of the assistance class. The following two sections describe how you can do that.

3.9.1 Online Text Repository

The *Online Text Repository* (OTR) enables you to use texts of up to 255 characters multiple times and to manage those texts. In the OTR, you can use an alias to define a text and assign the text to any number of view element properties. OTR texts are automatically included in the translation process. You can use Transaction SE63 to translate them into other languages. The system already provides various texts and messages that occur frequently in several languages in the package SOTR_VOCABULARY_BASIC.

You can navigate to the selection of OTR texts by clicking on the icon to the right of the input field for the text (see Figure 3.87). Alternatively, you can also select the menu item **Goto · Online Text Repository Browser** from the ABAP Workbench.

Property	Value		Binding
Properties (Button)			
ID	BTN_BACK		
Layout Data	MatrixHeadData	📄	
design	standard	📄	
enabled	✓		
explanation			
imageFirst	✓		
imageSource			
text	$OTR:SOTR_VOCABULARY_BASIC/BACK	🔗	
textDirection	inherit	📄	

Figure 3.87 Calling the OTR Text Selection

To create new texts, you must enter the alias name into the corresponding text field. Make sure you use the correct syntax when specifying the package. The syntax will most probably look as follows:

$OTR:[package_name]/[alias_name]

Thus, the OTR text assigned to the **text** property of the Button view element BTN_BACK is stored in package SOTR_VOCABULARY. You can create a new OTR text with the alias TEST_SEARCH in package TEST_WDY_BOOK_02 by entering the following string for the **text** property of a Button view element:

$OTR:TEST_WDY_BOOK_02/TEST_SEARCH

The text can be edited in the **Create Text** popup that displays next (see Figure 3.88). Note that the length indication is correct for the translation. Because you cannot always tell into how many languages the application will be translated at the time of development, you should specify a higher value than that of the length of the original text here.

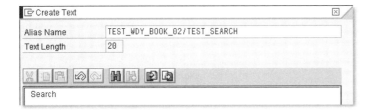

Figure 3.88 Editing an OTR Text

To access OTR Texts at runtime, the CL_WD_UTILITIES class provides the get_otr_text_by_alias() method. For example, the text created in Figure 3.88 could be read by using the following statement:

```
DATA lv_otr type string.
lv_otr = cl_wd_utilities=>get_otr_text_by_alias(
                          'TEST_WDY_BOOK_02/TEST_SEARCH' ).
```

3.9.2 Assistance Class

You can define an assistance class for each WD4A component. If this class inherits data from the abstract class CL_WD_COMPONENT_ASSISTANCE, then you can use various functions for the integration of text symbols. The assistance class is instantiated by the WD4A framework when the component is created. The wd_assist attribute provides a reference to the class. This attribute is then available in each controller of the component (see Figure 3.89).

The texts are generated in the class via the **Goto · Text Elements** menu. Each new text requires a constant with the corresponding text ID that has the type **WDR_TEXT_KEY**.

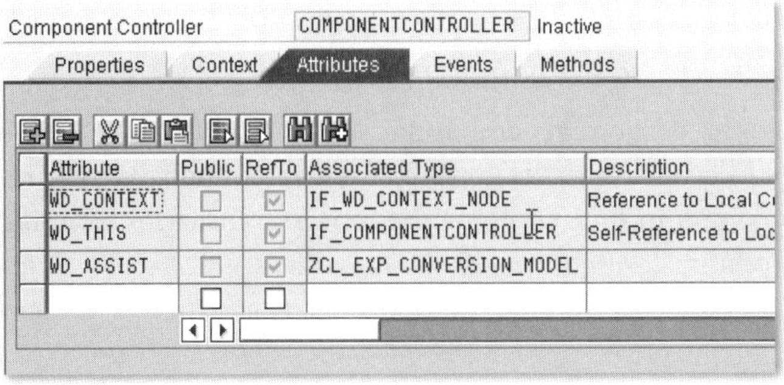

Figure 3.89 Reference to the Assistance Class in the Component Controller

The access to a text in the component, which has been created in the assistance class using the `CO_BUTTON_SAVE` constant, for example, occurs in the methods of a controller by calling the `if_wd_component_assistance~get_text()` method and transferring the corresponding constant:

```
DATA lv_text type string.
lv_text = wd_assist->if_wd_component_assistance~get_text(
                                   wd_assist->co_button_save ).
```

You can maintain the text symbols (see Figure 3.90) from the component by selecting **Goto · Text Symbols** from the menu.

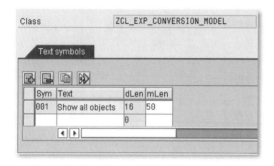

Figure 3.90 Creating Text Symbols

3.10 Customization, Configuration, Personalization

If an application is used by a larger number of users, user-specific requirements to the application often arise. The reason for these requirements can be due, for example, to the industry in which the application is used, or they can be caused by regional or country-specific situations. To meet specific configuration and customization requirements without having to change the implementation of components, you can create configuration data records for WD4A components and applications.

You can configure both components and applications. In this context, you must first define the relevant configurations for the components. When creating the application, you can then combine the required scenarios from the set of available component configurations.

3.10.1 Implicit and Explicit Configurations

A component can be configured in two ways:

- The *implicit configuration* enables the overriding of view element properties. For example, in a configuration data record, you can define whether a view element should be displayed. The implicit configuration does not require any additional implementation work, since the settings are made solely by the configurator.

- Apart from manipulating view element properties, you can also include additional context node attributes in the configuration. These attributes can then enable you to manipulate individual processes and the layout at runtime. This is referred to as an *explicit configuration*. The context to be configured is implemented in a specific custom controller, which is referred to as the configuration controller. Contrary to the implicit confuration that doesn't require any further implementation, the explicit configuration requires additional development work. This work involves the creation of context nodes and attributes, as well as data administration methods.

3.10.2 Configuring Components and Applications

We'll now use an example to describe the operation of the component configurator, the creation of a configuration controller, and the definition of different applications based on different component configurations. In this example, users of the sample application are supposed to maintain the personal data of software developers and store their preferred technology for the creation of web-based applications.

We want to configure the application for two groups of developers:

1. Software developers with predominantly ABAP experience
2. Software developers with predominantly Java experience

Moreover, we want the application to accept country-specific configurations: It should be used in countries where people have a middle name and in countries where people usually have only a first name, even though the latter is just hypothetical. Furthermore, we assume that the majority of developers prefer Web Dynpro. For this reason, we will check the checkbox that refers to the Web Dynpro technology by default for each entry that is to be newly created.

3 | Developing WD4A Applications

First, all the necessary input fields are created in the implementation of the component. In our example, the component is called ZEXP_CONFIGURATION. The layout consists of three InputField view elements and four CheckBox view elements (see Figure 3.91). The **value** properties of the InputField view elements are bound to STRING type context attributes; the **checked** property of the CheckBox view elements are bound to **WDY_BOOLEAN** type attributes.

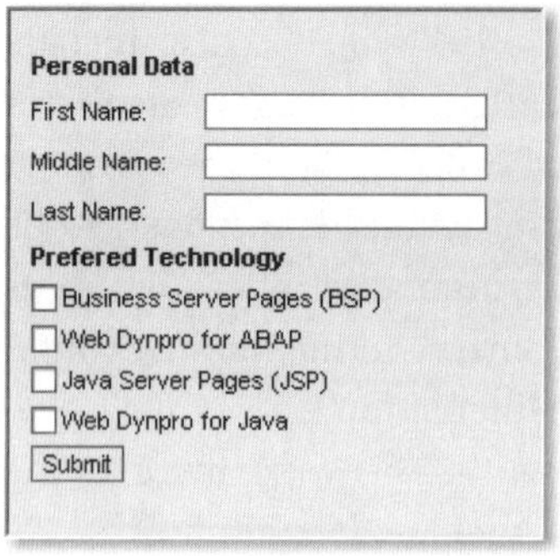

Figure 3.91 Component Output without Configuration

Table 3.5 lists the configurations that result from the application requirements. You can use implicit configuration to set the visibility of the input field for the middle name as well as the checkboxes. Explicit configuration is necessary to set a default value for the technology preference. Thus, there are four different possible configurations: ABAP_DE, ABAP_US, JAVA_DE, and JAVA_US. The following sections describe the configurator settings for these configurations.

Configuration ID	Platform (implicit)	Middle Name (implicit)	Technology Preference (explicit)
ABAP_DE	ABAP	no	Web Dynpro for ABAP
ABAP_US	ABAP	yes	Web Dynpro for ABAP
JAVA_DE	Java	no	Web Dynpro for Java
JAVA_US	Java	yes	Web Dynpro for Java

Table 3.5 Possible Configurations for the Sample Component

To create a configuration, open the context menu of the relevant component and select **Create/Change Configuration** (see Figure 3.92). A new window opens in which the configurator is active. The configurator itself is also implemented as a Web Dynpro application.

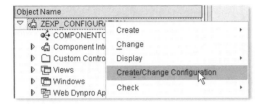

Figure 3.92 Creating a Component Configuration

We'll now create the four configurations one after the other and begin with configuration ABAP_DE. Enter the name of the configuration in the **Konfiguration** ("configuration") field and click on the **Create** link under **Functions**. Select the **implizite Konfiguration** ("implicit configuration") tab in the right-hand pane. Similar to the display in the view layout, the system now displays the view element hierarchy in a tree structure. The view element properties that are available for implicit configuration are displayed on the right when a corresponding view element is selected. Figure 3.93 shows the configuration options for the InputField view element INP_MIDDLENAME.

Apart from the visibility, you can also make other configurations. For example, you can define the tooltip, the length of the input field, and the orientation of the input field within the layout. You can save, delete, and copy the current configuration into another configuration in the **Functions** area on the left. You can also define variants for an existing configuration.

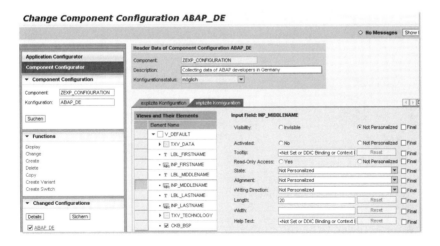

Figure 3.93 Configurator with Implicit Configuration

According to the default values we defined in Table 3.5, we want to hide the label and the input field for the middle name as well as the Java-relevant checkboxes in the configuration for ABAP_DE. Therefore, we'll select the **Invisible** radio button for the Label view element LBL_MIDDLENAME, for the InputField view element INP_MIDDLENAME, and for the CheckBox view elements CHK_JSP and CHK_WD4J. After that, you should create the remaining implicit configurations defined in Table 3.5 that are responsible for the visibility of input fields and checkboxes in the same manner. You can enter a descriptive text for each new configuration in the **Description** field. Once you have created all configurations, they should display upon clicking the **Suchen** ("search") button (see Figure 3.94).

Figure 3.94 Search Result for the Newly Created Configurations

Then, close the configurator window and return to the ABAP Workbench to continue editing the component. After refreshing the display, the new configurations are displayed in the object tree of the component (see Figure 3.95).

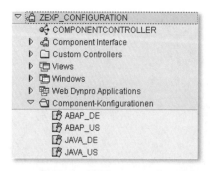

Figure 3.95 Component with Configurations

Now we want to carry out the explicit configuration, which, in our example, consists of setting two checkboxes by default. Because we want to preselect the checkboxes using the configurator, we have to create a controller that is visible to the configurator. That can be done by creating a custom controller and defining it as a configuration controller. Each component can have several custom controllers, but there can only be one configuration controller.

We'll call the custom controller CONFIGCONTROLLER. You can define the custom controller as a configuration controller by selecting **(Re)Set as Config. Controller** from the context menu of the controller name (see Figure 3.96).

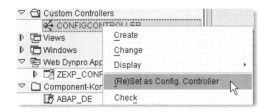

Figure 3.96 Defining the Custom Controller as a Configuration Controller

The context of the configuration controller consists of a context node called DEFAULTVALUES and two **WDY_BOOLEAN** type attributes called TWD4A and TWD4J. Because we want to use the two attributes in the view controller for setting the default values of the two checkboxes to **Web Dynpro for ABAP** and **Web Dynpro for Java**, they must first be mapped into the component controller and then into the view controller.

Next, we'll use the wddoinit() method of the view controller to assign the content of the two attributes from the configuration controller to the two attributes that are bound to the **checked** properties of the corresponding CheckBox view elements. Listing 3.30 contains the statements required to transfer the values.

```
METHOD wddoinit.
  DATA  lr_conf_node   TYPE REF TO if_wd_context_node.
  DATA  ls_default     TYPE if_v_default=>element_defaultvalues.
  DATA  lr_data_node   TYPE REF TO if_wd_context_node.
  DATA  ls_content     TYPE if_v_default=>element_content.
*--- Read default values from config controller context
  lr_conf_node = wd_context->get_child_node( 'DEFAULTVALUES' ).
  lr_conf_node->get_static_attributes( IMPORTING
                                 static_attributes = ls_default ).
*--- Assign values to context
  ls_content-webd4a = ls_default-twd4a.
  ls_content-webd4j = ls_default-twd4j.
  lr_data_node = wd_context->get_child_node( 'CONTENT' ).
```

```
lr_data_node->bind_structure( new_item = ls_content ).
ENDMETHOD.
```

Listing 3.30 Transferring the Values from the Configuration Controller

The default values are set by calling the configurator and selecting the relevant configuration. To do that, go to the right-hand side of the configurator and select the **explizite Konfiguration** ("explicit configuration") tab. Here you can set the values of the attributes of the configuration controller context DEFAULTVALUES according to our specifications. Figure 3.97 displays the configuration for ABAP_DE in which we want to set the **Web Dynpro for ABAP** checkbox (context attribute twd4a) by default.

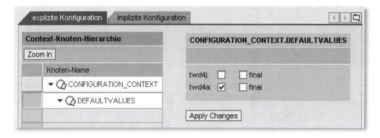

Figure 3.97 Defining the Explicit Configuration

After that you should complete the explicit configurations for the other examples listed in Table 3.5.

The last step consists of the creation of the WD4A applications for each of the configurations. The configurator for the application can also be started via the context menu, which you can display by right-clicking on the name of the WD4A application. Figure 3.98 displays the WD4A application ZEXP_CONFIGURATION with configuration APP_ABAP_DE that uses component ZEXP_CONFIGURATION with configuration ABAP_DE. You can call the application including its component configuration by clicking on the **Test** button in the top left-hand corner.

Figure 3.99 shows the component fields displayed according to configuration ABAP_DE from Table 3.5. The input field for the middle name and the checkboxes for the Java-relevant technologies are hidden, while the **Web Dynpro for ABAP** checkbox is set by default.

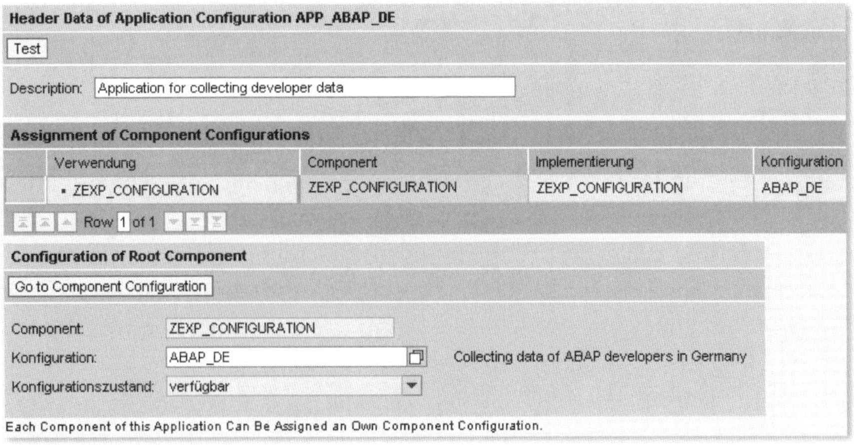

Figure 3.98 Configuration of the Application

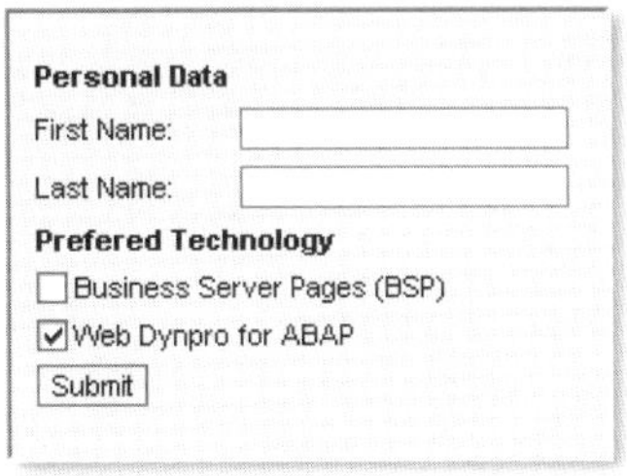

Figure 3.99 Output with Component Configuration ABAP_DE

In addition to the configuration of components and applications that is carried out during the development, the WD4A framework provides a function for user-specific personalization. In the context of personalization, the user of an application can customize the display in the client according to his or her personal habits and individual requirements and show or hide additional fields. In this respect, it is also possible to undo settings that have been made in the context of implicit configuration.

User-specific modifications of the layout can be done at runtime by pressing the **Ctrl** key and right-clicking on the relevant field in order to open the context menu. In Figure 3.100, the personalization was called for the input field for the first name. As you can see, you can now change the visibility of the first name input field and you can undo the settings that have been made by implicit configuration.

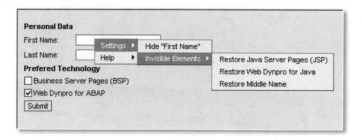

Figure 3.100 Personalizing the Client Output

Using existing components accelerates the development process of WD4A applications. Structuring and combining interrelated tasks in components increases clarity and ease of maintenance; and using design patterns in the structuring process makes the applications easier to understand and to extend. This chapter addresses all these aspects.

4 Multi-Component Applications

4.1 A Model of Layer Separation

The underlying concept of the Model View Controller (MVC) design pattern is based on separating the application business logic from its user interface layer. The objective here is to create a modular system in which the controller acts as the connection between the model and the view, and controls them both. The benefit of this kind of architecture is that it enables you to develop different views to represent the same information and to reuse components that provide and process this information. In a system that is developed in accordance with the MVC design pattern, the individual components are independent of one another, and can be exchanged and extended.

The goal of using the MVC design pattern is to reduce development time, to enable software reuse, and to minimize the time and effort required for maintenance.

Figure 4.1 shows a conceptual representation of the MVC design pattern. As you can see, the user initiates a request, which the client then sends to the controller. The controller evaluates the request, and sends the data and instructions from the request to the appropriate model. The model processes the data and returns the results to the controller. The controller then sends the data to the appropriate view, which formats it for display in the user interface.

The controller analyzes requests and formats data only to the point whereby the relevant decisions (i.e., regarding sending on the data to the model) can be made, thus enabling the model to process the data independently of the display-related information. No data formatting logic—logic that refers to

XML or HTML tags, for example—should be implemented in the model itself. Conversely, the controller accepts the results that the model has calculated and sends them on to the view.

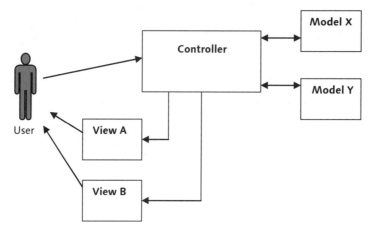

Figure 4.1 MVC Design Pattern and Interaction of the Components

The view, for its part, is responsible only for implementing display-specific logic. It does not handle any logic that interprets application-related conditions and therefore affects how the data is displayed, for example. You can only take advantage of the benefits of the MVC design pattern if you divide up the overall logic into subtasks and assign these tasks to the components that are responsible for each task when developing an application.

In this way, the MVC design pattern acts as a guide for implementing the presentation, control, and application logic in the components intended for these purposes. To clarify this structure and to discuss the effects of overlaps between the individual areas, we will now turn our attention to the *three-tier model*, which is familiar to us from client-server architecture (see Figure 4.2).

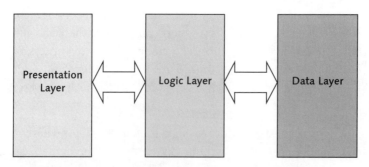

Figure 4.2 The Three-Tier Model

The three-tier model has the following characteristics:

- The subtasks of an application are structured and assigned to the appropriate tier or layer (in this chapter, we use the term "layer").
- Every layer can communicate only with the layers that are its direct neighbors.
- Communication takes place via interfaces.
- The interfaces encapsulate the tasks that are implemented in each individual layer.

Depending on how the MVC model overlaps with the three-tier model, the separation of the presentation, control, and application logic areas will be *strict* or *light*. We will discuss these kinds of separation in the next two sections.

4.1.1 Strict Separation

Figure 4.3 contains a schematic representation of how the layers of the three-tier model are almost completely overlapped by the components of the MVC model. The view components are assigned to the presentation layer only, while part of the controller component is also assigned to the presentation layer. This is because the controller analyzes incoming data packages and formats them for further processing by the model in accordance with the technology underlying the presentation layer. The model and the controller are completely decoupled from each other.

The view, controller, and model areas are strictly separated, with the exception of the overlap between the controller and the presentation layer. The controller has sole control over the communication between the view and the model. It implements logic that is necessary for the purposes of communication and data formatting only. Clearly defined interfaces between the components provide only the data that is necessary for interaction between the areas, and all other functionalities and implementations are unavailable outside the component in question. Similarly, implementations inside a component that are not specified in the interface for that component are invisible to other components and cannot be accessed by them.

4 | Multi-Component Applications

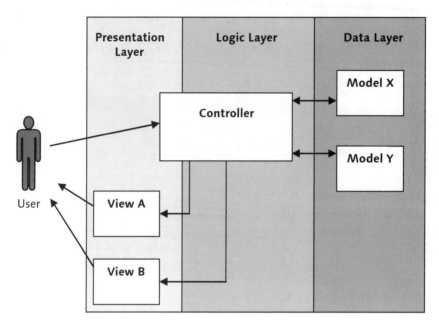

Figure 4.3 Schematic Representation of Strict Separation

4.1.2 Light Separation

Figure 4.4 contains a schematic representation of light separation. As with strict separation, there is also a slight overlap between the controller and the presentation layer here. The controller is always linked to the technology of the presentation layer to a certain degree, as it is responsible for analyzing and formatting incoming requests. However, there is also overlap here with the data layer of the three-tier model. This is necessary if, for example, the controller contained references to data type definitions that were made in the data layer, or if the controller were to format data in accordance with the structures defined in the data layer.

We can also see that the views overlap with parts of the data layer. An example of where this is necessary is the request-response cycle for calling and displaying popups for the input help texts associated with input fields. In this case, the view directly accesses the definitions in the data layer without the need for the controller to perform its control functions. Note that to implement the examples that lead to the overlaps illustrated here in order to create separation between the layers is in many cases either very difficult or requires a lot of development work.

A Model of Layer Separation | 4.1

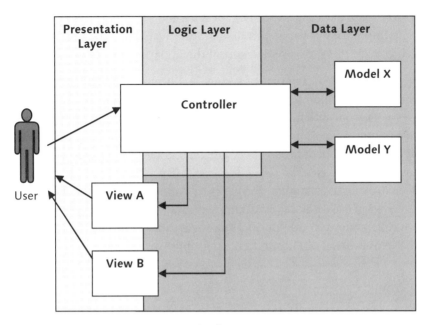

Figure 4.4 Schematic Representation of Light Separation

In certain cases, using strict separation can also cause user-friendliness to deteriorate, that is, having an architecture based on the strict separation of MVC layers does not give the developer the freedom to implement user-friendly interactions and requires a greater degree of implementation effort.

4.1.3 Strict versus Light Separation

The concept of light separation between the layers affects the exchangeability of the individual components that correspond to the MVC design pattern and thus has a negative effect on reusability. Light separation can also reduce the clarity of the implementation and thereby incur higher maintenance costs. A benefit of light separation, on the other hand, is the (in some cases) direct access to the data layer, which reduces the time and effort required for implementation, avoids redundant program areas, and increases user-friendliness. However, the functionality that is possible with light separation can sometimes also be achieved with strict separation by investing more time and effort in the implementation. The greater degree of reusability and the easier maintenance can then compensate for the higher implementation costs.

Therefore, when deciding which type of separation to use, you need to consider the future uses of the application and the available resources. In many cases, however, this decision depends on the underlying system landscape.

Figure 4.5 shows two examples of system architectures that affect the MVC design pattern. In the *coupled implementation* architecture, the application accesses data from different physical systems that are interconnected by a network. Strict separation is more or less obligatory here, and you would simply have to compensate for its disadvantages by investing more time in the development phase. The *closed implementation* architecture, on the other hand, enables light separation. In this case, you would need to ensure that light separation is used in the actual implementation, in accordance with any relevant instructions in the specification for creating an application, such as any that prescribe reusability and exchangeability of components.

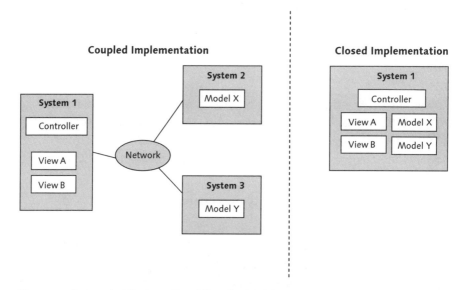

Figure 4.5 System Architectures That Affect the MVC Design Pattern

4.1.4 MVC Concepts in the WD4A Framework

The MVC design pattern is implemented in the WD4A framework with some modifications. For example, it does not have just a single controlling element; it has multiple controllers that are responsible for the individual parts of the WD4A components, including component, custom, view, and window controllers.

For simple WD4A applications, in which all processes can be implemented inside a single component, the separation of the layers of the MVC design pattern is predefined in the WD4A framework. The layout is defined in different views, independently of the model; only view-specific processes are handled in the methods of the view controller. The component controller context and the component controller methods perform the model's tasks and make their data and functions available to the views via mapping and referencing.

Note that this concept should be implemented only for simple applications, such as those that we looked at in Chapter 3. If applications that are based on only one component are used in more complex processes, this can result in confusion and a lack of clarity. Also, the MVC design pattern should be used throughout all components to increase reusability. This means that the WD4A application should be based on a design that takes into account separate WD4A components for the model, the user interface, and the controlling element. The model in this case can be implemented via a separate component that is responsible solely for data retention and processing and does not implement any user interface elements, such as a view or a window. Data is retained in the component's context, while processing takes place in the component controller methods that will be implemented. Uses of this model component are defined in the user interface component or the controller component, or both, and data can therefore be exchanged.

Another option is to implement and define the application logic for the model in an *assistance class* (see Figure 4.6). In Chapter 3, we described how to define and use an assistance class in the context of creating translatable texts; however, it is also possible to implement additional methods containing the business process logic in the assistance class. The functionality of these methods can be accessed via the `wd_assist` attribute, which is contained in every controller of the component.

Web Dynpro Component	ZEXP_CONVERSION_RM_MAIN		Active	
Description	Controller component - roadmap implementation			
Assistance-Klasse				
Created By	UHOFFMAN	Created On	31.10.2005	
Last Changed By	UHOFFMAN	Changed On	12.11.2005	
Package	TEST_WDY_BOOK_02		AccessibilityChecks Active	☑

Figure 4.6 Defining the Assistance Class in the Component

4 | Multi-Component Applications

4.2 Defining WD4A Component Usages

More complex WD4A applications usually consist of multiple components. The WD4A component uses its interface controller to define the components that it makes available externally.

- **Window**
  When it creates a window, the WD4A framework generates a corresponding interface view that can be embedded by other components. The important thing to know here is which inbound plug of the interface view is marked as Interface. Only this inbound plug is visible in the component that defines the usage.

- **Methods**
  Only methods of the component controller can be added to the interface controller and are thus part of the component interface; this is not possible with methods of the view controller, window controller, or custom controller. A method of the component controller is marked as **Interface** in the **Methods** tab (see Figure 4.7).

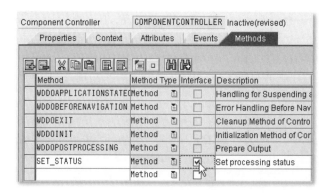

Figure 4.7 Adding a Method to the Interface of a Component

- **Events**
  Events can be defined in the component controller, and event handler methods can register themselves to these methods. If you want to register an event handler method to an event that is defined in another component, this event has to be marked as **Interface** in the **Events** tab (see Figure 4.8).

- **Context node**
  Context node mapping can be done between different components only if the **Interface** property of the required context node of the component to be used is marked accordingly (see Figure 4.9).

Component Controller
COMPONENTCONTROLLER Inactive(revised)
Properties
Context
Attributes
Events
Methods
Event
Interface
Description
CHANGE_STATUS
Change processing status

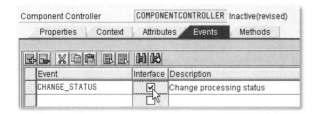

Figure 4.8 Adding an Event to the Interface of a Component

Context COMPONENTCONTROLLER
CONTEXT
CONTENT
Property
Value
Nodes
Node Name
CONTENT
Interface Node
Input Element (Ext.)
Dictionary structure
Cardinality
0..n
Selection
0..1

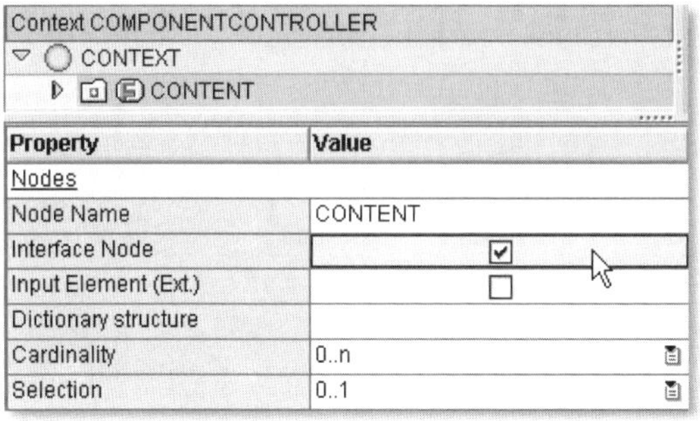

Figure 4.9 Adding a Context Node to the Interface of a Component

To be able to access the context nodes, events, methods, and windows or interface views that are defined as interface controller components of another component, you have to define a usage. You can define this usage in the **Used Components** tab of the component (see Figure 4.10).

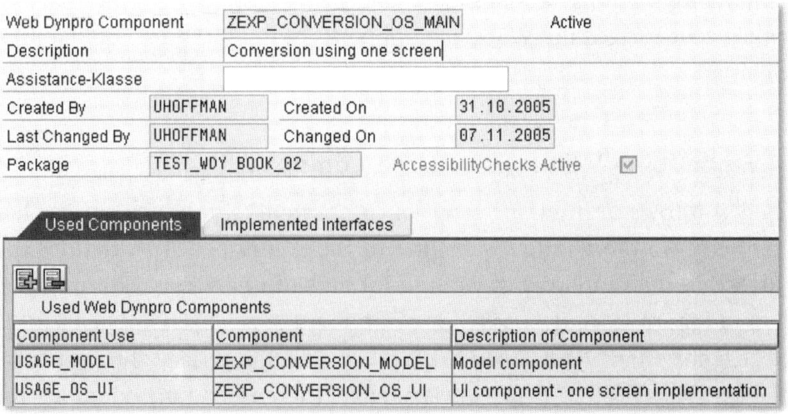

Web Dynpro Component
ZEXP_CONVERSION_OS_MAIN
Active
Description
Conversion using one screen
Assistance-Klasse
Created By
UHOFFMAN
Created On
31.10.2005
Last Changed By
UHOFFMAN
Changed On
07.11.2005
Package
TEST_WDY_BOOK_02
AccessibilityChecks Active
Used Components
Implemented interfaces
Used Web Dynpro Components
Component Use
Component
Description of Component
USAGE_MODEL
ZEXP_CONVERSION_MODEL
Model component
USAGE_OS_UI
ZEXP_CONVERSION_OS_UI
UI component - one screen implementation

Figure 4.10 Defining a Usage in a Component

4 | Multi-Component Applications

This definition allows you to embed windows of the component that you intend to use. Thus, the usage defined in Figure 4.10 would allow you to embed every window of the ZEXP_CONVERSION_OS_UI component in your own window. To access the context nodes, events, and methods of the interface controller of the other component from inside the various controllers, you have to define the usage separately in each controller in the **Properties** tab.

For the usage defined in the component controller in Figure 4.11, it is now possible to access methods, events, and context nodes of the ZEXP_CONVERSION_MODEL component that belong to the interface of that component.

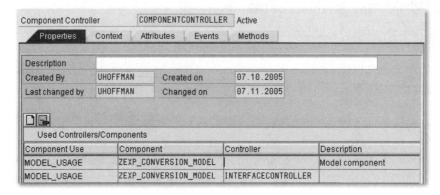

Figure 4.11 Defining Usages in a Controller

In the following sections, we'll demonstrate how to implement the usage of a component and access the WD4A components of the interface controller of components.

4.2.1 Embedding Windows of Used Components

To embed windows or interface views of components, for which a usage has been defined into the window structure of the component that defines the use, proceed in the same way as you did for embedding views. For example, as shown in Figure 4.10, if a usage for component ZEXP_CONVERSION_OS_UI is defined in component ZEXP_CONVERSION_OS_MAIN, all interface views of component ZEXP_CONVERSION_OS_UI are available for embedding windows for interface views in component ZEXP_CONVERSION_OS_MAIN. In the example in Figure 4.12, this would be interface view W_DEFAULT of component ZEXP_CONVERSION_OS_UI.

Defining WD4A Component Usages | **4.2**

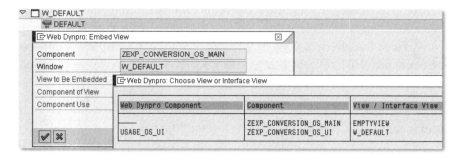

Figure 4.12 Embedding Interface Views from Components for which a Usage Has Been Defined

4.2.2 Calling Methods of Used Components

The easiest way to combine statements for calling methods in other components is to use the Code Wizard. Select **Method Call in Used Controller** and use the input help to select the **Component Name** and the **Component Use**. The methods that are accessible via the interface controller are also listed (see Figure 4.13).

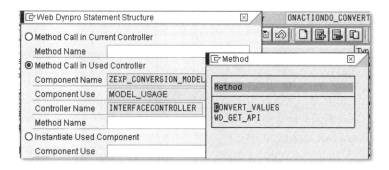

Figure 4.13 Calling a Method in a Used Component

After you select the method, the Code Wizard then combines the variable declarations and the syntax for calling the method. You can, of course, also adapt the logic thus created to suit your own programming conventions. After the method `convert_values()` shown in Figure 4.13 is selected, the Code Wizard creates the following declarations and statements:

```
DATA  lr_if_controller TYPE REF TO ziwci_exp_conversion_model.
lr_if_controller = wd_this->wd_cpifc_model_usage( ).
lr_if_controller->convert_values( ).
```

195

In order to call the method of a used component at runtime, the component must be instantiated. This is done either automatically via the WD4A framework, when the interface view of the used component is displayed, or it can be done manually. You can also use the Code Wizard to create the instantiation statements.

The code for creating an instance of component ZEXP_CONVERSION_OS_UI in component ZEXP_CONVERSION_OS_MAIN is as follows:

```
DATA lr_cmp_usage TYPE REF TO if_wd_component_usage.
lr_cmp_usage =   wd_this->wd_cpuse_model_usage( ).
IF lr_cmp_usage->has_active_component( ) IS INITIAL.
  lr_cmp_usage->create_component( ).
ENDIF.
```

4.2.3 Triggering Cross-Component Events

Figure 4.14 shows how to create an event handler method and register it to an event that is triggered by a used component. The event handler method is invalidate_nodes(), while the event to which invalidate_nodes() is to be registered is DIM_SELECTED and is triggered in the component ZEXP_CONVERSION_DIM_UI. Note that only components that define the usage can be registered to events of the used component. The opposite is not possible; that is, the used component cannot be registered to events of the component that defines the usage.

If some usage definitions exist across multiple layers, you will have to register the events in every layer and redefine them. For example, if component A defines the usage of a component B, which, in turn, uses component C, and component A wants to register itself to an event in component C, it can do so only via component B.

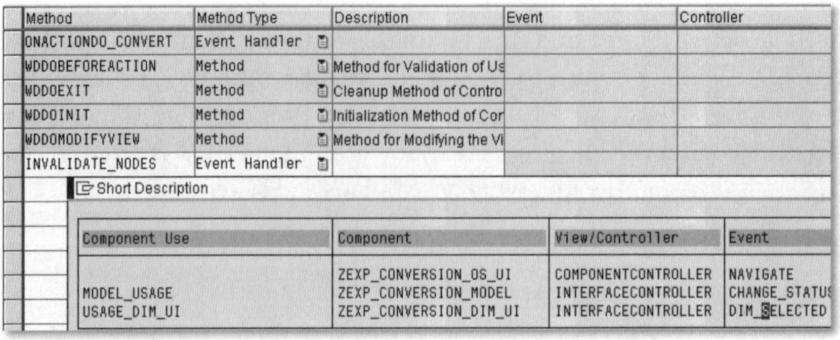

Method	Method Type	Description	Event	Controller
ONACTIONDO_CONVERT	Event Handler			
WDDOBEFOREACTION	Method	Method for Validation of Us		
WDDOEXIT	Method	Cleanup Method of Contro		
WDDOINIT	Method	Initialization Method of Cor		
WDDOMODIFYVIEW	Method	Method for Modifying the Vi		
INVALIDATE_NODES	Event Handler			

Component Use	Component	View/Controller	Event
	ZEXP_CONVERSION_OS_UI	COMPONENTCONTROLLER	NAVIGATE
MODEL_USAGE	ZEXP_CONVERSION_MODEL	INTERFACECONTROLLER	CHANGE_STATUS
USAGE_DIM_UI	ZEXP_CONVERSION_DIM_UI	INTERFACECONTROLLER	DIM_SELECTED

Figure 4.14 Registering a Component to an Event of a Used Component

4.2.4 External Context Access Using Direct Mapping

To copy or map (or both) the context of a used component to the context of the component that defines the use, you must define the usage in the **Properties** tab of the relevant controller (see Figure 4.11). The nodes of the component contexts that are marked as **Interface** then appear on the right-hand side in the **Context** tab. As shown in Figure 4.15, the context nodes UNITS, CONVERSION, and DIMENSION belong to the interface controller of the component ZEXP_CONVERSION_MODEL and can be defined, copied, or mapped in the context of the component controller that defines the usage of the component ZEXP_CONVERSION_MODEL. There has to be a valid instance of this component (see Section 4.2.2) when the context nodes of the used component ZEXP_CONVERSION_MODEL are accessed at runtime. In the example shown here, the context data of component ZEXP_CONVERSION_MODEL is used. This kind of mapping, in which the data of the used component is accessed directly, is called *direct mapping*.

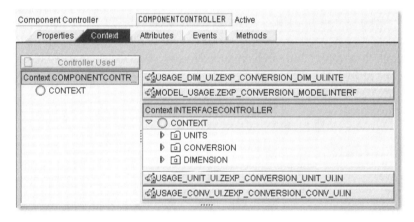

Figure 4.15 Contexts of Used Components

In Figure 4.16, the main component A implements a view plus context. Main component A also defines a usage of subcomponent B. The data of the context of subcomponent B should be output in the view of main component A. This is done by directly mapping the context of subcomponent B to the context of main component A.

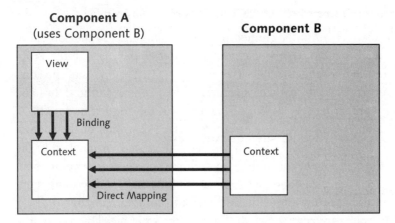

Figure 4.16 Schematic Representation of Direct Mapping

4.2.5 External Context Access Using Reverse Mapping

In cases in which interface views of used components are displayed, but the data displayed in the interface views is made available by the component that defines the use, *reverse mapping* should be used. For reverse mapping to be possible, the context node to be mapped has to be explicitly marked in the component to be used. To do this, check the **Input Element (Ext.)** property (see Figure 4.17).

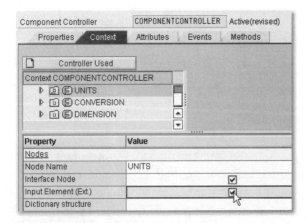

Figure 4.17 Marking the Context Node for Reverse Mapping

In Figure 4.18, the main component A implements a view without a context. For the display to be created, a view (or, to be more precise, an interface view) of subcomponent B for which a usage is defined in main component A is embedded in main component A.

However, it is the data in the context of main component A that needs to be displayed. Therefore, the context of main component A is mapped to the context of subcomponent B. Here, reverse mapping is used. To map a context node to a context node that is intended to be used for reverse mapping, navigate in the object tree of the main component to **Component Usages**. Underneath this, you will find the entry for the used subcomponent (MODEL_ USAGE in our example here). Use the context menu of the sub-component to create a controller usage (**Create Controller Usage**) containing the context node that is intended for reverse mapping (see Figure 4.19).

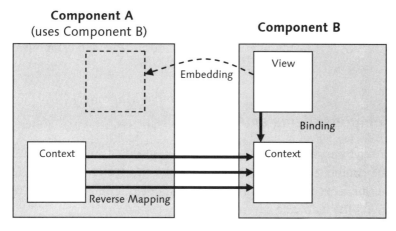

Figure 4.18 Schematic Representation of Reverse Mapping

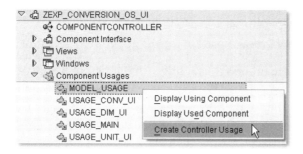

Figure 4.19 Creating a Controller Usage

If you now select the controller usage that you just created, the context nodes marked Interface and the context node intended for reverse mapping appear on the right-hand side of the screen. In Figure 4.20, the context node is UNITS.

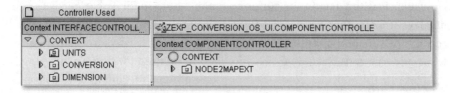

Figure 4.20 Context Nodes of the Controller Usage

For mapping to be possible, you still have to click on the **Controller Used** button and define the component controller of the main component as a use. This button is located on the left-hand side, as shown in Figure 4.20. You can now use drag and drop to map the relevant context node of the main component (NODE2MAPEXT) to the relevant context node of the sub-component (UNITS).

4.3 Componentizing an Application

In Chapter 3, we encountered a range of WD4A applications that were based on only one component; however, it would be very difficult to implement complex business processes within a single component. Componentizing an application has the following advantages:

- Enables you to divide up tasks within project teams
- Enables you to model and structure the application
- Facilitates component reusability
- Enables you to use the MVC design pattern for the application structure

In this section, we explain the process of creating a componentized application, based on the MVC design pattern. We show you how, by using componentization, the amount of time and effort required to make any requested changes to the user interface of an application is much less than that required when a single component is used.

In Section 3.5, we looked at an application for converting units of measure. The application included the various dimensions, such as distance, volume, and temperature, and the relevant units, such as Celsius, Kelvin, and Fahrenheit. Table T006D contains the data and needs to be made available in every system. Every time the user selects a new dimension, the units associated with the dimension are re-identified. The user interface was implemented using the RoadMap view element and the application was accordingly divided up into individual phases, through which the user is guided by the interface. The functions for identifying the units after the user selects the dimension and for converting the units are all implemented in the same component, which also contains the areas that are relevant to the user interface.

If changes are made to the user interface or the program logic, the component has to be recreated; existing functionalities cannot be reused. We want to minimize the work involved in such cases by structuring this single-component-based application into multiple components that are organized on the basis of the MVC design pattern. We will then use a design for a new user interface to show how this kind of change can be implemented by reusing components, without needing to adapt, copy, or change existing program logic. User interaction in the unit conversion application will be based on forms instead of on the `RoadMap` view element.

4.3.1 Structure of the Sample Application

The functionality of the sample application is based on the `ZEXP_ROADMAP` component (see Section 3.5). The functionality and the components of the user interface are separated here and implemented in individual components that correspond to their function. The name of the new WD4A application will be `ZEXP_CONVERSION_RM`, and the functions of the individual components are as follows:

- **Component `ZEXP_CONVERSION_RM_MAIN`**
  This component is the main component or controller component. It instantiates the model component and the user interface component, and is the starting-point for the application.

- **Component `ZEXP_CONVERSION_RM_UI`**
  This component implements the user interface functionality. It is the framework for other subcomponents of the user interface. In our example, `ZEXP_CONVERSION_RM_UI` implements the `RoadMap` view element. The view elements displayed in every RoadMap step are implemented in the subcomponents. Component `ZEXP_CONVERSION_RM_UI` instantiates the subcomponents and thus functions as a kind of controller component for other user interface components.

- **Component `ZEXP_CONVERSION_MODEL`**
  This component implements the selection and conversion of units and therefore maps functionalities of the model. It does not have any visual parts, and so it does not require any view controllers or window control-

lers. All data and processes are organized in the context and the methods of the component controller.

- **Component ZEXP_CONVERSION_DIM_UI**
  This component provides the visual part of the dimension selection process. In our example, this is a DropDownByIndex view element. This component is used by the component ZEXP_CONVERSION_RM_UI, and gets its data from the model component via reverse mapping.

- **Component ZEXP_CONVERSION_UNIT_UI**
  This component provides the visual part for selecting the unit and accepting the value to be converted. The layout consists of an InputField view element, two DropDownByIndex view elements, and the associated labels. This component is used by the component ZEXP_CONVERSION_RM_UI, and gets its data from the model component by means of reverse mapping.

- **Component ZEXP_CONVERSION_CONV_UI**
  This component provides the visual part for displaying the results of the conversion. The layout consists of inactive InputField view elements and TextView view elements. This component is used by the component ZEXP_CONVERSION_RM_UI, and gets its data from the model component via reverse mapping. Conversion is done in the model component.

4.3.2 Implementing the Components

In the next few sections, we'll develop the individual components and their interaction with each other step by step.

Component ZEXP_CONVERSION_DIM_UI

Component ZEXP_CONVERSION_DIM_UI is used to display the list of dimensions (see Figure 4.21).

Figure 4.21 Output Created by ZEXP_CONVERSION_DIM_UI

To display the selection list, the context node DIMENSION of the type **T006T** is created in the component controller of component ZEXP_CONVERSION_DIM_UI. The **Cardinality** property with the value **0..n** is assigned to this context node. Component ZEXP_CONVERSION_RM_UI transfers data at runtime to the context node, which has to be configured for reverse mapping. Fields DIMID and TXDIM are transferred from the ABAP Dictionary structure T006T and used as attributes (see Figure 4.22).

Property	Value	Transfer attri...
Nodes		
Node Name	DIMENSION	
Interface Node	✓	
Input Element (Ext.)	✓	
Dictionary structure	T006T	
Cardinality	0..n	
Selection	0..1	
Initialization Lead Selection	✓	
Singleton	✓	
Supply Function		

Figure 4.22 Component Controller Context

The view layout of component ZEXP_CONVERSION_DIM_UI consists of a Label view element and a DropDownByIndex view element that allow the dimension to be input. The DIMENSION context node is mapped from the component controller to the view controller. The **texts** property of the DropDownByIndex view element is bound to the TXDIM context attribute. The view is embedded in the W_DEFAULT window, which, in turn, has an inbound plug marked **Interface**.

Component ZEXP_CONVERSION_UNIT_UI

Component ZEXP_CONVERSION_UNIT_UI is used to input the conversion value and to display the dropdown lists for "Convert value from unit" and "Convert value to unit" (see Figure 4.23).

Figure 4.23 Output Created by ZEXP_CONVERSION_UNIT_UI

A context node called UNITS is created in the component controller of the component to display the input field for the conversion value and the dropdown lists for the units. An attribute called IVALUE of the **STRING** type is assigned to the context node and is used for the conversion value. Also, two subordinate context nodes—FROMUNIT and TOUNIT—are assigned to the UNITS context node. These subordinate nodes have the cardinality **0..n** and are used to display the list of units. They have the type **T006A_INT** and use the UNIT_INT and UNIT_TXT_L fields from the structure.

Component ZEXP_CONVERSION_RM_UI transfers data at runtime to the UNITS context node, which has to be configured for reverse mapping. The **Interface** and **Input Element (Ext.)** properties should therefore be marked for this purpose. The UNITS context node is mapped from the component controller to the view controller.

The view layout of the component consists of the view element INP_VALUE for inputting the conversion value, two DropDownByIndex view elements (DDI_FROM and DDI_TO) for specifying the source and target units, and the corresponding Label view elements (see Figure 4.24).

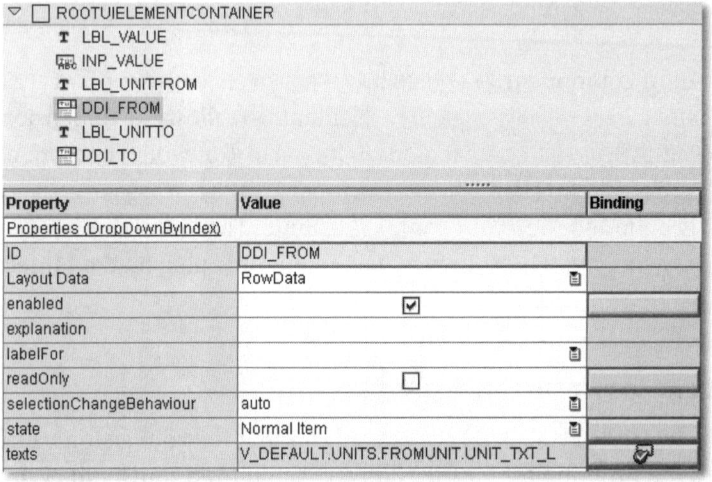

Property	Value		Binding
Properties (DropDownByIndex)			
ID	DDI_FROM		
Layout Data	RowData		
enabled		✓	
explanation			
labelFor			
readOnly		☐	
selectionChangeBehaviour	auto		
state	Normal Item		
texts	V_DEFAULT.UNITS.FROMUNIT.UNIT_TXT_L		

Figure 4.24 Layout of the View

In the next step, we will bind all required properties of the view elements to the corresponding context nodes or context node attributes. This applies to the **value** property of the view element INP_VALUE, which is bound to the IVALUE attribute.

The **texts** property of the DDI_FROM view element and the **texts** property of DDI_TO are both bound to the UNIT_TXT_L attribute of the FROM_UNIT context node. The V_DEFAULT view of component ZEXP_CONVERSION_UNIT_UI is embedded in the W_DEFAULT window, which, in turn, has an inbound plug marked **Interface**.

Component ZEXP_CONVERSION_CONV_UI

The UI component ZEXP_CONVERSION_CONV_UI is used to display the results of the conversion. The view layout of the component consists of TextView view elements and inactive InputField view elements for displaying the original value, the result, and the units (see Figure 4.25).

Figure 4.25 Output Created by ZEXP_CONVERSION_CONV_UI

The context in the component controller consists of two context nodes: context node UNITS has the same properties as it has in component ZEXP_CONVERSION_UNIT_UI, while context node CONVERSION has just one attribute called CVALUE of the type **STRING**. Both context nodes need to be marked for reverse mapping and are mapped to the view controller (see Figure 4.26).

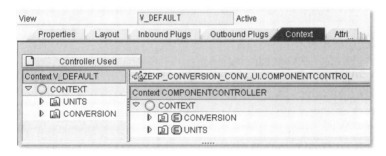

Figure 4.26 View Controller Context ZEXP_CONVERSION_CONV_UI

This component also has a view called V_DEFAULT. The layout of this view is made up of the following view elements: TXV_IVALUE, INP_FROMUNIT, TXV_SEPARATOR, TXV_CVALUE, and INP_TOUNIT (see Figure 4.27). We now bind the **texts** property of TXV_IVALUE to the IVALUE attribute of the UNITS context node. The **value** property of the InputField view elements INP_FROMUNIT and INP_TOUNIT is bound to the UNIT_TEXT_L attribute of the FROMUNIT and TOUNIT context nodes. The TXV_CVALUE view element displays the result of the conversion. The **texts** property of this view element is bound to the CVALUE attribute of the CONVERSION context node.

The component also has a window called W_DEFAULT, and the V_DEFAULT view is included in this window. The W_DEFAULT window has an inbound plug that is marked **Interface**.

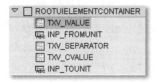

Figure 4.27 Layout of the V_DEFAULT View

Component ZEXP_CONVERSION_RM_UI

The `ZEXP_CONVERSION_RM_UI` component controls the user guidance process via the `RoadMap` view element (see Figure 4.28).

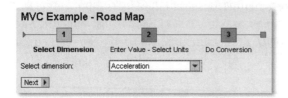

Figure 4.28 Output Created by ZEXP_CONVERSION_RM_UI

Unlike the example in Section 3.5, in which the `RoadMap` view element was used as a kind of container that displays the view that is assigned to the current step in each case and hides all other views, we'll now implement these views using the components described above. To do this, the three components are now integrated into the component that contains the `RoadMap` view element, `ZEXP_CONVERSION_RM_UI`. The layout of the `V_DEFAULT` view contains the `RMP_CONVERSION` view element with the following three `RoadMapStep` view elements: `STP_DIMENSION`, `STP_INPUT`, and `STP_RESULT`.

The `VCU_ROADMAP` view element is used as a container for the UI components that display the individual process steps. We also use a `ButtonRow` view element that contains a `Button` view element for advancing to the relevant process steps (see Figure 4.29).

The component requires data in the context in order to control the display of each active process step, and to set the Next button to active or inactive as required. For this purpose, a context node called `ROADMAP` (property **Cardinality** with the value **1..1**) and two attributes, `STEP` of the type **STRING** and `NEXT_ENABLED` of the type **WDY_BOOLEAN**, are created in the view controller. The **enabled** property of the `Button` view element `BTN_NEXT` is bound to the `NEXT_ENABLED` context attribute, and the **selectedStep** property of the `RoadMap` view element is bound to the `STEP` context attribute.

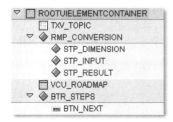

Figure 4.29 View Layout of ZEXP_CONVERSION_RM_UI

When the user clicks on the **Next** button, the next process step should open. The DO_NEXT action is defined for this purpose and is bound to the **onAction** property of the Button view element. The event handler method for the DO_NEXT action is onactiondo_next().

The input value is converted after the user inputs it and selects the source and target units. The conversion logic is implemented in a method of the model component, which accordingly has to be called when the Next button is clicked. However, because we are using the MVC design pattern, the view cannot directly access the model component. Instead, it accesses the model component via the controller component. For this reason, we implement an event called CONVERT_VALUES in the ZEXP_CONVERSION_RM_UI component, and the ZEXP_CONVERSION_RM_MAIN component registers itself to this event. The event is defined in the component controller of the ZEXP_CONVERSION_RM_UI component and is marked **Interface** (see Figure 4.30).

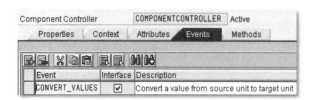

Figure 4.30 Definition of CONVERT_VALUES Event

The event handler method in the ZEXP_CONVERSION_RM_MAIN component then calls the relevant method in the model component. The CONVERT_VALUES event is triggered in the onactiondo_next() event handler method. The following sequence is implemented in this event handler method:

- Set follow-on step
- Determine visibility of **Next** button
- Trigger outbound plug for view of the follow-on step

4 | Multi-Component Applications

Listing 4.1 shows how the `onactiondo_next()` method is implemented.

```
METHOD onactiondo_next.
    DATA    lr_node             TYPE REF TO     if_wd_context_node.
    DATA    ls_roadmap          TYPE if_v_default=>element_roadmap.
    DATA    lv_step             TYPE            string.
*---- Determine current step
    lr_node = wd_context->get_child_node( 'ROADMAP' ).
    lr_node->get_attribute( EXPORTING name  = 'STEP'
                            IMPORTING value = lv_step ).
*---- Set next step depending on current step
    CASE lv_step.
      WHEN 'STP_DIMENSION'.
        ls_roadmap-step         = 'STP_INPUT'.
        ls_roadmap-next_enabled = abap_true.
        wd_this->fire_op_to_v_units_plg( ).
      WHEN 'STP_INPUT'.
        ls_roadmap-step         = 'STP_RESULT'.
        ls_roadmap-next_enabled = abap_false.
*---- Trigger calculation of conversion
        wd_comp_controller->fire_convert_values_evt( ).
        wd_this->fire_op_to_v_result_plg( ).
      WHEN OTHERS.
        ls_roadmap-next_enabled = abap_false.
    ENDCASE.
    lr_node->set_static_attributes( ls_roadmap ).
ENDMETHOD.
```

Listing 4.1 Implementation of onactiondo_next() Method

Before you activate the `onactiondo_next()` event handler method, you have to define the outbound plugs; otherwise, there will be a compilation error. The three outbound plugs `OP_TO_V_DIMENSION`, `OP_TO_V_RESULT`, and `OP_TO_V_UNITS` are used to implement the function for navigating to the views that display the individual process steps. Define these outbound plugs in the view controller of the `V_DEFAULT` view in the **Outbound Plugs** tab. Once the outbound plugs are defined, the WD4A framework creates the corresponding fire methods that are called in the `onactiondo_next()` method.

The view that is to be called by each outbound plug is defined in the window controller. In the window controller, first embed the `V_DEFAULT` view of its own `ZEXP_CONVERSION_RM_MAIN` component. The view of each current process step should now be displayed in the `ViewContainerUIElement` view element of the `V_DEFAULT` view. To embed interface views that display the process steps but belong to the other components, you have to define their uses.

You do this in the general data view of the component and in the window controller in the **Used Components** tab (see Figure 4.31).

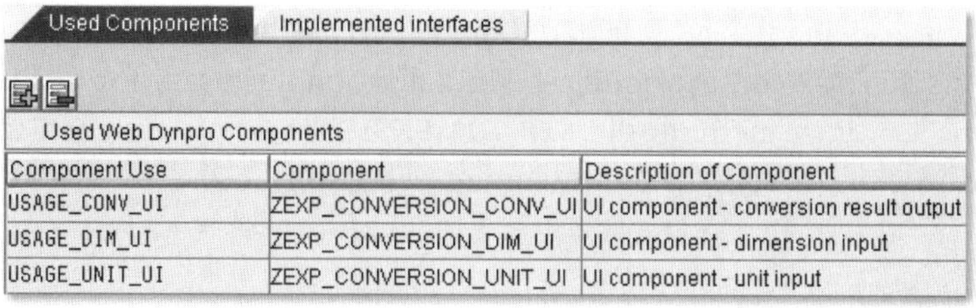

Component Use	Component	Description of Component
USAGE_CONV_UI	ZEXP_CONVERSION_CONV_UI	UI component - conversion result output
USAGE_DIM_UI	ZEXP_CONVERSION_DIM_UI	UI component - dimension input
USAGE_UNIT_UI	ZEXP_CONVERSION_UNIT_UI	UI component - unit input

Figure 4.31 Defining Uses for Individual Components

To define the structure of the window, you then embed the interface views of the components that display the individual process steps in the VCU_ROAD-MAP view element. You can then link the three outbound plugs OP_TO_V_DIMENSION, OP_TO_V_RESULT, and OP_TO_V_UNITS with the default inbound plugs of each interface view. Carry out these steps as shown in Figure 4.32.

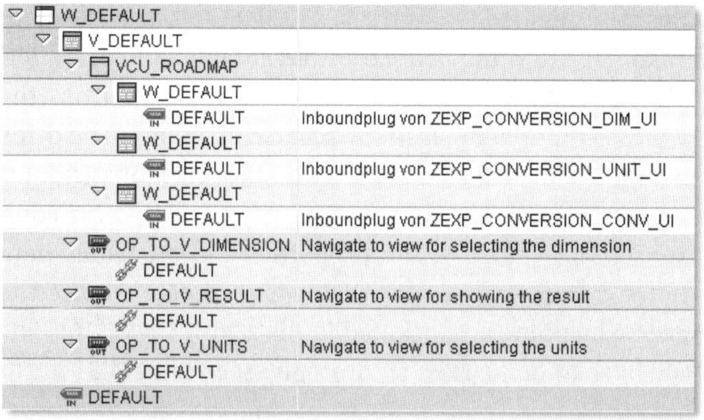

```
▽ ☐ W_DEFAULT
  ▽ ☐ V_DEFAULT
    ▽ ☐ VCU_ROADMAP
      ▽ ☐ W_DEFAULT
          ⚑ DEFAULT        Inboundplug von ZEXP_CONVERSION_DIM_UI
      ▽ ☐ W_DEFAULT
          ⚑ DEFAULT        Inboundplug von ZEXP_CONVERSION_UNIT_UI
      ▽ ☐ W_DEFAULT
          ⚑ DEFAULT        Inboundplug von ZEXP_CONVERSION_CONV_UI
    ▽ ⚑ OP_TO_V_DIMENSION  Navigate to view for selecting the dimension
        ⚑ DEFAULT
    ▽ ⚑ OP_TO_V_RESULT     Navigate to view for showing the result
        ⚑ DEFAULT
    ▽ ⚑ OP_TO_V_UNITS      Navigate to view for selecting the units
        ⚑ DEFAULT
  ⚑ DEFAULT
```

Figure 4.32 Defining the Window Structure and Navigation

The conversion process begins when the user enters the dimension. The first thing that has to be displayed is the view of component ZEXP_CONVERSION_DIM_UI. You do this by setting the **Default** property of the embedded W_DEFAULT interface view of the component. Only one view can be set as the default view in the window structure definition. By default, the WD4A framework always sets the **Default** property in the first view embedded in a window. If you have embedded the ZEXP_CONVERSION_DIM_UI component in a different order, set the **Default** property manually by checking the corresponding checkbox.

To ensure that the current step is highlighted in color by the `RoadMap` view element in the graphical display of the process steps, you have to assign the ID of the current `RoadMapStep` view element to the **selectedStep** property of the `RoadMap` view element. The **selectedStep** property is bound to the `STEP` attribute of the `ROADMAP` context node. The initialization necessary for this is done in the `wddoinit()` method: the **STP_DIMENSION** value is assigned to the `STEP` attribute of the `ROADMAP` context node (see Listing 4.2).

```
METHOD wddoinit.
   DATA lr_road_node    TYPE REF TO if_wd_context_node.
   DATA ls_road_data    TYPE        if_v_default=>element_roadmap.
*--- Set starting step
   lr_road_node             = wd_context->get_child_node( 'ROADMAP' ).
   ls_road_data-step        = 'STP_DIMENSION'.
   ls_road_data-next_enabled = abap_true.
   lr_road_node->set_static_attributes( ls_road_data ).
ENDMETHOD.
```

Listing 4.2 Initializing the RoadMap Context Node

Data is assigned to the views embedded in the `ZEXP_CONVERSION_RM_UI` component via reverse mapping from the context of the component controller. (The `ZEXP_CONVERSION_RM_UI` component, in turn, gets the data from the `ZEXP_CONVERSION_RM_MAIN` component, again by reverse mapping.) The three context nodes `DIMENSION`, `UNITS`, and `CONVERSION`, and the relevant attributes are created in the component controller of the `ZEXP_CONVERSION_RM_UI` component for this purpose. The values of the properties and attributes here must be the same as the values specified in previous sections. Because the context nodes for reverse mapping are included in the `ZEXP_CONVERSION_RM_MAIN` component, they have to be marked accordingly (see Figure 4.33).

Figure 4.33 Component Controller Context

Next, create the `USAGE_DIM_UI`, `USAGE_CONV_UI`, and `USAGE_UNIT_UI` interface controller usages for the `ZEXP_CONVERSION_DIM_UI`, `ZEXP_CONVERSION_UNITS_UI`, and `ZEXP_CONVERSION_CONV_UI` components (see Section 4.2.5). Figure 4.34 shows the result. Define the component controller usage of `ZEXP_CONVERSION_RM_UI` for every controller usage. You can then map each context node of the component controller context to the controller usages.

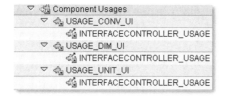

Figure 4.34 Creating Controller Usages

Component ZEXP_CONVERSION_MODEL

The ZEXP_CONVERSION_MODEL component implements the program logic for the conversion and provides the context nodes with data about the conversion units. In our structure, it is equivalent to the model component, in accordance with the MVC design pattern. The component contains the context nodes for data retention, which are mapped to the individual UI components, and the whole conversion logic. Only the component controller is used for this purpose; the view and window controllers are not required. As we know from the ZEXP_CONVERSION_RM_UI component, the context of the component controller consists of the three context nodes DIMENSION, UNITS, and CONVERSION. Their properties and those of the context attributes are summarized in Table 4.1 and Table 4.2. Note that the FROMUNIT and TOUNIT context nodes are subnodes of the UNITS context node. The DIMENSION, FROMUINT, and TOUNIT context nodes have supply function methods.

Context Node	Cardinality	Dictionary Structure	Supply Function Method
DIMENSION	1..1		supply_dimension()
UNITS	1..1		
FROMUNIT	0..n	T006A_INT	supply_unit()
TOUNIT	0..n	T006A_INT	supply_unit()
CONVERSION	1..1		

Table 4.1 Properties of the Context Nodes

Context Attribute	Context Node	Type
DVALUE	DIMENSION	DIMID
UNIT_INT	FROMUNIT TOUNIT	T006A_INT-UNIT_INT

Table 4.2 Properties of the Context Attributes

4 | Multi-Component Applications

Context Attribute	Context Node	Type
UNIT_TXT_L	FROMUNIT TOUNIT	**T006A_INT- UNIT_TXT_L**
IVALUE	UNITS	**STRING**
CVALUE	CONVERSION	**STRING**

Table 4.2 Properties of the Context Attributes (cont.)

Listing 4.3 shows how the `supply_dimension()` supply function method is implemented. The dimension data is read from Table T006T.

```
METHOD supply_dimension.
  DATA lt_dimension  TYPE    if_componentcontroller=>elements_dimension.
  DATA ls_dimension  TYPE    if_componentcontroller=>element_dimension.
*--- Get dimensions from data base
  SELECT DISTINCT * FROM t006t INTO TABLE lt_dimension WHERE
                                                          spras = sy-langu.
*--- Delete first row (it includes a dummy entry)
  DELETE lt_dimension INDEX 1.
*--- Sort list of dimension by their text description
  SORT lt_dimension BY txdim ASCENDING.
*--- Fill context
  node->bind_table( new_items = lt_dimension ).
ENDMETHOD.
```

Listing 4.3 Implementing supply_dimension()

Listing 4.4 shows how the `supply_unit()` supply function method is implemented. The function module UNITS_GET_FOR_DIMENSION is used to determine the units for a dimension.

```
METHOD supply_unit.
  DATA   lr_node     TYPE REF TO if_wd_context_node.
  DATA   lr_element  TYPE REF TO if_wd_context_element.
  DATA   ls_dim      TYPE if_componentcontroller=>element_dimension.
  DATA   lt_unit     TYPE if_componentcontroller=>elements_fromunit.
  lr_node    = wd_context->get_child_node( 'DIMENSION' ).
  lr_element = lr_node->get_lead_selection( ).
  lr_element->get_static_attributes( IMPORTING
                                     static_attributes = ls_dim ).
  CALL FUNCTION 'UNITS_GET_FOR_DIMENSION'
    EXPORTING
      dimension          = ls_dim-dimid
      language           = sy-langu
    TABLES
```

```abap
        units_of_measurement = lt_unit
    EXCEPTIONS
        dimension_not_found  = 1
        OTHERS               = 2.
  IF sy-subrc EQ 0.
    node->bind_table( new_items          = lt_unit
                      set_initial_elements = abap_true ).
  ENDIF.
ENDMETHOD.
```

Listing 4.4 Implementing supply_units()

The method `convert_values()` is called to convert the units. The input value and the selected units are read from the relevant context nodes, the result of the conversion is calculated, and the result value is assigned to the CONVERSION context node. Because you must be able to call the `convert_values()` method from inside other components, this method has to be marked as **Interface**. Listing 4.5 shows you how to implement the `convert_values()` method.

```abap
METHOD convert_values.
  DATA  ls_conv         TYPE  if_componentcontroller=>element_conversion.
  DATA  lr_input_node   TYPE REF TO if_wd_context_node.
  DATA  lr_sub_node     TYPE REF TO if_wd_context_node.
  DATA  lv_fromunit     TYPE       t006-msehi.
  DATA  lv_tounit       TYPE       t006-msehi.
  DATA  lv_value        TYPE       string.
  DATA  lv_denominator  TYPE       f.
  DATA  lv_numerator    TYPE       f.
  DATA  lv_nomout       TYPE       dzaehl.
  DATA  lv_denomout     TYPE       nennr.
  DATA  lr_node         TYPE REF TO if_wd_context_node.

  lr_input_node = wd_context->get_child_node( 'UNITS' ).
  lr_input_node->get_attribute( EXPORTING name  = 'IVALUE'
                                IMPORTING value = lv_value ).
  lr_sub_node     = lr_input_node->get_child_node( 'FROMUNIT' ).
  lr_sub_node->get_attribute( EXPORTING name  = 'UNIT_INT'
                              IMPORTING value = lv_fromunit ).
  lr_sub_node     = lr_input_node->get_child_node( 'TOUNIT' ).
  lr_sub_node->get_attribute( EXPORTING name  = 'UNIT_INT'
                              IMPORTING value = lv_tounit ).
  CALL FUNCTION 'CONVERSION_FACTOR_GET'
    EXPORTING
      no_type_check       = 'X'
```

```abap
        unit_in              = lv_fromunit
        unit_out             = lv_tounit
      IMPORTING
        denominator          = lv_denominator
        numerator            = lv_numerator
      EXCEPTIONS
        conversion_not_found = 1
        overflow             = 2
        type_invalid         = 3
        units_missing        = 4
        unit_in_not_found    = 5
        unit_out_not_found   = 6
        OTHERS               = 7.
    IF sy-subrc <> 0.
      RETURN.
    ELSE.
      CALL FUNCTION 'CONVERT_TO_FRACT10'
        EXPORTING
          nomin              = lv_numerator
          denomin            = lv_denominator
        IMPORTING
          nomout             = lv_nomout
          denomout           = lv_denomout
        EXCEPTIONS
          conversion_overflow = 1
          OTHERS              = 2.
      IF sy-subrc <> 0.
        RETURN.
      ELSE.
        ls_conv-cvalue = lv_value * ( lv_nomout / lv_denomout ).
      ENDIF.
*--- Supply node with data
      lr_node = wd_context->get_child_node( 'CONVERSION' ).
      lr_node->bind_structure( new_item           = ls_conv
                               set_initial_elements = abap_true ).
    ENDIF.
ENDMETHOD.
```

Listing 4.5 Implementing convert_values()

Component ZEXP_CONVERSION_RM_MAIN

The `ZEXP_CONVERSION_RM_MAIN` component is the controller component and defines the usage of the `ZEXP_CONVERSION_MODEL` model component and the `ZEXP_CONVERSION_RM_UI` view component. It can also control the lifecycle of the model component and view component, and is used as a starting-point for defining the WD4A application. Figure 4.35 illustrates the structure of the underlying application of the MVC design pattern, and the interconnections between the components.

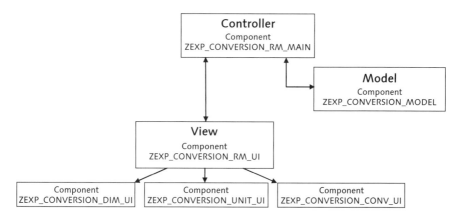

Figure 4.35 Components of the RoadMap Sample Application Based on the MVC Concept

The context nodes that are used across all components and the program processes are implemented in the ZEXP_CONVERSION_MODEL model component. Multiple UI components are responsible for the implementation of the view area. The ZEXP_CONVERSION_DIM_UI, ZEXP_CONVERSION_UNIT_UI, and ZEXP_CONVERSION_CONV_UI components display the individual process steps, and the ZEXP_CONVERSION_RM_UI component serves as a kind of container for these.

In the ZEXP_CONVERSION_RM_MAIN component, at runtime, the instances of the used components ZEXP_CONVERSION_MODEL and ZEXP_CONVERSION_RM_UI are created in the wddoinit() method of the component controller (see Listing 4.6).

```
METHOD wddoinit.
  DATA lr_usage    TYPE REF TO   if_wd_component_usage.
*---- Create model component
  lr_usage =   wd_this->wd_cpuse_usage_model( ).
  IF lr_usage->has_active_component( ) IS INITIAL.
    lr_usage->create_component( ).
  ENDIF.
*---- Create RoadMap UI component
  lr_usage =   wd_this->wd_cpuse_usage_rm_ui( ).
  IF lr_usage->has_active_component( ) IS INITIAL.
    lr_usage->create_component( ).
```

```
  ENDIF.
ENDMETHOD.
```

Listing 4.6 Instantiating Used Components

The `ZEXP_CONVERSION_RM_MAIN` component needs only one window, which we'll call `W_DEFAULT`. The interface view of the `ZEXP_CONVERSION_RM_UI` view component is embedded in this window. In our application, this component is the central view component. Therefore, it is the point from which the other view components are called, in accordance with the selected process step (see Figure 4.36).

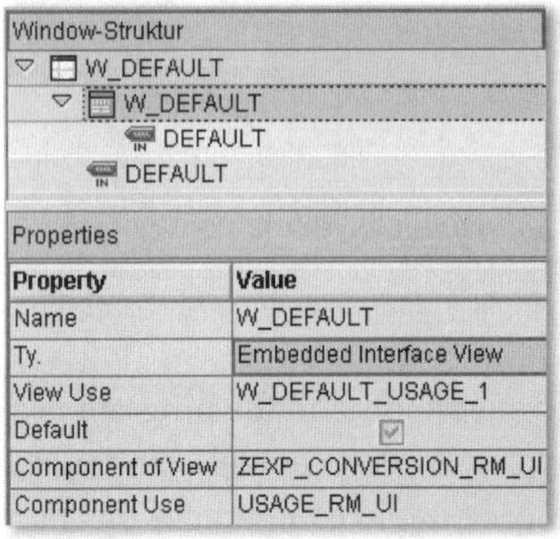

Window-Struktur	
▽ ☐ W_DEFAULT	
▽ 🗔 W_DEFAULT	
📄 DEFAULT	
📄 DEFAULT	

Properties	
Property	**Value**
Name	W_DEFAULT
Ty.	Embedded Interface View
View Use	W_DEFAULT_USAGE_1
Default	☑
Component of View	ZEXP_CONVERSION_RM_UI
Component Use	USAGE_RM_UI

Figure 4.36 Embedding the Interface View of the View Component

The controller component provides the link between the model component and the view component. It is used to transfer the context data in the model component to the view component, and the requirements created in the view component to the model component.

In our example, data transfer from the model component to the view component goes through the controller component via both direct and reverse mapping. The controller component also controls the process of calling program logic in the model component in response to events triggered in the view component. Furthermore, it registers itself to the `CONVERT_VALUES` event of the view component (see Figure 4.37).

The relevant method of the model component is called in `on_convert_values()`, the event handler method implemented for the event. Listing 4.7 shows how to implement the `on_convert_values()` event handler method.

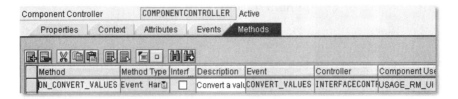

Figure 4.37 Registration of the Controller Component to an Event of the View Component

```
METHOD on_convert_values.
  DATA lr_interfacecontroller TYPE REF TO ziwci_exp_conversion_model.
  lr_interfacecontroller = wd_this->wd_cpifc_usage_model( ).
*--- Call to model component
  lr_interfacecontroller->convert_values( ).
ENDMETHOD.
```

Listing 4.7 Implementing on_convert_values()

The required context nodes of the model component are created by the ZEXP_CONVERSION_RM_MAIN component in the component controller via copying and mapping. We use reverse mapping to create the link to the view component ZEXP_CONVERSION_RM_UI. To do this, we first have to create the interface controller usage for the USAGE_RM_UI usage, as described in Section 4.2.5.

First, define the usage of the component controller of ZEXP_CONVERSION_RM_MAIN. Then, you can map each context node of the component controller context to the controller usages (see Figure 4.38).

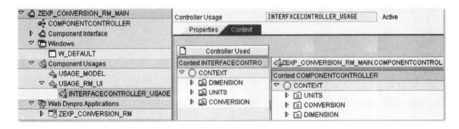

Figure 4.38 Reverse Mapping to View Component Context Nodes

The WD4A application is then also defined in the controller component. We call this application ZEXP_CONVERSION_RM. Once the application is started, the user selects the dimension, and the first step of the user guidance process is displayed.

4.3.3 Result of Componentization

After restructuring the single-component application ZEXP_ROADMAP to create an application based on the MVC design pattern, we now have a component-based structure that enables us to reuse the functionalities that we implemented in the application. The ZEXP_CONVERSION_MODEL model component can thus be used independently of the view components of other WD4A components at any time. Furthermore, you can use the individual view components for purposes other than converting units of measure. Componentization and the reusability that it enables within the WD4A framework enable you to create applications faster and more cost-effectively.

In the following sections, we'll redesign the user interface of our sample application, and explore ways of reusing some of the components that we discussed and developed in Section 4.3.2.

4.3.4 Redesigning the Sample Application

We'll now take our sample application for converting units of measure, using the RoadMap view element for user guidance, and redesign it as an application with a form-based user interface. The goal here is to provide the user with all the required fields and view elements in the client at the same time, and to avoid changing the structure of the displayed layout during user interaction.

To do this, the user selects the dimension that he requires from the list of dimensions. This selection causes the units to be set in accordance with the selected dimension. The user can now enter a value to be converted and select the units he requires. Then, the user clicks on the **Convert** button and the conversion is carried out.

Figure 4.39 shows the modified structure of the new WD4A application. The new application is called ZEXP_CONVERSION_FB. The ZEXP_CONVERSION_MAIN_FB and ZEXP_CONVERSION_FB_UI components are new and replace the ZEXP_CONVERSION_MAIN_RM and ZEXP_CONVERSION_RM_UI components used in the ZEXP_CONVERSION_RM application.

The ZEXP_CONVERSION_MODEL model component and the ZEXP_CONVERSION_DIM_UI, ZEXP_CONVERSION_UNIT_UI, and ZEXP_CONVERSION_CONV_UI components, which display the individual view areas, are reused. The structure of the newly added components is explained in the next two sections.

Componentizing an Application | **4.3**

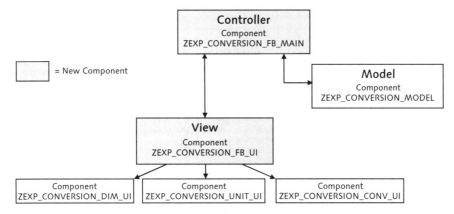

Figure 4.39 Components of the New Sample Application

Component ZEXP_CONVERSION_FB_UI

The new ZEXP_CONVERSION_FB_UI component controls how the view elements to be displayed in the client are arranged and sorted. You need to define the usages of the three components (ZEXP_CONVERSION_DIM_UI, ZEXP_CONVERSION_UNITS_UI, and ZEXP_CONVERSION_CONV_UI) in the **Used Components** tab.

The layout of the V_DEFAULT view (see Figure 4.40) contains three ViewContainerUIElement view elements: VCO_DIM, VCO_UNITS, and VCO_CONV. These view elements are used to embed the interface views from the ZEXP_CONVERSION_DIM_UI, ZEXP_CONVERSION_UNIT_UI, and ZEXP_CONVERSION_CONV_UI components. The Button view element BTN_CONVERT triggers the conversion process at runtime.

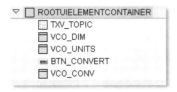

Figure 4.40 View Layout of ZEXP_CONVERSION_FB_UI

The view doesn't need any data from the context of the view controller and can remain empty. The DO_CONVERT action is linked to the **onAction** property of the Button view element. The CONVERT_VALUES event, which is defined in the component controller, is triggered in the onactiondo_convert() event handler method of the DO_CONVERT action. Besides the CONVERT_VALUES event,

219

the component controller also contains the definition for the DIM_SELECTED event, which is then triggered in the on_dim_selected() event handler method (see Figure 4.41). The event handler method contains only one statement for triggering the event (see Listing 4.8).

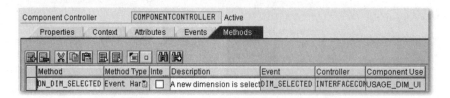

Figure 4.41 Registering to an Event of the Used Component

```
METHOD on_dim_selected.
  wd_this->fire_dim_selected_evt( ).
ENDMETHOD.
```

Listing 4.8 Implementing on_dim_selected()

Both events, CONVERT_VALUES and DIM_SELECTED, belong to the interface of the component. The event handler method has registered itself to the DIM_SELECTED event of the ZEXP_CONVERSION_DIM_UI component. Once the user selects a new dimension, this should cause the selection lists of the units to be reset via the controller component.

The individual components are instantiated in the wddoinit() method of the component controller. Listing 4.9 shows the statements used to implement this method.

```
METHOD wddoinit.
  DATA lr_ui_usage      TYPE REF TO    if_wd_component_usage.
*---- Create dimension UI component
  lr_ui_usage =   wd_this->wd_cpuse_usage_dim_ui( ).
  IF lr_ui_usage->has_active_component( ) IS INITIAL.
    lr_ui_usage->create_component( ).
  ENDIF.
*---- Create unit UI component
  lr_ui_usage =   wd_this->wd_cpuse_usage_unit_ui( ).
  IF lr_ui_usage->has_active_component( ) IS INITIAL.
    lr_ui_usage->create_component( ).
  ENDIF.
*---- Create conversion UI component
  lr_ui_usage =   wd_this->wd_cpuse_usage_conv_ui( ).
  IF lr_ui_usage->has_active_component( ) IS INITIAL.
    lr_ui_usage->create_component( ).
```

```
  ENDIF.
ENDMETHOD.
```

Listing 4.9 Generating the UI Component Instances

Figure 4.42 shows the structure of the `W_DEFAULT` window. The interface views of the used components are embedded in the relevant `ViewContainerUIElement` view elements.

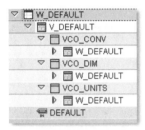

Figure 4.42 Window Structure

Data is assigned to the interface views embedded in the `ZEXP_CONVERSION_FB_UI` component via reverse mapping from the context of the component controller. (The `ZEXP_CONVERSION_FB_UI` component, in turn, gets the data from the `ZEXP_CONVERSION_FB_MAIN` component, again by reverse mapping.) To this end, the three context nodes `DIMENSION`, `UNITS`, and `CONVERSION` and the related attributes are created in the component controller of the `ZEXP_CONVERSION_RM_UI` component. The values of the properties and attributes are the same as those in Tables 4.1 and 4.2.

Because the context nodes for reverse mapping are included in the `ZEXP_CONVERSION_FB_MAIN` component, you need to set their **Interface Node** and **Input Element (Ext.)** properties. Then create the interface controller usage for the `USAGE_DIM_UI`, `USAGE_CONV_UI`, and `USAGE_UNIT_UI` usages of the `ZEXP_CONVERSION_DIM_UI`, `ZEXP_CONVERSION_UNITS_UI`, and `ZEXP_CONVERSION_CONV_UI` components (see Section 4.2.5). Next, define the usage of the component controller of `ZEXP_CONVERSION_FB_UI` for every controller usage. You can then map each context node of the component controller context to the controller usages.

Component ZEXP_CONVERSION_FB_MAIN

The `ZEXP_CONVERSION_FB_MAIN` component is the controller component. This component defines the usage of the `ZEXP_CONVERSION_MODEL` model compo-

4 | Multi-Component Applications

nent and the `ZEXP_CONVERSION_FB_UI` view component. It can also control the lifecycle of the model component and view component, and is used as a starting-point for defining the WD4A application. In the `ZEXP_CONVERSION_FB_MAIN` component, at runtime, the instances of the used components `ZEXP_CONVERSION_MODEL` and `ZEXP_CONVERSION_RM_UI` are created in the `wddoinit()` method of the component controller (see Listing 4.10).

```
METHOD wddoinit.
  DATA lr_usage    TYPE REF TO    if_wd_component_usage.
*---- Create model component
  lr_usage =   wd_this->wd_cpuse_usage_model( ).
  IF lr_usage->has_active_component( ) IS INITIAL.
    lr_usage->create_component( ).
  ENDIF.
*---- Create form based UI component
  lr_usage =   wd_this->wd_cpuse_usage_fb_ui( ).
  IF lr_usage->has_active_component( ) IS INITIAL.
    lr_usage->create_component( ).
  ENDIF.
ENDMETHOD.
```

Listing 4.10 Instantiating Used Components

This component requires only one window, which we'll call `W_DEFAULT` and into which the interface view of the `ZEXP_CONVERSION_FB_UI` view component is embedded. The controller component registers itself to the `CONVERT_VALUES` and `DIM_SELECTED` events of the view component (see Figure 4.43). The relevant method of the model component is called in `on_convert_values()`, the event handler method implemented for the event. Listing 4.11 shows you how to implement this event handler method.

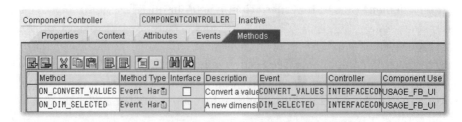

Figure 4.43 Registration of the Controller Component to Events of the View Component

```
METHOD on_convert_values.
  DATA lr_interfacecontroller TYPE REF TO ziwci_exp_conversion_model.
  lr_interfacecontroller = wd_this->wd_cpifc_usage_model( ).
*--- Call to model component
```

```
  lr_interfacecontroller->convert_values( ).
ENDMETHOD.
```

Listing 4.11 Implementing on_convert_values()

In the `on_dim_selected( )` event handler method implemented for the event, you need to invalidate the context nodes that provide the data for the units and the result. When the context nodes are accessed again, this invalidation causes any supply function methods that exist to be called. In our example, the data for the selection lists is determined in accordance with the newly selected dimensions. Listing 4.12 shows how to implement the `on_dim_selected( )` event handler method.

```
METHOD on_dim_selected.
  DATA lr_interfacecontroller TYPE REF TO ziwci_exp_conversion_model .
  lr_interfacecontroller =   wd_this->wd_cpifc_usage_model( ).
  lr_interfacecontroller->invalidate_nodes( ).
ENDMETHOD.
```

Listing 4.12 Implementing on_dim_selected()

The required context nodes of the model component are created in the component controller of the ZEXP_CONVERSION_FB_MAIN component via copying and mapping. We use reverse mapping to create the link to the view component ZEXP_CONVERSION_FB_UI. To do this, we first have to create the interface controller usage for the USAGE_FB_UI usage, as described in Section 4.2.5. First, define the usage of the component controller of ZEXP_CONVERSION_FB_MAIN. Then map each context node of the component controller context to the controller usages. The result should be the same as that for the ZEXP_CONVERSION_RM_MAIN component (see Figure 4.38).

In the last step, create the WD4A application called ZEXP_CONVERSION_FB. After the application is started, the display shown in Figure 4.44 should appear in the client.

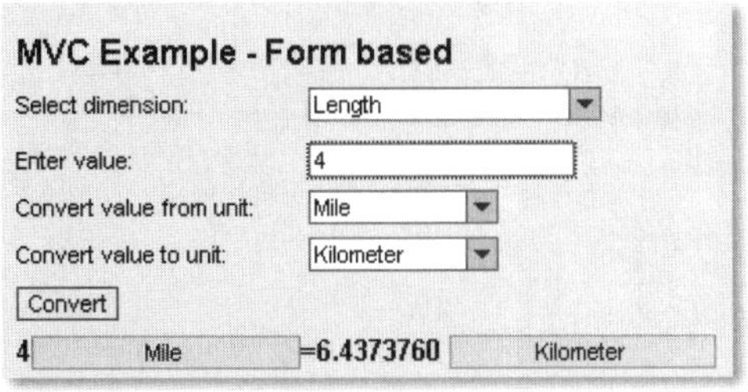

Figure 4.44 Converting Units Using a Form-Based UI

4.3.5 Overview of Used Components and Sample Applications

Table 4.3 contains an overview of the components developed in this chapter and their functions, and Table 4.4 gives an overview of the two sample applications that we developed and their components (the application-specific ones and the reused ones).

Component Name	Function
ZEXP_CONVERSION_RM_MAIN	Fulfills the controller function for converting units via user guidance.
ZEXP_CONVERSION_FB_MAIN	Fulfills the controller function for converting units via a form-based display.
ZEXP_CONVERSION_RM_UI	Component for displaying the individual steps with user guidance implemented via the RoadMap view element.
ZEXP_CONVERSION_FB_UI	Component for displaying the individual steps via a form-based display.
ZEXP_CONVERSION_MODEL	Contains the program logic for conversion and data management.
ZEXP_CONVERSION_DIM_UI	Component for selecting the dimension.
ZEXP_CONVERSION_UNIT_UI	Component for selecting the units and inputting the conversion value.
ZEXP_CONVERSION_CONV_UI	Component for displaying the results.

Table 4.3 Components and Functions

WD4A Application	Application-Specific Components	Reused Components
ZEXP_CONVERSION_RM (Sample application for converting units with user guidance)	▶ ZEXP_CONVERSION_RM_MAIN ▶ ZEXP_CONVERSION_RM_UI	▶ ZEXP_CONVERSION_MODEL ▶ ZEXP_CONVERSION_DIM_UI ▶ ZEXP_CONVERSION_UNIT_UI ▶ ZEXP_CONVERSION_CONV_UI
ZEXP_CONVERSION_FB (Sample application for converting units using forms)	▶ ZEXP_CONVERSION_FB_MAIN ▶ ZEXP_CONVERSION_FB_UI	

Table 4.4 Sample Applications of the Components

In many scenarios, we need to respond to changing conditions that cannot be defined at the time of development. Dynamic programming enables us to implement flexible and generic processes. This chapter describes how the Web Dynpro for ABAP (WD4A) framework can facilitate and accelerate the development process of dynamic applications.

5 Dynamic Component Applications

5.1 Types of Dynamic Changes

The examples we have developed so far were predominantly based on the following process flow:

1. Create the component.
2. Define the context nodes in the different controllers.
3. Define the structure of the layout in the view designer.
4. Bind the view element properties to the context.
5. Modify the hook methods.
6. Implement the event handler method.
7. Embed the views into the window.
8. Define the navigation within the window.
9. Create the application.

For this process to work, the user interaction, the data structure to be displayed, and the design of the user interface must all be known completely at the time of development.

However, the status at program runtime often requires changes to the user interface or to the downstream processes. In simple cases, you can control such changes by modifying the properties of view elements that can be manipulated by the program logic at runtime, providing that they are bound to context elements. Modifications such as the enabling and disabling of input fields thus can be controlled by modifying the bound context

5 | Dynamic Component Applications

attributes at runtime. The layout can still be generated declaratively, all view elements that are needed in the application are compiled in the user interface (UI) hierarchy, and the visibility and properties of the view elements are controlled through the context.

But those runtime changes are no longer sufficient if you have to deal with more complex requirements, such as occur when implementing comprehensively configurable applications or developing generic components that are to be reused in many different scenarios. In such cases, the WD4A framework allows for the manipulation of different parts of the components at runtime. That includes the following:

- Dynamic modification of the properties
- Dynamic modification of the UI hierarchy
- Dynamic binding of properties
- Dynamic modification of the context structure
- Dynamic modification of action assignments

The following sections describe those types of dynamic programming in greater detail, using examples to demonstrate the implementation of various functions.

5.1.1 Dynamic Modification of the Properties

Properties of view elements that can be bound to context nodes or context attributes can be identified by a button in the **Binding** column. In Figure 5.1, these are the properties **alignment**, **enabled**, **length**, **passwordField**, and **readOnly**. The **ID** and **explanation** properties can only be assigned static values.

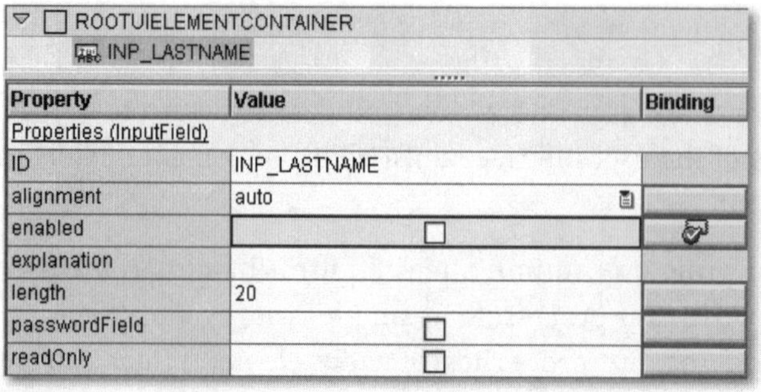

Figure 5.1 Some Properties of an InputField View Element

If a property is bound to a context node or a context attribute, this is indicated by an icon in the **Binding** column. In the example in Figure 5.1, the **enabled** property of the view element INP_LASTNAME is bound to a context attribute. Note that when you bind view-element properties to context attributes, the context attributes are assigned the correct types. Some types can be derived from the WD4A framework view: For example, the context attribute type to which properties are always bound using a checkbox is **WDY_BOOLEAN**. Text outputs require the **STRING** type, and for length indications you should use the **I** type (integer). To control the visibility of view elements, you should use the type **WDY_MD_UI_VISIBILITY**.

The IF_WDL_CORE interface contains the constants that enable you to show the view element (IF_WDL_CORE=>VISIBILITY_VISIBLE) and hide it (IF_WDL_CORE=>VISIBILITY_NONE). This is true for controlling the visibility of all view elements except for the tabs of the TabStrip view element that use the type **WDY_BOOLEAN**.

For other properties, you can derive the type from the name of the view element and of the property in the following way:

WDY_MD_[name of view element]_[name of property]

If that does not give the result you need, you should use the following combination:

WDUI_[name of view element]_[name of property]

Thus, for the **alignment** property of the InputField view element shown in Figure 5.1, you can determine the type **WDUI_INPUT_FIELD_ALIGNMENT**.

There are two other ways to determine the values that can be assigned to the context attribute. Originally, the values were stored in constants in the IF_WDL_STANDARD interface. With regard to the **alignment** property of the InputField view element shown in Figure 5.1, we have the following options:

- IF_WDL_STANDARD=>INPUTFIELDALIGNMENT_AUTO
- IF_WDL_STANDARD=>INPUTFIELDALIGNMENT_CENTER
- IF_WDL_STANDARD=>INPUTFIELDALIGNMENT_FORCEDLEFT
- IF_WDL_STANDARD=>INPUTFIELDALIGNMENT_ENDOFLINE
- IF_WDL_STANDARD=>INPUTFIELDALIGNMENT_FORCEDRGHT
- IF_WDL_STANDARD=>INPUTFIELDALIGNMENT_BGNOFLINE

A more recent concept involves accessing the name of the constant through the view element class. For the `InputField` view element, this would be the CL_WD_INPUT_FIELD class. For this purpose, you must go to the Class Builder (Transaction SE24) and find the name of the attribute in the **Attributes** tab. The attribute consists of an initial "E_," which stands for *enumeration*, and the name of the property. For the **alignment** property, we thus get the attribute E_ALIGNMENT (see Figure 5.2).

Figure 5.2 Determining the Values of Enumerations

For the `InputField` view element, however, the values are defined in the superclass. For this reason, you should navigate via the **Properties** tab to the superclass CL_WD_ABSTRACT_INPUT_FIELD. Figure 5.3 shows this class with two of its attributes, E_ALIGNMENT and T_STATE. Via the **Types** tab or the **Direct Type Entry** button you can navigate to the list of values for E_ALIGNMENT. Figure 5.4 shows a part of it.

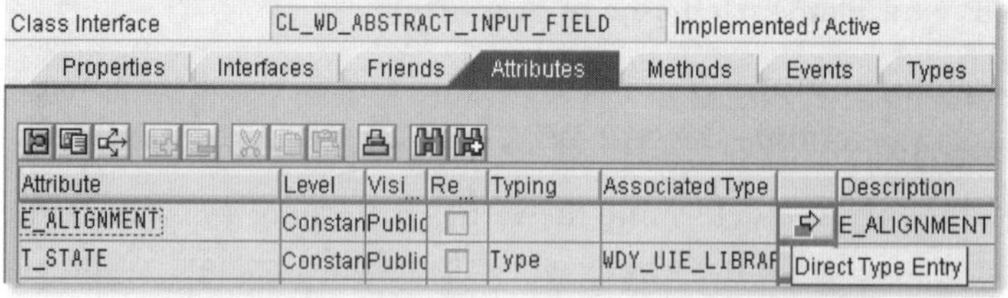

Figure 5.3 Defining the Enumeration Values in the Superclass

```
Public section           Active
     21  ⊟     BEGIN OF E_ALIGNMENT,
     22         AUTO TYPE WDY_UIE_LIBRARY_ENUM_TYPE VALUE '03',
     23         " InputFieldAlignment.auto,
```

Figure 5.4 Defining the Values for E_ALIGNMENT

In many cases, you don't need to follow this somewhat inconvenient method because you can simply derive the syntax of the constant from the name of the value. For example, if you want to use automatic enumeration, as shown in Figure 5.1 (enumeration value auto), you can derive the name of the constant as follows:

```
cl_wd_input_field=>e_alignment-auto
```

You should not use absolute values for assignments, given that the values can change over time and thus result in incompatible changes to your implementations.

5.1.2 Dynamic Modification of the UI Hierarchy

As described in Section 5.1.1, we can manipulate properties not only by binding them to context attributes, but also by accessing the objects in the UI hierarchy. This is possible in the hook method wddomodify() in the view controller. Only here does the WD4A framework allow you to access an instance of the view at runtime. It provides a parameter called VIEW of the type **IF_WD_VIEW**.

Let us now see how you can access the InputField view element and its **alignment** property in the wddomodify() method. We'll use the get_element() method to determine a reference to the instance of the view element in question by specifying the ID (here: INP_LASTNAME). Make sure you use the type-cast operator ?= for the return value:

```
DATA    lr_inputfield    TYPE REF TO    cl_wd_input_field.
  lr_inputfield ?= view->get_element( 'INP_LASTNAME' ).
```

The class in which the functions and properties of the InputField view element are implemented is CL_WD_INPUT_FIELD. CL_WD_INPUT_FIELD provides several different methods for determining and changing properties values. You can easily recognize those methods by the prefixes set_* and get_*. The available methods for the **alignment** property are set_alignment() and get_alignment(). Consequently, the statements for reading and changing the **alignment** property can look as follows:

```
DATA    lv_alignmnt    TYPE    wdui_input_field_alignment.
  lv_alignmnt    = lr_inputfield->get_alignment( ).
  lr_inputfield->set_alignment( IMPORTING value =
                   IF_WDL_STANDARD=>INPUTFIELDALIGNMENT_CENTER).
```

Structuring Views

Apart from changing the properties of declaratively created views, you can also generate new view elements and add them to the UI hierarchy, and you also can remove existing view elements. To better understand the individual steps and options involved in this, we must look more closely at the structure of a view.

Until now, we have used the term *view element* for any element that is to be arranged in a view. However, view elements can be categorized according to their usage, function, and properties. A view element represents a component in a view that can be referenced within the view by an ID. The following components are special cases of view elements: *UI element*, *layout*, and *layout data*. The *UI element container* represents a special case of the UI element. The classes listed in Table 5.1 represent those view components in the WD4A framework.

View Component	Name of ABAP Class
View element	CL_WDR_VIEW_ELEMENT
UI element	CL_WD_UI_ELEMENT
UI element container	CL_WD_UI_ELEMENT_CONTAINER
Layout	CL_WD_LAYOUT
Layout data	CL_WD_LAYOUT_DATA

Table 5.1 Components of a View and Associated Classes

Within a view, the hierarchy of view elements is built upon the root node. The root node always consists of a `TransparentContainer` view element that has the ID ROOTUIELEMENTCONTAINER. Based on this name, you can determine the specialization, namely the UI element container.

Deleting a View Element

Manipulations of the UI hierarchy always begin with the root node. Thus, the first step in those processes is the referencing of the view via the ID ROOTUIELEMENTCONTAINER:

```
DATA lr_container    TYPE REF TO  cl_wd_transparent_container.
  lr_container ?= view->get_element( 'ROOTUIELEMENTCONTAINER' ).
```

In the subsequent steps, you can then manipulate the hierarchy below the root node. For example, if you want to remove the `INP_LASTNAME` view element, you should use the following statement:

```
lr_container->remove_child( EXPORTING id = 'INP_LASTNAME' ).
```

You need to know that view components can have a certain specialization. In dynamic programming, this knowledge enables you to access the additional functions of those specializations.

For example, you only can perform add or delete actions for UI element container components. If, on the other hand, you had used the following statement to reference the root node, the delete function would not be available to you:

```
DATA  lr_container    TYPE REF TO   cl_wdr_view_element.
  lr_container = view->get_element( 'ROOTUIELEMENTCONTAINER' ).
```

In the ABAP Objects context, this means that the CL_WD_TRANSPARENT_CONTAINER class inherits the properties of its superclass and is enhanced by functions for manipulating components of the UI hierarchy, such as deletion and addition of view elements.

Figure 5.5 displays a simplified model of the inheritance hierarchy for the CL_WD_TRANSPARENT_CONTAINER class. Methods and attributes are not included for the sake of simplicity.

To obtain the name of a view element class, you must combine the prefix cl_wd with the name of the view element.

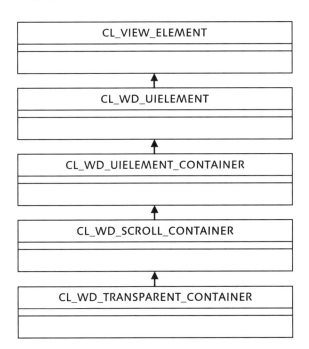

Figure 5.5 Class Diagram for CL_WD_TRANSPARENT_CONTAINER

Generating a New View Element

We already demonstrated how you can delete a view element from the UI hierarchy. Now let's look at how we can generate a new view element. The layout shown in Figure 5.1 is to be complemented with a `TextView` view element. To do that, we must perform the following steps:

1. **Create an instance of the new view element**
   The class of the view element contains a method that begins with the prefix `new_`. For the `TextView` view element, this is `new_text_view()`. The parameters of the `new_` methods more or less correspond to the properties that are provided by the view designer. Usually, you generate a new instance by specifying the parameters `ID` and `VIEW`, but those parameters are optional. If no `ID` is transferred, the WD4A framework automatically generates it. If the `VIEW` parameter remains blank, the system uses the view in which the `wddomodify()` method has been implemented. For our example, the implementation would look as follows:

   ```
   DATA lr_textview    TYPE REF TO   cl_wd_text_view.
     lr_textview = cl_wd_text_view=>new_text_view( id   = 'TXV_TOPIC'
                                                   view = view
                                                   text = 'HELLO!' ).
   ```

2. **Generate a layout data object**
   For embedding the view element into the layout, you need data that specifies the arrangement of the view element. This data depends on the layout type (`FlowLayout`, `RowLayout`, `MatrixLayout`, `GridLayout`) of the UI element container into which you want to embed the new view element. For example, layout type `MatrixLayout` allows you to specify the width and height of the cell.

   Our example uses layout type `FlowLayout`. Accordingly we need a new instance of the CL_WD_FLOW_DATA class (see Table 5.2). The implementation thus looks as follows:

   ```
   DATA lr_flow_data    TYPE REF TO cl_wd_flow_data.
     lr_flow_data = cl_wd_flow_data=>new_flow_data(
                                       element = lr_textview ).
   ```

Layout Type	Layout Data Class
FlowLayout	CL_WD_FLOW_DATA
RowLayout	CL_WD_ROW_DATA
	CL_WD_ROW_HEAD_DATA
MatrixLayout	CL_WD_MATRIX_DATA
	CL_WD_MATRIX_HEAD_DATA
GridLayout	CL_WD_GRID_DATA

Table 5.2 Layout Data Classes

3. **Add new view element to UI element container**

   The `add_child()` method enables you to attach a view element to the UI hierarchy. You can use the INDEX parameter to define the position within the UI element container.

   In our example, we want to the new view element to follow the Input-Field view element. For this reason we don't need to define the position explicitly. The implementation contains the following statements:

```
DATA  lr_container   TYPE REF TO   cl_wd_transparent_container.
  lr_container = view->get_element('ROOTUIELEMENTCONTAINER' ).
   lr_container->add_child( lr_textview ).
```

The `wddomodify()` method summarizes the implementation of the individual steps (see Listing 5.1).

```
METHOD wddomodifyview.
  DATA  lr_textview  TYPE REF TO cl_wd_text_view.
  DATA  lr_flow_data TYPE REF TO cl_wd_flow_data.
  DATA  lr_container TYPE REF TO cl_wd_transparent_container.
  IF first_time EQ abap_true.
    lr_textview = cl_wd_text_view=>new_text_view( id   = 'TXV_TOPIC'
                                                  view = view
                                                  text = 'Hello!' ).
    lr_flow_data = cl_wd_flow_data=>new_flow_data(
                                      element = lr_textview ).
    lr_container ?= view->get_element( 'ROOTUIELEMENTCONTAINER' ).
    lr_container->add_child( lr_textview ).
  ENDIF.
ENDMETHOD.
```

Listing 5.1 Implementing wddomodify()

The `FIRST_TIME` parameter is provided by the WD4A framework in order to ensure that the manipulation of the UI hierarchy occurs only once within the lifetime of the view. The client output looks as shown in Figure 5.6.

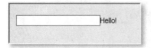

Figure 5.6 Display with Dynamically Generated TextView View Element

The `wddomodify()` method should only be used for manipulating view elements. Within `wddomodify()` you should neither manipulate the context, nor transfer messages to the Message Manager, nor trigger navigation by calling outbound plugs.

5.1.3 Dynamic Binding of Properties

The properties of dynamically generated view elements can be bound to the context, as is the case with a declaratively created view layout. This can occur during the creation of the instance of the new view element by transferring parameters in the `new_` methods. In that case, the parameters provided for binding the properties to the context are marked by the `BIND_` prefix (see Figure 5.7).

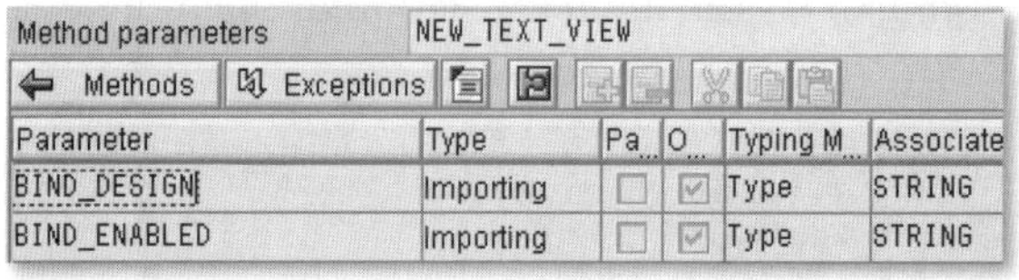

Method parameters	NEW_TEXT_VIEW				
← Methods ᵴ Exceptions					
Parameter	Type	Pa	O	Typing M	Associate
BIND_DESIGN	Importing	☐	☑	Type	STRING
BIND_ENABLED	Importing	☐	☑	Type	STRING

Figure 5.7 Context Binding Parameters

Another way to bind the properties to the context is to use a separate method and to overwrite the declaratively programmed binding. In this case, too, the methods of the corresponding view element classes contain the prefix `BIND_`.

You must specify the absolute path in order to bind properties to context attributes. You cannot use an index that refers to the position of the attribute in the context hierarchy.

The path results from the stringing together of context nodes and the relevant context attribute names, separated by periods:

```
[Context-Node_1].[Context-Node_2]...[Context-Node_n].[Context-Attribut]
```

The names of the context nodes and the context attribute consist of capital letters. Thus, we get the following notation for the context shown in Figure 5.8:

```
CONTROL.IFIELD.ENABLED
```

Figure 5.8 Sample Context for Dynamic Binding

The call of a method of the `InputField` view element to bind the **enabled** property would be implemented as shown in Listing 5.2.

```
DATA   lr_inputfield   TYPE REF TO cl_wd_input_field.
  lr_inputfield ?= view->get_element( 'INP_LASTNAME' ).
  lr_inputfield->bind_enabled( 'CONTROL.IFIELD.ENABLED' ).
```

Listing 5.2 Dynamic Binding of Properties

In order to delete the binding of a property to a context attribute, you must call the corresponding `bind_` method with an empty string.

5.1.4 Dynamic Modification of the Context

Each context node contains *node info* that describes its properties. This node info is used for dynamically modifying the context. In order to create a reference to the node info of a context node, the following two options are available:

1. Determine the reference to the node info through the root node:

    ```
    DATA lr_node_info TYPE REF TO if_wd_context_node_info.
      lr_node_info ?= wd_context->get_node_info( ).
      lr_node_info = lr_node_info->get_node_info('CONTROL' ).
    ```

2. Determine the reference to the node info through the context node:

    ```
    DATA lr_node_info TYPE REF TO if_wd_context_node_info.
    DATA lr_node      TYPE REF TO if_wd_context_node.
      lr_node = wd_context->get_child_node( 'CONTROL' ).
      lr_node_info ?= lr_node->get_node_info( ).
    ```

You can add attributes via the node info of the corresponding context node by calling the `add_attribute()` method. The parameter to be transferred, which contains the data for the new attribute, has the type **WDR_CONTEXT_ATTRIBUTE_INFO**. The name of the attribute should be unique with regard to the entire context. The type is transferred as text in parameter `TYPE_NAME` or as runtime object in parameter `RTTI`. Listing 5.3 contains the statements for adding a `READONLY` attribute to the `CONTROL` context node.

```
DATA lr_node_info TYPE REF TO if_wd_context_node_info.
DATA ls_attribute  TYPE  wdr_context_attribute_info.
  lr_node_info ?= wd_context->get_node_info( ).
  lr_node_info = lr_node_info->get_node_info( 'CONTROL' ).
  ls_attribute-name       = 'ENABLED'.
  ls_attribute-type_name = 'WDY_BOOLEAN'.
  lr_node_info->add_attribute( EXPORTING
                               attribute_info = ls_attribute ).
```

Listing 5.3 Example of the Dynamic Structure of the Context

We write and determine values of dynamically generated attributes by using the `get_attribute()` and `set_attribute()` methods of the interfaces `IF_WD_CONTEXT_NODE` and `IF_WD_CONTEXT_ELEMENT` respectively. New context nodes can be added to the corresponding context node by using the `add_new_child_node()` method in the node info.

5.1.5 Dynamic Modification of Action Assignments

View elements can trigger events that can be bound to actions. The definition of an action automatically involves the definition of an event handler method that is called at runtime when the event is triggered.

You can specify actions either dynamically or by a separate call during the creation of a view element instance. The `DropDownByIndex` view element, for example, uses the `ON_SELECT` parameter in its `new_dropdown_by_idx()` method (class CL_WD_DROPDOWN_BY_IDX). This parameter is used to bind the **onSelect** event to an action. A separate binding of the event can be achieved via the `set_on_select()` method. You can bind an icon to several different events of view elements. You can identify the ID of the view element that has triggered an event via the `WDEVENT` parameter in the event handler method that is associated with the action. Listing 5.4 shows an example of this.

```
METHOD onactiondo_submit.
  DATA lv_id    TYPE string.
  lv_id = wdevent->get_string( 'ID' ).
```

```
  CASE lv_id.
    WHEN 'BTN_PERSON'.
*--- Button to submit person data was pressed
    WHEN 'BTN_PRODUCT'.
*--- Button to submit product data was pressed
  ENDCASE.
ENDMETHOD.
```

Listing 5.4 Identifying the View Elements That Trigger an Event

5.2 Dynamic Programming—A Sample Application

We now want to implement the functions for the dynamic programming of WD4A components described in Section 5.1 in a sample application. For this purpose, we'll focus on the issue of country-specific address formats, an issue that often causes problems in the administration of business-partner data.

5.2.1 Dynamic Display of Address Data

The hierarchy and sequence of address fields differs from country to country. This makes it difficult to find a layout that can be applied to all address formats when designing a view. The effort to develop separate views for each country-specific format is too high.

In this respect, it is a good idea to create the view at runtime, depending on the required country-specific format. The view elements that represent the address components are arranged dynamically and based on metadata that describe the country-specific format. Table 5.3 shows address formats as they are used in the US and Great Britain. Note the differences in the building and room descriptions and in the ZIP codes.

Country	Sample Address	Address Components
USA	New Stuff Inc. Suite 370 31 West 52nd Street New York, NY 10019—7000 USA	▶ New Stuff: company name ▶ Inc.: Incorporated (type of company, stock corporation) ▶ Suite: room or several rooms in an office building ▶ 370: room number

Table 5.3 Country-Specific Address Formats

Country	Sample Address	Address Components
		▶ 31: building number ▶ West: part of the district ▶ 52nd Street: street name ▶ New York: city ▶ NY: standardized abbreviation for the state ▶ 10019: ZIP code ▶ 7000: four-digit code used for postal delivery ▶ USA: United States of America (country)
GB	Design Consulting Ltd. Stanton House 20 Lensfield Road CAMBRIDGE Cambridgeshire CB2 3EA UK	▶ Design Consulting: company name ▶ Ltd.: Limited (type of company, limited liability company) ▶ Stanton House: building name ▶ 20: building number ▶ Lensfield Road: street name ▶ Cambridge: city (usually in capital letters) ▶ Cambridgeshire: county ▶ CB2 3EA: postal code (either after blank space or in a new line) ▶ UK: country

Table 5.3 Country-Specific Address Formats (cont.)

The objective of our sample application is to present four fictitious companies from the US and Great Britain in their country-specific address format (see Table 5.4).

Sample Addresses	
New Stuff Inc. 31 West 52nd Street, Suite 370 New York, NY 10019–7000 USA	TechWare Corporation 900 West Chimes Street, Suite 2250 Baton Rouge, LA 70802–5814 USA

Table 5.4 Sample Addresses for the Application

Sample Addresses	
Design Consulting Ltd.	International Publishing Ltd.
Stanton House	Kingsbury House
20 Lensfield Road	9 Golden Ball Street
Cambridge	Norwich
Cambridgeshire CB2 3EA	Norfolk NR1 3EH
UK	UK

Table 5.4 Sample Addresses for the Application (cont.)

These addresses are maintained in the system via Transaction BP, while the WD4A application displays the address in the country-specific format. Moreover, the user should have the option of viewing the location of the companies through Google Maps (*http://maps.google.com*). We'll implement a separate link for this purpose.

Once the application ZEXP_DYNAMIC_BPA is started, a list of the implemented countries should first be displayed. The layout of this list will be created declaratively, which means it is defined in the view editor at runtime. Figure 5.9 shows the output of the declaratively created component of the view at runtime in the client.

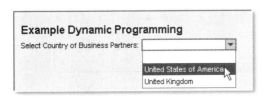

Figure 5.9 Selecting the Country of the Business Partner

When you have the selected the country, the corresponding addresses are determined. The layout is dynamically created in compliance with the country-specific default values and then output in the client (see Figure 5.10). Clicking the Create Link button creates a link (**Locate at Google Maps**) to the Google Maps API. If you click on that link, the Google Maps API outputs the location of the selected business partner in a new window corresponding to the selected type of display (see Figure 5.11). The user can choose between the following different display types:

5 | Dynamic Component Applications

- **Satellite**
  Display of the location in a satellite picture
- **Map**
  Cartographic display of the location
- **Hybrid**
  Display of the location in a satellite picture with indication of street names

Figure 5.10 Displaying the Address in Country-Specific Format

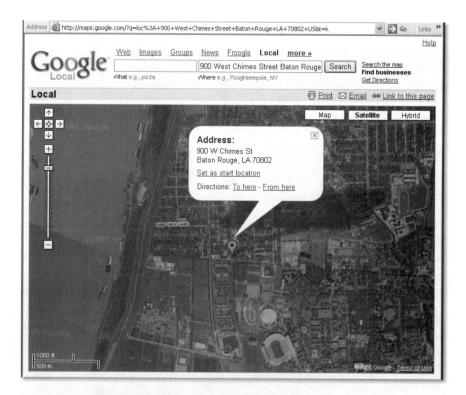

Figure 5.11 Displaying the Company Location Via Google Maps

5.2.2 Creating Business Partners

You can create business partners via Transaction BP. Select **Create · Organization** from the menu (see Figure 5.12).

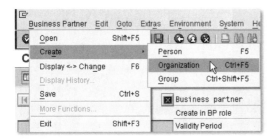

Figure 5.12 Creating Business Partners

The number for the new business partner is assigned automatically. Use the **Business Partner (Gen.)** role that is assigned by default. For our simple example it is not necessary to assign the business partner to a more specific role such as Financial Services or Prospect. The data listed in Table 5.4 must now be entered in the **Address** tab: Start with the **Name** of the company. Enter the string "WD4A" in the **Search Term 1/2** field. This way you can make sure that at runtime it will be possible to call data only for those business partners that we want to use for the sample application.

Figures 5.13 through 5.16 show the input fields for the remaining data. If you don't see the required input fields on your screen, then just click on the **More Fields** icon in the bottom right corner of the screen in order to display all available input fields.

Street address						
Building Code	SUITE	Room	370	Floor		
Street/House number	West 52nd Street			31		
Postal Code/City	10019-7000	New York				
Country	US	USA		Region	NY	New York
Time zone						

Figure 5.13 Address Data for New Stuff Inc.

Street address						
Street/House number	West Chimes Street			900		
Postal Code/City	70802-5814	Baton Rouge				
Country	US	USA		Region	LA	Louisiana
Time zone	CST					

Figure 5.14 Address Data for TechWare Corporation

5 | Dynamic Component Applications

Street address				
Building Code	Stanton House	Room	Floor	
Street/House number	Lensfield Road		20	
Postal Code/City	CB2 3EA	Cambridge		
Country	GB	United Kingdom	Region	CA	Cambridgeshire
Time zone	GMTUK			

Figure 5.15 Address Data for Design Consulting Ltd.

Street address				
Building Code	Kingsbury Ho	Room	Floor	
Street/House number	Golden Ball Street		9	
Postal Code/City	NR1 3EH	Norwich		
Country	GB	United Kingdom	Region	NK	Norfolk
Time zone	GMTUK			

Figure 5.16 Address Data for International Publishing Ltd.

The business partners have now been created and can be read by the WD4A application by using the corresponding APIs. The necessary statements to do that are described in the following sections.

5.2.3 Metadata for the Address Formats

In order to output the individual address components at the correct positions, we'll use a pattern in which the position of each field is defined by coordinates. The coordinates of the address fields are provided as metadata for each country. Based on those position details, the address is dynamically output. The arrangement of the fields is shown in Figure 5.17. Table 5.5 summarizes the country-specific metadata.

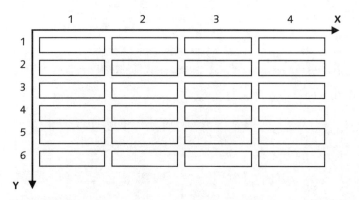

Figure 5.17 Pattern for Defining the Position of Address Fields

Field Name	Country	Y Position	X Position
DESCR	US	1	1
CITY	US	3	1
POSTL_COD1	US	3	3
STREET	US	2	2
HOUSE_NO	US	2	1
BUILDING	US	2	3
ROOM_NO	US	2	4
COUNTRY	US	4	1
REGION	US	3	2
DESCR	UK	1	1
CITY	UK	4	1
POSTL_COD1	UK	5	2
STREET	UK	3	2
HOUSE_NO	UK	3	1
BUILDING	UK	2	1
COUNTRY	UK	6	1
REGION	UK	5	1

Table 5.5 Metadata for the Address Field Positions

We create the metadata repository at the initialization time of the WD4A component. The component is assigned the name ZEXP_DYNAMIC_BPA. The context node META_ADDRESS is filled in the wddoinit() method in the component controller. The **Cardinality** property of the context node META_ADDRESS has the value **0..n**. The context attribute FIELD_NAME has the type **STRING**, and the context attribute COUNTRY has the type **LAND1**. The two context attributes for defining the position of an address field, POSITION_X and POSITION_Y, have the type **I**. The context attribute LONG indicates whether the region is to be output as full text (e.g., Norfolk) or in short form (e.g., LA); for this purpose the **WDY_BOOLEAN** type is used (see Figure 5.18).

5 | Dynamic Component Applications

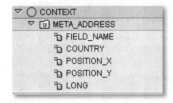

Figure 5.18 Context Node for Address Metadata

Listing 5.5 shows the implementation of the data listed in the Table 5.5 method `wddoinit()` of the component controller.

```
METHOD wddoinit.
  DATA  lr_node         TYPE REF TO if_wd_context_node.
  DATA  ls_meta_address TYPE
               ig_componentcontroller=>element_meta_address.
  DATA  lt_meta_address TYPE
               ig_componentcontroller=>elements_meta_address.
*--- Meta data - US addresses
  ls_meta_address-field_name = 'DESCR'.
  ls_meta_address-country    = 'US'.
  ls_meta_address-position_x = 1.
  ls_meta_address-position_y = 1.
  APPEND ls_meta_address TO lt_meta_address.
  ls_meta_address-field_name = 'CITY'.
  ls_meta_address-country    = 'US'.
  ls_meta_address-position_x = 1.
  ls_meta_address-position_y = 3.
  APPEND ls_meta_address TO lt_meta_address.
  ls_meta_address-field_name = 'POSTL_COD1'.
  ls_meta_address-country    = 'US'.
  ls_meta_address-position_x = 3.
  ls_meta_address-position_y = 3.
  APPEND ls_meta_address TO lt_meta_address.
  ls_meta_address-field_name = 'STREET'.
  ls_meta_address-country    = 'US'.
  ls_meta_address-position_x = 2.
  ls_meta_address-position_y = 2.
  APPEND ls_meta_address TO lt_meta_address.
  ls_meta_address-field_name = 'HOUSE_NO'.
  ls_meta_address-country    = 'US'.
  ls_meta_address-position_x = 1.
  ls_meta_address-position_y = 2.
  APPEND ls_meta_address TO lt_meta_address.
  ls_meta_address-field_name = 'BUILDING'.
```

```abap
  ls_meta_address-country    = 'US'.
  ls_meta_address-position_x = 3.
  ls_meta_address-position_y = 2.
  APPEND ls_meta_address TO lt_meta_address.
  ls_meta_address-field_name = 'ROOM_NO'.
  ls_meta_address-country    = 'US'.
  ls_meta_address-position_x = 4.
  ls_meta_address-position_y = 2.
  APPEND ls_meta_address TO lt_meta_address.
  ls_meta_address-field_name = 'COUNTRY'.
  ls_meta_address-country    = 'US'.
  ls_meta_address-position_x = 1.
  ls_meta_address-position_y = 4.
  APPEND ls_meta_address TO lt_meta_address.
  ls_meta_address-field_name = 'REGION'.
  ls_meta_address-country    = 'US'.
  ls_meta_address-position_x = 2.
  ls_meta_address-position_y = 3.
  APPEND ls_meta_address TO lt_meta_address.
*--- Meta data - UK addresses
  ls_meta_address-field_name = 'DESCR'.
  ls_meta_address-country    = 'GB'.
  ls_meta_address-position_x = 1.
  ls_meta_address-position_y = 1.
  APPEND ls_meta_address TO lt_meta_address.
  ls_meta_address-field_name = 'CITY'.
  ls_meta_address-country    = 'GB'.
  ls_meta_address-position_x = 1.
  ls_meta_address-position_y = 4.
  APPEND ls_meta_address TO lt_meta_address.
  ls_meta_address-field_name = 'POSTL_COD1'.
  ls_meta_address-country    = 'GB'.
  ls_meta_address-position_x = 2.
  ls_meta_address-position_y = 5.
  APPEND ls_meta_address TO lt_meta_address.
  ls_meta_address-field_name = 'STREET'.
  ls_meta_address-country    = 'GB'.
  ls_meta_address-position_x = 2.
  ls_meta_address-position_y = 3.
  APPEND ls_meta_address TO lt_meta_address.
  ls_meta_address-field_name = 'HOUSE_NO'.
  ls_meta_address-country    = 'GB'.
  ls_meta_address-position_x = 1.
  ls_meta_address-position_y = 3.
  APPEND ls_meta_address TO lt_meta_address.
```

```
        ls_meta_address-field_name = 'BUILDING'.
        ls_meta_address-country     = 'GB'.
        ls_meta_address-position_x = 1.
        ls_meta_address-position_y = 2.
        APPEND ls_meta_address TO lt_meta_address.
        ls_meta_address-field_name = 'COUNTRY'.
        ls_meta_address-country     = 'GB'.
        ls_meta_address-position_x = 1.
        ls_meta_address-position_y = 6.
        APPEND ls_meta_address TO lt_meta_address.
        ls_meta_address-field_name = 'REGION'.
        ls_meta_address-country     = 'GB'.
        ls_meta_address-position_x = 1.
        ls_meta_address-position_y = 5.
        ls_meta_address-long        = abap_true.
        APPEND ls_meta_address TO lt_meta_address.
        lr_node = wd_context->get_child_node( 'META_ADDRESS' ).
        lr_node->bind_table( new_items          = lt_meta_address
                             set_initial_elements = abap_true ).
ENDMETHOD.
```

Listing 5.5 Compiling the Metadata in Method wddoinit()

5.2.4 Implementation and Layout of the Component

The view of component `ZEXP_DYNAMIC_BPA` contains a `TextView` view element, a `Label` view element, and a `DropDownByIndex` view element. These view elements represent the declaratively created part of the layout. `RowLayout` (see Figure 5.19) is the layout type that was chosen in the ROOTUIELE-MENTCONTAINER. The layout type must be taken into account later for the dynamically created view elements.

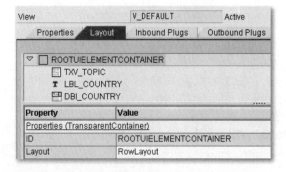

Figure 5.19 Static View Elements in RowLayout

The view controller requires the data of the component controller context node META_ADDRESS. For this reason, the context node is copied into the view-controller context, and a mapping is defined between the attributes of both context nodes. In addition, the view-controller context is assigned a context node called CONTENT under which the data to be displayed is grouped. The COUNTRY context node that is supposed to manage the list of countries is created under the context node CONTENT so that the country-selection list can be filled with data. The **texts** property of the DropDownByIndex view element DBI_COUNTRY is bound to the LANDX50 attribute of context node COUNTRY. The two attributes of the context node—LANDX50 and LAND1—are filled in the supply function method supply_country(). Listing 5.6 shows the implementation.

```
METHOD supply_country.
  DATA ls_country    TYPE    if_v_default=>element_country.
  DATA lt_country    TYPE    if_v_default=>elements_country.
*--- Add initial line to dropdown list
  APPEND ls_country TO lt_country.
*--- Add USA
  ls_country-land1    = 'US'.
  ls_country-landx50 = 'United States of America'.
  APPEND ls_country TO lt_country.
*--- Add UK
  ls_country-land1    = 'GB'.
  ls_country-landx50 = 'United Kingdom'.
  APPEND ls_country TO lt_country.
*--- Bind to context node
  node->bind_table( new_items          = lt_country
                    set_initial_elements = abap_true ).
ENDMETHOD.
```

Listing 5.6 Supply Function Method for Filling the Countries List

Actions in the View Controller

Two actions—DO_DISPLAY_BP and DO_CREATELINK—are defined in the **Actions** tab. Once a country has been selected, the DO_DISPLAY_BP action is to be triggered at runtime through the **onSelect** event of the DBI_COUNTRY view element. The event-handler method for this action is assigned the role of retrieving the address data. When implementing the event-handler method onactiondo_display_bp(), you must perform the following steps:

1. Determine the selected country.
2. Find all business partners of the selected country.

3. Determine the detail data for the business partners.

4. Bind the data to the context node ADDRESS_DATA.

5. The context node ADDRESS_DATA contains the data of the business partners you have determined. The properties of the dynamically created view elements are bound to the attributes of the context node ADDRESS_DATA (see Figure 5.20).

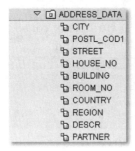

Figure 5.20 Attributes of Context Node ADDRESS_DATA

6. Except for the attributes DESCR and PARTNER, the types correspond to those of the fields with the same names in ABAP Dictionary structure BAPIBUS1006_ADDRESS. Context attribute DESCR has the type **BUS000FLDS-DESCRIP**, while context attribute PARTNER has type **BU_PARTNER**.

Determining Business Partner Data

Once the selected country has been read through the lead selection of context node COUNTRY, the business partner from the country must be determined. For this purpose, function module BUPA_SEARCH is used. We transfer the string "WD4A" in parameter iv_sort1. This string enables us to limit the search result to the business-partner data we created in Section 5.2.2. We then use the function modules BUP_PARTNER_DESCRIPTION_GET and BUPA_ADDRESS_GET_DETAIL to determine additional details of the address data, which we'll store in the internal table lt_address_data. This table is then bound to context node ADDRESS_DATA.

Listing 5.7 shows how the onactiondo_display_bp() method is implemented.

```
METHOD onactiondo_display_bp.
  DATA  ls_bapibus1006_addr  TYPE bapibus1006_address.
  DATA  ls_address_data      TYPE if_v_default=>element_address_data.
```

```abap
  DATA lt_address_data     TYPE if_v_default=>elements_address_data.
  DATA lt_bupa_result      TYPE TABLE OF bus020_search_result.
  DATA ls_bupa_result      TYPE          bus020_search_result.
  DATA ls_search_address   TYPE          bupa_addr_search.
  DATA lr_node             TYPE REF TO   if_wd_context_node.
  DATA lr_sub_node         TYPE REF TO   if_wd_context_node.
  DATA lr_element          TYPE REF TO   if_wd_context_element.
*--- Get country selection from context node
  lr_node = wd_context->get_child_node( 'CONTENT' ).
  lr_sub_node = lr_node->get_child_node( 'COUNTRY' ).
  lr_element = lr_sub_node->get_lead_selection( ).
  lr_element->get_attribute( EXPORTING name  = 'LAND1'
             IMPORTING value = ls_search_address-country ).
*--- Search for business partners of the selected country
  CALL FUNCTION 'BUPA_SEARCH'
    EXPORTING
      is_address      = ls_search_address
      iv_partner      = '*'
      iv_sort1        = 'WD4A'
    TABLES
      et_search_result = lt_bupa_result.
*--- Get detailed data of search result
  LOOP AT lt_bupa_result INTO ls_bupa_result.
*------ Get business partner name
    CALL FUNCTION 'BUP_PARTNER_DESCRIPTION_GET'
      EXPORTING
        i_partner         = ls_bupa_result-partner
      IMPORTING
        e_description_name = ls_address_data-descr
      EXCEPTIONS
        partner_not_found = 1
        wrong_parameters  = 2
        internal_error    = 3
        OTHERS            = 4.
    IF sy-subrc EQ 0.
*------ Get business partner detailed address data
      CALL FUNCTION 'BUPA_ADDRESS_GET_DETAIL'
        EXPORTING
          iv_partner = ls_bupa_result-partner
        IMPORTING
          es_address = ls_bapibus1006_addr.
      ls_address_data-partner = ls_bupa_result-partner.
      MOVE-CORRESPONDING ls_bapibus1006_addr TO ls_address_data.
      APPEND ls_address_data TO lt_address_data.
    ENDIF.
```

```
    ENDLOOP.
*--- Bind address detailed data to context node
  lr_sub_node = lr_node->get_child_node( 'ADDRESS_DATA' ).
  lr_sub_node->bind_table( new_items            = lt_address_data
                           set_initial_elements = abap_true ).
ENDMETHOD.
```

Listing 5.7 Implementation of onactiondo_display_bp()

Display Options in Google Maps

The user can choose between different types of display (**Satellite**, **Map**, and **Hybrid**) that are provided by Google Maps. For this purpose, we add the context node OPTION, which contains the attributes KEY and VALUE, to the view controller context under context node CONTENT. The context node is filled with data by using the supply function method supply_option().

In our application, radio buttons are used for the selection. These radio buttons are also generated dynamically at the end of the address data display. A selection is only valid for one business partner. Listing 5.8 shows the implementation of supply function method supply_option().

```
METHOD supply_option.
  DATA  ls_text_design  TYPE if_v_default=>element_option.
  DATA  lt_text_designs TYPE if_v_default=>elements_option.
*----- Create value-key list of different
  ls_text_design-key   = 'k'.
  ls_text_design-value = 'Satellite'.
  APPEND ls_text_design TO lt_text_designs.
  ls_text_design-key   = ''.
  ls_text_design-value = 'Map'.
  APPEND ls_text_design TO lt_text_designs.
  ls_text_design-key   = 'h'.
  ls_text_design-value = 'Hybrid'.
  APPEND ls_text_design TO lt_text_designs.
*----- Fill context node
  node->bind_elements( new_items = lt_text_designs ).
ENDMETHOD.
```

Listing 5.8 Supply Function Method for Filling the Display Options

Dynamic View Composition: Initialization

Once a country has been selected, the address data is determined in the event handler method onactiondo_display_bp(). The address data is now to be output in the country-specific format. The dynamic composition of the view layout is carried out in the wddomodify() method.

To better understand the implementation, we should look separately at the individual fragments of the method. First, a reference to ROOTUIELEMENT-CONTAINER must be determined. The view is to be rebuilt with each request-response cycle. We therefore delete the view elements that have been dynamically created earlier.

```
lr_container ?= view->get_element( 'ROOTUIELEMENTCONTAINER' ).
*--- Initialize dynamic UI Tree-remove all dynamic view elements
LOOP AT wd_this->mt_child_ids INTO lv_child_id .
  lr_container->remove_child( EXPORTING id = lv_child_id ).
ENDLOOP.
```

Class CL_WD_UIELEMENT_CONTAINER provides two different methods for deletions: The first one is remove_all_children(). This method removes all view elements, not only the ones that have been created dynamically. However, because we want to be able to select the country, we must separately remove the view elements that have been dynamically added to the UI hierarchy.

To separate the statically created view elements from the dynamically created ones we store the IDs of the dynamically created view elements in an internal table, which has been defined as a view controller attribute. When a view element is added to the UI hierarchy, its ID is stored in table mt_child_ids. The remove_child() method is used at the beginning of wddomodify() to delete all dynamically created view elements by transferring the corresponding IDs.

Dynamic View Composition: Determining Address Metadata

In the next step, we'll read the address data that has been determined for the selected country by the event-handler method onactiondo_display_bp():

```
lr_node    = wd_context->get_child_node( 'CONTENT' ).
lr_sub_node = lr_node->get_child_node( 'ADDRESS_DATA' ).
lr_sub_node->get_static_attributes_table( IMPORTING
                                    table = lt_addr_data ).
```

lt_addr_data now contains the address data of the business partners for the selected country. We want to determine the metadata for the country in question in order to be able to output the address in compliance with the country's conventions. The next step accesses the metadata:

```
lr_node = wd_context->get_child_node( 'META_ADDRESS' ).
lr_node->get_static_attributes_table( IMPORTING
                                      table = lt_meta_addr ).
```

We now need a process for sorting according to the position values so that the UI hierarchy can be built up sequentially.

```
SORT lt_meta_address BY position_y position_x.
```

The LOOP statement is used to determine the position of each address field in the view based on the metadata. The Y position is temporarily stored and compared with the newly determined metadata values. If the values do not match, a new row must be created. This is done using the layout data class of the corresponding layout type (see Section 5.1.2).

The UI element container into which the dynamically created view elements are embedded contains a RowData layout type. A view element is positioned in a new row by creating a layout data object of the CL_WD_ROW_HEAD_DATA class:

```
lr_row_head = cl_wd_row_head_data=>new_row_head_data(
                                   element = lr_textview ).
```

Dynamic View Composition: Adding Display Options

Once the address has been completely composed, the selection options for creating the link to Google Maps are compiled. The statements needed for that have been previously stored in separate methods. The compilation of the RadioButton view elements is implemented in method add_option() (see Listing 5.9).

```
METHOD add_option.
   DATA lr_container        TYPE REF TO cl_wd_uielement_container.
   DATA lr_row_head_data    TYPE REF TO cl_wd_row_head_data.
   DATA lr_radiobutton      TYPE REF TO cl_wd_radiobutton_group_by_idx.
   DATA lv_child_id         TYPE        string.
   DATA lv_bind_texts       TYPE        string.
   lr_container ?= ir_view->get_element( 'ROOTUIELEMENTCONTAINER' ).
   lv_bind_texts = 'CONTENT.OPTION.VALUE'.
   CONCATENATE iv_id 'RBN' INTO lv_child_id.
   lr_radiobutton =
     cl_wd_radiobutton_group_by_idx=>new_radiobutton_group_by_idx(
                          view       = ir_view
                          id         = lv_child_id
                          bind_texts = lv_bind_texts ).
*------ Create new line
```

```abap
  lr_row_head_data = cl_wd_row_head_data=>new_row_head_data(
                                      element = lr_radiobutton ).
  lr_radiobutton->set_layout_data( lr_row_head_data ).
  lr_container->add_child( lr_radiobutton ).
  APPEND lv_child_id TO wd_this->mt_child_ids.
ENDMETHOD.
```

Listing 5.9 Implementing add_option()

The method that implements the dynamic creation of the Button view element with the **Create Link** label is add_button() (see Listing 5.10). The DO_CREATELINK action is linked to the **onAction** event of the Button view element. The ID of the Button view element is used to determine which button was pushed: If, for each business partner, the button is dynamically added to the layout by calling the add_button() method, the view element ID includes the letter B and the partner number.

```abap
METHOD add_button.
  DATA lr_container     TYPE REF TO cl_wd_uielement_container.
  DATA lr_row_head_data TYPE REF TO cl_wd_row_head_data.
  DATA lr_button        TYPE REF TO cl_wd_button.
  DATA lv_child_id      TYPE        string.
  lr_container ?= ir_view->get_element('ROOTUIELEMENTCONTAINER' ).
  CONCATENATE 'B' iv_partner INTO lv_child_id.
  CONDENSE lv_child_id NO-GAPS.
  lr_button = cl_wd_button=>new_button( view      = ir_view
                                        id        = lv_child_id
                                        text      = 'Create Link'
                                        on_action = 'DO_CREATELINK' ).
  APPEND lv_child_id IO wd_this->mt_child_ids.
*------ Create new line
  lr_row_head_data = cl_wd_row_head_data=>new_row_head_data(
                                      element = lr_button ).
  lr_button->set_layout_data( lr_row_head_data ).
  lr_container->add_child( lr_button ).
ENDMETHOD.
```

Listing 5.10 Implementing add_button()

When the **Create Link** button is pushed, the Uniform Resource Identifier (URI) for determining the business partner location is created based on the selected option (**Satellite**, **Map**, or **Hybrid**) and integrated into the view by means of a LinkToUrl view element (see Figure 5.21). The partner number is extracted from the view element ID after the first character in method onactiondo_createlink().

```
wdevent->get_data( EXPORTING name  = 'ID'
                   IMPORTING value = lv_id ).
lv_partner = lv_id+1(10).
```

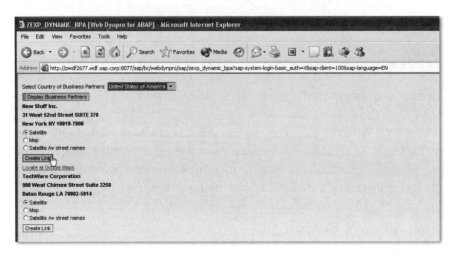

Figure 5.21 Address Display and Link Creation

The partner number is then used to read the exact address data of the business partner, which is needed for the creation of the link.

```
lt_addr_data = wd_this->read_address_data( ).
READ TABLE lt_addr_data INTO ls_addr_data WITH KEY
                                    partner = lv_partner.
```

The client only displays a Google Maps link for one business partner. To be able to tell for which partner the event-handler method onactiondo_createlink() was called, the partner number is stored in view controller attribute mv_link4partner (**BU_PARTNER** type) and queried in method wddomodifyview() when view elements are added.

```
IF wd_this->mv_link4partner EQ ls_addr_data-partner.
  wd_this->add_linktourl( ir_view   = view ).
ENDIF.
```

Table 5.6 lists the parameters used in the URI, including their functions.[1]

---

[1] You can find more information in the online API documentation for Google Maps at http://www.google.com/apis/maps.

5.2 Dynamic Programming—A Sample Application

Parameter	Function	Sample Values
hl	Language definition	en, de
t	Definition of display format	h (hybrid), k (satellite), no value (map)
q	Search term for the location	q=loc... (address)

Table 5.6 Parameters Used in Links to Google Maps

The URI creation occurs in event-handler method `onactiondo_createlink()` (see Listing 5.11).

```
METHOD onactiondo_createlink.
  DATA  lt_splittab   TYPE string_table.
  DATA  ls_split      TYPE string.
  DATA  lr_node       TYPE REF TO if_wd_context_node.
  DATA  lr_sub_node   TYPE REF TO if_wd_context_node.
  DATA  lv_id         TYPE string.
  DATA  lt_addr_data  TYPE if_v_default=>elements_address_data.
  DATA  ls_addr_data  TYPE if_v_default=>element_address_data.
  DATA  lv_partner    TYPE bu_partner.
  DATA  lv_street     TYPE string.
  DATA  lv_city       TYPE string.
  DATA  ls_t005u      TYPE t005u.
  DATA  ls_option     TYPE if_v_default=>element_option.
  DATA  lr_element    TYPE REF TO if_wd_context_element.
  DATA  lv_option_key TYPE c.
*--- Determine partner number from view element ID
  wdevent->get_data( EXPORTING name  = 'ID'
                     IMPORTING value = lv_id ).
  lv_partner = lv_id+1(10).
*--- Determine type of Google Maps display, i.e. map, hybrid etc.
  lr_node = wd_context->get_child_node( 'CONTENT' ).
  lr_sub_node  = lr_node->get_child_node( 'OPTION' ).
  lr_element = lr_sub_node->get_lead_selection( ).
  lr_element->get_attribute( EXPORTING  name = 'KEY'
                             IMPORTING value = lv_option_key ).
*--- Read address data for the selected country
  lr_node     = wd_context->get_child_node( 'CONTENT' ).
  lr_sub_node = lr_node->get_child_node( 'ADDRESS_DATA' ).
  lr_sub_node->get_static_attributes_table( IMPORTING
                                           table = lt_addr_data ).
  READ TABLE lt_addr_data INTO ls_addr_data WITH KEY
                                           partner = lv_partner.
  IF sy-subrc EQ 0.
    SPLIT ls_addr_data-street AT space INTO TABLE lt_splittab.
```

```abap
        LOOP AT lt_splittab INTO ls_split.
          CONCATENATE lv_street ls_split '+' INTO lv_street.
        ENDLOOP.
        CLEAR lt_splittab.
        SPLIT ls_addr_data-city AT space INTO TABLE lt_splittab.
        LOOP AT lt_splittab INTO ls_split.
          CONCATENATE lv_city ls_split '+' INTO lv_city.
        ENDLOOP.
        IF ls_addr_data-country EQ 'US'.
*--- Create a link to Google Maps for an US address
          CONCATENATE 'http://maps.google.com/?q=loc%3A+'
                      ls_addr_data-house_no '+' lv_street lv_city
                      ls_addr_data-region '+' ls_addr_data-postl_cod1(5)
                      '+' ls_addr_data-country '&t=' lv_option_key
                      INTO wd_this->mv_url.
        ELSEIF ls_addr_data-country EQ 'GB'.
          SELECT SINGLE * FROM t005u INTO ls_t005u
                                  WHERE land1 = ls_addr_data-country
                                  AND   bland = ls_addr_data-region
                                  AND   spras = sy-langu.
*--- Create a link to Google Maps for an UK address
          CONCATENATE 'http://maps.google.com/?q=loc%3A+'
                      lv_street lv_city
                      ls_t005u-bezei '+' ls_addr_data-postl_cod1(3) '+'
                      ls_addr_data-country '&t=' lv_option_key
                      INTO wd_this->mv_url.
        ENDIF.
*--- Keep partner number for which the link was created
        wd_this->mv_link4partner = lv_partner.
      ENDIF.
ENDMETHOD.
```

Listing 5.11 Compiling the Links to Google Maps

Method `add_linktourl()` implements the statements for adding the `Link-ToUrl` view element to the view (see Listing 5.12).

```abap
METHOD add_linktourl.
  DATA lr_container      TYPE REF TO cl_wd_uielement_container.
  DATA lr_row_head       TYPE REF TO cl_wd_row_head_data.
  DATA lr_linktourl      TYPE REF TO cl_wd_link_to_url.
  DATA lv_child_id       TYPE        string.
  lr_container ?= ir_view->get_element( 'ROOTUIELEMENTCONTAINER' ).
  lv_child_id = 'LTU_MAP'.
  lr_linktourl = cl_wd_link_to_url=>new_link_to_url(
                         id        = lv_child_id
```

```abap
                              reference = wd_this->mv_url
                              text      = 'Locate at Google Maps' ).
  lr_row_head   = cl_wd_row_head_data=>new_row_head_data(
                                        element = lr_linktourl ).
  lr_linktourl->set_layout_data( lr_row_head ).
  lr_container->add_child( lr_linktourl ).
  APPEND lv_child_id TO wd_this->mt_child_ids.
ENDMETHOD.
```

Listing 5.12 Adding a LinkToUrl View Element

Dynamic View Composition: Compiling the Calls

Finally, Listing 5.13 shows the entire process of the dynamic view composition in method wddomodify().

```abap
METHOD wddomodifyview.
  DATA lr_node       TYPE REF TO if_wd_context_node.
  DATA lr_sub_node   TYPE REF TO if_wd_context_node.
  DATA lr_container  TYPE REF TO cl_wd_uielement_container.
  DATA lr_row_head   TYPE REF TO cl_wd_row_head_data.
  DATA ls_addr_data  TYPE if_v_default=>element_address_data.
  DATA lt_addr_data  TYPE if_v_default=>elements_address_data.
  DATA lt_meta_addr  TYPE ig_componentcontroller=>elements_meta_address.
  DATA ls_meta_addr  TYPE ig_componentcontroller=>element_meta_address.
  DATA lv_position_y TYPE i.
  DATA lr_textview   TYPE REF TO cl_wd_text_view.
  DATA lv_text       TYPE string.
  DATA lv_sytabix1   TYPE string.
  DATA lv_sytabix2   TYPE string.
  DATA lv_child_id   TYPE string.
  DATA ls_t005u      TYPE t005u.
  FIELD-SYMBOLS: <lv_content>     TYPE ANY.
  IF first_time IS INITIAL.
    lr_container ?= view->get_element( 'ROOTUIELEMENTCONTAINER' ).
*--- Initialize dynamic UI tree - remove all dynamic view elements
    LOOP AT wd_this->mt_child_ids INTO lv_child_id .
      lr_container->remove_child( EXPORTING id = lv_child_id ).
    ENDLOOP.
*--- Read address data for the selected country
    lr_node     = wd_context->get_child_node( 'CONTENT' ).
    lr_sub_node = lr_node->get_child_node( 'ADDRESS_DATA' ).
    lr_sub_node->get_static_attributes_table( IMPORTING
                                              table = lt_addr_data ).
*--- Read meta data of address format
    lr_node = wd_context->get_child_node( 'META_ADDRESS' ).
```

```abap
      lr_node->get_static_attributes_table( IMPORTING
                                     table = lt_meta_addr ).
   SORT lt_meta_addr BY position_y position_x.
   LOOP AT lt_addr_data INTO ls_addr_data.
     CLEAR: lv_position_y, lv_text.
     lv_sytabix1 = sy-tabix.
     LOOP AT lt_meta_addr INTO ls_meta_addr WHERE
                          country EQ ls_addr_data-country.
       lv_sytabix2 = syst-tabix.
       ASSIGN COMPONENT ls_meta_addr-field_name
                  OF STRUCTURE ls_addr_data TO <lv_content>.
       IF sy-subrc = 0.
         IF ls_meta_addr-long IS NOT INITIAL.
*------ Read region description
           SELECT SINGLE * FROM t005u INTO ls_t005u
                             WHERE land1 = ls_addr_data-country
                             AND   bland = <lv_content>
                             AND   spras = sy-langu.
           IF sy-subrc = 0. <lv_content> = ls_t005u-bezei. ENDIF.
         ENDIF.
         IF lv_position_y NE ls_meta_addr-position_y
                          AND lv_position_y IS NOT INITIAL.
           lr_textview = cl_wd_text_view=>new_text_view( view  = view
                                         id    = lv_child_id
                       design = cl_wd_text_view=>e_design-emphasized
                                         text  = lv_text   ).
           APPEND lv_child_id TO wd_this->mt_child_ids.
           lv_position_y = ls_meta_addr-position_y.
*--- Create a new line
           lr_row_head = cl_wd_row_head_data=>new_row_head_data(
                                         element = lr_textview ).
           lr_textview->set_layout_data( lr_row_head ).
           lr_container->add_child( lr_textview ).
           lv_text = <lv_content>.
           CONCATENATE  ls_meta_addr-field_name lv_sytabix1
                     lv_sytabix2 lv_child_id INTO lv_child_id.
           CONDENSE lv_child_id NO-GAPS.
         ELSE.
*--- Append to the same line
           CONCATENATE lv_text <lv_content> INTO lv_text
                                         SEPARATED BY space.
           CONCATENATE  ls_meta_addr-field_name lv_sytabix1
                      lv_sytabix2 lv_child_id INTO lv_child_id.
           CONDENSE lv_child_id NO-GAPS.
           lv_position_y = ls_meta_addr-position_y.
```

```
            ENDIF.
          ENDIF.
        ENDLOOP.
*--- Add option of Google Maps display type
        wd_this->add_option( ir_view = view
                             iv_id   = lv_child_id ).
*--- Add button to trigger the creation of a link
        wd_this->add_button( ir_view   = view
                             iv_partner = ls_addr_data-partner ).
        IF wd_this->mv_link4partner EQ ls_addr_data-partner.
*--- Add url link to navigate to Google Maps
          wd_this->add_linktourl( ir_view   = view ).
        ENDIF.
      ENDLOOP.
    ENDIF.
ENDMETHOD.
```

Listing 5.13 Creating the Dynamic Address Output in wddomodify()

Reuse of software components allows faster development cycles and reduces expenses. Web Dynpro for ABAP (WD4A) supports these development processes using a constantly growing library of predefined components. In this chapter, you will learn how to manage your WD4A applications more efficiently by using predefined components in your developments, instead of implementing the relevant functions manually.

6 Reusing WD4A Components

6.1 Comparing Classes and Components

Before we discuss the use of existing WD4A components and specific factors in developing WD4A components for multiple uses, we will briefly look at the basic principles in component-based software development. Software manufacturing is increasingly seeing the introduction and implementation of concepts intended to further "industrialize" the development process. This includes the building of applications from components that can be combined.

The goal is to increasingly automate the process of the development of software systems in the same way that cars are assembled from various components such as bodywork, engine, chassis, and so on. To achieve this, software development initially focused on structured and procedural processes: Absolute jump instructions were to be avoided, and related program areas were to be organized by control structures. A further step was the introduction of modular programming: Here, tasks were divided into logical subparts, individually planned, developed and tested, and then finally linked together. Frequently used routines were grouped as independent programs or program parts in the form of modules or procedures. These then could be implemented at any point in the actual application and, ideally, were also available for other uses.

Modular programming was perfected with the adoption of object-oriented programming. Thanks to the object-oriented concepts, systems no longer sequentially ran individual function areas of an algorithm, but rather the program logic developed in communication and the internal status changes of the objects from which the program is built. The step had been completed from the *module*, which encapsulated related data and processes, to the *object*, which was characterized by the following features:

- **Abstraction**
  The ability of an object to process data, change status, and exchange messages, without having to reveal details for the implementation of these processes.

- **Encapsulation**
  An object only allows other objects to access functions through the restricted definitions of its interface that change its internal status. This allows changes to the implementation of an object that do not cause any change or adjustment of the interface, providing they do not affect the interface of the object. Encapsulation therefore primarily seeks to allow the flexible grouping of related information, rather than to protect against uncontrolled status changes.

- **Polymorphism**
  The interfaces of objects can be the same. Depending on their type, different objects can react differently to the same query.

- **Inheritance**
  New types of objects are created based on existing objects. Encapsulation and polymorphism can be used to add new components and characteristics or to swap existing ones.

Accordingly, objects are units that encapsulate status and behavior and have unique identities. The behavior and structure of objects are defined by classes, and a class here has several purposes: It implements the concept of the *abstract data type* (ADT) and provides an abstract description of the behavior of its objects. Classes are frequently used as types in type-related systems, as is the case with ABAP Objects, for example. A class is used to generate objects, an occurrence known as the *instance* of a class.

In software technology, components are very similar to classes. Like classes, components also define object behavior and create objects. Objects created using components are described as *component instances*. Classes and components make their implemented functions available to the interface through abstract behavior descriptions. Components cannot be used as types, as is common for classes. Furthermore, the concepts of inheritance cannot be applied to components. There is a wide divergence of definitions in software technology. Some common definitions are from Grady Booch, the Meta Group, and Jed Harris:

> "A reusable software component is a logically cohesive, loosely coupled module that denotes a single abstraction." (Grady Booch, 1987)

> "Software components are defined as prefabricated, pre-tested, self-contained, reusable software modules—bundles of data and procedures—that perform specific functions." (Meta Group, 1994)

> "A component is a piece of software small enough to create and maintain, big enough to deploy and support, and with standard interfaces for interoperability." (Jed Harris, 1995)

The WD4A framework is primarily geared towards component-based development in the area of the user interfaces. Reusable components are supposed to avoid any recurring structures, processes, and display formats in programs that need to be repeatedly re-developed from scratch. In future, the library of WD4A components available for reuse will therefore grow, both through development of new components by SAP and by developments from third-party providers.

6.2 ALV Component SALV_WD_TABLE

The *ABAP List Viewer* (ALV) offers extensive functionality for the tabular display of data and was originally developed for the SAP GUI. The ALV component SALV_WD_TABLE now offers the developer functions that are comparable with the SAP GUI implementation and also enhances the limited possibilities of the Table view element. The ABAP List Viewer therefore is not implemented as a view element in the WD4A framework, but rather as a component that integrates various view elements, and implements extended functionalities. These functions include the following:

- Optional header and footer areas display additional information.
- You can display and hide table columns.
- Columns can be sorted by clicking on column headers.
- Multiple sort criteria can be combined.
- Calculations (addition, calculating averages, displaying minimum and maximum values, and so on) can be performed.
- Table cells can be edited.

6 | Reusing WD4A Components

- Settings can be saved by the user in various different views.
- The data that is displayed can be exported to Microsoft Excel or as a print version in PDF format.

6.2.1 Using the ALV Component

We now will provide an example to show how the display of the country table T005T (shown in Chapter 3, Section 6) is performed using the ALV component. We will access its functions using usage definitions and reverse mapping.

Our sample component is given the name ZEXP_ALV_SIMPLE. For the component characteristics, define the use of the ALV component SALV_WD_TABLE and describe the component use as USAGE_ALV. In the component controller, create a context node COUNTRIES of the type **T005T** with the attributes LAND1, LANDX, NATIO, LANDX50, and NATIO50 and then delete the type specification again for the context node COUNTRIES. This is necessary because the ALV component shows the entire structure for existing ABAP Dictionary types, regardless of what attributes were defined in the context node. Assign the value **0..n** to the **Cardinality** property. The context node is supplied with data through the supply function method supply_countries() (see Listing 6.1).

```
METHOD supply_countries.
  DATA lt_countries   TYPE STANDARD TABLE OF t005t.
*--- Get country data
  SELECT * FROM t005t INTO TABLE lt_countries WHERE spras EQ sy-langu.
  IF sy-subrc EQ 0.
    node->bind_table( new_items = lt_countries ).
  ENDIF.
ENDMETHOD.
```

Listing 6.1 Filling the COUNTRIES Context Node

In the view layout of the V_DEFAULT view, add a ViewContainerUIElement view element, which will serve as a container for the views implemented in the ALV component. Embed the view in the W_DEFAULT window.

The ALV component has various interface views, but to begin with we are only interested in the table display. Of the various interface views offered when you embed into the ViewContainerUIElement view element, select the one with the name TABLE (see Figure 6.1). You can also embed the TABLE interface view directly in the window without using a view of your own component. However, in that case you do not have the option of displaying additional view elements together with the ALV table.

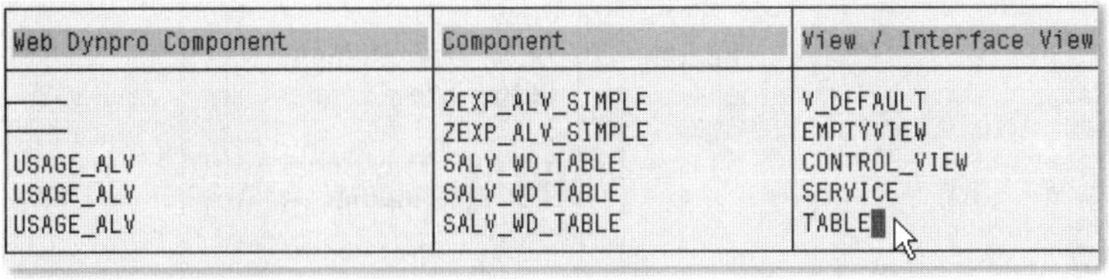

Web Dynpro Component	Component	View / Interface View
———	ZEXP_ALV_SIMPLE	V_DEFAULT
———	ZEXP_ALV_SIMPLE	EMPTYVIEW
USAGE_ALV	SALV_WD_TABLE	CONTROL_VIEW
USAGE_ALV	SALV_WD_TABLE	SERVICE
USAGE_ALV	SALV_WD_TABLE	TABLE

Figure 6.1 Selecting the TABLE Interface View of the ALV Component

Now, the data of the ALV component that is in the context node COUNTRIES must also be provided. This is done via reverse mapping. To do this, navigate in the object tree of the component ZEXP_ALV_SIMPLE to the entry **Component Usages**. Here you will find the entry for the ALV component USAGE_ALV that is used. For the reverse mapping, we need an interface controller usage.

Figure 6.2 shows such a usage. If this is not available, create it using the context menu of the component usage USAGE_ALV. The context nodes to which the system is to map will then appear on the right. You also must now define the usage of the component controller context node COUNTRIES and then map this to the DATA context node (see Figure 6.3).

Figure 6.2 Component Usage of SALV_WD_COMPONENT

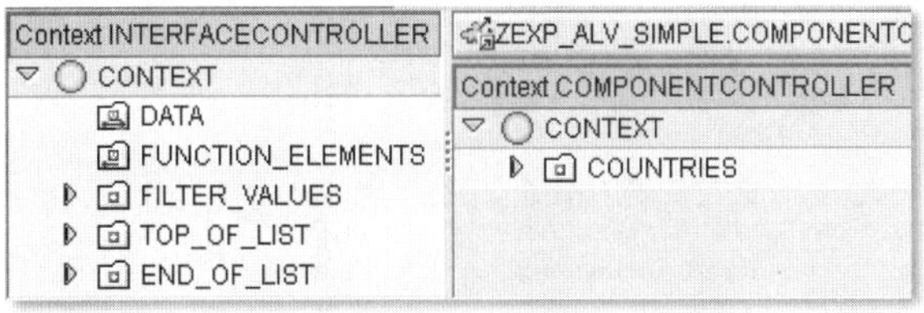

Context INTERFACECONTROLLER	ZEXP_ALV_SIMPLE.COMPONENTC
▽ ○ CONTEXT	Context COMPONENTCONTROLLER
DATA	▽ ○ CONTEXT
FUNCTION_ELEMENTS	▷ COUNTRIES
▷ FILTER_VALUES	
▷ TOP_OF_LIST	
▷ END_OF_LIST	

Figure 6.3 Interface Context Nodes of SALV_WD_TABLE

Figure 6.4 displays the relationships between the application component ZEXP_ALV_SIMPLE and the ALV component SALV_WD_TABLE. The view elements are fully implemented in the ALV component. The data supply for the view is performed from the component ZEXP_ALV_SIMPLE.

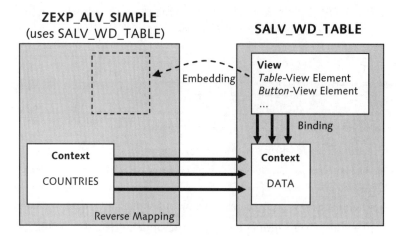

Figure 6.4 Schematic Display of the ALV Component Usage

After the application is created and started, the display shown in Figure 6.5 appears in the client. You can identify the buttons **Excel** for exporting the data displayed into Microsoft Excel and **Print Version** for creating a print version in PDF format. When you click on the **Filter** link, a row is shown under the column headers with input fields for the filter values for each column. When you activate the **Settings** link, an area appears above the table in which you can make various settings such as showing and hiding columns and sort parameters, through to configuring the print output. These are among the extensive functions automatically available when you use the ALV component. They are intended to make it easier for the user to work with, and manipulate, data contained in a tabular structure.

View [Standard View] | Excel | Print Version | Filter Settings

Country	Name	Nation.	Name	Nation.
AD	Andorra	Andorran	Andorra	Andorran
AE	Utd.Arab Emir.	Unit.Arab Emir.	United Arab Emirates	United Arab Emirates
AF	Afghanistan	Afghan	Afghanistan	Afghan
AG	Antigua/Barbuda	Antiguan	Antigua and Barbuda	Antiguan
AI	Anguilla	Anguilla	Anguilla	Anguillian
AL	Albania	Albanian	Albania	Albanian
AM	Armenia	Armenian	Armenia	Armenian
AN	Dutch Antilles	Dutch	Dutch Antilles	Dutch
AO	Angola	Angolan	Angola	Angolan
AQ	Antarctica	Antarctica	Antarctica	From Antarctica

Row 1 of 240

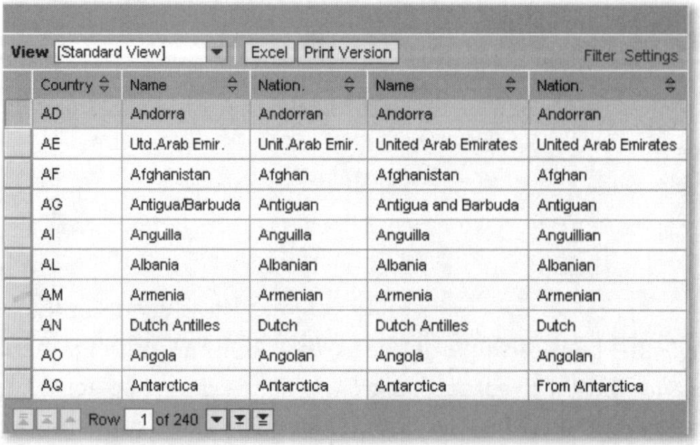

Figure 6.5 Country Display Using SALV_WD_TABLE

The values of the ABAP Dictionary data elements are used for the column headers. The number of rows to be initially displayed (in our case, 10 rows) is defined within the ALV component. Below, we want to add a tooltip to the column header of the first column and restrict the display to two rows, using the ALV configuration model.

6.2.2 Accessing the ALV Configuration Model

For manipulating the ALV output, the *ALV configuration model* is available. It is implemented in the class CL_SALV_WD_CONFIG_TABLE. The implemented interfaces and their methods provide an overview of the possible changes (see Table 6.1). This overview of the individual interface methods that are implemented will make it easier for you to find the functions that meet your needs.

Interface	Function
IF_SALV_WD_COLUMN_SETTINGS	Allows access to the columns in the table and the deletion and creation of new columns
IF_SALV_WD_CONFIG_ADMIN	Allows the storage of administrative data, such as times for creating and changing
IF_SALV_WD_EXPORT_SETTINGS	Allows access to the settings for data export to Microsoft Excel
IF_SALV_WD_FIELD_SETTINGS	Allows access to the individual fields for the internal data table, for example for performing calculations
IF_SALV_WD_FUNCTION_SETTINGS	Allows the definition of and access to functions you have defined yourself. These can be executed using elements in the toolbar, for example
IF_SALV_WD_PDF_SETTINGS	Allows access to the settings for data export to PDF format
IF_SALV_WD_STD_FUNCTIONS	Allows access to standard functions of the ALV table, such as the visibility of buttons and the activation of the sort function
IF_SALV_WD_TABLE_SETTINGS	Allows display options such as the width and design to be changed for the ALV table

Table 6.1 Interfaces of the ALV Configuration Model

To meet our objective of changing the number of rows that are initially displayed, the method `set_visible_row_count()` can be used in the interface `IF_SALV_WD_TABLE_SETTINGS`.

The tooltip for the column header can be accessed on several levels. We can get a reference to the relevant column via the `get_column()` method implemented in the `IF_SALV_WD_COLUMN_SETTINGS` interface. Via the column object of the type **CL_SALV_WD_COLUMN**, we receive a reference to the column header by calling the method `get_header()`. The header object is of the type **CL_SALV_WD_COLUMN_HEADER**. The method `set_tooltip()` allows a tooltip to be specified.

Because all changes to be made to the ALV table should be valid for the full duration that the table is displayed, we implement these in the method `wddoinit()` of the V_DEFAULT view. In the case of runtime-dependent changes, the relevant implementation would be performed in the method `wddomodify()` of the V_DEFAULT view. To further extend the developments from the example ZEXP_ALV_SIMPLE, copy the component ZEXP_ALV_SIMPLE into the new component ZEXP_ALV_CONFIG. Given that we access the ALV component in this component in the method `wddoinit()` of the V_DEFAULT view, we must first define its use in the view controller in the **Properties** tab (see Figure 6.6).

Component Use	Component	Controller
	ZEXP_ALV_CONFIG	COMPONENTCONTROLLER
USAGE_ALV	SALV_WD_TABLE	
USAGE_ALV	SALV_WD_TABLE	INTERFACECONTROLLER

Figure 6.6 Using the ALV Component in the View Controller

If one or several interface views are displayed from a component that is used, the instantiation is transferred from the WD4A framework. You must perform the instantiation manually when you access the implemented logic of the component. The Code Wizard generates the instructions for the method `wddoinit()` that are required for this:

```
lr_cmp_usage =   wd_this->wd_cpuse_usage_alv( ).
IF lr_cmp_usage->has_active_component( ) IS INITIAL.
  lr_cmp_usage->create_component( ).
ENDIF.
```

Using the reference to the interface controller of the ALV component, you can now access the configuration model of the type **CL_SALV_WD_CONFIG_**

TABLE. Here, the Code Wizard again offers the relevant assistance in compiling the instructions:

```
lr_if_controller = wd_this->wd_cpifc_usage_alv( ).
lr_config_mdl    = lr_if_controller->get_model( ).
```

The number of rows to be displayed can be changed using the method set_visible_row_count() of the interface IF_SALV_WD_TABLE_SETTINGS:

```
lr_cmdl->if_salv_wd_table_settings~set_visible_row_count( '2' ).
```

To write a tooltip, a reference is first determined to the corresponding column, through which the header is then determined:

```
lr_col = lr_cmdl->if_salv_wd_column_settings~get_column('LAND1').
lr_header = lr_col->get_header( ).
lr_header->set_tooltip( EXPORTING
                        value = 'Country Internal Key ' ).
```

Listing 6.2 shows the complete implementation of the method wddoinit().

```
METHOD wddoinit.
  DATA lr_cmp_usage     TYPE REF TO if_wd_component_usage.
  DATA lr_if_controller TYPE REF TO iwci_salv_wd_table.
  DATA lr_cmdl          TYPE REF TO cl_salv_wd_config_table.
  DATA lr_col           TYPE REF TO cl_salv_wd_column.
  DATA lr_header        TYPE REF TO cl_salv_wd_column_header.
*--- Instantiate ALV component
  lr_cmp_usage =  wd_this->wd_cpuse_usage_alv( ).
  IF lr_cmp_usage->has_active_component( ) IS INITIAL.
    lr_cmp_usage->create_component( ).
  ENDIF.
*--- Get reference to model
  lr_if_controller =  wd_this->wd_cpifc_usage_alv( ).
  lr_cmdl          = lr_if_controller->get_model( ).
*--- Modify visible row count
  lr_cmdl->if_salv_wd_table_settings~set_visible_row_count( '2' ).
*--- Set tooltip of column header
  lr_col = lr_cmdl->if_salv_wd_column_settings~get_column( 'LAND1' ).
  lr_header = lr_col->get_header( ).
  lr_header->set_tooltip( EXPORTING value = 'Country Internal Key ' ).
ENDMETHOD.
```

Listing 6.2 Instructions for the Changes to the ALV Configuration Model

Figure 6.7 shows the resulting display: The number of rows displayed has been reduced to two, and the column header for the first column contains a tooltip with the text "Country Internal Key."

6 | Reusing WD4A Components

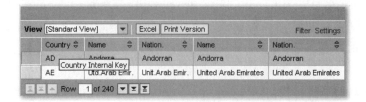

Figure 6.7 Country Display after Modifications to the Configuration Model

6.3 OVS Component WDR_OVS

In addition to the simple input helps—already discussed in Chapter 3, Section 8—the OVS (*Object value selector*) component WDR_OVS provides the option of implementing extended search functionalities. WDR_OVS builds on a uniform process and a uniform layout that allow the developer to implement search helps for any values and objects while always retaining the same user interaction.

To achieve this, the following demands must be noted:

- Navigation within the application
- Layout of the screen elements
- Validation of entries and error handling
- Reusability of business process logic
- Data-abstraction support

The component using the OVS component WDR_OVS registers to the OVS event and in the corresponding event-handler method implements the various phases for which the OVS event is triggered. These phases can be defined as follows:

- **Phase 0**
  Configuration of the OVS component; this includes, among other things, setting the window caption, label texts, group headers and the number of columns and rows in the search results table
- **Phase 1**
  Definition of the selection fields and fixing of default values
- **Phase 2**
  Reading the search criteria made by the user and determining the search result

▶ **Phase 3**
  Reading the selected object from the search result and transferring to the context to which the entry field of the search help is linked

We will show the implementation of the phases through the example of the selection of units used earlier. The OVS component performs the selection of the dimension, the determining of the units for each dimension, and the transfer of the selected unit to the main view. The process runs as follows:

1. In Figure 6.8, the user has selected the icon to the right of the input field with the label **Unit**, and a dialog box then appears (**Object Value Selector**) for entering a dimension.

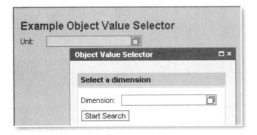

Figure 6.8 Calling the OVS Component

2. The dimension is selected using a simple input help (see Figure 6.9).

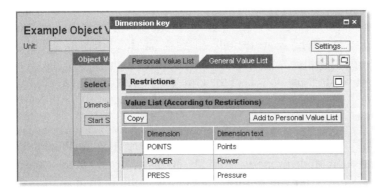

Figure 6.9 Using a Simple Input Help in the OVS Component

3. The selected value is copied into the input field for the dimension. After you click on **Start Search,** the units for the dimension are determined and displayed in a table in the **Object Value Selector** window (see Figure 6.10).

4. The transfer of a value from the search result is implemented in such a way that the description for the selected object (**Unit text** column) appears in the original input field (see Figure 6.11).

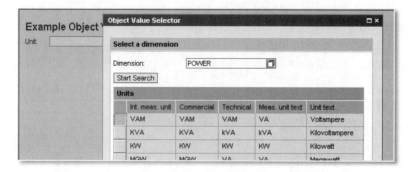

Figure 6.10 Search Result for the Selected Unit

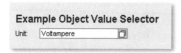

Figure 6.11 Copying from the Search Result

This scenario is implemented in component ZEXP_OVS. The usage of the OVS component WDR_OVS is defined in the **Used Components** tab with the name USAGE_OVS. The view controller of the V_DEFAULT view defines the use of the interface controller of USAGE_OVS. The context of the view controller consists of two context nodes: The context node CONTENT has the attribute UNIT, to which the property **value** of the InputField view element INP_UNIT is linked; the context attribute UNIT is of the type **T006A_INT-UNIT_TXT_L**. The context node PARAMS also only has one attribute called DIMENSION of the type **T006T-DIMID**.

The corresponding input help type must be set at the context attribute UNIT using the **Input Help Mode** property. You can set this according to the **Object Value Selector** value. After you confirm your entry, an input field appears in which the **OVS Component Usage** must be entered. In our example, this is USAGE_OVS (see Figure 6.12).

The view simply consists of a TextView, Label, and InputField view element. The property **value** of the InputField view element INP_UNIT is linked to the UNIT context attribute. In the **Methods** tab, we define an event-handler method on_ovs() that registers itself to the OVS event of USAGE_OVS.

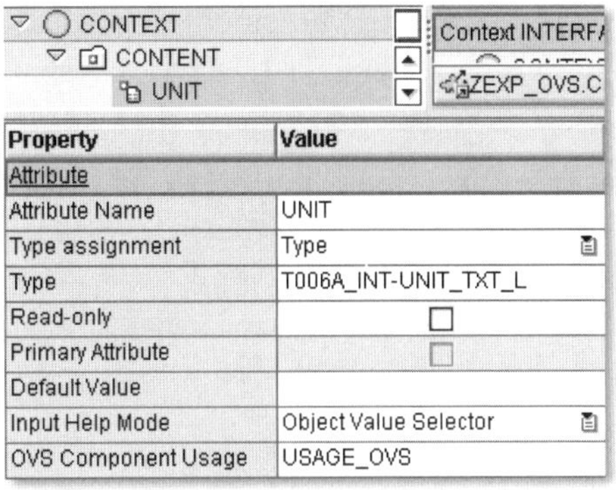

Property	Value
Attribute	
Attribute Name	UNIT
Type assignment	Type
Type	T006A_INT-UNIT_TXT_L
Read-only	☐
Primary Attribute	☐
Default Value	
Input Help Mode	Object Value Selector
OVS Component Usage	USAGE_OVS

Figure 6.12 Defining the Input Help Type

The phases outlined above are now implemented in the event-handler method on_ovs(). The functions are provided by the OVS_CALLBACK_OBJECT parameter transferred to the event-handler method, which is a reference to an object of the type IF_WDR_OVS. The implemented methods of interface IF_WDR_OVS are called in the individual phases.

The phases are determined using the PHASE_INDICATOR attribute; Phase 0 is for configuring the OVS component. In our example, we are primarily determining the texts of the labels and windows:

```
ls_text-name  = 'DIMID'.
ls_text-value = 'Dimension'.
APPEND ls_text TO lt_text.
ovs_callback_object->set_configuration(
                label_texts  = lt_text
                group_header = 'Select a dimension'
                window_title = 'Object Value Selector'
                table_header = 'Units' ).
```

In Phase 1, the input structure for the search criteria is assigned. In our example, this structure only contains one field; however, default values can also be set for the search criteria in this step:

```
ovs_callback_object->set_input_structure( input = ls_params )
```

Phase 2 transfers the search criteria and determines the search result. In our example, this is done by calling the UNITS_GET_FOR_DIMENSION function module. The last instruction in Phase 2 transfers the search result to the OVS component for display:

6 | Reusing WD4A Components

```
        ASSIGN ovs_callback_object->query_parameters->* TO <ls_params>.
        IF NOT <ls_params>-dimension EQ ''.
          CALL FUNCTION 'UNITS_GET_FOR_DIMENSION'
            EXPORTING
              dimension            = <ls_params>-dimension
              language             = sy-langu
            TABLES
              units_of_measurement = lt_unit
            EXCEPTIONS
              dimension_not_found  = 1
              OTHERS               = 2.
          IF sy-subrc EQ 0.
            ovs_callback_object->set_output_table( output = lt_unit ).
          ENDIF.
        ENDIF.
```

Phase 3 is run through once the user has selected and copied the required value from the search result. The selection is then determined and transferred to the context to which the corresponding input field is linked:

```
        ASSIGN ovs_callback_object->selection->* TO <ls_selection>.
        IF <ls_selection> IS ASSIGNED.
          lr_node = wd_context->get_child_node( name = 'CONTENT' ).
          lr_node->set_attribute( EXPORTING name  = 'UNIT'
                                  value = <ls_selection>-unit_txt_l ).
        ENDIF.
```

The entire implementation of the event-handler method on_ovs() is shown in Listing 6.3.

```
METHOD on_ovs.
    DATA lr_node        TYPE REF TO if_wd_context_node.
    DATA lt_text        TYPE  wdr_name_value_list.
    DATA ls_text        TYPE  wdr_name_value.
    DATA ls_params      TYPE  if_v_default=>element_params.
    DATA lt_unit        TYPE STANDARD TABLE OF t006a_int.
    FIELD-SYMBOLS:  <ls_params>     TYPE if_v_default=>element_params.
    FIELD-SYMBOLS:  <ls_selection> TYPE t006a_int.
    CASE ovs_callback_object->phase_indicator.
      WHEN ovs_callback_object->co_phase_0.
*--- Create text for field label
        ls_text-name  = 'DIMID'.
        ls_text-value = 'Dimension'.
        APPEND ls_text TO lt_text.
*--- Set configuration data of ovs popup window
        ovs_callback_object->set_configuration(
```

```
                label_texts  = lt_text
                group_header = 'Select a dimension'
                window_title = 'Object Value Selector'
                table_header = 'Units' ).
    WHEN ovs_callback_object->co_phase_1.
      ovs_callback_object->set_input_structure( input = ls_params ).
    WHEN ovs_callback_object->co_phase_2.
*--- Get parameter
      ASSIGN ovs_callback_object->query_parameters->* TO <ls_params>.
      IF NOT <ls_params>-dimension EQ ''.
*--- Call to search API
        CALL FUNCTION 'UNITS_GET_FOR_DIMENSION'
          EXPORTING
            dimension             = <ls_params>-dimension
            language              = sy-langu
          TABLES
            units_of_measurement  = lt_unit
          EXCEPTIONS
            dimension_not_found   = 1
            OTHERS                = 2.
        IF sy-subrc EQ 0.
          ovs_callback_object->set_output_table( output = lt_unit ).
        ENDIF.
      ENDIF.
    WHEN ovs_callback_object->co_phase_3.
*--- Get selection
      ASSIGN ovs_callback_object->selection->* TO <ls_selection>.
      IF <ls_selection> IS ASSIGNED.
*--- Write to context
        lr_node = wd_context->get_child_node( name = 'CONTENT' ).
        lr_node->set_attribute( EXPORTING name  = 'UNIT'
                                          value = <ls_selection>-unit_txt_l ).
      ENDIF.
  ENDCASE.
ENDMETHOD.
```

Listing 6.3 Event-Handler Method for Implementing the OVS Component Phases

6.4 SO Component WDR_SELECT_OPTIONS

Select Options (SO) provide different, and more complex, possibilities for defining search criteria. This includes, for instance, the definition of areas and individual values to be included in the search and to be excluded from the search. The functions of Select Options were copied from the classical

6 | Reusing WD4A Components

screen programming into the WD4A framework and are available in the component `WDR_SELECT_OPTIONS`.

Figure 6.13 shows a section from the initial screen for determining ABAP runtime errors in the classical SAP GUI (Transaction ST22). Selection criteria based on Select Options can be arranged here for the fields **Date**, **Time**, and **Host**, for example.

In Web Dynpro for ABAP you can use the interface view `WND_SELECTION_SCREEN` of the `WDR_SELECT_OPTIONS` component to define the area in the layout in which the selection fields are displayed. The fields can be added using the `add_selection_field()` method of the `IF_WD_SELECT_OPTIONS` interface. The interface has further methods for configuration, layout design, and value manipulations. We will use an example to illustrate at what points in the component you have to add the necessary instructions. The function shown in Figure 6.13 for determining runtime errors will serve us as a basis.

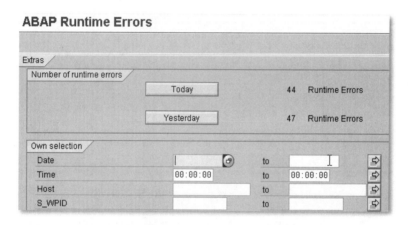

Figure 6.13 Select Options for Determining Runtime Errors

The selection screen will contain three fields for the date, time, and user name (see Figure 6.14). The result will be the output of a list of the runtime fields to which the search criteria apply. The sample component is given the name `ZEXP_SELECT_OPTIONS`. The usage of the `WDR_SELECT_OPTIONS` component is defined in the **Used Components** tab as `USAGE_SO`. The View Controller of the `V_DEFAULT` view defines the use of the interface controller of `USAGE_SO`.

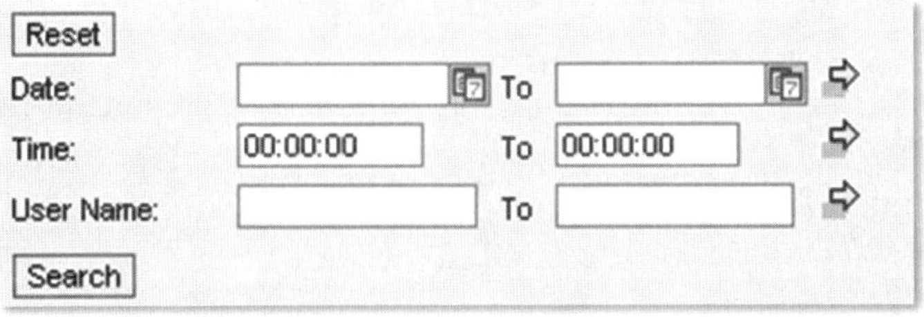

6.4 SO Component WDR_SELECT_OPTIONS

Figure 6.14 Displaying the Selection Fields with WDR_SELECT_OPTIONS

The context only consists of one DUMPS context node of the **SNAP_BEG** type with a cardinality of **0..n**. At runtime, the elements of the context node contain the search result. Add the following attributes to the context node: DATE, TIME, AHOST, UNAME, MANDT, and FLIST. The V_DEFAULT view consists of a ViewContainerUIElement view element for the area shown in Figure 6.14, a Button view element for initiating the search and the Table view element for displaying the results table. The **dataSource** property of the Table view element is linked to the DUMPS context node (see Figure 6.15).

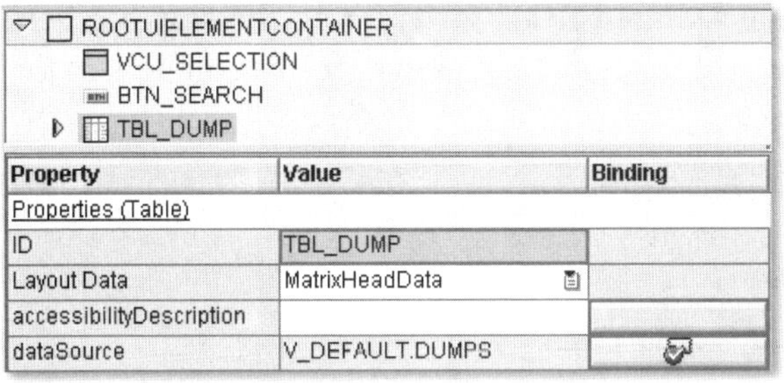

Figure 6.15 Layout of the View

Define a SEARCH action, and link the event **onAction** of the Button view element to this action. The V_DEFAULT view is embedded in the W_DEFAULT window, and the interface view WND_SELECTION_SCREEN of the Select Options component is embedded in the ViewContainerUIElement view element of the V_DEFAULT view (see Figure 6.16).

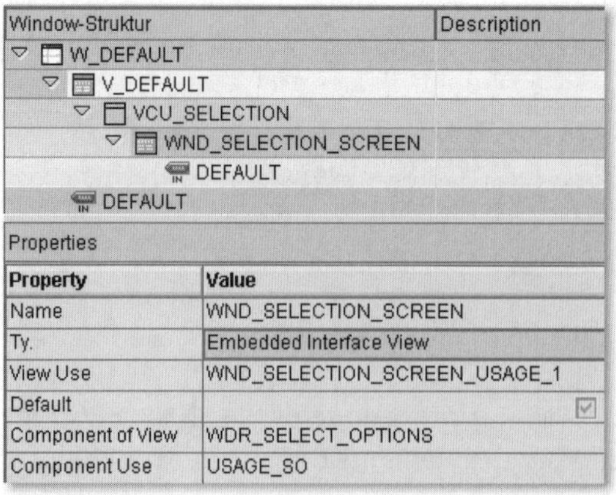

Window-Struktur	Description
▽ ☐ W_DEFAULT	
▽ ☐ V_DEFAULT	
▽ ☐ VCU_SELECTION	
▽ ☐ WND_SELECTION_SCREEN	
DEFAULT	
DEFAULT	

Properties	
Property	**Value**
Name	WND_SELECTION_SCREEN
Ty.	Embedded Interface View
View Use	WND_SELECTION_SCREEN_USAGE_1
Default	☑
Component of View	WDR_SELECT_OPTIONS
Component Use	USAGE_SO

Figure 6.16 Embedding the Interface View of the SO Component

In the view controller, we need an attribute that holds the reference to the instance of the Select Options component. This is necessary because at runtime we access this reference to the search criteria that have been entered in the event-handler method. The attribute is MR_SELOPT and it is of the type **IF_WD_SELECT_OPTIONS**. The required fields for entering the search criteria are compiled in the wddoinit() method. First, however, the component that is used must be instantiated:

```
lr_usage = wd_this->wd_cpuse_usage_so( ).
IF lr_usage->has_active_component( ) IS INITIAL.
  lr_usage->create_component( ).
ENDIF.
```

In the next step, the selection screen is initialized. The return value corresponds to the reference to the instance:

```
lr_if_controller = wd_this->wd_cpifc_usage_so( ).
wd_this->mr_selopt = lr_if_controller->init_selection_screen( ).
```

The interface of the SO component provides various methods for modifying the selection screen. We use the method set_global_options(), in order to hide all control buttons except for the **Reset** button, which is used to reset the search criteria that have been entered:

```
wd_this->mr_selopt->set_global_options(
                 i_display_btn_cancel  = abap_false
                 i_display_btn_check   = abap_false
                 i_display_btn_reset   = abap_true
                 i_display_btn_execute = abap_false ).
```

SO Component WDR_SELECT_OPTIONS | 6.4

Now the fields are created with their range tables, containing details on the areas to be included or excluded, which are to be used for the search. We define three fields for entering the search criteria: **DATE** for choosing and restricting the days, **TIME** for choosing and restricting the times, and **UNAME** for selecting and restricting the users for whom the runtime errors occurred:

```
lt_range = wd_this->mr_selopt->create_range_table(
                                 i_typename = 'DATE' ).
wd_this->mr_selopt->add_selection_field( i_id      = 'DATE'
                                 it_result = lt_range ).
lt_range = wd_this->mr_selopt->create_range_table(
                                 i_typename = 'TIME' ).
wd_this->mr_selopt->add_selection_field( i_id      = 'TIME'
                                 it_result = lt_range ).
lt_range = wd_this->mr_selopt->create_range_table(
                                 i_typename = 'UNAME' ).
wd_this->mr_selopt->add_selection_field( i_id      = 'UNAME'
                                 it_result = lt_range ).
```

Listing 6.4 shows the entire implementation of the method wddoinit().

```
METHOD wddoinit.
  DATA lt_range         TYPE REF TO data.
  DATA lr_range         TYPE REF TO data.
  DATA lv_type          TYPE string.
  DATA lr_comp_contr    TYPE REF TO ig_componentcontroller.
  DATA lr_usage         TYPE REF TO if_wd_component_usage.
  DATA lr_if_controller TYPE REF TO iwci_wdr_select_options.
*--- Instantiate select options component
  lr_usage = wd_this->wd_cpuse_usage_so( ).
  IF lr_usage->has_active_component( ) IS INITIAL.
    lr_usage->create_component( ).
  ENDIF.
*--- Initialize selection screen
  lr_if_controller = wd_this->wd_cpifc_usage_so( ).
  wd_this->mr_selopt = lr_if_controller->init_selection_screen( ).
*--- Configure layout options
  wd_this->mr_selopt->set_global_options(
                          i_display_btn_cancel  = abap_false
                          i_display_btn_check   = abap_false
                          i_display_btn_reset   = abap_true
                          i_display_btn_execute = abap_false ).
*--- Create range tables
  lt_range = wd_this->mr_selopt->create_range_table(
                                 i_typename = 'DATE' ).
```

```
          wd_this->mr_selopt->add_selection_field( i_id     = 'DATE'
                                                  it_result = lt_range ).
          lt_range = wd_this->mr_selopt->create_range_table(
                                              i_typename = 'TIME' ).
          wd_this->mr_selopt->add_selection_field( i_id     = 'TIME'
                                                  it_result = lt_range ).
          lt_range = wd_this->mr_selopt->create_range_table(
                                              i_typename = 'UNAME' ).
          wd_this->mr_selopt->add_selection_field( i_id     = 'UNAME'
                                                  it_result = lt_range ).
ENDMETHOD.
```

Listing 6.4 Implementing wddoinit()

After you enter the search criteria and click on the **Search button**, the onactionsearch() event-handler method is called. Here, in the first step, the search criteria that have been entered are determined. This is done using the reference stored in the view controller attribute MR_SELOPT to the instance of the SO component:

```
lr_date = wd_this->mr_selopt->get_range_table_of_sel_field(
                                             i_id = 'DATE' ).
ASSIGN lr_date->* TO <lt_date>.
lr_time = wd_this->mr_selopt->get_range_table_of_sel_field(
                                             i_id = 'TIME' ).
ASSIGN lr_time->* TO <lt_time>.
lr_user = wd_this->mr_selopt->get_range_table_of_sel_field(
                                             i_id = 'UNAME' ).
ASSIGN lr_user->* TO <lt_date>.
```

We can determine the corresponding result using the search criteria that are now contained in range tables. In our example, we directly access the SNAP_BEG table:

```
SELECT * FROM snap_beg INTO ls_snap_beg WHERE seqno = '000'
                              AND   date IN <lt_date>
                              AND   time IN <lt_time>
                              AND   uname IN <lt_user>
                    ORDER BY date DESCENDING time DESCENDING.
```

The program fragment that follows this edits the string that contains the type of runtime error; we will not go any further into the details of this. Finally, the search result must also be transferred to the DUMPS context node to which the Table view element joins.

```
lr_node = wd_context->get_child_node( name = 'DUMPS' ).
lr_node->bind_elements( lt_snap_beg ).
```

Figure 6.17 shows the result of a search for runtime errors using the WDR_SELECT_OPTIONS Select Options component. The declarations and instructions of the event-handler method onactionsearch() are shown in Listing 6.5.

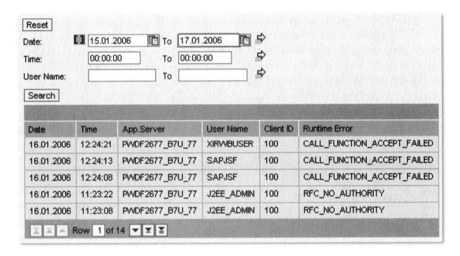

Figure 6.17 Entering the Search Criteria and Results with the SO Component

```
METHOD onactionsearch.
  DATA lt_snap_beg TYPE STANDARD TABLE OF snap_beg.
  DATA lr_node    TYPE REF TO if_wd_context_node.
  DATA lr_user    TYPE REF TO data.
  DATA lr_date    TYPE REF TO data.
  DATA lr_time    TYPE REF TO data.
  DATA lv_strlen  TYPE i.
  DATA ls_snap_beg TYPE snap_beg.
  FIELD-SYMBOLS <lt_user>  TYPE table.
  FIELD-SYMBOLS <lt_date>  TYPE table.
  FIELD-SYMBOLS <lt_time>  TYPE table.
*--- Retrieve the data from the select option
  lr_user = wd_this->mr_selopt->get_range_table_of_sel_field(
                      i_id = 'UNAME' ).
  ASSIGN lr_user->* TO <lt_user>.
  lr_date = wd_this->mr_selopt->get_range_table_of_sel_field(
                      i_id = 'DATE' ).
  ASSIGN lr_date->* TO <lt_date>.
  lr_time = wd_this->mr_selopt->get_range_table_of_sel_field(
                      i_id = 'TIME' ).
```

```
    ASSIGN lr_time->* TO <lt_time>.
*--- Read dump table
  SELECT * FROM snap_beg INTO ls_snap_beg WHERE seqno = '000'
                                    AND   date IN <lt_date>
                                    AND   time IN <lt_time>
                                    AND   uname IN <lt_user>
                   ORDER BY date DESCENDING time DESCENDING.
*--- Extract runtime error name
    lv_strlen = ls_snap_beg-flist+2(3).
    IF lv_strlen < 1 OR lv_strlen > 30.
      EXIT.
    ELSE.
      ls_snap_beg-flist   = ls_snap_beg-flist+5(lv_strlen).
    ENDIF.
    APPEND ls_snap_beg TO lt_snap_beg.
  ENDSELECT.
*--- Fill context node
  lr_node = wd_context->get_child_node( name = 'DUMPS' ).
  lr_node->bind_elements( lt_snap_beg ).
ENDMETHOD.
```

Listing 6.5 Implementing the Event-Handler Method

6.5 Developing Input-Help Components

If the different ways of integrating input helps do not meet your requirements, you also have the option of developing separate input-help components that can be used by other components. For the user, the procedure for this remains the same as that described in the previous sections. As a developer, after you click on an icon in the input field, a dialog box opens in which scenarios run for determining the corresponding input value.

These processes, as well as the visual areas, are implemented in a separate component and can be designed as the developer chooses. To guarantee a uniform interface between the input-help component and the application component, and thereby the reuse of the input-help components, the WD4A framework provides the IWD_VALUE_HELP interface. The interface has the method set_value_help_listener(), which is called by the WD4A framework and transfers a reference to the Listener. This reference then allows the dialog box in which the input help is displayed to be closed.

To allow access to the Listener, the reference is stored in a controller attribute. The interface also has two events, VH_WINDOW_OPENED and VH_

WINDOW_CLOSED, which are triggered when the input help dialog box is opened and closed. If the application needs to react to these events, they must be added to its interface controller in the input-help component. The interface has a view for the declaration of the visual area with the name WD_VALUE_HELP. Views that are to be displayed within the input-help component must be embedded in this interface view.

We want to show the development of an input-help component and describe how it is used by an application component. To do this, we will develop an input help for entering a country from the North American Free Trade Agreement area (NAFTA). This means that not all countries will be made available for selection, but rather only the member countries of NAFTA. ABAP Dictionary search helps (Transaction SE11) such as H_T005_LAND, for example, therefore cannot be used, as these display the entire country list. The restriction of the countries to be selected is therefore implemented in an input-help component.

6.5.1 Implementation of the Input-Help Component

The input-help component is given the name ZEXP_CUSTOM_SH_COMP. The interface IWD_VALUE_HELP is specified in the **Implemented Interfaces** tab. For the implementation of the interface, click on the **Reimplement** button (see Figure 6.18).

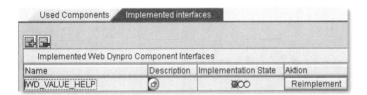

Figure 6.18 Implementation of Interface IWD_VALUE_HELP

The display in the **Implementation State** column then switches to green and the events and methods of the component interface of IWD_VALUE_HELP are visible in the component controller. The context of the component consists of a context node NAFTA, under which the three attributes LAND1, LANDX, and NATIO are located. The **Cardinality** property of the context node is assigned the value **0..n**. The context node SELECTION, which belongs to the component interface and provides the selected value to the application, also consists of the attributes LAND1, LANDX, and NATIO. The attribute type corresponds to that of the values of the same name of the DDIC type **T005T**.

6 | Reusing WD4A Components

The context node NAFTA is filled with data by the supply function method `supply_nafta()`. Here, the restriction is made to the three NAFTA member states of Canada, Mexico, and the USA. Listing 6.6 shows the implementation.

```
METHOD supply_nafta.
  DATA lt_countries   TYPE if_componentcontroller=>elements_nafta.
*--- Get NAFTA member data
  SELECT * FROM t005t INTO CORRESPONDING FIELDS OF TABLE lt_countries
                      WHERE spras EQ sy-langu AND ( land1 EQ 'US '
                                                OR  land1 EQ 'MX '
                                                OR  land1 EQ 'CA ' ).
  IF sy-subrc EQ 0.
    node->bind_table( new_items = lt_countries ).
  ENDIF.
ENDMETHOD.
```

Listing 6.6 Implementation of supply_nafta()

In the **Events** tab, we define the event DATA_SELECTED and add it to the component interface by setting the **Interface** identifier to the component interface. The application registers itself to this event and transfers the selected data in the corresponding event-handler method. We also add the VH_WINDOW_OPENED and VH_WINDOW_CLOSED events provided by the IWD_VALUE_HELP interface to the component interface (see Figure 6.19). The application is then also able to react separately to the opening or closing of the input-help dialog box.

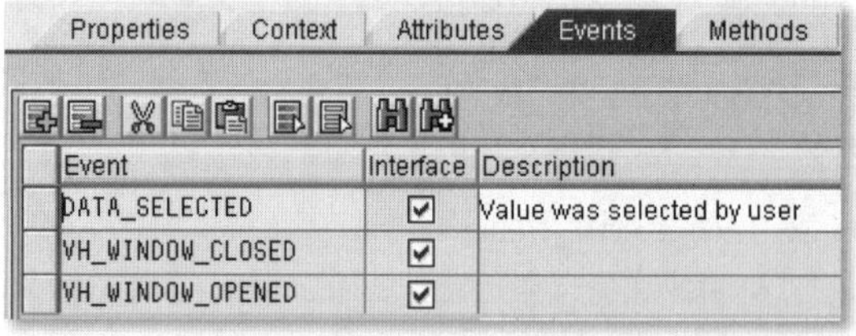

Event	Interface	Description
DATA_SELECTED	✓	Value was selected by user
VH_WINDOW_CLOSED	✓	
VH_WINDOW_OPENED	✓	

Figure 6.19 Events of the Input-Help Component

The `set_value_help_listener()` method must now be implemented (see Listing 6.7). This only consists of one instruction: Here, the reference to the Listener that is transferred is stored in a component controller attribute to be defined (VALUE_HELP_LISTENER of the type **IF_WD_VALUE_HELP_LISTENER**).

```
METHOD set_value_help_listener.
  wd_this->value_help_listener = listener.
ENDMETHOD.
```

Listing 6.7 Implementation of set_value_help_listener()

The V_DEFAULT view consists of a Table view element and a Button view element. The Table view element links to the NAFTA context node that is copied and mapped from the component controller. The action DO_COPY is joined to the **onAction** event of the Button view element.

In the corresponding event-handler method onactiondo_copy(), the selected value is first determined via lead selection and copied to the context node SELECTION, which forms the component interface. The DATA_SELECTED event is then triggered. The input help dialog box is closed by calling the close_window() method of the Listener. You can take these instructions from Listing 6.8.

```
METHOD onactiondo_copy.
  DATA   lr_node      TYPE REF TO if_wd_context_node.
  DATA   lr_element   TYPE REF TO if_wd_context_element.
  DATA   ls_nafta     TYPE if_v_default=>element_nafta.
  DATA   ls_selection TYPE if_v_default=>element_selection.
*--- Copy selected line to component interface
  lr_node = wd_context->get_child_node( 'NAFTA' ).
  lr_element = lr_node->get_lead_selection( ).
  lr_element->get_static_attributes( importing static_attributes =
                                     ls_nafta ).
  lr_node = wd_context->get_child_node( 'SELECTION' ).
  lr_node->bind_structure( new_item = ls_nafta ).
*--- Fire event, that data was selected
  wd_comp_controller->fire_data_selected_evt( ).
*--- Close window
  wd_comp_controller->value_help_listener->close_window( ).
ENDMETHOD.
```

Listing 6.8 Implementation of onactiondo_copy()

The WD_VALUE_HELP interface view belongs to the IWD_VALUE_HELP interface. The V_DEFAULT view is embedded in this interface view. The creation of the ZEXP_CUSTOM_SH_COMP input-help component that provides the NAFTA member states for selection is thus completed.

6.5.2 Using the Input-Help Component

We now want to integrate the input-help component we have created into an application that should only consist of an input field into which the NAFTA member state determined from the input help is copied.

We will call the component that is to use the input-help component ZEXP_CUSTOM_SH_COMP 'ZEXP_CUSTOM_SH_APP'. We define the usage USAGE_SH in the **Used Components** tab of ZEXP_CUSTOM_SH_APP. In our example, the component controller remains untouched. We must create the view V_DEFAULT and add the usage USAGE_SH in the **Properties** tab. The context of the view controller consists of the context node CONTENT with the attribute LANDX. The **value** property of the InputField view element is joined to the LANDX attribute.

To be able to call the input help at the input field, the **Input Help Mode** property of the LANDX context attribute must be set to the value **User-Defined Programming**. The usage USAGE_SH of the input-help component is then entered in the **Input Help Component Usage** property that appears underneath it (see Figure 6.20).

In the next step, the event-handler method is implemented that has registered to the event DATA_SELECTED of the input-help component (see Figure 6.21). At runtime, the data is copied from the SELECTION context node of the component interface of the input-help component and copied to the CONTENT context node, to which the InputField view element is joined.

Context V_DEFAULT	ZEXP_CUSTOM_SH_APP.COMPONENTCON
▽ ○ CONTEXT	USAGE_SH.ZEXP_CUSTOM_SH_COMP.INTE
▽ CONTENT	
LANDX	Context INTERFACECONTROLLER
▷ SELECTION	▽ ○ CONTEXT
	▷ SELECTION

Property	Value
Attribute	
Attribute Name	LANDX
Type assignment	Type
Type	T005T-LANDX
Read-only	☐
Primary Attribute	☐
Default Value	
Input Help Mode	User-Defined Programming
Input Help Component Usage	USAGE_SH

Figure 6.20 Usage Definition of the Input-Help Component in the View Controller

Developing Input-Help Components | 6.5

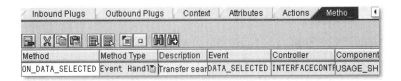

Figure 6.21 Defining the Event-Handler Method

The implementation of the transfer of the selected value in the event-handler method is shown in Listing 6.9.

```
METHOD on_data_selected.
  DATA lr_node    TYPE REF TO if_wd_context_node.
  DATA ls_content TYPE if_v_default=>element_content.
  DATA ls_sel     TYPE if_v_default=>element_selection.
*--- Read selected value from search help
  lr_node = wd_context->get_child_node( 'SELECTION' ).
  lr_node->get_static_attributes( IMPORTING
                                    static_attributes = ls_sel ).
  ls_content-landx = ls_sel-landx.
*--- Copy value to context
  lr_node = wd_context->get_child_node( 'CONTENT' ).
  lr_node->bind_structure( new_item = ls_content ).
ENDMETHOD.
```

Listing 6.9 Transferring the Selection from the Input-Help Component

After you start the application and call the input help, you will see the output in the client shown in Figure 6.22.

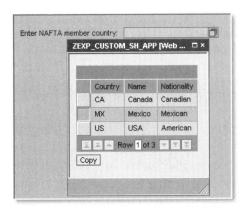

Figure 6.22 Output from the Application for the Input-Help Component

6.6 Enhancements of Components

When you reuse components, requirements can arise that necessitate changes or enhancements, building on the existing functionality of the component. If you were to attempt to implement these changes or enhancements by copying the component, for example, the component would be excluded from the future maintenance process of the supplier of the component.

For this reason, the possibility was introduced for modification-free implementation of changes and enhancements of components. These functions are part of the comprehensive *enhancement framework*, which allows not only modification-free enhancements of WD4A components, but also of a whole range of other objects and applications that are implemented in the SAP NetWeaver Application Server ABAP. Within a WD4A component you can make the corresponding enhancements to the following components (see Table 6.2).

Part of the component	Possible enhancements
1. View	▶ Adding view elements ▶ Hiding existing view elements ▶ Defining additional inbound and outbound plugs ▶ Defining additional actions
2. Controller	▶ Adding context nodes and context attributes ▶ Creating new methods and controller attributes ▶ Extending existing methods by implementing *pre-exit* and *post-exit* methods
3. Window	▶ Adding navigation links ▶ Hiding existing navigation links ▶ Defining a new navigation goal for an existing navigation link

Table 6.2 Possible Enhancements of Component Elements

To create an enhancement for a component, choose the element in the component for which the enhancement is to be implemented. You can then use the menu entry **[Component]** · **Enhance** to switch to enhancement mode in the main menu of the ABAP Workbench; note that you must be in display mode for this. In the dialog box that appears, assign a name to the enhancement and give a description (see Figure 6.23).

Create Enhancement Implementation	
Enh.Impl.	ZEXP_SH_AFTA
ShText	Example enhancement of search help

Figure 6.23 Creating an Enhancement

When you switch repeatedly to enhancement mode, you initially always get an overview of the enhancements that are already available for the component. You can manage several enhancements for each component. However, the changes you have made can only be edited in the enhancement in which they were originally implemented.

Our example will cover the enhancement to the input-help component ZEXP_CUSTOM_SH_COMP from Section 5.2 of this chapter, which provides an input help for the member states of the NAFTA trade agreement. Our objective now is to change the input-help component in such a way that the NAFTA member states are no longer provided for selection, but rather the member states of the Asian Free Trade Area (AFTA): Brunei, Indonesia, Malaysia, Philippines, Singapore, and Thailand.

In the component ZEXP_CUSTOM_SH_COMP, the determining of the NAFTA member countries has been implemented in the supply function method supply_nafta() in the component controller. We cannot change the instructions of this method in enhancement mode. However, it is possible to implement pre-exit and post-exit methods for the original method.

The pre-exit method has the same importing and changing parameters as the original method and is executed directly before the original method is called. Similarly, the post-exit method also makes the importing parameters of the original method available, unchanged, and is executed after the original method is called. The exporting, returning, and changing parameters of the original method can be edited as changing parameters in the post-exit method.

To implement the post-exit method, we decide to implement the supply function method supply_nafta(), since our objective is to replace the country table of the NAFTA member countries with a table of the AFTA member countries. To switch to the editor of the post-exit method, click on the corresponding button for the original method (see Figure 6.24). The implementation for the post-exit method is shown in Listing 6.10.

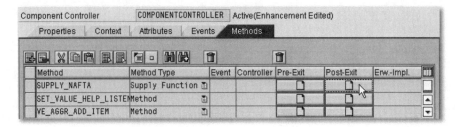

Figure 6.24 Editing the Post-Exit Method

```
METHOD _pst_01wynvic61k3c2dbtrv0e5gym.
  DATA lt_countries TYPE if_componentcontroller=>elements_nafta.
  DATA lt_elements  TYPE wdr_context_element_set.
  DATA lr_element   TYPE REF TO if_wd_context_element.
*--- Get AFTA member data
  SELECT * FROM t005t INTO CORRESPONDING FIELDS OF TABLE lt_countries
                  WHERE spras EQ sy-langu AND ( land1 EQ 'BN '
                     OR land1 EQ 'ID ' OR land1 EQ 'MY '
                     OR land1 EQ 'PH ' OR land1 EQ 'SG '
                     OR land1 EQ 'ID ' OR land1 EQ 'TH ' ).
  IF sy-subrc EQ 0.
    lt_elements = node->get_elements( ).
    LOOP AT lt_elements INTO lr_element.
*--- Remove original elements
      node->remove_element( lr_element ).
    ENDLOOP.
    node->bind_table( new_items = lt_countries ).
  ENDIF.
ENDMETHOD.
```

Listing 6.10 Implementing the Post-Exit Method

The name of the post-exit method is issued by the WD4A framework. First we determine the data on the member states from Table T005T, and then the context elements that were generated from the original method are deleted. The reference to the context node is also available in the post-exit method in the importing parameter NODE, so that the bind_table() method for filling the context node can be used with the newly created country list. The post-exit method must be activated as usual.

To use the input-help component we create a new test application with the name ZEXP_CUSTOM_SH_APP02. After you start the application and click on the input help icon in the input field, the display shown in Figure 6.25 appears with the list of AFTA member countries.

Enhancements of Components | **6.6**

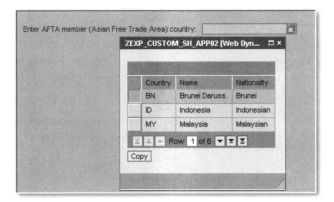

Figure 6.25 Output with Enhanced Input-Help Component

How well new technologies and frameworks can be integrated is integral to how readily they are accepted in heterogeneous system environments. In this respect, Web Dynpro for ABAP (WD4A), as a component of SAP NetWeaver, benefits from the extensive functions that the SAP NetWeaver components provide. In this chapter, we'll discuss the integration of WD4A applications into the SAP NetWeaver Portal, as well as integration with Adobe Interactive Forms. We will also show you how to display business graphics using the Internet Graphics Server.

7 Integrating WD4A Applications

7.1 Integration into the SAP NetWeaver Portal

The *SAP NetWeaver Portal* allows you to integrate applications that run on several backend systems, or different backend systems, by consolidating their display at the frontend. The smallest unit in the integration structure is the *iView*, which is a kind of container for the application to be integrated. iViews that are related in terms of content are grouped in *pages*. The *workset* forms the container for grouping mutually dependent tasks and processes. The portal also operates in a role-based manner: The individual users are assigned their tasks according to their access to functions in the portal.

There are three portal areas for creating links to the backend systems. User administration, including the assignment of roles, is performed in the *User Administrator*. In the *System Administrator*, you define the data for addressing the backend systems, such as the domain names of the servers and their port numbers. Here you can also assign aliases to the systems that are used in the *Content Administrator* in defining the application. The iView Wizard in the Content Administrator is used to define the connections to the applications that are implemented in the backend systems. Different iView Wizards exist for the various integration possibilities, such as the Web Dynpro for ABAP, Business Server Pages (BSP), or Portal Components.

SAP NetWeaver Portal allows the interaction between the applications running in the iViews, regardless of what technology they are based on or on what backend system they are operated. The functionality of the SAP NetWeaver Portal that allows this interaction is referred to as *portal eventing*. It is also possible to navigate from a WD4A application to various resources in the SAP NetWeaver Portal. You can specify both the relative and absolute paths of the resources in the SAP NetWeaver Portal. The *object-based navigation* (OBN) is another navigation model. Here, operations are executed using business objects. Business objects are the smallest logical units within a scenario that is based on business processes. Operations are assigned to the business objects via links. When you activate the links, this starts a new iView in which the operation that is executed is dependent on the business object.

7.1.1 Triggering Portal Events

The functions required for the portal integration of WD4A applications are provided by the IF_WD_PORTAL_INTEGRATION interface. An event is triggered by calling the method fire(). The data that must be transferred include a corresponding namespace in the PORTAL_EVENT_NAMESPACE parameter, the name of the event in the PORTAL_EVENT_NAME parameter, and a possible optional parameter in PORTAL_EVENT_PARAMETER.

In the WD4A component, the portal event should usually be triggered in an event-handler method. Listing 7.1 shows the instructions that are implemented in the event-handler method onactiondo_portal_eventing(). The value transferred in the PORTAL_EVENT_PARAMETER parameter is first read from the SOURCE context attribute of the CONTENT context node. You can use the Code Wizard to create the instructions for triggering the event.

```
METHOD onactiondo_portal_eventing.
  DATA lr_api_component   TYPE REF TO if_wd_component.
  DATA lr_portal_manager  TYPE REF TO if_wd_portal_integration.
  DATA lv_parameter       TYPE string.
  DATA ls_content         TYPE if_v_default=>element_content.
  DATA lr_node            TYPE REF TO if_wd_context_node.
*--- Read input value
  lr_node = wd_context->get_child_node( 'CONTENT' ).
  lr_node->get_static_attributes( IMPORTING
                                    static_attributes = ls_content ).
  lv_parameter = ls_content-source.
*--- Fire portal event
  lr_api_component  = wd_comp_controller->wd_get_api( ).
  lr_portal_manager = lr_api_component->get_portal_manager( ).
  CALL METHOD lr_portal_manager->fire
```

```
    EXPORTING
      portal_event_namespace = 'org.any'
      portal_event_name      = 'WD4A_EVENT'
      portal_event_parameter = lv_parameter.
ENDMETHOD.
```

Listing 7.1 Instructions for Triggering a Portal Event

To clarify the portal-eventing concept, we will integrate two WD4A applications into the SAP NetWeaver Portal. One of these serves as a source for a parameter value that is copied to the target application when an event is triggered, using the portal-eventing functionality.

ZEXP_PORTAL_SOURCE assumes the role of the source application, using the component of the same name. The function of the parameter transfer is fulfilled in the ZEXP_PORTAL_TARGET target application with the component of the same name. The ZEXP_PORTAL_SOURCE component consists of a Label, an InputField, and a Button view element. The **value** property of the InputField view element is linked to the SOURCE attribute of the CONTENT context node. The DO_PORTAL_EVENTING action was defined for the **onAction** event of the Button view element. The implementation of the corresponding event-handler method was presented in Listing 7.1.

7.1.2 Registration to Portal Events

Registration to a portal event within a WD4A component should be carried out when the component is initialized. The data for the namespace and for naming the event are required here. You perform registration in the same way you would when implementing the triggering of the event using the functions of the IF_WD_PORTAL_INTEGRATION interface; here we use the subscribe_event() method. You also need a reference to the view, which registers to the event, and the name of the action, which is triggered within the component. You must define this action manually in the **Actions** tab. In our example, it has the name ON_PORTAL_EVENT. The declarations and instructions for calling subscribe_event() can in turn be added with the Code Wizard. Listing 7.2 shows the implementation of the entire method.

```
METHOD wddoinit.
  DATA lr_api_component   TYPE REF TO if_wd_component.
  DATA lr_portal_manager  TYPE REF TO if_wd_portal_integration.
  DATA lr_view            TYPE REF TO if_wd_view_controller.
*--- Subscribe to portal event
  lr_view ?= wd_this->wd_get_api( ).
```

7 | Integrating WD4A Applications

```abap
    lr_api_component = wd_comp_controller->wd_get_api( ).
    lr_portal_manager = lr_api_component->get_portal_manager( ).
    CALL METHOD lr_portal_manager->subscribe_event
      EXPORTING
        portal_event_namespace = 'org.any'
        portal_event_name      = 'WD4A_EVENT'
        view                   = lr_view
        action                 = 'ON_PORTAL_EVENT'.
ENDMETHOD.
```

Listing 7.2 Registration to a Portal Event

At runtime, the event-handler method onactionon_portal_event() is called when you trigger the WD4A_EVENT portal event. You can access the value of the event parameter using the WDEVENT parameter copied to the event-handler method, which contains a reference to the instance of the object of the type **CL_WD_CUSTOM_EVENT**. The get_string() method returns the value of the event parameter. Since we want to output the parameter copied by the source application, we write the value that has been determined into the TARGET context attribute of the CONTENT context node. Listing 7.3 shows all instructions of the onactionon_portal_event() method.

```abap
METHOD onactionon_portal_event.
    DATA lr_node       TYPE REF TO if_wd_context_node.
    DATA ls_content    TYPE if_v_default=>element_content.
    DATA lv_parameter  TYPE string.
*--- Read parameter and write it to context
    lv_parameter = wdevent->get_string(
                             name = 'PORTAL_EVENT_PARAMETER' ).
    lr_node = wd_context->get_child_node( name = 'CONTENT' ).
    lr_node->set_attribute( EXPORTING name = 'TARGET'
                                      value = lv_parameter ).
ENDMETHOD.
```

Listing 7.3 Implementation of onactionon_portal_event()

The V_DEFAULT view of the ZEXP_PORTAL_TARGET component consists of the view elements Label and InputField. The **value** property of the InputField view element joins to the TARGET context attribute and outputs the value of the event parameter.

Figure 7.1 shows the output of the two WD4A applications in the SAP NetWeaver Portal. On the left-hand side in the iView, with the name **Source iView**, the ZEXP_PORTAL_SOURCE WD4A application is running. On the right-hand side in the **Target iView** iView you will see the output of the ZEXP_

PORTAL_TARGET WD4A application. The entry made in the input field of the **Source iView** iView is used as the event parameter. When you click on the **Trigger Event** button, the portal event is triggered with the name WD4A_EVENT in the onactiondo_portal_eventing() method of the ZEXP_PORTAL_SOURCE component, and the input value ("wd4a_message") is copied in the PORTAL_EVENT_PARAMETER parameter.

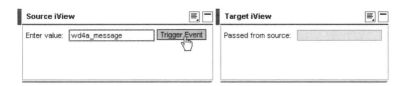

Figure 7.1 Output of Two WD4A Applications in the SAP NetWeaver Portal

The ZEXP_PORTAL_TARGET component has registered in the method wddoinit() to the event WD4A_EVENT and the event-handler method onactionon_portal_event() is therefore called. The PORTAL_EVENT_PARAMETER parameter is then read, and its value is copied to the context. The parameter value is displayed because the **value** property of the InputField view element is copied to the TARGET context attribute by the CONTENT context node. Figure 7.2 shows the status of the two applications in the SAP NetWeaver Portal, once the portal event has been triggered: The entry made in the input field of the WD4A application ZEXP_PORTAL_SOURCE "wd4a_message" is displayed in the WD4A application ZEXP_PORTAL_TARGET.

Figure 7.2 WD4A Applications After the Portal Event Is Triggered

7.2 Graphical Display of Data

The BusinessGraphics view element, thanks to the integration of the *Internet Graphics Server* (IGS), allows data to be displayed graphically in the WD4A framework. The BusinessGraphics view element allows a range of chart types to be displayed: For instance, the system supports the display of area charts (**area**), bar charts (**bars**), column charts (**columns**) and Gantt charts (**Gantt**). The setting for this is made using the **chartType** property (see Figure 7.3).

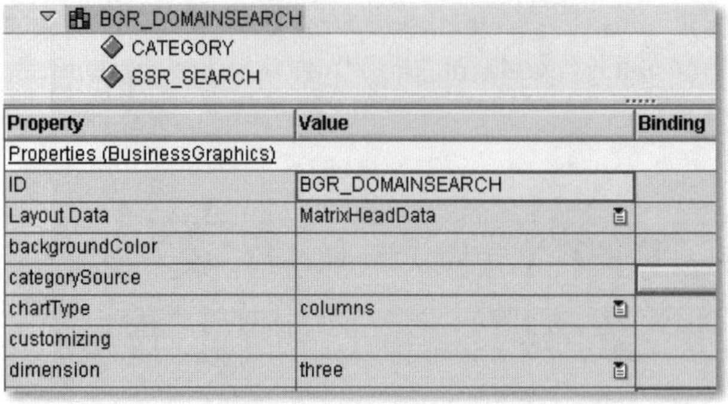

Figure 7.3 BusinessGraphics View Element

You also can manipulate the dimension of the graphic that is displayed using the **dimension** property. Two-dimensional (**two**), pseudo-three-dimensional[1] (**pseudo_three**), and three-dimensional (**three**) outputs are possible. Depending on the structure and type of the data volume to be displayed and the display type that is required, you can use different view elements that are subordinated to the BusinessGraphics view element that can be used in designing the graphics (see Table 7.1).

Design Type	Description
TimeValue	Used when time values are displayed.
Category	Used to group data into categories that are independent of each other. In column charts, categories are arranged horizontally beside each other, while the values are displayed vertically. In scatter or portfolio chart types, the Category view element cannot be used.
NumericValue	Used to display numeric values of the data type **double** and can determine, for example, the x-values for scatter charts or the y-values when you use the Category view element.
Point	Defines the number and type of the values of a dataset. The Point view element can have subordinate NumericValue or TimeValue view elements.

Table 7.1 Possible Design Types for Datasets

---

1 In a pseudo-three dimensional display, the z-axis is not displayed separately.

Design Type	Description
SimpleSeries	Used when you have a fixed number of numerical series that are fixed at the time of development. You use the SimpleSeries view element if the display is based on the Category view element and each category only has a y-value.
Series	Used to display more complex numerical series, for instance for scatter charts.

Table 7.1 Possible Design Types for Datasets (cont.)

You can modify the appearance of a special graphic using the *Chart Designer*; for example, you can change the colors, the lines, and the background of the graphical display. The Chart Designer is integrated into the development environment and is called through the context menu of the view element (**Edit Customizing**). The changes are stored as an XML file and converted by the IGS into a JPG or GIF file to be displayed.

In the following example, we want to display a category-based number quantity for the BusinessGraphics view element, using a column diagram. We want the graphic to illustrate the number of search results for a term within various Internet domains. The individual categories form the Internet domains .com, .us, .org, .edu, .net, and .de. The number of search results per domain is determined using the Google Web APIs Service and is copied to the WD4A application.

7.2.1 Using the BusinessGraphics View Element

Figure 7.4 shows the results of our sample component ZEXP_SEARCH_BY_DOMAIN. The search results were determined for the term "inheritance" for six different domains and were graphically implemented with the BusinessGraphics view element.

The data to be illustrated is provided in the form of a table of the name-value pairs by the data source. Table 7.2 shows an example of the search results that are determined.

7 | Integrating WD4A Applications

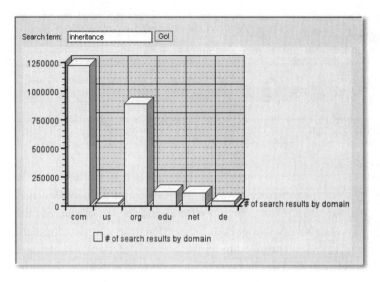

Figure 7.4 Graphic for Categorizing Search Results

Name	Value
.com	1244000
.us	31200
.org	880300
.edu	110120
.net	98000
.de	65800

Table 7.2 Format of a Randomly Chosen Numerical Series of Search Results

The table type of the internal table in which the search results are stored as name-value pairs is **TIHTTPNVP**. This table type is provided as standard by the ABAP Dictionary and is sufficient for managing the data in the example shown here. The context node DRESULT in the component controller is supplied from this internal table. To join the view element properties, this context node is copied and mapped by the component controller into the context of the view controller. The context node DRESULT is of the type **IHTTPNVP** and has the cardinality **0..n** (see Figure 7.5). The view-controller context also has two attributes, with the names SEARCHTERM of the type **STRING** and BGR_VSISBLE of the type **WDY_MD_UI_VISIBILITY**.

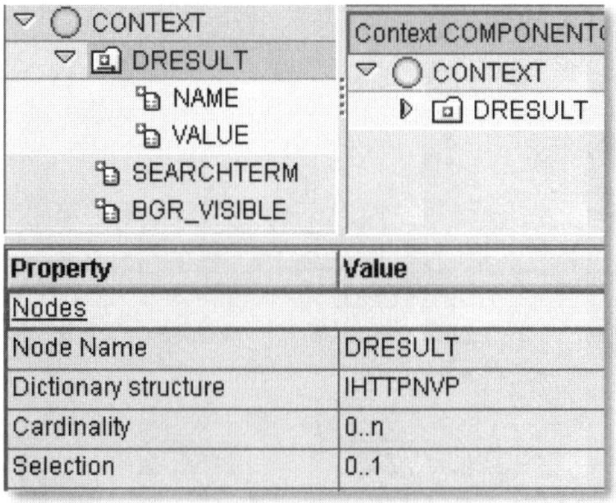

7.2 Graphical Display of Data

▽ ○ CONTEXT
   ▽ ▣ DRESULT
      🔸 NAME
      🔸 VALUE
      🔸 SEARCHTERM
      🔸 BGR_VISIBLE
	Context COMPONENTC
	  ▽ ○ CONTEXT
	    ▷ ▣ DRESULT

Property	Value
Nodes	
Node Name	DRESULT
Dictionary structure	IHTTPNVP
Cardinality	0..n
Selection	0..1

Figure 7.5 Context of the View Controller

The **value** property of the InputField view element that is used to enter the search term joins to the SEARCHTERM context attribute. The context attribute BGR_VSISBLE controls the visibility of the graphic; this should not be displayed until the search result is available. The V_DEFAULT view consists of a TransparentContainer view element TCO_INPUT, whose subordinate view elements are used to enter the search term and trigger the search. The **value** property of the InputField view element INP_SEARCH joins to the SEARCHTERM context attribute. The **onAction** event of the Button view element BTN_SEARCH joins to the DO_SEARCH action.

The data source for the BusinessGraphics view element is formed by the DRESULT context node. The **dataSource** property is thus joined to this context node. It is to be displayed using a column chart. The **columns** value is therefore chosen for the **chartType** property. You can show a three-dimensional display using the value **three** for the **dimension** property (see Figure 7.6).

The individual Internet domains form the categories that are displayed on the horizontal axis. A Category view element is therefore subordinated to the BusinessGraphics view element. The **description** property of the Category view element joins to the attribute NAME of the DRESULT context node. The names of the domains are available in this attribute at runtime in the elements of the context node (see Figure 7.7).

7 | Integrating WD4A Applications

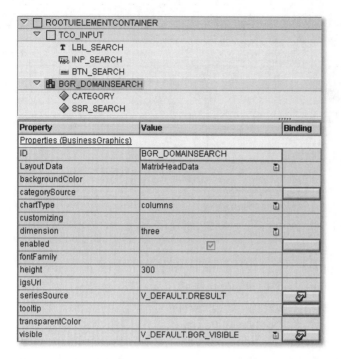

Figure 7.6 Setting the Properties of the BusinessGraphics View Element

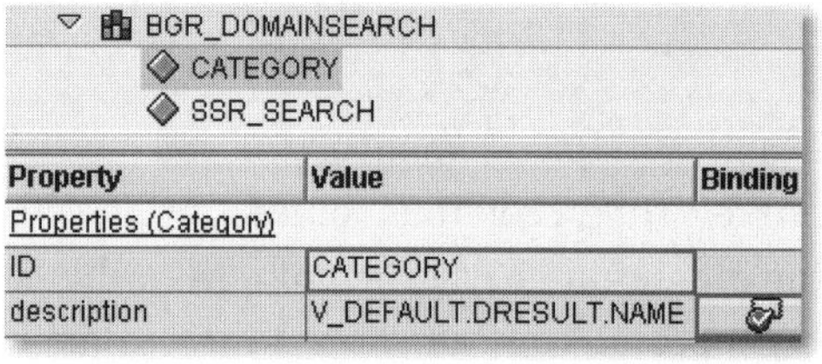

Figure 7.7 Using the Category View Element

Since every category or domain contains a value at runtime, we can use the `SimpleSeries` view element to display the y axis. Its **value** property is joined to the `VALUE` context attribute of the `DRESULT` context node (see Figure 7.8). At runtime, this contains the elements of the context node and the number of search results for each domain.

At runtime, clicking on the **Go!** button calls the event-handler method `onactiondo_search()`. Here, the search term is determined from the `SEARCH-TERM` context attribute, and a search is started by calling the `query_google()` method and copying the search term into the component controller. In the last step, the `BusinessGraphics` view element is shown.

Figure 7.8 Using the SimpleSeries View Element

You can find the instructions for the onactiondo_search() method in Listing 7.4.

```
METHOD onactiondo_search.
  DATA lv_searchterm   TYPE      string.
  DATA lt_result       TYPE      tihttpnvp.
  wd_context->get_attribute( EXPORTING name  = 'SEARCHTERM'
                             IMPORTING value = lv_searchterm ).
  wd_comp_controller->query_google( EXPORTING
                             iv_searchterm = lv_searchterm ).
  wd_context->set_attribute( EXPORTING name  = 'BGR_VISIBLE'
                   value = cl_wd_ui_element=>visibility_visible ).
ENDMETHOD.
```

Listing 7.4 Implementing the onactiondo_search() Event-Handler Method

7.2.2 Connecting the Data Source

To implement the search we use the Google Web APIs service[2] (*http://www.google.com/apis*), a program provided by Google that you can use to access Google's search functions via Web services, and whose functions can be integrated into your own applications. The application uses Web-service calls to access the Google Web APIs.

Communication is XML-based using the *Simple Object Access Protocol* (SOAP) via HTTP. In our case, the SAP NetWeaver Application Server ABAP, on which the WD4A application runs, acts as a client and triggers the query to

---

[2] At the time this book was written, the Google Web APIs Service was still at the beta stage. Non-commercial use of the Google Web APIs requires registration (which is free of charge), for which a Google account is created. Google then sends you a license key via email. This key must be used with every query you make using the Google Web APIs Service. The number of queries is restricted to 1,000 per day.

the Google Web APIs service. The Google Web APIs use the same syntax, which is also common in dialog-based searches through the Google website (*http://www.google.com*).

Three methods are responsible for communication with the Google Web APIs service in the component controller of ZEXP_SEARCH_BY_DOMAIN:

- wddoinit()
  Creates a HTTP client instance and sets the relevant header fields
- query_google()
  Compiles the search criteria, the triggering of the send operation, and the extraction of the search results data
- create_soap_env()
  Creates the SOAP envelope to be sent

The name-value pair for the domain search result is extracted from the message received from the Google Web APIs service via *XSL Transformation* (XSLT). The name of the XSL transformation is ZEXP_GOOGLE2ABAP. In the estimatedTotalResultsCount tag, the Google response contains the number of websites found for the search criterion. The search criterion, in turn, consists of the search term and domain and is contained in the searchQuery tag. You will find the instructions for the XSL transformation in Listing 7.5.

```
<xsl:transform version="1.0"
  xmlns:xsl="http://www.w3.org/1999/XSL/Transform"
  xmlns:sap="http://www.sap.com/sapxsl"
  xmlns:asx="http://www.sap.com/abapxml" >
<!-- Transform Google response to an abap structure -->
  <xsl:strip-space elements="*"/>
  <xsl:output indent="yes" />
  <xsl:template match="return">
    <asx:abap version="1.0">
      <asx:values>
        <ES_RESULT>
        <!-- Total number of results -->
        <VALUE>
          <xsl:value-of select="estimatedTotalResultsCount" />
        </VALUE>
        <!-- Search Parameter -->
        <NAME>
          <xsl:value-of select="searchQuery" />
        </NAME>
        </ES_RESULT>
      </asx:values>
```

```
        </asx:abap>
      </xsl:template>
    </xsl:transform>
```

Listing 7.5 XSL Transformation of the Google Response into an ABAP Structure

In the wddoinit() method of the component controller, an instance of the HTTP client is created specifying the URL. The Google URL to be used for this is *http://api.google.com/search/beta2*. In the **SoapAction** header field, you must use the value **doGoogleSearch**. You can take the values for the remaining header fields from Listing 7.6.

```
METHOD wddoinit.
*--- Create client by URL
  CALL METHOD cl_http_client=>create_by_url
    EXPORTING
      url           = 'http://api.google.com/search/beta2'
      proxy_host    = 'proxy'
      proxy_service = '8080'
    IMPORTING
      client        = wd_this->mr_http_client.
*--- Set header fields
  CALL METHOD wd_this->mr_http_client->request->set_header_field
    EXPORTING
      name  = '~request_method'
      value = 'POST'.
  CALL METHOD wd_this->mr_http_client->request->set_header_field
    EXPORTING
      name  = '~server_protocol'
      value = 'HTTP/1.1'.
  CALL METHOD wd_this->mr_http_client->request->set_header_field
    EXPORTING
      name  = 'Content-Type'
      value = 'text/xml; charset=utf-8'.
  CALL METHOD wd_this->mr_http_client->request->set_header_field
    EXPORTING
      name  = 'SOAPAction'
      value = 'doGoogleSearch'.
ENDMETHOD.
```

Listing 7.6 Generating the Client Instance in wddoinit()

The query_google() method has an input parameter iv_sterm of the type **STRING**. The method is called from the view controller, and the search term is transferred to it. The search is performed for each individual domain, which means that for each of the six domains *.com*, *.us*, *.org*, *.net*, *.edu*, and

.de in method `query_google()` a request is sent to the Google Web APIs Service, and the necessary values are extracted from the response via XSLT.

Listing 7.7 shows the implementation of `query_google()`.

```
METHOD query_google.
    DATA  lv_strlength      TYPE            string.
    DATA  lv_ilength        TYPE            i.
    DATA  lv_reponse        TYPE            xstring.
    DATA  lr_xslt_err       TYPE REF TO     cx_xslt_exception.
    DATA  lv_data           TYPE            string.
    DATA  ls_result         TYPE            ihttpnvp.
    DATA  lt_result         TYPE            tihttpnvp.
    DATA  lv_dummy          TYPE            string.
    DATA  lr_node           TYPE REF TO     if_wd_context_node.
*--- Loop for every of the six domains we want to analyze
    DO 6 TIMES.
*--- Create soap envelope
      wd_this->create_soap_env( EXPORTING iv_index      = sy-index
                                          iv_searchterm = iv_searchterm
                                IMPORTING ev_data       = lv_data ).
      lv_strlength = STRLEN( lv_data ).
*--- Set header field content length
      CALL METHOD wd_this->mr_http_client->request->set_header_field
        EXPORTING
          name  = 'Content-Length'
          value = lv_strlength.
*--- Put soap envelope into the request
      lv_ilength = lv_strlength.
      CALL METHOD wd_this->mr_http_client->request->set_cdata
        EXPORTING
          data   = lv_data
          offset = 0
          length = lv_ilength.
*--- Send request
      CALL METHOD wd_this->mr_http_client->send
        EXCEPTIONS
          http_communication_failure = 1
          http_invalid_state         = 2.
*--- Receive response
      CALL METHOD wd_this->mr_http_client->receive
        EXCEPTIONS
          http_communication_failure = 1
          http_invalid_state         = 2
          http_processing_failed     = 3.
*--- Get response as XML from the client response
      lv_reponse = wd_this->mr_http_client->response->get_data( ).
```

```
*--- Do XSL transformation
    TRY.
        CALL TRANSFORMATION ('ZEXP_GOOGLE2ABAP')
             SOURCE XML lv_reponse
             RESULT    es_result  = ls_result.
      CATCH cx_xslt_exception INTO lr_xslt_err.
*----- Do error handling here...
    ENDTRY.
    SPLIT ls_result-name AT '.' INTO lv_dummy ls_result-name.
    APPEND ls_result TO lt_result.
  ENDDO.
*--- Fill context node
  lr_node = wd_context->get_child_node( 'DRESULT' ).
  lr_node->bind_table( new_items         = lt_result
                       set_initial_elements = abap_true ).
ENDMETHOD.
```

Listing 7.7 Triggering the Search Queries for Google

The `create_soap_env()` method creates the SOAP notification to be sent. It has two input parameters: `iv_sterm` for the search term, and `iv_index` for determining the domain to be used. Here you should note the `key` tag, where your personal Google registration key must be entered. The search term for each domain is then formed using the loop index transferred to the method. The remaining settings correspond to the specifications in the Google Web APIs Service documentation. All of the instructions for this are summarized in Listing 7.8.

```
METHOD create_soap_env.
  CONCATENATE '<?xml version="1.0" encoding="UTF-8" ?>'
  '<SOAP-ENV:Envelope xmlns:SOAP-ENV='
  '"http://schemas.xmlsoap.org/soap/envelope/"'
  'xmlns:xsi="http://www.w3.org/1999/XMLSchema-instance"'
  'xmlns:xsd="http://www.w3.org/1999/XMLSchema"><SOAP-ENV:Body>'
  '<ns1:doGoogleSearch xmlns:ns1="urn:GoogleSearch" SOAP-ENV:'
  'encodingStyle="http://schemas.xmlsoap.org/soap/encoding/">'
  '<key xsi:type="xsd:string">[YOUR KEY BELONGS HERE]</key>'
  INTO ev_data.
  CASE iv_index.
    WHEN 1. CONCATENATE ev_data '<q xsi:type="xsd:string">'
        iv_sterm 'site:.com</q>' INTO ev_data SEPARATED BY space.
    WHEN 2. CONCATENATE ev_data '<q xsi:type="xsd:string">'
        iv_sterm 'site:.us</q>' INTO ev_data SEPARATED BY space.
    WHEN 3. CONCATENATE ev_data '<q xsi:type="xsd:string">'
        iv_sterm 'site:.org</q>' INTO ev_data SEPARATED BY space.
    WHEN 4. CONCATENATE ev_data '<q xsi:type="xsd:string">'
```

```abap
                iv_sterm 'site:.edu</q>' INTO ev_data SEPARATED BY space.
    WHEN 5. CONCATENATE ev_data '<q xsi:type="xsd:string">'
                iv_sterm 'site:.net</q>' INTO ev_data SEPARATED BY space.
    WHEN 6. CONCATENATE ev_data '<q xsi:type="xsd:string">'
                iv_sterm 'site:.de</q>' INTO ev_data SEPARATED BY space.
  ENDCASE.
  CONCATENATE ev_data
  '<start xsi:type="xsd:int">0</start>'
  '<maxResults xsi:type="xsd:int">10</maxResults>'
  '<filter xsi:type="xsd:boolean">true</filter>'
  '<restrict xsi:type="xsd:string" />'
  '<safeSearch xsi:type="xsd:boolean">false</safeSearch>'
  '<lr xsi:type="xsd:string" />'
  '<ie xsi:type="xsd:string">latin1</ie>'
  '<oe xsi:type="xsd:string">latin1</oe>'
  '</ns1:doGoogleSearch>'
  '</SOAP-ENV:Body>'
  '</SOAP-ENV:Envelope>'
  INTO ev_data.
ENDMETHOD.
```

Listing 7.8 Creating the SOAP Envelope

7.3 Interactive Forms Via Adobe Integration

With the SAP Web Application Server 6.40, SAP offers a functionality that is referred to as *Adobe Document Service* (ADC). The ADC allows the setting, display, and editing of interactive forms that are based on Adobe software. With Web Dynpro for ABAP, which is available with SAP NetWeaver Application Server ABAP (SAP NetWeaver Release 2004s), you can integrate interactive forms into WD4A applications or create interactive, PDF-based forms from Web Dynpro for ABAP.

Using Portable Document Format (PDF) in applications offers the following advantages over purely browser-based user interaction:

▶ PDF documents can be saved locally. This enables you to edit forms offline if you have no Internet connection, or if the Internet connection is interrupted, and then load them into the application later.

▶ PDF documents have a high-quality appearance. Users are more familiar with formula-based processes than they are with complicated online navigation scenarios.

▶ The print output corresponds exactly with the appearance on the screen. There are no changes in orientation, or in terms of font sizes.

- Special functions in Adobe Acrobat Reader allow digital signatures for interactive forms.
- The design tool developed by Adobe has a graphic development environment and is very easy to use.

7.3.1 System Requirements for Interactive Forms

You need at least Adobe Acrobat Reader 7.0.1 to work with Adobe Interactive Forms. Furthermore, to display Adobe Interactive Forms in your web browser, you also need the frontend components of the *SAP Active Component Framework* (ACF). Installation requires at least Microsoft Windows 2000 and Microsoft Internet Explorer 6.0. You must also make the following settings in Internet Explorer:

1. **Run ActiveX controls and plug-ins** must be set to **Enabled**
2. **Script ActiveX controls marked safe for scripting** must be set to **Enabled**
3. **Active scripting** must be set to **Enabled**

To ensure that there is a link to the Adobe Document Service, run the FP_PDF_TEST_00 program (Transaction SE38) on your server. A dialog box should then appear showing the version number of the installed ADS.

To be able to use the development environment of Adobe Interactive Forms — the *Adobe LifeCycle Designer* — it must be installed in the frontend as part of the SAP GUI installation. You can check this using the Form Builder (Transaction SFP) and by navigating to the layout of an Adobe form contained in your system.

7.3.2 Scenario for Using Interactive Forms

The WD4A framework allows interactive forms to be created both in the Form Builder (Transaction SFP) and from the Web Dynpro View Designer. The integration into the WD4A framework provides the advantage that an existing context in the View Controller is used to create the interface in the Form Builder. This lets you avoid unnecessary development work, because the attributes created in the context are immediately available in the Adobe LifeCycle Designer.

Our procedure for developing the sample application therefore begins with the creation of the WD4A component, which we will call ZEXP_INTERACTIVE_FORMS. We want application users to have the option of editing personal data (i.e., first name, last name, position, and company), either online in the web browser or offline in Adobe Acrobat Reader. After editing offline, we want users to be able to restart the application, load the document from the local PC into the WD4A application, and copy the data if they so choose. We also want them to have the option of checking the copied data by displaying it in a separate view.

In the component controller of the ZEXP_INTERACTIVE_FORMS component, we create a context node PERSON with the cardinality **1..1**. The context node receives four attributes, FIRSTNAME, LASTNAME, POSITION, and COMPANY, which are all of the type **STRING**. The context node is copied into the view controller context of the V_DEFAULT and V_CONFIRM views and mapped. V_DEFAULT displays the interactive form and the upload, the V_CONFIRM view displays and confirms the entries made offline by the user. The context of the V_DEFAULT view also contains a FILE context node with the attribute IFORM of the type **XSTRING**. In this attribute, the loaded PDF file is stored in binary format (see Figure 7.9).

The main components of the V_DEFAULT view are the FileUpload view element FUD_PDF and the InteractiveForm view element IFO_PERSON, along with two Button view elements, BTN_UPLOAD for triggering the upload process and BTN_SUBMIT for copying the data from the PDF into the view controller context (see Figure 7.10).

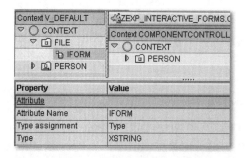

Figure 7.9 Context of the V_DEFAULT View

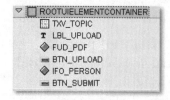

Figure 7.10 Layout of the V_DEFAULT View

The actions to which the **onAction** event of the Button view elements are joined are called DO_LOAD and DO_SUBMIT. The event-handler method of the DO_LOAD action does not have to be implemented; rather we merely need a server round trip to write the datastream into the context attribute. The OP_V_DEFAULT outbound plug is triggered in the onactiondo_submit() event-handler method, which should trigger the navigation to the V_CONFIRM view at runtime (see Listing 7.9). The V_DEFAULT view also has an inbound plug for navigating back from the V_CONFIRM view.

```
METHOD onactiondo_submit.
    wd_this->fire_op_v_default_plg( ).
ENDMETHOD.
```

Listing 7.9 Triggering the Outbound Plug

7.3.3 Using the InteractiveForm View Element

Figure 7.11 shows the view of the most important properties of the InteractiveForm view element. The **dataSource** property is joined to the PERSON context node, whose attributes are thus used when the Interactive Form is created in the Form Builder to generate the interface. The **pdfSource** property is joined to the IFORM context attribute of the FILE context node, which contains the PDF after uploading the file from the user's local PC. The **enabled** property is responsible for ensuring that the form's interactivity is released. These indicators are not set in the standard setting and interactive forms can only be displayed.

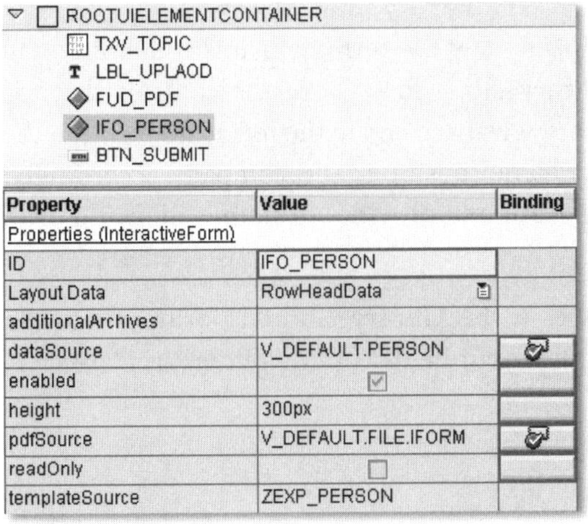

Property	Value	Binding
Properties (InteractiveForm)		
ID	IFO_PERSON	
Layout Data	RowHeadData	
additionalArchives		
dataSource	V_DEFAULT.PERSON	
enabled	☑	
height	300px	
pdfSource	V_DEFAULT.FILE.IFORM	
readOnly	☐	
templateSource	ZEXP_PERSON	

Tree structure:
- ROOTUIELEMENTCONTAINER
  - TXV_TOPIC
  - LBL_UPLAOD
  - FUD_PDF
  - IFO_PERSON
  - BTN_SUBMIT

Figure 7.11 Properties of the InteractiveForm View Element

All Adobe forms in the system, and as they are also listed in the Form Builder, are offered for selection when you select the icon for the input help in the input field for the **templateSource** property. However, in our example we want to create a new form that uses the settings made in the context. We therefore enter a new name in the input field for the **templateSource** property and call the new interactive form to be created ZEXP_PERSON. Once you confirm your entry, a dialog box appears to establish the interface to the new interactive form to be created. Name the interface as shown in Figure 7.12 as "Zexp_if_person."

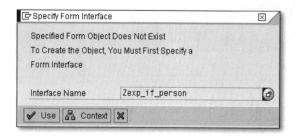

Figure 7.12 Creating the Interface for the Interactive Form

After you click on **Context**, you can choose a context node whose structure is used to create the interface. Here, choose the context node PERSON. The Adobe LifeCycle Designer integrated into the Form Builder, as shown in Figure 7.13, is then called. On the left-hand side, in the **Data View** tab, you can see the attributes of the PERSON context node, which now belong to the newly created interface ZEXP_IF_PERSON.

In the center of the screen, you can view the form, which is still empty. On the right-hand side, in the **Library** tab, you will see the controls that are available to build the form. We now want to create the form and position the input fields for first name, last name, position, and company accordingly. For this, the Adobe LifeCycle Designer provides a simple drag-and-drop functionality.

Use the **Text Field** control listed in the **Library** tab and position it in the form. A sample placement for two input fields is shown in Figure 7.14.

Interactive Forms Via Adobe Integration | 7.3

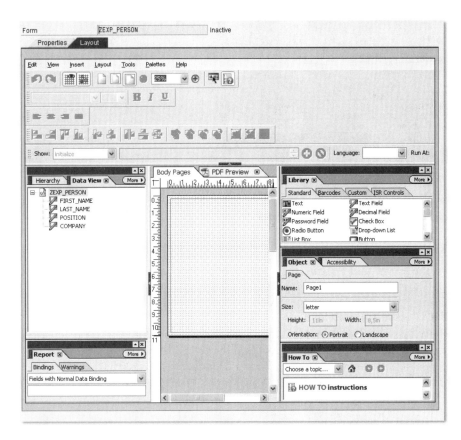

Figure 7.13 Creating an Interactive Form

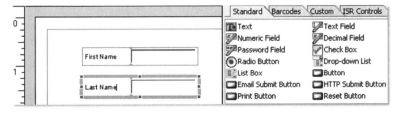

Figure 7.14 Positioning of Input Fields in the Form

Once you have created the four input fields in the form, join the attributes of the interface to the input fields. To do this, select the relevant input field and make the assignment in the **Binding** tab you can see on the right-hand side: Figure 7.15 shows the binding of the input field with the indicator "TextField1" for the interface attribute FIRST_NAME.

7 | Integrating WD4A Applications

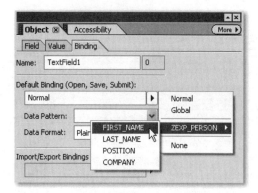

Figure 7.15 Binding the Interface Attributes

After all of the form's controls have been joined to the interface attributes, you can save and activate the form. You are then also requested to activate the newly created interface ZEXP_IF_PERSON, which you can confirm.

Back to the component ZEXP_INTERACTIVE_FORMS: Here you must also add the views V_DEFAULT and V_CONFIRM to the window and fix the navigation. Make these settings as shown in Figure 7.16.

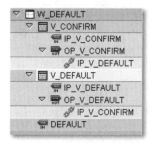

Figure 7.16 Structure of the Window

You can then activate the component and create and start the application. Figure 7.17 shows the output in the client: the form contains the **First Name**, **Last Name**, **Position**, and **Company** fields created by us in the Form Builder, which the user can edit online. However, you also have the possibility of saving the PDF file locally to the PC using the corresponding icon; the form can then be edited without linking to the WD4A application. Simple search helps are also available offline, depending on how the context has been configured. To upload the entries you have made in the WD4A application, the application must be restarted. You can use the **Browse...** button of the implemented FileUpload view element to choose the locally stored PDF file.

The **Load Data** button loads the PDF file into the WD4A application. The entries made by the user are now displayed in the online form (see Figure 7.18). The data, however, is not yet included in the context; it is not copied until you press the **Submit Data** button at the bottom of the screen. In our sample application, clicking on **Submit Data** causes you to navigate to a second view, in which the content of the context that is now filled is displayed for checking. Figure 7.19 shows the result of this output.

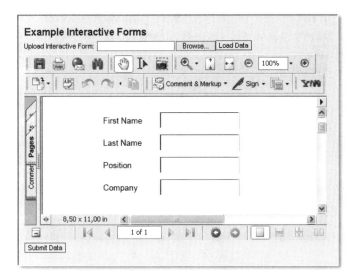

Figure 7.17 View for Applying Interactive Forms

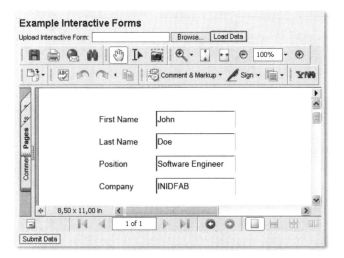

Figure 7.18 Copying the Offline Entries

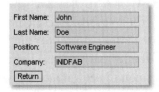

Figure 7.19 Displaying the Context Content

As well as supporting the integration for generating interactive forms, our simple scenario has also shown that this process, thanks to the WD4A framework's model-driven approach, can run declaratively and without having to create ABAP statements manually.

A Classes and Interfaces

The ability to access interfaces and objects directly in the Web Dynpro for ABAP (WD4A) framework is required mainly in dynamic programming. Chapter 5 already introduced some of these options. The following sections in this Appendix provide a complete overview of the classes and interfaces of the WD4A components that are available at runtime. This includes various examples of declarations and statements.

A.1 Component

A.1.1 IF_WD_COMPONENT

The `IF_WD_COMPONENT` interface enables you to access the properties of a WD4A component. The declarations and calls of the respective methods are described in the following sections. By calling `wd_get_api()` within the component controller, you can access the component object reference.

```
DATA lr_comp_api TYPE REF TO if_wd_component.
lr_comp_api = wd_this->wd_get_api( ).
```

- You can obtain the component ID by calling the `get_id()` method.

    ```
    DATA lv_comp_id TYPE string.
    lv_comp_id = lr_comp_api->get_id( ).
    ```

- Input data that hasn't been written to the context yet can be deleted by calling the `remove_pending_input()` method.

    ```
    lr_comp_api->remove_pending_input( ).
    ```

- If you call the `get_window_manager()` method, you can obtain a reference to the Window Manager.

    ```
    DATA lr_window_manager TYPE REF TO if_wd_window_manager.
    lr_window_manager = lr_comp_api->get_window_manager( ).
    ```

- You can determine information data on the component by calling the `get_component_info()` method.

    ```
    DATA lr_comp_info TYPE REF TO if_wd_rr_component.
    lr_comp_info = lr_comp_api->get_component_info( ).
    ```

- The result is of the **IF_WD_RR_COMPONENT** type. You then can access the implemented interfaces via the component information. This is done by calling the `get_impl_components()` method.

  ```
  DATA lt_impl TYPE string_table.
  lt_impl = lr_comp_info->get_impl_components( [InterfaceName] ).
  ```

- The component usages can be obtained by calling the `get_component_usage()` method.

  ```
  DATA lr_usage TYPE REF TO if_wd_rr_component_usage.
  lr_usage = lr_comp_info->get_component_usage( [ComponentUsageName] ).
  ```

- When calling the `get_controller()` method, the component information returns a reference to the metadata of the corresponding controller.

  ```
  DATA lr_controller TYPE REF TO if_wd_rr_controller.
  lr_controller = lr_comp_info->get_controller( [ControllerName] ).
  ```

- When calling the `get_view()` method, the component information returns a reference to the metadata of the corresponding view.

  ```
  DATA lr_view  TYPE REF TO if_wd_rr_view.
  lr_view = lr_comp_info->get_view( [ViewName] ).
  ```

- When calling the `get_window()` method, the component information returns a reference to the metadata of the corresponding window.

  ```
  DATA lr_window  TYPE REF TO if_wd_rr_window.
  lr_window = lr_comp_info->get_window( [WindowName] ).
  ```

- You can determine the component name by calling the `get_name()` method.

  ```
  DATA lv_name  TYPE STRING.
  lv_name  = lr_comp_info->get_name( ).
  ```

- Calling the `get_portal_manager()` method enables you to obtain a reference to the Portal Manager.

  ```
  DATA lr_portal_man TYPE REF TO if_wd_portal_integration.
  lr_portal_man = lr_comp_api->get_portal_manager( ).
  ```

- The `get_configuration_key()` method enables you to determine the ID of a configuration.

  ```
  DATA lv_config_key TYPE wdy_config_key.
  lv_config_key = lr_comp_api->get_configuration_key( ).
  ```

The `add_event_handler()` method enables the dynamic registration of an event-handler method for an event that is triggered in a different controller. The parameters to be transferred for this purpose have the following properties:

- LISTENER_NAME
  Name of the controller in which the event-handler method was implemented
- HANDLER_NAME
  Name of the event-handler method
- CONTROLLER_NAME
  Name of the controller in which the event is triggered
- EVENT_NAME
  Name of the event

  ```
  DATA lv_listener   TYPE string.
  DATA lv_handler    TYPE string.
  DATA lv_controller TYPE string.
  DATA lv_event      TYPE string.
  lr_comp_api->add_event_handler( EXPORTING
                                  listener_name   = lr_listener
                                  handler_name    = lv_handler
                                  controller_name = lv_controller
                                  event_name      = lv_event ).
  ```

  You also can undo the registration of an event-handler method for an event by calling the `remove_event_handler()` method.

  ```
  lr_comp_api->remove_event_handler( EXPORTING
                                  listener_name   = lv_listener
                                  handler_name    = lv_handler
                                  controller_name = lv_controller
                                  event_name      = lv_event ).
  ```

- The call of the `cancel_navigation()` method does not allow any navigation for the current request-response cycle.

  ```
  lr_comp_api->cancel_navigation( ).
  ```

- Calling the `get_personalization_manager()` method enables you to obtain a reference to the Personalization Manager object. The return value is of type **IF_WD_PERSONALIZATION**.

  ```
  DATA lr_pers_manager TYPE REF TO if_wd_personalization.
  lr_pers_manager = lr_comp_api->get_personalization_manager( ).
  ```

▶ Access to the IF_WD_APPLICATION interface (see Section A.6.1) occurs via the get_application() method.

```
DATA lr_appl_api  TYPE REF TO if_wd_application.
lr_appl_api = lr_comp_api->get_application( ).
```

You can obtain a reference to the object of a component usage group via the get_cmp_usage_group() method. Prior to that, you can use the has_cmp_usage_group() method to check whether a component usage group exists. A component usage group summarizes all usages that refer to the same component.

```
DATA lr_usage_group      TYPE REF TO if_wd_cmp_usage_group.
DATA lv_usage_gr_exists  TYPE WDY_BOOLEAN.
lv_usage_gr_exists = lr_comp_api->has_cmp_usage_group( [GroupName] ).
IF lv_usage_gr_exists EQ abap_true.
  lr_usage_group = lr_comp_api->get_cmp_usage_group( [GroupName] ).
ENDIF.
```

You can create a component usage group by using the create_cmp_usage_group() method. A freely definable group name and the name of the component for which the different usages have been defined are then transferred.

```
DATA lr_usage_group TYPE REF TO if_wd_cmp_usage_group.
lr_usage_group = lr_comp_api->create_cmp_usage_group( EXPORTING
                                    name            = [GroupName]
                                    used_component  = [ComponentName ).
```

A.1.2 IF_WD_COMPONENT_USAGE

Within a defined component usage, you can access the used component through the IF_WD_COMPONENT_USAGE interface.

```
DATA  lr_comp_usage TYPE REF TO if_wd_component_usage.
lr_comp_usage = wd_this->wd_cpuse_[NameOfUsage]( ).
```

The instance of a used component can be created by calling the create_component() method. You need that instance to access methods, events, and the context in the interface controller of the used component. If you only use the interface view of the used component, the WD4A framework will automatically generate the instance. If an instance of the used component already exists, a runtime error will be generated. For this reason, you should first use the has_active_component() method in order to check whether or not an instance already exists.

```
IF lr_comp_usage->has_active_component( ) IS INITIAL.
  lr_comp_usage->create_component( ).
ENDIF.
```

You can delete an existing instance of a used component by using the `delete_component()` method.

```
IF lr_comp_usage->has_active_component( ) IS INITIAL.
  lr_comp_usage->delete_component( ).
ENDIF.
```

The reference to the interface controller of the used component can be obtained by calling the `get_interface_controller()` method. The type of the return value depends on the structure of the corresponding interface controller. In Listing A.1, an `on_convert_values()` method of a component to be used is called. The name of the component is ZEXP_CONVERSION_MODEL, and the type of the interface controller is ZIWCI_EXP_CONVERSION_MODEL. The declarations and the combination of the statements are made available to you by the Code Wizard.

```
METHOD on_convert_values.
  DATA lr_if_contr   TYPE REF TO  ziwci_exp_conversion_model.
  DATA lr_comp_usage TYPE REF TO if_wd_component_usage.
  lr_comp_usage = wd_this->wd_cpuse_usage_model( ).
  lr_if_contr ?= lr_comp_usage->get_interface_controller( ).
  lr_if_contr->convert_values( ).
ENDMETHOD.
```

Listing A.1 Access to a Method of the Interface Controller

As is the case with the IF_WD_COMPONENT interface (see Section A.1.1), you can dynamically register an event-handler method for an event. The parameters to be transferred for this purpose have the following properties:

- LISTENER_NAME
  Name of the controller in which the event-handler method was implemented

- HANDLER_NAME
  Name of the event-handler method

- CONTROLLER_NAME
  Name of the controller in which the event is triggered

- EVENT_NAME
  Name of the event

In the following listing you can see the declarations of the `add_event_handler()` method parameters and their calls.

```
DATA lr_listener    TYPE REF TO if_wd_controller.
DATA lv_handler     TYPE string.
DATA lv_controller  TYPE string.
DATA lv_event       TYPE string.
*--- ... coding to define event handler data comes here
lr_comp_usage->add_event_handler( EXPORTING
                                  listener        = lr_listener
                                  handler_name    = lv_handler
                                  controller_name = lv_controller
                                  event_name      = lv_event ).
```

The registration can be deleted by calling the `remove_event_handler()` method.

```
lr_comp_usage->remove_event_handler( EXPORTING
                                     listener        = lr_listener
                                     handler_name    = lv_handler
                                     controller_name = lv_controller
                                     event_name      = lv_event ).
```

It is possible to create a component usage of the same type: that is, of the same used component. This function is carried out by the `create_comp_usage_of_same_type()` method.

```
DATA  lr_comp_usage2 TYPE REF TO if_wd_component_usage.
lr_comp_usage2 = lr_comp_usage->create_comp_usage_of_same_type( ).
```

By using the `enter_referencing_mode()` method you can force several components to work with the same instance of a component usage. The component that instantiates the component to be used via the `create_component()` method transfers the reference to that instance to all other components that use the same component. Those other components then use the `enter_referencing_mode()` method in order to work with the same object.

```
lr_comp_usage->enter_referencing_mode( ir_usage ).
```

Let us, for example, suppose that three components exist with the following names: `Z_MAIN`, `Z_DATA`, and `Z_RESULT`. Components `Z_MAIN` and `Z_RESULT` are supposed to use the same instance of component `Z_DATA`. Component `Z_MAIN` is the entry component of the application and instantiates the usage of component `Z_DATA`. There are two ways to ensure that component `Z_RESULT` uses the same instance of `Z_DATA` as component `Z_MAIN`:

1. You can implement a `set_usage()` method in the component controller of component Z_RESULT. The method receives the reference for the usage of component Z_DATA in the `ir_usage` parameter of type **IF_WD_COMPONENT_USAGE** and is called by component Z_MAIN. The usage definitions of component Z_DATA and component Z_RESULT in Z_MAIN are assigned the names USAGE_Z_DATA and USAGE_Z_RESULT.

   ```
   DATA lr_usage TYPE REF TO if_wd_component_usage.
     lr_usage = wd_this->wd_cpuse_usage_z_data( ).
     lr_usage->enter_referencing_mode( ir_usage ).
   ```

   The flow in the `wddoinit()` method of component Z_MAIN is as follows:

   ```
   DATA lr_usage TYPE REF TO if_wd_component_usage.
   DATA lr_if_ctr_z_result TYPE REF TO iwci_z_result.
   DATA lr_data_usage TYPE REF TO if_wd_component_usage.
   *-- Create instance of z_data
   lr_data_usage = wd_this->wd_cpuse_usage_z_data( ).
   IF lr_data_usage->has_active_component( ) IS INITIAL.
   lr_data_usage->create_component( ).
   ENDIF.
   *-- Create instance of z_result
   lr_usage = wd_this->wd_cpuse_usage_z_result( ).
   IF lr_usage->has_active_component( ) IS INITIAL.
   lr_usage->create_component( ).
   ENDIF.
   *-- Set usage
   lr_if_ctr_z_result = wd_this->wd_cpifc_usgae_z_result( ).
   lr_if_ctr_z_result->set_usage( model_usage = lr_usage).
   ```

2. The second option is to use the MODEL_USAGE parameter in the `create_component()` method. If you want two components to exchange only one common reference, you can achieve this more easily by using the following statement:

   ```
   DATA lr_data_usage TYPE REF TO if_wd_component_usage.
   DATA lr_usage      TYPE REF TO if_wd_component_usage.
   lr_data_usage = wd_this->wd_cpuse_usage_z_data( ).
   IF lr_data_usage->has_active_component( ) IS INITIAL.
     lr_data_usage->create_component( ).
   ENDIF.
   lr_usage = wd_this->wd_cpuse_usage_z_result( ).
   IF lr_usage->has_active_component( ) IS INITIAL.
     lr_usage->create_component( model_usage = lr_data_usage ).
   ENDIF.
   ```

   A prerequisite for this is that you assign the name MODEL_USAGE to the usage in component Z_RESULT.

You can terminate the referencing of a component usage via the `leave_referencing_mode()` method.

```
lr_comp_usage->leave_referencing_mode( ).
```

Then you can use the `is_referencing()` method to find out whether a component usage references another component usage.

```
DATA lv_is_referencing TYPE abap_bool.
lv_is_referenced = lr_comp_usage->is_referencing( ).
```

The `is_referenced()` method enables you to determine if a component usage is referenced by another component usage.

```
DATA lv_is_referenced TYPE abap_bool.
lv_is_referenced = lr_comp_usage->is_referenced( ).
```

The metadata of a component usage, such as its name, can be obtained by calling the `get_component_usage_info()` method.

```
DATA lr_cusage_info TYPE REF TO if_wd_rr_component_usage.
DATA lv_comp_nameTYPE STRING.
lr_cusage_info = lr_comp_usage->get_comp_usage_info( ).
lv_comp_name   = lr_cusage_info->get_name( ).
```

A.1.3 IF_WD_COMPONENT_USAGE_GROUP

Within one component, you can define several usages that are all based on the same component. To make it easier to manage those usages, you can arrange them in component usage groups. A component usage group can be generated by calling the `create_cmp_usage_group()` method of the `IF_WD_COMPONENT` interface. We already described this in Section A.1.1. When you call the `get_component_usage()` method, a reference to the required component usage is returned.

```
DATA lr_comp_usage TYPE REF TO if_wd_component_usage.
lr_comp_usage = lr_usage_group->get_comp_usage( [UsageName] ).
```

By calling the `get_component_usages()` method, you can obtain a list of references to all usages.

```
DATA lt_comp_usages TYPE wdapi_component_usages.
DATA ls_comp_usage  TYPE wdapi_component_usage.
DATA lr_comp_usage  TYPE REF TO if_wd_component_usage.
lt_comp_usages = lr_usage_group->get_component_usages( ).
LOOP AT lt_comp_usages INTO ls_comp_usage.
   lr_comp_usage = ls_comp_usage-component_usage.
```

```
*-- ... other coding might come here
ENDLOOP.
```

To add another component usage or instance to an existing component usage group, you must use the `add_component_usage()` method. This method automatically generates an instance, which is then added to the component usage group.

```
DATA   lv_name              TYPE STRING.
DATA   lv_lifecycle_control TYPE STRING.
DATA   lv_position          TYPE STRING.
DATA   lv_used_component    TYPE STRING.
DATA   lr_usage             TYPE REF TO if_wd_component_usage.
*-- ... other coding might come here
lr_usage = lr_usage_group->add_component_usage(
                    name              = lv_name
                    lifecycle_control = lv_lifecycle_control
                    embedding_position = lv_position
                    used_component    = lv_used_component ).
```

- To delete a component usage from a component usage group, you must use the `remove_component_usage()` method.

    ```
    DATA   lr_comp_usageTYPE REF TO if_wd_component_usage.
    *-- ... other coding might come here
    lr_usage_group->remove_component_usage( lr_comp_usage ).
    ```

- You can delete all component usages by calling the `remove_all_cmp_usages()` method.

    ```
    lr_usage_group->remove_all_cmp_usages( ).
    ```

- The properties of a component usage within a component usage group can be changed via the `set()` method.

    ```
    DATA   lv_component_usage_name TYPE STRING.
    DATA   lv_embedding_position   TYPE STRING.
    DATA   lv_used_component       TYPE STRING.
    lr_usage_group->set( component_usage_name = lv_component_usage_name
                         embedding_position   = lv_embedding_position
                         used_component       = lv_used_component ).
    ```

A.1.4 IF_WD_PERSONALIZATION

You can establish a reference to an IF_WD_PERSONALIZATION object at runtime within the component controller by using the following statements:

```
DATA lr_comp_api      TYPE REF TO if_wd_component.
DATA lr_pers_manager  TYPE REF TO if_wd_personalization.
lr_comp_api = wd_this->wd_get_api( ).
lr_pers_manager  = lr_comp_api->get_personalization_manager( ).
```

Several methods are provided through the IF_WD_PERSONALIZATION interface. These methods enable you to dynamically implement the options that can be declaratively defined by means of configuration, adjustment, and personalization.

A.2 Context

A.2.1 IF_WD_CONTEXT

IF_WD_CONTEXT enables you to reference the context of a node. At runtime, you can establish such a reference by using the following call:

```
DATA lr_context TYPE if_wd_context.
lr_context = wd_context->get_context( ).
```

By accessing the context you can monitor user entries. The logging mode can be activated via the enable_context_change_log( ) method.

```
lr_context->enable_context_change_log( ).
```

To disable the logging mode you must call the disable_context_change_log( ) method.

```
lr_context->disable_context_change_log( ).
```

To read the change logs, you can use the get_context_change_log( ) method. Here, you can use the AND_RESET parameter to define whether you want to reset the log table.

```
DATA lv_reset       TYPE abap_bool.
DATA lt_change_list TYPE wdr_context_change_list.
lv_reset        = abap_false.
lt_change_list = lr_context->get_context_change_log( lv_reset ).
```

The context change log is stored in a table of the **WDR_CONTEXT_CHANGE_LIST** type. The individual fields have the following meanings:

- NODE_NAME
  Name of the context node in which the changes have been carried out
- SEQUENCE
  Sequential numbering of the changes

- NODE
  Reference to the instance of the context node in which the changes have been carried out
- NODE_PATH
  Path to the context node in which the changes have been carried out
- CHANGE_KIND
  Information on the type of change. It is possible to change an attribute, the lead selection, the collection of elements, and the selection. The type of change is indicated by the following constants located in the IF_WD_CONTEXT interface:
  - IF_WD_CONTEXT=>CHANGED_ATTRIBUTE
  - IF_WD_CONTEXT=>CHANGED_LEADSELECTION
  - IF_WD_CONTEXT=>CHANGED_COLLECTION
  - IF_WD_CONTEXT=>CHANGED_SELECTION
- ELEMENT_INDEX
  Index of the context element in compliance with its position in the collection
- ATTRIBUTE_NAME
  Name of the attribute that has been changed
- OLD_VALUE
  Contains a reference to the previous value of the attribute
- NEW_VALUE
  Contains a reference to the new value of the attribute

You can use the reset_context_change_log() method to explicitly reset the change logs.

```
lr_context->reset_context_change_log( ).
```

Changes to a context attribute that is populated with data via an input help (OVS or freely programmed) are not included automatically into the log. If you want this to happen, you must explicitly call the add_context_attribute_change() method.

```
DATA lv_element              TYPE REF TO if_wd_context_element.
DATA lv_attribute_name       TYPE STRING.
DATA lv_new_value            TYPE DATA.
DATA lv_delegate_to_original TYPE wdy_booelan.
DATA lv_force_entry          TYPE wdy_boolean.
DATA lv_entry_added          TYPE wdy_boolean.
```

```
*-- ... other coding might come here
lv_entry_added = lr_context->add_context_attribute_change(
                element              = lv_element
                attribute_name       = lv_attribute_name
                new_value            = lv_new_value
                delegate_to_original = lv_delegate_to_original
                force_entry          = lv_force_entry ).
```

A.2.2 IF_WD_CONTEXT_NODE

The `IF_WD_CONTEXT_NODE` interface provides several methods that enable you to obtain read and write access to the properties, attributes, elements, and the subordinate structures of a context node.

Here, we want to describe a scenario for compiling elements and the groups of methods that are characterized by various prefixes in greater detail. You must perform several steps in order to add elements to a context node that has the properties shown in Figure A.1.

Context V_DEFAULT	
▽ OPTION	
KEY	
VALUE	

Property	Value
Nodes	
Node Name	OPTION
Dictionary structure	SHSVALSTR2
Cardinality	0..n
Selection	0..1

Figure A.1 Sample Context Node

1. First you must create an instance of a new element.

    ```
    DATA  lr_node    TYPE REF TO if_wd_context_node.
    DATA  lr_element TYPE REF TO if_wd_context_element.
    lr_element = lr_node->create_element( ).
    ```

2. Then you must fill the attributes of the new context element with values.

    ```
    lr_element->set_attribute( name = 'KEY'   value = 'A_KEY_01' ).
    lr_element->set_attribute( name = 'VALUE' value = 'A_VALUE_01' ).
    ```

3. Finally, you must bind the new context element to the context node.

    ```
    lr_node->bind_element( new_item = lr_element ).
    ```

The following list describes the methods that are characterized by common prefixes and their functions.

- `bind_*()` methods
  `bind_*()` methods are used to fill the entire context node and to create new elements. The `bind_structure()` and `bind_table()` methods optimize the performance in cases where context nodes are based on data types that were defined in the ABAP Dictionary.

- `set_*()` methods
  The `set_*()` methods enable you to directly access attributes of context elements. For this to be possible, however, the elements must exist.

- `move_*()` methods
  By using the `move_element()` method you can move an element if you specify the index. All other `move_*()` methods are used to manipulate the lead selection.

- `path_get_*()` methods
  You can access context attributes and subordinate context nodes by navigating through the tree step by step, but it is more efficient to specify the path.

  ```
  DATA lv_attribute TYPE DATA.
  lv_attribute = lr_node->path_get_attribute( 'CONTENT.VALUE' ).
  ```

- `get_*()` methods
  You can access the individual elements of the context node via the `get_*()` methods. For example, you can reference the context node information by calling the `get_node_info()` method.

  ```
  DATA lr_node_info TYPE REF TO if_wd_context_node_info.
  lr_node_info = lr_node->get_node_info( ).
  ```

A.2.3 IF_WD_CONTEXT_NODE_INFO

The `IF_WD_CONTEXT_NODE_INFO` interface enables you to access and change some of the properties of a context node at runtime. You also can add and remove attributes and subordinate context nodes at runtime via the context node information. The **Cardinality** property that was used in the declarative development is determined by the `IS_MANDATORY` and `IS_MULTIPLE` attributes in the `IF_WD_CONTEXT_NODE_INFO` interface. Table A.1 provides an overview of the relationships between the attribute values and the resulting cardinality.

IS_MULTIPLE	IS_MANDATORY	Cardinality
abap_false	abap_false	**0..1**
abap_false	abap_true	**1..1**
abap_true	abap_false	**0..n**
abap_true	abap_true	**1..n**

Table A.1 Comparison of Dynamic and Declarative Determination of the Cardinality

The number of available context node elements that are contained in view elements such as the Table view element, must be defined declaratively via the **Selection** property. Definitions that are carried out at runtime must use the IS_MANDATORY_SELECTION and IS_MULTIPLE_SELECTION attributes. Table A.2 provides an overview of the relationships between the values of these attributes and the resulting selection types.

IS_MULTIPLE_SELECTION	IS_MANDATORY_SELECTION	Selection
abap_false	abap_false	**0..1**
abap_false	abap_true	**1..1**
abap_true	abap_false	**0..n**
abap_true	abap_true	**1..n**

Table A.2 Comparison of Dynamic and Declarative Determination of the Selection Types

You can use the add_new_child_node() method in the context-node information to assign a new context node as a child node to the parent node. The context node that is declaratively created in Figure A.2 would have to be dynamically defined using the following statements:

```
DATA lv_supply_method       TYPE string.
DATA lv_static_element_type TYPE string.
DATA lv_name                TYPE string.
DATA lv_mandatory           TYPE abap_bool.
DATA lv_mandatory_selection TYPE abap_bool.
DATA lv_multiple            TYPE abap_bool.
DATA lv_multiple_selection  TYPE abap_bool.
DATA lv_singleton           TYPE abap_bool.
DATA lv_init_lead_selection TYPE abap_bool.
DATA lr_child_node_info     TYPE REF TO  if_wd_context_node_info.
  lv_supply_method       = 'SUPPLY_UNIT'.
  lv_static_element_type = 'T006A_INT'.
```

```
lv_name                   = 'FROMUNIT'.
lv_mandatory              = abap_false.
lv_mandatory_selection    = abap_false.
lv_multiple               = abap_true.
lv_multiple_selection     = abap_false.
lv_singleton              = abap_true.
lv_init_lead_selection    = abap_true.
lr_child_node_info = lr_node_info->add_new_child_node(
    supply_method                = lv_supply_method
    static_element_type          = lv_static_element_type
    name                         = lv_name
    is_mandatory                 = lv_mandatory
    is_mandatory_selection       = lv_mandatory_selection
    is_multiple                  = lv_multiple
    is_multiple_selection        = lv_multiple_selection
    is_singleton                 = lv_singleton
    is_initialize_lead_selection = lv_init_lead_selection ).
```

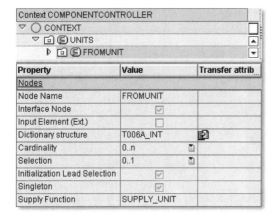

Figure A.2 Declaratively Created Context Node

When accessing the attribute properties, you sometimes have to distinguish between the declaratively created attributes and the dynamically created ones. The declaratively created attributes have the indicator static in their method names. Thus, the return value of the get_static_attributes_type() method refers only to the declaratively created attributes: that is, attributes that have been created during the development phase. The remove_dynamic_attributes() method, in turn, deletes only the dynamically created attributes, that is, attributes that have been created at runtime. Attribute-related methods that don't have the static and dynamic indicators in their names apply to both types of attributes, whether these have been created declaratively or dynamically.

A.2.4 IF_WD_CONTEXT_ELEMENT

The access to and modification of elements of a context node at runtime is controlled by the `IF_WD_CONTEXT_ELEMENT` interface. There is a number methods of the `IF_WD_CONTEXT_NODE` interface that return references to elements. You can access an element via its index in the collection.

```
DATA  lr_node    TYPE REF TO if_wd_context_node.
DATA  lr_element TYPE REF TO if_wd_context_element.
  lr_node    = wd_context_node->get_child_node( '[NAME_OF_NODE]' ).
  lr_element = lr_node->get_elment( index = 3 ).
```

If no index is specified, the lead selection element will be returned. The lead selection can also be determined directly via the `get_lead_selection()` method.

```
lr_element = lr_node->get_lead_selection( ).
```

You can use set and get methods in order to access the attributes of context element and change their values. For individual attributes those methods are the `set_attribute()` and `get_attribute()` methods; here, you can also use dynamically created attributes. The `set_static_attributes()` and `get_static_attributes()` methods, on the other hand, can only be used for declaratively created attributes.

A.2.5 CL_WD_CONTEXT_SERVICES

The `get_context_change_log()` method of the `IF_WD_CONTEXT` interface (see Section A.2.1) enables you to log the context changes that were initiated by the user entries. The functions needed to query context changes involving program changes are implemented in the CL_WD_CONTEXT_SERVICES class.

First, a list of context nodes whose changes are to be logged is transferred to the `subscribe_to_node_changes()` method. Once the list has been transferred, the log function is activated. To deactivate it you can use the `deactivate_subscriptions()` method, whereas the `activate_subscriptions()` method causes its reactivation. You can query the changes by using the `get_change_list()` method.

A second group of methods contained in class CL_WD_CONTEXT_SERVICES is used to identify the data of context nodes to be mapped and the relationship between the mapped and the original context nodes. Those methods are primarily used in dynamic programming. The following examples demonstrate how you can call the methods.

Method get_mapped_node_for_controller()

```
DATA lr_view_ctx_node TYPE REF TO if_wd_context_node.
DATA lr_mapped_node   TYPE REF TO if_wd_context_node.
DATA lr_ctr           TYPE REF TO if_wd_controller.
*-- ... other coding might come here
CALL METHOD cl_wd_context_services=>get_mapped_node_for_controller
  EXPORTING
    node       = lr_view_ctx_node
    controller = lr_ctr
  RECEIVING
    new_node   = lr_new_node.
```

Method get_node_metapath_for_controller()

```
DATA lr_view_ctx_node TYPE REF TO if_wd_context_node.
DATA lr_ctr           TYPE REF TO if_wd_controller.
DATA lv_path          TYPE string.
*-- ... other coding might come here
CALL METHOD cl_wd_context_services=>get_node_metapath_for_ctrl
  EXPORTING
    node       = lr_view_ctx_node
    controller = lr_ctr
  RECEIVING
    path       = lv_path.
```

Method get_original_node()

The get_original_node() method enables you to determine the original context node of a mapped context node. In Figure A.3, for example, context node LEVEL02 of the component controller has been copied to the view controller and then mapped. In the view controller, context node LEVEL02 is located directly under the root context node.

A | Classes and Interfaces

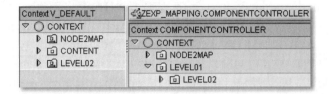

Figure A.3 Identifying the Original Node (Example)

The following statements first determine a reference to the original context node.

```
DATA lr_view_ctx_node TYPE REF TO if_wd_context_node.
DATA lv_path          TYPE string.
lr_view_ctx_node = wd_context->get_child_node( 'LEVEL02' ).
CALL METHOD cl_wd_context_services=>get_original_node
  EXPORTING
    in_node  = lr_view_ctx_node
  RECEIVING
    out_node = lr_orig_node.
lv_path = lr_orig_node->get_meta_path( ).
```

The path of the original context node in the component controller is then output in the `lv_path` variable. In our example, this is `COMPONENTCONTROLLER.LEVEL01.LEVEL02`.

Method get_element_path_for_ctrl()

```
DATA lr_element TYPE REF TO if_wd_context_element.
DATA lr_ctr     TYPE REF TO if_wd_controller.
DATA lv_path    TYPE string.
*-- ... other coding might come here
CALL METHOD cl_wd_context_services=>get_element_path_for_ctrl
  EXPORTING
    element    = lr_element
    controller = lr_ctr
  RECEIVING
    path = lv_path.
```

A.3 View

A.3.1 IF_WD_ACTION

The interface IF_WD_ACTION allows for the modification of specific attributes of an action that is created in the view controller. The set() method can be used to modify the following attributes:

- Activation indicator of the action ENABLED
- Validation indicator VALIDATING
- Descriptive text TEXT
- Original URL of an image file IMAGE

If you use the same action for several event-triggering view elements, the triggering view element can be identified through the ID in the case of declarative programming. In dynamic programming, the ID of a view element is often arbitrarily generated at runtime and therefore cannot be used as a distinctive feature during the development phase. In that case, IF_WD_ACTION enables access to parameters that can help you implement a distinction. Let's suppose, for example, that two Button view elements are created in the wddomodify() method, one for transferring customer data and the other one for transferring supplier data.

```
lr_cust_btn = cl_wd_button=>new_button( view = ir_view
                                text = 'Submit Customer Data'
                                on_action = 'DO_SUBMIT' ).
*-- ... other coding might come here
lr_vend_btn = cl_wd_button=>new_button( view = ir_view
                                text = 'Submit Vendor Data'
                                on_action = 'DO_SUBMIT' ).
```

Both Button view elements use the same action: DO_SUBMIT. The ID is assigned generically by the WD4A framework. In order to distinguish the two elements, we add an IV_TYPE parameter that is assigned to the Button view elements.

```
ls_params-name = 'SUBMIT_TYPE'.
ls_params-value = 'CUSTOMER'.
APPEND ls_params TO lt_params.
lr_cust_btn->map_on_action( lt_params ).
*-- ... other coding might come here
ls_params-name = 'SUBMIT_TYPE'.
ls_params-value = 'VENDOR'.
```

```
APPEND ls_params TO lt_params.
lr_vend_btn->map_on_action( lt_params ).
```

The actual distinction for the action is then made in the event-handler method by means of parameter values that are determined via the `IF_WD_ACTION` interface. Listing A.2 provides the corresponding statements.

```
METHOD onactiondo_submit.
   DATA    lt_params    TYPE wdr_name_value_list.
   DATA    ls_params    TYPE wdr_name_value.
   DATA    lr_action    TYPE REF TO if_wd_action.
   DATA    lr_api       TYPE REF TO if_wd_controller.
   lr_api    = wd_this->wd_get_api( ).
   lr_action = lr_api->get_action( name = 'DO_SUBMIT' ).
   lt_params = lr_action->parameters.
   READ TABLE lt_params INTO ls_params WITH KEY
                                       value = 'SUBMIT_TYPE'.
   IF sy-subrc EQ 0.
     CASE ls_params-name.
       WHEN 'CUSTOMER'.
*---- Handle customer specific tasks
       WHEN 'VENDOR'.
*---- Handle vendor specific tasks
     ENDCASE.
   ENDIF.
ENDMETHOD.
```

Listing A.2 A.2: Using IF_WD_ACTION

A.3.2 IF_WD_VIEW

The `IF_WD_VIEW` interface provides you with access to view data. A reference to an instance of the view is only available in the hook method `wddomodify()` in the `VIEW` parameter. The `get_element()` method provides access to all view elements and their properties by specifying the corresponding IDs.

```
DATA    lr_button    type ref to    cl_wd_button.
lr_lr_button ?= view->get_element( 'BTN_SUBMIT' ).
```

The `get_root_element()` method determines a reference to the root node in the UI hierarchy.

```
DATA  lr_root TYPE REF TO  cl_wd_transparent_container.
lr_root ?= view->get_root_element( ).
```

You can use the `get_view_usage()` method in order to determine data on the usage of the view, such as the name of the window in which the view is embedded or the name of the usage that has been assigned by the WD4A framework.

```
DATA lr_view_usage TYPE REF TO if_wd_rr_view_usage.
DATA lr_window     TYPE REF TO if_wd_rr_window.
DATA lv_embed_name TYPE string.
lr_view_usage = view->get_view_usage( ).
lr_window     = lr_view_usage->get_window( ).
lv_embed_name = lr_view_usage->get_name( ).
```

You can focus on a specific view element by using the `request_focus_on_view_elem()` method.

```
DATA   lr_button TYPE REF TO if_wd_view_element.
lr_button = view->get_element( 'BTN_SAVE' ).
view->request_focus_on_view_elem( lr_button ).
```

To be able to reset a view to its original status when dynamically created or added view elements are used, you can call the `reset_view()` method to delete all dynamically created view elements.

```
view->reset_view( ).
```

A.3.3 IF_WD_VIEW_CONTROLLER

The `IF_WD_VIEW_CONTROLLER` interface provides access to the data of a view controller. This interface is an enhancement of the `IF_WD_CONTROLLER` interface, which means it contains all functions of `IF_WD_CONTROLLER` that we will describe in Section 7 of this appendix. You can determine a reference to the object of the view controller within the view controller by calling the `wd_get_api()` method.

```
DATA lr_view_ctr TYPE REF TO if_wd_view_controller.
lr_view_ctr = wd_this->wd_get_api( ).
```

Dynamically created plugs are triggered by the `fire_plug()` method. The interface of the method contains the name of the plug and an optional table of parameters.

```
lr_view_ctr->fire_plug( plug_name = 'OP_TO_CONFIRM' ).
```

You can determine a reference of the window controller that embeds the view by calling the `get_embedding_window_ctlr()` method. The result is of the `IF_WD_WINDOW_CONTROLLER` type (see Section A.4.2).

```
DATA lr_window_ctr TYPE REF TO if_wd_window_controller.
lr_window_ctr = lr_view_ctr->get_embedding_window_ctlr( ).
```

The view info provides information such as the name and description and enables you to change the lifecycle of the view. When you call the `get_view_info()` method, you obtain the reference to the corresponding object.

```
DATA lr_view_info TYPE REF TO if_wd_rr_view.
DATA lv_view_name TYPE string.
lr_view_info = lr_view_ctr->get_view_info( ).
lv_view_name = lr_view_info->get_name( ).
```

The `get_current_action()` method provides access to the current action that belongs to the event triggered by the user. Note that this method can only be called in the hook method `wddobeforeaction()`.

```
DATA lr_action  TYPE REF TO if_wd_action.
lr_action = lr_view_ctr->get_current_action( ).
```

You can set the focus by specifying the view element ID or by specifying an action. This function is enabled by calling the `request_focus_on_action()` method in the `IF_WD_VIEW_CONTROLLER` interface.

```
DATA lr_action  TYPE REF TO if_wd_action.
lr_action = lr_view_ctr->if_wd_controller~get_action( 'DO_SUBMIT' ).
lr_view_ctr->request_focus_on_action( lr_action ).
```

A.3.4 IF_WD_VIEW_ELEMENT

The `IF_WD_VIEW_ELEMENT` interface provides a simple interface to any view element of a view. You can request the ID and a reference to the view that contains the view element.

```
DATA lr_view_element TYPE REF TO if_wd_view_element.
DATA lv_id           TYPE       string.
DATA lr_view         TYPE REF TO if_wd_view.
*-- ... other coding might come here
lv_id   = lr_view_element->get_id( ).
lr_view = lr_view_element->get_view( ).
```

A.3.5 IF_WD_VALIDATION

The `IF_WD_VALIDATION` interface enables you to request and manipulate the validation results for user entries that have been determined by the WD4A framework at runtime. You thus can interfere with the flow defined by the phase model of the WD4A framework.

```
DATA lr_node     TYPE REF TO if_wd_context_node.
DATA lr_element  TYPE REF TO if_wd_context_element.
```

```abap
DATA lr_validation TYPE REF TO if_wd_validation.
DATA lv_time_valid TYPE abap_bool.
*-- ... other coding might come here
lr_node = wd_context->get_child_node( 'CONTENT' ).
lr_element = lr_node->get_element( ).
lv_time_valid = lr_validation->is_attribute_valid(
                                     element = lr_element
                                     attribute_name = 'TIME' ).
IF lv_time_valid EQ abap_false.
  lr_validation->set_attribute_valid( element = lr_element
                                      attribute_name = 'TIME' ).
ENDIF.
```

A.4 Window

A.4.1 IF_WD_WINDOW

When you create a window by using the Window Manager, a reference to an IF_WD_WINDOW object is created. This step is usually performed when popup dialogs are used.

```abap
DATA lr_window_manager TYPE REF TO if_wd_window_manager.
DATA lr_component_api  TYPE REF TO if_wd_component.
DATA lr_compcontroller TYPE REF TO ig_componentcontroller.
DATA lr_window         TYPE REF TO if_wd_window.
lr_compcontroller = wd_this->get_componentcontroller_ctr( ).
lr_component_api  = lr_comp_controller->wd_get_api( ).
lr_window_manager = lr_component_api->get_window_manager( ).
lr_window = lr_window_manager->create_window(
                               window_name = 'W_POPUP' ).
```

The methods used for showing and hiding pop-up windows are open() and close():

```abap
lr_window->open().
lr_window->close().
```

The shape and position of the window are defined by the set_window_position(), set_window_position_control(), and set_window_size() methods. If no specific unit is indicated, the values are interpreted as pixels.

```abap
DATA lv_width  TYPE string.
DATA lv_height TYPE string.
lv_width  = '200'.
lv_height = '300'.
```

```
lr_window->set_window_size( width  = lv_width
                            height = lv_height ).
```

The position of the window can either be specified as a relative value within the parent window or by entering absolute values that indicate the distance from the left and top edges of the parent window.

- Relative indication of the position:

    ```
    DATA lv_position  TYPE string.
    lv_position = if_wd_window=>co_bottom.
    lr_window->set_window_position( position = lv_position ).
    ```

- Indication of the distance:

    ```
    DATA lv_left_margin  TYPE i.
    DATA lv_top_margin   TYPE i.
    lv_left_margin = 100.
    lv_top_margin  = 200.
    lr_window->set_window_position( left = lv_left_margin
                                    top  = lv_top_margin ).
    ```

To define the relative position of the window, the IF_WD_WINDOW interface provides several constants of the type **STRING**. Those constants are:

- IF_WD_WINDOW=>CO_BOTTOM
- IF_WD_WINDOW=>CO_LEFT
- IF_WD_WINDOW=>CO_CENTER
- IF_WD_WINDOW=>CO_RIGHT
- IF_WD_WINDOW=>CO_TOP

- You can use the set_window_position_control() method to define the position of a pop-up window in relation to a view element within a view.

    ```
    DATA lv_id   TYPE string.
    DATA lv_view TYPE REF TO if_wd_view.
    *- Coding for setting view reference and view element ID comes here
    lr_window->set_window_position_control( id   = lv_id
                                            view = lv_view ).
    ```

- The action that is to be carried out when the window is being closed can be defined using the set_on_close_action() method.

    ```
    DATA lv_view TYPE REF TO if_wd_view.
    *- Coding for setting view reference comes here
    lr_window->set_onclose_action( view        = lv_view
                                   action_name = 'DO_SUBMIT' ).
    ```

- The `set_button_kind()` method can be used to define the types of standard buttons that are displayed at the bottom of the window. The possible combinations for arranging the buttons are defined via constants that are also contained in the `IF_WD_WINDOW` interface. For example, the statement for arranging the **Yes**, **No**, and **Close** buttons is as follows:

  ```
  lr_window->set_button_kind( button_kind =
                              if_wd_window=>co_buttons_yesnocancel ).
  ```

- Then you can use the `subscribe_to_button_event()` method to assign actions to the buttons of the pop-up window.

  ```
  DATA lv_view TYPE REF TO if_wd_view.
  *- Coding for setting view reference comes here
  lr_compcontroller->mr_window->subscribe_to_button_event(
                  button      = if_wd_window=>co_buttons_ok
                  action_name = 'DO_SUBMIT'
                  action_view = lr_view ).
  ```

- The `set_message_type()` method defines the different types of messages such as warnings, errors, or informational messages. This involves the display of a corresponding icon in the pop-up window.

  ```
  lr_window->set_message_type(
            message_type = if_wd_window=>co_msg_type_warning ).
  ```

A.4.2 IF_WD_WINDOW_CONTROLLER

The `IF_WD_WINDOW_CONTROLLER` interface enhances the `IF_WD_VIEW_CONTROLLER` interface and thus contains the attributes of the `IF_WD_CONTROLLER` and `IF_WD_NAVIGATION_SERVICES` interfaces. Additional methods here are `get_window()`, which determines a reference to the pop-up window if such a references exists, and `get_window_info()` for identifying the information data of the window.

A.5 Integration

A.5.1 CL_WDR_PORTAL_OBNWEB_SERVICE

When integrating WD4A applications into the SAP NetWeaver Portal, you can use object-based navigation as an implementation option. The CL_WDR_PORTAL_OBNWEB_SERVICE class provides several different functions that enable an easy handling of the interface via Web services.

A.5.2 IF_WD_PORTAL_INTEGRATION

The Portal Manager implements the `IF_WD_PORTAL_INTEGRATION` interface that provides functions for triggering and intercepting portal-based events and for implementing the object-based navigation.

```
DATA lr_api_component  TYPE REF TO if_wd_component.
DATA lr_portal_manager TYPE REF TO if_wd_portal_integration.
lr_api_component  = wd_comp_controller->wd_get_api( ).
lr_portal_manager = lr_api_component->get_portal_manager( ).
```

A.5.3 CL_WD_ADOBE_SERVICES

Using the methods implemented in class CL_WD_ADOBE_SERVICES, you can dynamically access the XML-based PDF document (`parse_xml_data()` method) and the XML schema that corresponds to the context (`parse_xml_schema()` method): that is, at runtime. The class also contains methods that are called by the WD4A framework during the development phase if `InteractiveForms` view elements are used.

A.6 Application

A.6.1 IF_WD_APPLICATION

The `IF_WD_APPLICATION` interface enables you to access some attributes of the WD4A application. The following information is currently output:

- `get_is_accessible()` method
  Information on the set accessibility
- `get_is_rtl()` method
  Information on the possible RTL changeover *(right to left)*
- `get_application_info()` method
  Information on the name and start window of the application

The determination of the name and start window of the application occurs through the `IF_WD_RR_APPLICATION` interface. The following list contains the necessary declarations and statements for determining properties of the application:

```
DATA lr_comp_api  TYPE REF TO if_wd_component.
DATA lr_appl_api  TYPE REF TO if_wd_application.
DATA lr_appl_info TYPE REF TO if_wd_rr_application.
```

```
DATA lr_window     TYPE REF TO if_wd_rr_window.
DATA lv_appl_name TYPE string.
DATA lv_is_rtl     TYPE wdy_boolean.
DATA lv_is_acc     TYPE wdy_boolean.
lr_comp_api  = wd_this->wd_get_api( ).
lr_appl_api  = lr_comp_api->get_application( ).
lr_appl_info = lr_appl_api->get_application_info( ).
lv_appl_name = lr_appl_info->get_name( ).
lr_window    = lr_appl_info->get_startup_window( ).
lv_is_rtl    = lr_appl_api->get_is_rtl( ).
lv_is_acc    = lr_appl_api->get_is_accessible( ).
```

A.7 Other

A.7.1 IF_WD_CONTROLLER

The components and functions of individual controllers are addressed through the IF_WD_CONTROLLER interface. This interface enables you to access the context, actions, the Message Manager, and the Personalization Manager. The following statement provides you with a reference to your own controller:

```
DATA  lr_controller  type ref to  if_wd_controller.
  lr_controller = wd_this->wd_get_api( ).
```

If, within a controller, you want to access the API of another controller, the Code Wizard can assist you in compiling the declarations and statements.

1. Declaration and statement for accessing the component controller from a separate controller:

   ```
   DATA  lr_controller TYPE REF TO if_wd_component.
     lr_controller = wd_comp_controller->wd_get_api( ).
   ```

2. Declaration and statement for accessing the window controller of a window called W_DEFAULT from a separate controller:

   ```
   DATA lr_w_default    TYPE REF TO ig_w_default.
   DATA lr_controller   TYPE REF TO if_wd_controller.
     lr_w_default    = wd_this->get_w_default_ctr( ).
     lr_controller   = lr_w_default->wd_get_api( ).
   ```

3. The `get_message_manager()` method provides access to the Message Manager (see Section A.7.2).

   ```
   DATA lr_msg_manager TYPE REF TO if_wd_message_manager.
     lr_msg_manager = lr_controller->get_message_manager( ).
   ```

A.7.2   IF_WD_MESSAGE_MANAGER

The Message Manager supports the management of different types of messages. The methods used for displaying text messages are as follows:

- `report_attribute_error_message()`
  Enables the creation of a message based on a static text and the binding to a context attribute.

  ```
  CALL METHOD lr_message_manager->report_attribute_error_message
      EXPORTING
        message_text   = 'Please enter a dimension type.'
        element        = lr_element
        attribute_name = 'DVALUE'.
  ```

- `report_success()`
  Enables the creation of a success message.

  ```
  CALL METHOD lr_message_manager->report_success
      EXPORTING
        message_text = 'The record was successfully saved.'
  ```

- `report_warning()`
  Enables the creation of a message that is output as a warning.

  ```
  CALL METHOD lr_message_manager->report_warning
      EXPORTING
        message_text = 'The max. number of records is reached.'.
  ```

- `report_error_message()`
  Enables the creation of a message based on a static text without binding to a context attribute.

  ```
  CALL METHOD lr_message_manager->report_error_message
      EXPORTING
        message_text   = 'Please enter a dimension type.'.
  ```

- `report_fatal_error_message()`
  Enables the creation of a fatal error message based on a static text.

```
CALL METHOD lr_message_manager->report_fatal_error_message
  EXPORTING
    message_text = 'Error when accessing the sel. object.'
```

The methods used for outputting exceptions are as follows:

- report_exception()
  Enables the creation of an error message based on an exception.

```
DATA  lr_message_object    TYPE REF TO if_message.
DATA  lv_number            TYPE string.
DATA  lv_int               TYPE i.
DATA  lr_sy_conv           TYPE REF TO
                             cx_sy_conversion_no_number.
*-- ... other coding might come here
TRY.
   MOVE lv_number TO lv_int.
   CATCH cx_sy_conversion_no_number INTO lr_sy_conv.
   lr_message_object ?= lr_sy_conv.
     CALL METHOD lr_message_manager->report_exception
       EXPORTING
         message_object = lr_message_object.
ENDTRY.
```

- report_attribute_exception()
  Enables the creation of an error message based on an exception and the binding to a context attribute.

```
TRY.
    MOVE lv_number TO lv_int.
  CATCH cx_sy_conversion_no_number INTO lr_sy_conv.
    lr_message_object ?= lr_sy_conv.
    CALL METHOD lr_message_manager->report_attribute_exception
      EXPORTING
        message_object = lr_message_object
        element        = lr_element
        attribute_name = 'DVALUE'.
ENDTRY.
```

- report_fatal_exception()
  Creates a fatal message for an exception.

To be able to output T100 messages, you must first create those messages via the message maintenance (Transaction SE91). In the following example, the name of the message class is ZEXP_WD4A_MSG and the message number is 007. The methods used for outputting T100 messages are as follows:

▶ `report_t100_message()`

Enables creation of a message based on a T100 entry.

```
CALL METHOD lr_message_manager->report_t100_message
  EXPORTING
    msgid       = 'ZEXP_WD4A_MSG'
    msgno       = '007'
    msgty       = 'E'.
```

▶ `report_attribute_t100_message()`

Enables the creation of a message based on a T100 entry and the binding to a context attribute. The elements of the T100 message are transferred through a structure of the SYMSG type.

```
DATA ls_msg  TYPE  symsg.
ls_msg-msgid = 'ZEXP_WD4A_MSG'.
ls_msg-msgno = '007'.
ls_msg-msgty = 'E'.
CALL METHOD lr_message_manager->report_attribute_t100_message
  EXPORTING
    msg            = ls_msg
    element        = lr_element
    attribute_name = 'DVALUE'.
```

A.7.3 IF_WD_NAVIGATION_SERVICES

The navigation that is declaratively created in the window during development can also be implemented dynamically if you use the corresponding statements. Here, you have two options:

1. The navigation is defined when the component is called (for example in the `wddoinit()` method) and is then run in an event-handler method when an outbound plug is triggered. The navigation is defined using the `prepare_dynamic_navigation()` method.

```
DATA lr_nav_services   TYPE REF TO if_wd_navigation_services.
lr_nav_services ?= wd_this->wd_get_api( ).
CALL METHOD lr_nav_services->prepare_dynamic_navigation
  EXPORTING
    source_window_name  = 'W_DEFAULT'
    source_vusage_name  = 'V_ONE_USAGE_1'
    source_plug_name    = 'OP_TO_V_TWO'
    target_view_name    = 'V_TWO'
    target_plug_name    = 'IP_V_TWO'.
```

In the call of the `prepare_dynamic_navigation()` method shown above, the `source_window_name` parameter is used to assign a name to the window in which the navigation occurs. In our example, this is the `W_DEFAULT` window. The `source_vusage_name` parameter describes the usage of the start view that is assigned by the WD4A framework during the embedding of a view. You can determine this view in the **View Use** property in the window editor (see Figure A.4).

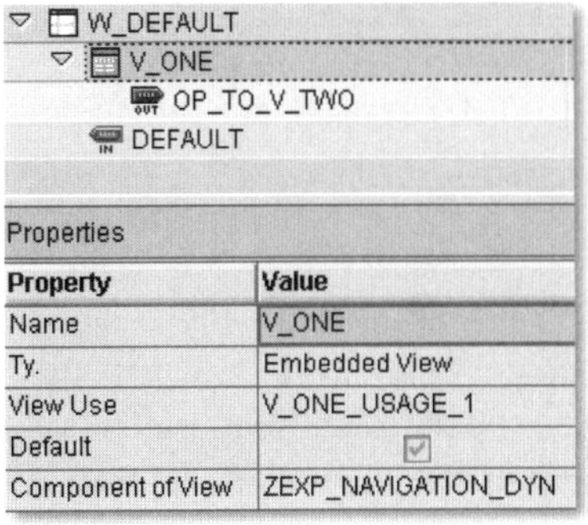

W_DEFAULT	
▽ V_ONE	
OP_TO_V_TWO	
DEFAULT	

Properties	
Property	**Value**
Name	V_ONE
Ty.	Embedded View
View Use	V_ONE_USAGE_1
Default	☑
Component of View	ZEXP_NAVIGATION_DYN

Figure A.4 Name of Embedding and View Use

The `source_plug_name` parameter defines the plug which the navigation is based on; in declarative programming that means the outbound plug. In our example, this plug is called `OP_TO_V_TWO` and is defined in the `V_ONE` view. The view to which you want to navigate is defined by the `target_view_name` parameter. In our example, the target view is `V_TWO`. The plug of the target view is determined by the `target_plug_name` parameter. This plug is defined as an inbound plug in the `V_TWO` view and is called `IP_V_TWO`.

At runtime, the navigation is triggered in an event-handler method by calling the fire method for the outbound plug `OP_TO_V_TWO`:

```
wd_this->fire_op_to_v_two_plg( ).
```

2. When an event-handler method is called, the navigation is defined and executed. The `do_dynamic_navigation()` method controls the definition and execution of the navigation.

```
DATA lr_nav_services    TYPE REF TO if_wd_navigation_services.
lr_nav_services ?= wd_this->wd_get_api( ).
CALL METHOD lr_nav_services->do_dynamic_navigation
  EXPORTING
    source_window_name = 'W_DEFAULT'
```

```
source_vusage_name = 'V_ONE_USAGE_1'
source_plug_name   = 'OP_TO_V_TWO'
target_view_name   = 'V_TWO'
target_plug_name   = 'IP_V_TWO'.
```

As you can see, no changes are made to the interface parameters of the do_dynamic_navigation( ) method as compared to the prepare_dynamic_navigation( ) method. The only difference is that the navigation is triggered within the do_dynamic_navigation( ) method, that is, an explicit call of a fire method is not necessary.

A.7.4 CL_WD_CUSTOM_EVENT

The event-handler methods generated by the WD4A framework during the creation of actions or events contain an importing parameter called CUSTOM_EVENT of the **CL_WD_CUSTOM_EVENT** type. Within the event-handler method, this parameter enables the access to properties and parameters of a triggered action, to properties and parameters of the view element that the event is based on, and to the parameters of the triggered event.

If the view contains a Button view element with the ID BTN_SUBMIT and the user clicks on this button at runtime, the following calls can be used in the event-handler method to determine, for example, information on the ID of the view element that triggers the event and information on the event name:

```
DATA lv_id         TYPE string.
DATA lv_event_name TYPE string.
lv_id = wdevent->get_string( 'ID' ).  "Result = BTN_SUBMIT
lv_event_name = wdevent->get_name( ). "Result = ON_ACTION
```

A.7.5 CL_WD_RUNTIME_SERVICES

The CL_WD_RUNTIME_SERVICES class is used to provide enhanced functionalities of the Web Dynpro Runtime. In the current service package and release status, the class contains only one method, which enables the download of files that are located or created on the server. The name of this method is attach_file_to_response( ). In the following example, we'll generate a Word file that is transferred to the HTTP response.

```
DATA lr_conv        TYPE REF TO cl_abap_conv_out_ce.
DATA lv_transaction TYPE tcode.
DATA lv_data        TYPE string.
DATA lv_xfile       TYPE xstring.
lv_data = 'Example text, which will be opened in MS Word.'.
```

```
CALL METHOD cl_abap_conv_out_ce=>create
  RECEIVING
    conv = lr_conv.
lr_conv->convert( EXPORTING data   = lv_data
                  IMPORTING buffer = lv_xfile ).
CALL METHOD cl_wd_runtime_services=>attach_file_to_response
  EXPORTING
    i_filename  = 'wd4a.doc'
    i_content   = lv_xfile
    i_mime_type = 'application/msword'.
```

In this example, the parameters I_IN_NEW_WINDOW (default value: abap_false) and I_INPLACE (default value: abap_false) have not been changed. You can use the I_IN_NEW_WINDOW parameter to specify whether you want to display the file in a new window. The I_INPLACE parameter can be used to define whether you want to overwrite the contents of the client window in which the request was triggered. If that parameter is set to abap_false, a prompt is displayed that asks you to open or save the downloaded file.

A.7.6 CL_WD_UTILITIES

In the current service package and release status, the CL_WD_UTILITIES class contains four methods that we'll briefly describe in the following sections.

Method calc_width4ddlbbykey()

The calc_width4ddlbbykey() method dynamically calculates the approximate width of a DropDownByKey view element based on the potential length of the descriptions output in the list. For this purpose, the following parameters must be transferred to the method:

- Parameter ROOT_NODE
  Reference to the root context node

- Parameter PATH
  Path to the attribute to which the **selectedKey** property of the DropDownByKey view element binds

- Parameter ALGORITHM (optional)
  Defines the type of calculation. There are four possibilities that are derived from the maximum length (maxLen) of a string to be displayed. The length unit is ex (see Table A.3). By default, the ALGORITHM parameter is set to **1**.

Value of ALGORITHM	Type of Calculation
1	maxLen *1,2 + 2
2	maxLen * 1,2
3	maxLen +2
4	maxLen

Table A.3 Types of Calculation for the Width of a DropDownByKey View Element

In the following example, the **selectedKey** property of the DropDownByKey view element is bound to the context attribute WIDTH. The elements of the selection list are managed in the context node TEXT_DESIGNS.

```
DATA lv_path  TYPE string.
DATA lv_width TYPE string.
DATA lr_node  TYPE REF TO if_wd_context_node.
lv_path  = 'TEXT_DESIGNS.KEY'.
lv_width = cl_wd_utilities=>calc_width4ddlbbykey(
                          root_node = wd_context
                          path      = lv_path ).
  wd_context->set_attribute( exporting name  = 'WIDTH'
                                       value = lv_width ).
```

Method set_width_4ddlbbykey()

The set_width_4ddlbbykey() calculates the approximate width of a DropDownByKey view element based on the potential length of the descriptions output in the list and sets the width dynamically. Unlike the calc_width4ddlbbykey() method set_width_4ddlbbykey() only requires a reference to the corresponding DropDownByKey view element. This means that the method can only be used in the hook method wddomodifyview(). The type of calculation can be determined as shown in Table A.3. Here, the ALGORITHM parameter is also optional and is set to **1** by default.

```
DATA lr_ddlb TYPE REF TO cl_wd_dropdown_by_key.
lr_ddlb ?= view->get_element( 'DLB_DESIGNS' ).
CALL METHOD cl_wd_utilities=>set_width_4ddlbbykey
  EXPORTING
    ddlb      = lr_ddlb
    algorithm = 2.
```

Method get_otr_text_by_alias()

The dynamic assignment of OTR texts is handled by the `get_otr_text_by_alias()` method. The parameters to be transferred are the alias of the OTR text and the required language. If the language is not defined, the text is returned in the login language.

```
DATA lv_btn TYPE string.
lv_btn = cl_wd_utilities=>get_otr_text_by_alias(
            'SOTR_VOCABULARY_BASIC/CONFIRM' ).
```

Method construct_wd_url()

This method enables you to determine individual components of the URL of a WD4A application (for example the port or host name), the local URL of an application on the respective server, and the absolute URL that you can store in the list of favorites in your client, for instance. The following example determines the absolute URL of the application `ZEXP_DDLB_KEY`.

```
DATA   lv_url     TYPE string.
CALL METHOD cl_wd_utilities=>construct_wd_url
  EXPORTING
    application_name = 'ZEXP_DDLB_KEY'
  IMPORTING
    out_absolute_url = lv_url.
```

B Bibliography

- Calishain, Tara; Dornfest, Rael: *Google Hacks*. O'Reilly 2005.
- Carnell, Jojn; Linwood, Jeff; Zawadzki, Maciej: *Professional Struts Applications*. Wrox Press 2003.
- Flanagan, David: *JavaScript—The Definitive Guide*. O'Reilly 2002.
- Goebel, Arnd; Ritthaler, Dirk: *SAP Enterprise Portal—Technology and Programming*. SAP PRESS 2005.
- Heineman, George T.; Councill, William T.: *Component-Based Software Engineering*. Addison-Wesley 2001.
- Heinemann, Frédéric; Rau, Christian: *Web Programming in ABAP with the SAP Web Application Server*. 2nd edition, SAP PRESS 2005.
- Husted, Ted; Dumoulin, Cedric; Franciscus, George; Winterfeldt, David: *Struts in Action*. Manning Publications 2003.
- Keller, Horst; Krüger, Sascha: *ABAP Objects—An Introduction to Programming SAP Applications*. Addison-Wesley 2002.
- McKellar, Brian; Jung, Thomas: *Advanced BSP Programming*. SAP PRESS 2006.
- Sells, Chris; Gethland, Justin: *Windows Forms Programming in Visual Basic .NET*. Addison-Wesley 2004.
- Szyperski, Clemens; Gruntz, Dominik; Murer, Stephan: *Component Software*. ACM PRESS 2002.

C The Author

Ulli Hoffmann studied information technology at the Technical College in Coburg, Germany, where he graduated in electrical engineering. He also studied computer engineering at Louisiana State University (LSU), where he received a Master of Science degree. After finishing his studies, he worked in various positions at AMD, Inc. and the AMD European Microelectronic Center.

Ulli was introduced to SAP technology when he worked in the Application Link Enabling (ALE) area. In recent years, he has focused more on ABAP-based web technologies (e.g., Business Server Pages and Web Dynpro for ABAP).

Today, Ulli Hoffmann is the founder and Managing Director of INIDFAB Computing GmbH, a consulting firm that specializes in the design and development of web-based applications. As a development consultant, he is involved in various projects at SAP AG and SAP customers.

Index

A

ABAP Dictionary 28, 173, 203
ABAP List Viewer 263
ABAP Objects 14, 262
ABAP runtime 35
Abstract data types 262
Abstraction 262
Action 80, 104, 207, 236
Active Server Pages (ASP) 27
ADC 308
Adobe Document Service 308
Adobe LifeCycle Designer 309
Adobe Reader 309
ADT 262
ALV component 263, 264
ALV configuration model 267
Application class 27
Assistance class 175, 191
Attribute info 116, 123, 124
Automatic forwarding 109

B

Bar chart 297
BSP extensions 29
Business object 294
Business Server Pages (BSP) 27, 293

C

Cardinality 63
Cascading Style Sheets (CSS) 15, 59
Cell editor 155
Cell variant 159
Chart Designer 299
CL_SALV_WD_COLUMN 268
CL_SALV_WD_COLUMN_HEADER 268
CL_SALV_WD_CONFIG_TABLE 267
CL_WD_ABSTRACT_INPUT_FIELD 228
CL_WD_ADOBE_SERVICES 342
CL_WD_COMPONENT_ASSISTANCE 175
CL_WD_CONTEXT_SERVICES 333
CL_WD_CUSTOM_EVENT 296, 348

CL_WD_INPUT_FIELD 228
CL_WD_POPUP_FACTORY 163, 164, 165, 166
CL_WD_RUNTIME_SERVICES 348
CL_WD_TRANS_PARENT_CONTAINER 231
CL_WD_UTILITIES 175, 349
CL_WDR_PORTAL_OBNWEB_SERVICE 341
Classes 317
Client technologies 33
Client-server architecture 186
close_window() 285
Closed implementation 190
Column chart 297, 301
Component 38, 51, 317
  Enhancement 288
Component concept 32
Component configurator 177
Component controller 39, 72, 78, 220
Component interface 38
Component usage 199, 265
Component use 73
Component-based software development 261
Configuration 176
  application 182
  component 179
  explicit 177
  implicit 177
Configuration controller 181
Context 61, 326
Context attribute 61, 75
Context binding 62
Context mapping 85
Context node 61, 77, 192, 234
Controller usage 210
Conventions 18
Coupled implementation 190
Custom controller 39, 78
Customer namespace 44

D

Default view 99, 103, 109

Index

Development environment 37
Dialog boxes 282
Direct mapping 197, 216
Drag&Drop 13
Dynamic programming
 actions 226, 236
 binding properties 226, 234
 context 226, 235
 UI hierarchy 226, 229

E

Encapsulation 262
Enhancement framework 288
Entry component 52, 54
estimatedTotalResultsCount 304
Event 196
 DATA_SELECTED 286
 onAction 277, 295, 301
Event-handler method 80, 82, 236
Explicit configuration 177
External context access 197

F

F4 help 171
Fire method 83, 88, 143, 208
Form Builder 309

G

Gantt chart 298
GIF 299
Google Maps 239, 250
Google Web APIs service 299, 303
Graphical user interface (GUI) 25

H

Hook method 80, 151, 229
HTML 186
HTMLB tag library 29
HTTP 23, 61, 303

I

IF_SALV_WD_TABLE_SETTINGS 268
IF_WD_ACTION 335
IF_WD_APPLICATION 342

IF_WD_COMPONENT 93, 317, 321
IF_WD_COMPONENT_USAGE 320
IF_WD_COMPONENT_USAGE_GROUP 324
IF_WD_CONTEXT 326
IF_WD_CONTEXT_ELEMENT 236, 332
IF_WD_CONTEXT_NODE 236, 328
IF_WD_CONTEXT_NODE_INFO 329
IF_WD_CONTROLLER 343
IF_WD_MESSAGE_MANAGER 150, 344
IF_WD_NAVIGATION_SERVICES 346
IF_WD_PERSONALIZATION 325
IF_WD_PORATL_INTEGRATION 294, 342
IF_WD_VALIDATION 338
IF_WD_VIEW 161, 336
IF_WD_VIEW_CONTROLLER 337
IF_WD_VIEW_ELEMENT 338
IF_WD_WINDOW 165, 339
IF_WD_WINDOW_CONTROLLER 341
IF_WD_WINDOW_MANAGER 163
IF_WDL_CORE 227
IF_WDL_STANDARD 227
IF_WDR_OVS 273
IGS 297
Implicit configuration 177
Inbound plug 46, 51, 61, 87, 96
 default type 209
 interface type 203, 204
 startup type 49, 100
 type startup 54
Inheritance 262
Input help 171, 270, 282
Input-help component 283
Instance method 82
Instantiating used components 196
Interactive Forms 308
Interface controller 78, 192
Interface view 49, 53, 192, 194, 268
 inbound plug 54
Interfaces 283, 317
Internationalization 172
Internet Communication Manager (ICM) 27
Internet Connection Framework (ICF) 27
Internet Graphics Server (IGS) 297
Internet Transaction Server (ITS) 26
IWD_VALUE_HELP 282

J

Java Server Pages (JSP) 27
JPG 299

K

Keywords, reserved 21

L

Layout 230
Layout category 39
 FlowLayout 57
 GridLayout 58
 MatrixLayout 59
 RowLayout 58
Layout data 230
Layout type 232
 FlowLayout 232
 MatrixLayout 232
 RowData 252
 RowLayout 246
Lead selection 66, 113, 115, 129, 157, 248

M

Mainframes 24
Mapping 192
Message handling 148
Message Manager 234
MIME 39, 131
MIME Repository 131
Model View Controller (MVC) 13, 29, 185, 200
MODEL_USAGE 323

N

Navigation 87, 100, 109
Node info 235

O

Object tree 37, 38
Object value selector 270
Object-based navigation 294
Online text repository 173
Open SQL 34
OTR 173
Outbound plug 46, 83, 87
OVS 172
OVS component 270
OVS_CALLBACK_OBJECT 273

P

PDF 266, 308, 310
Personalization 183
Phase model 91
PHASE_INDICATOR 273
Plug name 49
Polymorphism 262
Popup windows 163
Portal event
 registering to 295
 trigger 294
Portal eventing 294
Post-exit method 289
Pre-exit method 289
Prefixes 20
Program
 FP_PDF_TEST_00 309
Programming
 declarative 30
 dynamic 30
Property
 alignment 226, 228
 cardinality 153, 264
 chartType 298, 301
 dataSource 129, 153, 277, 301, 311
 description 301
 design 47, 113
 Dictionary Search Help 172
 Dictionary structure 153
 dimension 298, 301
 enabled 226, 235, 311
 explanation 226
 ID 226
 Input Element (Ext.) 204
 Input Help Component Usage 286
 Input Help Mode 171, 286
 Interface 204
 onAction 104
 passwordField 226
 pdfSource 311
 readOnly 226

selectedCellVariant 160
selectedKey 123
selectedStep 210
Selection 158
selectionMode 158
Singleton 129
supply function 154
templateSource 312
text 47
texts 113
value 272, 295

R

Radio buttons 121
Repository Browser 43
Request/response cycle 23, 28, 91, 103, 251
Reuse 51, 282
Reverse mapping 198, 202, 216, 221
Rich Client 32
ROOTUIELEMENTCONTAINER 39, 56

S

SALV_WD_TABLE 264
SAP Developer Network (SDN) 13
SAP GUI 27
SAP Help Portal 13
SAP NetWeaver Application Server ABAP 27, 34, 288, 303
SAP NetWeaver Portal 293
 iView 293, 296
 page 293
 workset 293
SAP R/2 24
SAP Smart Board 34
SAP Web Application Server 44
searchQuery 304
Select Options 275
selectionMode 69
Server-Side Rendering (SSR) 34
set_global_options() 278
set_lead_selection_index() 116
Simple Object Access Protocol (SOAP) 303
Singleton 66, 133
Smart Client 32

Supply function method 70, 76, 289
Support package 44

T

T100 message 150
Tables 152
Thin client 32
Three-tier model 187
Tooltip 269
Transaction
 BP 239, 241
 SE11 172, 283
 SE38 309
 SE80 37, 43, 131
 SFP 309
 ST22 65, 276
Trees
 recursive 131
 sequential 126

U

UI element 230
UI element container 230, 252
UI technology 31
Uniform Resource Identifier (URI) 49, 95, 100, 253
 parameter 95, 109, 254

V

Value help component 286
Value set 117
VH_WINDOW_CLOSED 283, 284
VH_WINDOW_OPENED 282, 284
View 39
 lifetime 84, 234
View controller 39, 79, 87
View designer 41
View editor 39
View element 39, 41, 56, 230
 BusinessGraphics 297
 Button 107, 169, 206
 ButtonRow 206
 Caption 154
 Category 301
 Composite 42, 152

DropDownByIndex 112, 113, 203, 204, 236, 246
DropDownByKey 116
FileUpload 310, 314
InputField 146, 204, 227, 295
InteractiveForm 310
label 113, 246
LinkToUrl 159, 253
MessageArea 149
property 47, 56
RadioButton 252
RadioButtonGroupByIndex 121
RadioButtonGroupByKey 121, 123
RoadMap 137, 200, 206, 210
RoadMapStep 206
simple 42
SimpleSeries 302
table 152, 263, 277
TableColumn 152, 160
TabStrip 227
TextView 232, 246
TimedTrigger 105
TransparentContainer 230, 301
Tree 125
TreeItemType 129
TreeNodeType 130
ViewContainerUIElement 206, 208, 219, 221, 264, 277
View element library 39, 46, 111
View element property 42
View layout 56

W

wd_assist 175, 191
wd_this 82
WD_VALUE_HELP 283
WD4A application 45, 49, 51
WD4A components 31, 44, 52
WD4A framework 13, 29, 35, 37, 38, 317
WD4A runtime 34
wddobeforeaction() 82, 92, 151
wddobeforenavigation() 81, 92
wddoexit() 81
wddoinit() 81, 93, 268
wddomodify() 257
wddomodifyview() 81, 93, 107, 108, 161

wddoonclose() 82
wddopostprocessing() 81, 92, 93
WDEVENT 130, 236
WDR_CONTEXT_ATTRIBUTE_INFO 236
WDR_CONTEXT_ELEMENT_SET 158
WDR_OVS 270
WDR_POPUP_BUTTON_KIND 165
WDR_POPUP_MSG_TYPE 165
WDR_SELECT_OPTIONS 276
WDUI_TEXT_VIEW_DESIGN 119
WDY_BOOLEAN 107
WDY_KEY_VALUE_TABLE 116, 117, 123
WDY_MD_UI_VISIBILITY 227
Web Dynpro Code Wizard 151, 195, 268, 294
Web Dynpro Explorer 37, 49
Web Dynpro for ABAP 30, 35
Window 39, 60, 192, 221
Window controller 39, 54, 78, 97
Window editor 48
Window Manager 168
Window structure 48
WND_SELECTION_SCREEN 276

X

XML 186, 299, 303

New 2nd Edition of the bestselling programmers' guide — fully updated and expanded

New sections on architecture, integration topics, and migrating legacy applications

Up-to-date for SAP NetWeaver 7.1

550 pp., 2007, 2. edition, 69,95 Euro / US$ 69.95
ISBN 978-1-59229-092-5

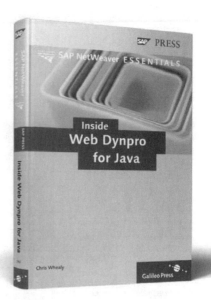

Inside Web Dynpro for Java

www.sap-press.com

Chris Whealy

Inside Web Dynpro for Java

This updated and completely revised second edition of "Inside Web Dynpro for Java" covers everything you need to know to leverage the full power of Web Dynpro for Java — taking you well beyond the standard drag and drop functionality.
Benefit from expert guidance on how to create your own Web Dynpro applications, with volumes of practical insights on the dos and don'ts of Web Dynpro Programming. The author provides you with detailed sections on the use of the Adaptive RFC layer, as well as Dynamic Programming techniques, to name just a few. This exceptional book is complemented by an in-depth class and interface reference, which further assists readers in their efforts to modify existing objects, design custom controllers, and much more.

Interested in reading more?

Please visit our Web site for all
new book releases from SAP PRESS.

www.sap-press.com